GNU Scientific Library

Reference Manual
Edition 1.8, for GSL Version 1.8
August 2006

Mark Galassi
Los Alamos National Laboratory

Jim Davies
Department of Computer Science, Georgia Institute of Technology

James Theiler
Astrophysics and Radiation Measurements Group,
Los Alamos National Laboratory

Brian Gough
Network Theory Limited

Gerard Jungman
Theoretical Astrophysics Group, Los Alamos National Laboratory

Michael Booth
Department of Physics and Astronomy, The Johns Hopkins University

Fabrice Rossi
University of Paris-Dauphine

A catalogue record for this book is available from the British Library.

Second edition, First printing, February 2002 (14/2/2002)
Revised and updated, Second printing, March 2005 (17/3/2005)
Revised for version 1.8, Third printing, August 2006 (23/8/2006)

Published by Network Theory Limited.

15 Royal Park
Bristol
BS8 3AL
United Kingdom

Email: info@network-theory.co.uk

ISBN 0-9541617-3-4

Original cover design by David Nicholls.

Further information about this book is available from
http://www.network-theory.co.uk/gsl/manual/

This book has an unconditional guarantee. If you are not fully satisfied
with your purchase for any reason, please contact the publisher at the
address above.

The Texinfo source for this manual may be obtained from
http://www.network-theory.co.uk/gsl/manual/src/

Table of Contents

Preface

This manual documents the use of the GNU Scientific Library, a numerical library for C and C++ programmers.

The GNU Scientific Library is *free software*. The term "free software" is sometimes misunderstood—it has nothing to do with price. It is about freedom. It refers to your freedom to run, copy, distribute, study, change and improve the software. With the GNU Scientific Library you have all these freedoms.

The GNU Scientific Library is part of the GNU Project. The GNU Project was launched in 1984 to develop a complete Unix-like operating system which is free software: the GNU system. It was conceived as a way of bringing back the cooperative spirit that prevailed in the computing community in earlier days, by removing the obstacles to cooperation imposed by the owners of proprietary software.

The Free Software Foundation is a tax-exempt charity that raises funds for work on the GNU Project and is dedicated to promoting the freedom to modify and redistribute computer programs. You can support the GNU Project by becoming an associate member of the Free Software Foundation and paying regular membership dues. For more information, visit the website www.fsf.org.

Brian Gough
Publisher
August 2006

1 Introduction

The GNU Scientific Library (GSL) is a collection of routines for numerical computing. The routines have been written from scratch in C, and present a modern Applications Programming Interface (API) for C programmers, allowing wrappers to be written for very high level languages. The source code is distributed under the GNU General Public License.

1.1 Routines available in GSL

The library covers a wide range of topics in numerical computing. Routines are available for the following areas,

Complex Numbers	Roots of Polynomials
Special Functions	Vectors and Matrices
Permutations	Combinations
Sorting	BLAS Support
Linear Algebra	CBLAS Library
Fast Fourier Transforms	Eigensystems
Random Numbers	Quadrature
Random Distributions	Quasi-Random Sequences
Histograms	Statistics
Monte Carlo Integration	N-Tuples
Differential Equations	Simulated Annealing
Numerical Differentiation	Interpolation
Series Acceleration	Chebyshev Approximations
Root-Finding	Discrete Hankel Transforms
Least-Squares Fitting	Minimization
IEEE Floating-Point	Physical Constants
Wavelets	

The use of these routines is described in this manual. Each chapter provides detailed definitions of the functions, followed by example programs and references to the articles on which the algorithms are based.

Where possible the routines have been based on reliable public-domain packages such as FFTPACK, QUADPACK and MINPACK, which the developers of GSL have reimplemented in C with modern coding conventions.

1.2 GSL is Free Software

The subroutines in the GNU Scientific Library are "free software"; this means that everyone is free to use them, and to redistribute them in other free programs. The library is not in the public domain; it is copyrighted and there are conditions on its distribution. These conditions are designed to permit everything that a good cooperating citizen would want to do. What is not allowed is to try to prevent others from further sharing any version of the software that they might get from you.

Specifically, we want to make sure that you have the right to share copies of programs that you are given which use the GNU Scientific Library, that you receive their source code or else can get it if you want it, that you can change these programs or use pieces of them in new free programs, and that you know you can do these things.

To make sure that everyone has such rights, we have to forbid you to deprive anyone else of these rights. For example, if you distribute copies of any code which uses the GNU Scientific Library, you must give the recipients all the rights that you have received. You must make sure that they, too, receive or can get the source code, both to the library and the code which uses it. And you must tell them their rights. This means that the library should not be redistributed in proprietary programs.

Also, for our own protection, we must make certain that everyone finds out that there is no warranty for the GNU Scientific Library. If these programs are modified by someone else and passed on, we want their recipients to know that what they have is not what we distributed, so that any problems introduced by others will not reflect on our reputation.

The precise conditions for the distribution of software related to the GNU Scientific Library are found in the GNU General Public License (see [GNU General Public License], page 561). Further information about this license is available from the GNU Project webpage *Frequently Asked Questions about the GNU GPL*,

    http://www.gnu.org/copyleft/gpl-faq.html

1.3 Obtaining GSL

The source code for the library can be obtained in different ways, by copying it from a friend, purchasing it on CDROM (see below) or downloading it from the internet. A list of public ftp servers which carry the source code can be found on the GNU website,

> http://www.gnu.org/software/gsl/

Downloaded files can be checked by following the procedure described in Appendix E [GPG verification], page 557.

The preferred platform for the library is a GNU system, which allows it to take advantage of additional features in the GNU C compiler and GNU C library. However, the library is fully portable and should compile on most systems with a C compiler. Instructions for building GSL can be found in the source code 'README' file.

Announcements of new releases, updates and other relevant events are made on the info-gsl@gnu.org mailing list. To subscribe to this low-volume list, send an email of the following form:

> To: info-gsl-request@gnu.org
> Subject: subscribe

You will receive a response asking you to reply in order to confirm your subscription.

1.4 No Warranty

The free software described in this manual has no warranty, it is provided "as is". It is your responsibility to validate the behavior of the routines and their accuracy using the source code provided, or to purchase support and warranties from commercial redistributors. Consult the GNU General Public license for further details (see [GNU General Public License], page 561).

1.5 Commercial Support

Commercially supported versions of GSL with warranties are available on CD from Network Theory Ltd (www.network-theory.com). The money raised from the sales of CDs and maintenance contracts by Network Theory Ltd supports the development of the library (see [Commercial support for GSL], page 559).

1.6 Reporting Bugs

A list of known bugs can be found in the 'BUGS' file included in the GSL distribution. Details of other compilation problems can be found in the 'INSTALL' file.

If you find a bug which is not listed in these files, please report it to bug-gsl@gnu.org.

All bug reports should include:

- The version number of GSL
- The hardware and operating system
- The compiler used, including version number and compilation options
- A description of the bug behavior
- A short program which exercises the bug

It is useful if you can check whether the same problem occurs when the library is compiled without optimization. Thank you.

Any errors or omissions in this manual can also be reported to the same address.

1.7 Further Information

Additional information, including online copies of this manual, links to related projects, and mailing list archives are available from the website mentioned above.

Any questions about the use and installation of the library can be asked on the mailing list help-gsl@gnu.org. To subscribe to this list, send an email of the following form:

```
To: help-gsl-request@gnu.org
Subject: subscribe
```

This mailing list can be used to ask questions not covered by this manual, and to contact the developers of the library.

If you would like to refer to the GNU Scientific Library in a journal article, the recommended way is to cite this reference manual, e.g. *M. Galassi et al, GNU Scientific Library Reference Manual (2nd Ed.), ISBN 0954161734.*

If you want to give a url, use "http://www.gnu.org/software/gsl/".

1.8 Conventions used in this manual

This manual contains many examples which can be typed at the keyboard. A command entered at the terminal is shown like this,

    $ command

The first character on the line is the terminal prompt, and should not be typed. The dollar sign '$' is used as the standard prompt in this manual, although some systems may use a different character.

The examples assume the use of the GNU operating system. There may be minor differences in the output on other systems. The commands for setting environment variables use the Bourne shell syntax of the standard GNU shell (bash).

2 Using the library

This chapter describes how to compile programs that use GSL, and introduces its conventions.

2.1 An Example Program

The following short program demonstrates the use of the library by computing the value of the Bessel function $J_0(x)$ for $x = 5$,

```
#include <stdio.h>
#include <gsl/gsl_sf_bessel.h>

int
main (void)
{
  double x = 5.0;
  double y = gsl_sf_bessel_J0 (x);
  printf ("J0(%g) = %.18e\n", x, y);
  return 0;
}
```

If GSL is installed in its default location, the command to compile this program and link to the necessary libraries is,

```
$ gcc -Wall example.c -lgsl -lgslcblas -lm
```

The result of running the program is shown below, and should be correct to double-precision accuracy,

```
J0(5) = -1.775967713143382920e-01
```

The compilation and linking procedure may vary on different platforms—full details are given in the following sections.

2.2 Compiling and Linking

The library header files are installed in their own 'gsl' directory. You should write any preprocessor include statements with a 'gsl/' directory prefix thus,

```
#include <gsl/gsl_math.h>
```

If the directory is not installed on the standard search path of your compiler you will also need to provide its location to the preprocessor as a command line flag. The default location of the 'gsl' directory is '/usr/local/include/gsl'. A typical compilation command for a source file 'example.c' with the GNU C compiler gcc is,

```
$ gcc -Wall -I/usr/local/include -c example.c
```
This results in an object file 'example.o'. The default include path for
gcc searches '/usr/local/include' automatically so the -I option can
actually be omitted when GSL is installed in its default location.

2.2.1 Linking programs with the library

The library is installed as a single file, 'libgsl.a'. A shared version of
the library 'libgsl.so' is also installed on systems that support shared
libraries. The default location of these files is '/usr/local/lib'. If this
directory is not on the standard search path of your linker you will also
need to provide its location as a command line flag.

To link against the library you need to specify both the main library
and a supporting CBLAS library, which provides standard basic linear algebra subroutines. A suitable CBLAS implementation is provided in the
library 'libgslcblas.a' if your system does not provide one. The following example shows how to link an application with the library,

```
$ gcc -L/usr/local/lib example.o -lgsl -lgslcblas -lm
```
The default library path for gcc searches '/usr/local/lib' automatically
so the -Lpath option can be omitted when GSL is installed in its default
location.

2.2.2 Linking with an alternative BLAS library

The following command line shows how you would link the same application with an alternative CBLAS library called 'libcblas',

```
$ gcc example.o -lgsl -lcblas -lm
```
For the best performance an optimized platform-specific CBLAS library
may be used for -lcblas. The library must conform to the CBLAS standard. The ATLAS package provides a portable high-performance BLAS
library with a CBLAS interface. It is free software and can be used with
GSL in place of 'libgslcblas.a'. The following command line will link
with the ATLAS library and its CBLAS interface instead,

```
$ gcc example.o -lgsl -lcblas -latlas -lm
```
For more information see Chapter 12 [BLAS Support], page 149.

2.3 Shared Libraries

To run a program linked with the shared version of the library the operating system must be able to locate the corresponding '.so' file at runtime. If the library cannot be found, the following error will occur:

```
$ ./a.out
./a.out: error while loading shared libraries:
libgsl.so.0: cannot open shared object file: No such
file or directory
```

To avoid this error, define the shell variable LD_LIBRARY_PATH to include the directory where the library is installed.

For example, in the Bourne shell (/bin/sh or /bin/bash), the library search path can be set with the following commands:

```
$ LD_LIBRARY_PATH=/usr/local/lib:$LD_LIBRARY_PATH
$ export LD_LIBRARY_PATH
$ ./example
```

In the C-shell (/bin/csh or /bin/tcsh) the equivalent command is,

```
% setenv LD_LIBRARY_PATH /usr/local/lib:$LD_LIBRARY_PATH
```

The standard prompt for the C-shell in the example above is the percent character '%', and should not be typed as part of the command.

To save retyping these commands each session they should be placed in an individual or system-wide login file.

To compile a statically linked version of the program, use the -static flag in gcc,

```
$ gcc -static example.o -lgsl -lgslcblas -lm
```

For more information about trouble-shooting compilation and linking problems, see the book *An Introduction to GCC* listed in the appendix [Other books from the publisher], page 579.

2.4 ANSI C Compliance

The library is written in ANSI C and is intended to conform to the ANSI C standard (C89). It should be portable to any system with a working ANSI C compiler.

The library does not rely on any non-ANSI extensions in the interface it exports to the user. Programs you write using GSL can be ANSI compliant. Extensions which can be used in a way compatible with pure ANSI C are supported, however, via conditional compilation. This allows the library to take advantage of compiler extensions on those platforms which support them.

When an ANSI C feature is known to be broken on a particular system the library will exclude any related functions at compile-time. This should make it impossible to link a program that would use these functions and give incorrect results.

To avoid namespace conflicts all exported function names and variables have the prefix gsl_, while exported macros have the prefix GSL_.

2.5 Inline functions

The inline keyword is not part of the original ANSI C standard (C89) and the library does not export any inline function definitions by default. However, the library provides optional inline versions of performance-critical functions by conditional compilation. The inline versions of these functions can be included by defining the macro HAVE_INLINE when compiling an application,

```
$ gcc -Wall -c -DHAVE_INLINE example.c
```

If you use autoconf this macro can be defined automatically. If you do not define the macro HAVE_INLINE then the slower non-inlined versions of the functions will be used instead.

Note that the actual usage of the inline keyword is extern inline, which eliminates unnecessary function definitions in GCC. If the form extern inline causes problems with other compilers a stricter autoconf test can be used, see Appendix C [Autoconf Macros], page 537.

2.6 Long double

The extended numerical type long double is part of the ANSI C standard and should be available in every modern compiler. However, the precision of long double is platform dependent, and this should be considered when using it. The IEEE standard only specifies the minimum precision of extended precision numbers, while the precision of double is the same on all platforms.

In some system libraries the stdio.h formatted input/output functions printf and scanf are not implemented correctly for long double. Undefined or incorrect results are avoided by testing these functions during the configure stage of library compilation and eliminating certain GSL functions which depend on them if necessary. The corresponding line in the configure output looks like this,

```
checking whether printf works with long double... no
```

Consequently when long double formatted input/output does not work on a given system it should be impossible to link a program which uses GSL functions dependent on this.

If it is necessary to work on a system which does not support formatted long double input/output then the options are to use binary formats or to convert long double results into double for reading and writing.

2.7 Portability functions

To help in writing portable applications GSL provides some implementations of functions that are found in other libraries, such as the BSD math library. You can write your application to use the native versions of these functions, and substitute the GSL versions via a preprocessor macro if they are unavailable on another platform.

For example, after determining whether the BSD function hypot is available you can include the following macro definitions in a file 'config.h' with your application,

```
/* Substitute gsl_hypot for missing system hypot */

#ifndef HAVE_HYPOT
#define hypot gsl_hypot
#endif
```

The application source files can then use the include command #include <config.h> to replace each occurrence of hypot by gsl_hypot when hypot is not available. This substitution can be made automatically if you use autoconf, see Appendix C [Autoconf Macros], page 537.

In most circumstances the best strategy is to use the native versions of these functions when available, and fall back to GSL versions otherwise, since this allows your application to take advantage of any platform-specific optimizations in the system library. This is the strategy used within GSL itself.

2.8 Alternative optimized functions

The main implementation of some functions in the library will not be optimal on all architectures. For example, there are several ways to compute a Gaussian random variate and their relative speeds are platform-dependent. In cases like this the library provides alternative implementations of these functions with the same interface. If you write your application using calls to the standard implementation you can select an alternative version later via a preprocessor definition. It is also possible to introduce your own optimized functions this way while retaining portability. The following lines demonstrate the use of a platform-dependent choice of methods for sampling from the Gaussian distribution,

```
#ifdef SPARC
#define gsl_ran_gaussian gsl_ran_gaussian_ratio_method
#endif
#ifdef INTEL
#define gsl_ran_gaussian my_gaussian
#endif
```

These lines would be placed in the configuration header file 'config.h' of the application, which should then be included by all the source files. Note that the alternative implementations will not produce bit-for-bit identical results, and in the case of random number distributions will produce an entirely different stream of random variates.

2.9 Support for different numeric types

Many functions in the library are defined for different numeric types. This feature is implemented by varying the name of the function with a type-related modifier—a primitive form of C++ templates. The modifier is inserted into the function name after the initial module prefix. The following table shows the function names defined for all the numeric types of an imaginary module gsl_foo with function fn,

gsl_foo_fn	double
gsl_foo_long_double_fn	long double
gsl_foo_float_fn	float
gsl_foo_long_fn	long
gsl_foo_ulong_fn	unsigned long
gsl_foo_int_fn	int
gsl_foo_uint_fn	unsigned int
gsl_foo_short_fn	short
gsl_foo_ushort_fn	unsigned short
gsl_foo_char_fn	char
gsl_foo_uchar_fn	unsigned char

The normal numeric precision double is considered the default and does not require a suffix. For example, the function gsl_stats_mean computes the mean of double precision numbers, while the function gsl_stats_int_mean computes the mean of integers.

A corresponding scheme is used for library defined types, such as gsl_vector and gsl_matrix. In this case the modifier is appended to the type name. For example, if a module defines a new type-dependent struct or typedef gsl_foo it is modified for other types in the following way,

gsl_foo	double
gsl_foo_long_double	long double
gsl_foo_float	float
gsl_foo_long	long
gsl_foo_ulong	unsigned long
gsl_foo_int	int
gsl_foo_uint	unsigned int
gsl_foo_short	short
gsl_foo_ushort	unsigned short
gsl_foo_char	char

```
      gsl_foo_uchar                    unsigned char
```

When a module contains type-dependent definitions the library provides individual header files for each type. The filenames are modified as shown in the below. For convenience the default header includes the definitions for all the types. To include only the double precision header file, or any other specific type, use its individual filename.

```
#include <gsl/gsl_foo.h>              All types
#include <gsl/gsl_foo_double.h>       double
#include <gsl/gsl_foo_long_double.h>  long double
#include <gsl/gsl_foo_float.h>        float
#include <gsl/gsl_foo_long.h>         long
#include <gsl/gsl_foo_ulong.h>        unsigned long
#include <gsl/gsl_foo_int.h>          int
#include <gsl/gsl_foo_uint.h>         unsigned int
#include <gsl/gsl_foo_short.h>        short
#include <gsl/gsl_foo_ushort.h>       unsigned short
#include <gsl/gsl_foo_char.h>         char
#include <gsl/gsl_foo_uchar.h>        unsigned char
```

2.10 Compatibility with C++

The library header files automatically define functions to have extern "C" linkage when included in C++ programs. This allows the functions to be called directly from C++.

To use C++ exception handling within user-defined functions passed to the library as parameters, the library must be built with the additional CFLAGS compilation option '-fexceptions'.

2.11 Aliasing of arrays

The library assumes that arrays, vectors and matrices passed as modifiable arguments are not aliased and do not overlap with each other. This removes the need for the library to handle overlapping memory regions as a special case, and allows additional optimizations to be used. If overlapping memory regions are passed as modifiable arguments then the results of such functions will be undefined. If the arguments will not be modified (for example, if a function prototype declares them as const arguments) then overlapping or aliased memory regions can be used safely.

2.12 Thread-safety

The library can be used in multi-threaded programs. All the functions are thread-safe, in the sense that they do not use static variables. Memory is always associated with objects and not with functions. For functions which use *workspace* objects as temporary storage the workspaces should be allocated on a per-thread basis. For functions which use *table* objects as read-only memory the tables can be used by multiple threads simultaneously. Table arguments are declared const in function prototypes to indicate when they may be safely accessed by different threads.

There are a small number of static global variables which are used to control the overall behavior of the library (e.g. whether to use range-checking, the function to call on fatal error, etc). These variables are set directly by the user, so they should be initialized once at program startup and not modified by different threads.

2.13 Deprecated Functions

From time to time, it may be necessary for the definitions of some functions to be altered or removed from the library. In these circumstances the functions will first be declared *deprecated* and then removed from subsequent versions of the library. Functions that are deprecated can be disabled in the current release by setting the preprocessor definition GSL_DISABLE_DEPRECATED. This allows existing code to be tested for forwards compatibility.

2.14 Code Reuse

Where possible the routines in the library have been written to avoid dependencies between modules and files. This should make it possible to extract individual functions for use in your own applications, without needing to have the whole library installed. You may need to define certain macros such as GSL_ERROR and remove some #include statements in order to compile the files as standalone units. Reuse of the library code in this way is encouraged, subject to the terms of the GNU General Public License.

3 Error Handling

This chapter describes the way that GSL functions report and handle errors. By examining the status information returned by every function you can determine whether it succeeded or failed, and if it failed you can find out what the precise cause of failure was. You can also define your own error handling functions to modify the default behavior of the library.

The functions described in this section are declared in the header file 'gsl_errno.h'.

3.1 Error Reporting

The library follows the thread-safe error reporting conventions of the POSIX threads library. Functions return a non-zero error code to indicate an error and 0 to indicate success.

```
int status = gsl_function (...)

if (status) { /* an error occurred */
  .....
  /* status value specifies the type of error */
}
```

The routines report an error whenever they cannot perform the task requested of them. For example, a root-finding function would return a non-zero error code if could not converge to the requested accuracy, or exceeded a limit on the number of iterations. Situations like this are a normal occurrence when using any mathematical library and you should check the return status of the functions that you call.

Whenever a routine reports an error the return value specifies the type of error. The return value is analogous to the value of the variable errno in the C library. The caller can examine the return code and decide what action to take, including ignoring the error if it is not considered serious.

In addition to reporting errors by return codes the library also has an error handler function gsl_error. This function is called by other library functions when they report an error, just before they return to the caller. The default behavior of the error handler is to print a message and abort the program,

```
gsl: file.c:67: ERROR: invalid argument supplied by user
Default GSL error handler invoked.
Aborted
```

The purpose of the gsl_error handler is to provide a function where a breakpoint can be set that will catch library errors when running under

the debugger. It is not intended for use in production programs, which
should handle any errors using the return codes.

3.2 Error Codes

The error code numbers returned by library functions are defined in
the file 'gsl_errno.h'. They all have the prefix GSL_ and expand to
non-zero constant integer values. Error codes above 1024 are reserved for
applications, and are not used by the library. Many of the error codes
use the same base name as the corresponding error code in the C library.
Here are some of the most common error codes,

int GSL_EDOM   Macro
> Domain error; used by mathematical functions when an argument
> value does not fall into the domain over which the function is defined
> (like EDOM in the C library)

int GSL_ERANGE   Macro
> Range error; used by mathematical functions when the result value is
> not representable because of overflow or underflow (like ERANGE in
> the C library)

int GSL_ENOMEM   Macro
> No memory available. The system cannot allocate more virtual mem-
> ory because its capacity is full (like ENOMEM in the C library). This
> error is reported when a GSL routine encounters problems when trying
> to allocate memory with malloc.

int GSL_EINVAL   Macro
> Invalid argument. This is used to indicate various kinds of problems
> with passing the wrong argument to a library function (like EINVAL
> in the C library).

The error codes can be converted into an error message using the
function gsl_strerror.

const char * gsl_strerror (const int *gsl_errno*)   Function
> This function returns a pointer to a string describing the error code
> *gsl_errno*. For example,
>
>   printf ("error: %s\n", gsl_strerror (status));
>
> would print an error message like error: output range error for a
> status value of GSL_ERANGE.

3.3 Error Handlers

The default behavior of the GSL error handler is to print a short message and call abort. When this default is in use programs will stop with a core-dump whenever a library routine reports an error. This is intended as a fail-safe default for programs which do not check the return status of library routines (we don't encourage you to write programs this way).

If you turn off the default error handler it is your responsibility to check the return values of routines and handle them yourself. You can also customize the error behavior by providing a new error handler. For example, an alternative error handler could log all errors to a file, ignore certain error conditions (such as underflows), or start the debugger and attach it to the current process when an error occurs.

All GSL error handlers have the type gsl_error_handler_t, which is defined in 'gsl_errno.h',

gsl_error_handler_t   Data Type
    This is the type of GSL error handler functions. An error handler will be passed four arguments which specify the reason for the error (a string), the name of the source file in which it occurred (also a string), the line number in that file (an integer) and the error number (an integer). The source file and line number are set at compile time using the __FILE__ and __LINE__ directives in the preprocessor. An error handler function returns type void. Error handler functions should be defined like this,

```
void handler (const char * reason,
              const char * file,
              int line,
              int gsl_errno)
```

To request the use of your own error handler you need to call the function gsl_set_error_handler which is also declared in 'gsl_errno.h',

gsl_error_handler_t * gsl_set_error_handler   Function
      (gsl_error_handler_t *new_handler*)
    This function sets a new error handler, *new_handler*, for the GSL library routines. The previous handler is returned (so that you can restore it later). Note that the pointer to a user defined error handler function is stored in a static variable, so there can be only one error handler per program. This function should be not be used in multi-threaded programs except to set up a program-wide error handler from a master thread. The following example shows how to set and restore a new error handler,

```
/* save original handler, install new handler */
old_handler = gsl_set_error_handler (&my_handler);

/* code uses new handler */
.....

/* restore original handler */
gsl_set_error_handler (old_handler);
```

To use the default behavior (abort on error) set the error handler to NULL,

```
old_handler = gsl_set_error_handler (NULL);
```

gsl_error_handler_t * gsl_set_error_handler_off ()   *Function*
> This function turns off the error handler by defining an error handler which does nothing. This will cause the program to continue after any error, so the return values from any library routines must be checked. This is the recommended behavior for production programs. The previous handler is returned (so that you can restore it later).

The error behavior can be changed for specific applications by recompiling the library with a customized definition of the GSL_ERROR macro in the file 'gsl_errno.h'.

3.4 Using GSL error reporting in your own functions

If you are writing numerical functions in a program which also uses GSL code you may find it convenient to adopt the same error reporting conventions as in the library.

To report an error you need to call the function gsl_error with a string describing the error and then return an appropriate error code from gsl_errno.h, or a special value, such as NaN. For convenience the file 'gsl_errno.h' defines two macros which carry out these steps:

GSL_ERROR (*reason, gsl_errno*)   *Macro*
> This macro reports an error using the GSL conventions and returns a status value of gsl_errno. It expands to the following code fragment,
> ```
> gsl_error (reason, __FILE__, __LINE__, gsl_errno);
> return gsl_errno;
> ```
> The macro definition in 'gsl_errno.h' actually wraps the code in a do { ... } while (0) block to prevent possible parsing problems.

Here is an example of how the macro could be used to report that a routine did not achieve a requested tolerance. To report the error the routine needs to return the error code GSL_ETOL.

```
if (residual > tolerance)
  {
     GSL_ERROR("residual exceeds tolerance", GSL_ETOL);
  }
```

GSL_ERROR_VAL (*reason*, *gsl_errno*, *value*)   Macro
This macro is the same as GSL_ERROR but returns a user-defined value of *value* instead of an error code. It can be used for mathematical functions that return a floating point value.

The following example shows how to return a NaN at a mathematical singularity using the GSL_ERROR_VAL macro,

```
if (x == 0)
  {
     GSL_ERROR_VAL("argument lies on singularity",
               GSL_ERANGE, GSL_NAN);
  }
```

3.5 Examples

Here is an example of some code which checks the return value of a function where an error might be reported,

```
#include <stdio.h>
#include <gsl/gsl_errno.h>
#include <gsl/gsl_fft_complex.h>

...
  int status;
  size_t n = 37;

  gsl_set_error_handler_off();

  status = gsl_fft_complex_radix2_forward (data, n);

  if (status) {
    if (status == GSL_EINVAL) {
       fprintf (stderr, "invalid argument, n=%d\n", n);
    } else {
       fprintf (stderr, "failed, gsl_errno=%d\n",
                   status);
    }
```

```
    exit (-1);
  }
...
```

The function `gsl_fft_complex_radix2` only accepts integer lengths which are a power of two. If the variable n is not a power of two then the call to the library function will return `GSL_EINVAL`, indicating that the length argument is invalid. The function call to `gsl_set_error_handler_off` stops the default error handler from aborting the program. The `else` clause catches any other possible errors.

4 Mathematical Functions

This chapter describes basic mathematical functions. Some of these functions are present in system libraries, but the alternative versions given here can be used as a substitute when the system functions are not available.

The functions and macros described in this chapter are defined in the header file 'gsl_math.h'.

4.1 Mathematical Constants

The library ensures that the standard BSD mathematical constants are defined. For reference, here is a list of the constants:

M_E   The base of exponentials, e

M_LOG2E   The base-2 logarithm of e, $\log_2(e)$

M_LOG10E   The base-10 logarithm of e, $\log_{10}(e)$

M_SQRT2   The square root of two, $\sqrt{2}$

M_SQRT1_2   The square root of one-half, $\sqrt{1/2}$

M_SQRT3   The square root of three, $\sqrt{3}$

M_PI   The constant pi, π

M_PI_2   Pi divided by two, $\pi/2$

M_PI_4   Pi divided by four, $\pi/4$

M_SQRTPI   The square root of pi, $\sqrt{\pi}$

M_2_SQRTPI
               Two divided by the square root of pi, $2/\sqrt{\pi}$

M_1_PI   The reciprocal of pi, $1/\pi$

M_2_PI   Twice the reciprocal of pi, $2/\pi$

M_LN10   The natural logarithm of ten, $\ln(10)$

M_LN2   The natural logarithm of two, $\ln(2)$

M_LNPI   The natural logarithm of pi, $\ln(\pi)$

M_EULER   Euler's constant, γ

4.2 Infinities and Not-a-number

GSL_POSINF   Macro
 This macro contains the IEEE representation of positive infinity, $+\infty$.
 It is computed from the expression +1.0/0.0.

GSL_NEGINF   Macro
 This macro contains the IEEE representation of negative infinity, $-\infty$.
 It is computed from the expression -1.0/0.0.

GSL_NAN   Macro
 This macro contains the IEEE representation of the Not-a-Number
 symbol, NaN. It is computed from the ratio 0.0/0.0.

int gsl_isnan (const double x)   Function
 This function returns 1 if x is not-a-number.

int gsl_isinf (const double x)   Function
 This function returns $+1$ if x is positive infinity, -1 if x is negative
 infinity and 0 otherwise.

int gsl_finite (const double x)   Function
 This function returns 1 if x is a real number, and 0 if it is infinite or
 not-a-number.

4.3 Elementary Functions

The following routines provide portable implementations of functions
found in the BSD math library. When native versions are not available
the functions described here can be used instead. The substitution can
be made automatically if you use autoconf to compile your application
(see Section 2.7 [Portability functions], page 13).

double gsl_log1p (const double x)   Function
 This function computes the value of $\log(1+x)$ in a way that is accurate
 for small x. It provides an alternative to the BSD math function
 log1p(x).

double gsl_expm1 (const double x)   Function
 This function computes the value of $\exp(x)-1$ in a way that is accurate
 for small x. It provides an alternative to the BSD math function
 expm1(x).

double gsl_hypot (const double x, const double y)   Function
 This function computes the value of $\sqrt{x^2+y^2}$ in a way that avoids
 overflow. It provides an alternative to the BSD math function
 hypot(x,y).

double `gsl_acosh` (const double x)   Function
    This function computes the value of $\mathrm{arccosh}(x)$. It provides an alternative to the standard math function `acosh(x)`.

double `gsl_asinh` (const double x)   Function
    This function computes the value of $\mathrm{arcsinh}(x)$. It provides an alternative to the standard math function `asinh(x)`.

double `gsl_atanh` (const double x)   Function
    This function computes the value of $\mathrm{arctanh}(x)$. It provides an alternative to the standard math function `atanh(x)`.

double `gsl_ldexp` (double x, int e)   Function
    This function computes the value of $x * 2^e$. It provides an alternative to the standard math function `ldexp(x,e)`.

double `gsl_frexp` (double x, int * e)   Function
    This function splits the number x into its normalized fraction f and exponent e, such that $x = f * 2^e$ and $0.5 \leq f < 1$. The function returns f and stores the exponent in e. If x is zero, both f and e are set to zero. This function provides an alternative to the standard math function `frexp(x, e)`.

4.4 Small integer powers

A common complaint about the standard C library is its lack of a function for calculating (small) integer powers. GSL provides some simple functions to fill this gap. For reasons of efficiency, these functions do not check for overflow or underflow conditions.

double `gsl_pow_int` (double x, int n)   Function
    This routine computes the power x^n for integer n. The power is computed efficiently—for example, x^8 is computed as $((x^2)^2)^2$, requiring only 3 multiplications. A version of this function which also computes the numerical error in the result is available as `gsl_sf_pow_int_e`.

double `gsl_pow_2` (const double x)   Function
double `gsl_pow_3` (const double x)   Function
double `gsl_pow_4` (const double x)   Function
double `gsl_pow_5` (const double x)   Function
double `gsl_pow_6` (const double x)   Function
double `gsl_pow_7` (const double x)   Function
double `gsl_pow_8` (const double x)   Function
double `gsl_pow_9` (const double x)   Function
    These functions can be used to compute small integer powers x^2, x^3, etc. efficiently. The functions will be inlined when possible so that

use of these functions should be as efficient as explicitly writing the
corresponding product expression.

```
#include <gsl/gsl_math.h>
double y = gsl_pow_4 (3.141)   /* compute 3.141**4 */
```

4.5 Testing the Sign of Numbers

GSL_SIGN (x)   Macro

This macro returns the sign of x. It is defined as `((x) >= 0 ? 1 : -1)`.
Note that with this definition the sign of zero is positive (regardless of
its IEEE sign bit).

4.6 Testing for Odd and Even Numbers

GSL_IS_ODD (n)   Macro

This macro evaluates to 1 if n is odd and 0 if n is even. The argument
n must be of integer type.

GSL_IS_EVEN (n)   Macro

This macro is the opposite of GSL_IS_ODD(n). It evaluates to 1 if n is
even and 0 if n is odd. The argument n must be of integer type.

4.7 Maximum and Minimum functions

GSL_MAX (a, b)   Macro

This macro returns the maximum of a and b. It is defined as `((a) >
(b) ? (a):(b))`.

GSL_MIN (a, b)   Macro

This macro returns the minimum of a and b. It is defined as `((a) <
(b) ? (a):(b))`.

extern inline double GSL_MAX_DBL (double a, double b)   Function

This function returns the maximum of the double precision numbers
a and b using an inline function. The use of a function allows for type
checking of the arguments as an extra safety feature. On platforms
where inline functions are not available the macro GSL_MAX will be
automatically substituted.

extern inline double GSL_MIN_DBL (double a, double b)   Function

This function returns the minimum of the double precision numbers a
and b using an inline function. The use of a function allows for type
checking of the arguments as an extra safety feature. On platforms
where inline functions are not available the macro GSL_MIN will be
automatically substituted.

extern inline int GSL_MAX_INT (int a, int b)   Function
extern inline int GSL_MIN_INT (int a, int b)   Function

These functions return the maximum or minimum of the integers a and b using an inline function. On platforms where inline functions are not available the macros GSL_MAX or GSL_MIN will be automatically substituted.

extern inline long double GSL_MAX_LDBL (long double a,   Function
        long double b)
extern inline long double GSL_MIN_LDBL (long double a,   Function
        long double b)

These functions return the maximum or minimum of the long doubles a and b using an inline function. On platforms where inline functions are not available the macros GSL_MAX or GSL_MIN will be automatically substituted.

4.8 Approximate Comparison of Floating Point Numbers

It is sometimes useful to be able to compare two floating point numbers approximately, to allow for rounding and truncation errors. The following function implements the approximate floating-point comparison algorithm proposed by D.E. Knuth in Section 4.2.2 of *Seminumerical Algorithms* (3rd edition).

int gsl_fcmp (double x, double y, double epsilon)   Function

This function determines whether x and y are approximately equal to a relative accuracy epsilon.

The relative accuracy is measured using an interval of size 2δ, where $\delta = 2^k \epsilon$ and k is the maximum base-2 exponent of x and y as computed by the function frexp.

If x and y lie within this interval, they are considered approximately equal and the function returns 0. Otherwise if $x < y$, the function returns -1, or if $x > y$, the function returns $+1$.

The implementation is based on the package fcmp by T.C. Belding.

5 Complex Numbers

The functions described in this chapter provide support for complex numbers. The algorithms take care to avoid unnecessary intermediate underflows and overflows, allowing the functions to be evaluated over as much of the complex plane as possible.

For multiple-valued functions the branch cuts have been chosen to follow the conventions of Abramowitz and Stegun in the *Handbook of Mathematical Functions*. The functions return principal values which are the same as those in GNU Calc, which in turn are the same as those in *Common Lisp, The Language (Second Edition)*[1] and the HP-28/48 series of calculators.

The complex types are defined in the header file 'gsl_complex.h', while the corresponding complex functions and arithmetic operations are defined in 'gsl_complex_math.h'.

5.1 Complex numbers

Complex numbers are represented using the type gsl_complex. The internal representation of this type may vary across platforms and should not be accessed directly. The functions and macros described below allow complex numbers to be manipulated in a portable way.

For reference, the default form of the gsl_complex type is given by the following struct,

```
typedef struct
{
   double dat[2];
} gsl_complex;
```

The real and imaginary part are stored in contiguous elements of a two element array. This eliminates any padding between the real and imaginary parts, dat[0] and dat[1], allowing the struct to be mapped correctly onto packed complex arrays.

gsl_complex gsl_complex_rect (double x, double y)   *Function*
    This function uses the rectangular cartesian components (x,y) to return the complex number $z = x + iy$.

gsl_complex gsl_complex_polar (double r, double theta)   *Function*
    This function returns the complex number $z = r \exp(i\theta) = r(\cos(\theta) + i \sin(\theta))$ from the polar representation $(r, theta)$.

---

[1] Note that the first edition uses different definitions.

GSL_REAL (z) Macro
GSL_IMAG (z) Macro
> These macros return the real and imaginary parts of the complex number z.

GSL_SET_COMPLEX $(zp,\ x,\ y)$ Macro
> This macro uses the cartesian components (x,y) to set the real and imaginary parts of the complex number pointed to by zp. For example,
>
>   GSL_SET_COMPLEX(&z, 3, 4)
>
> sets z to be $3 + 4i$.

GSL_SET_REAL (zp,x) Macro
GSL_SET_IMAG (zp,y) Macro
> These macros allow the real and imaginary parts of the complex number pointed to by zp to be set independently.

5.2 Properties of complex numbers

double gsl_complex_arg (gsl_complex z)   Function
> This function returns the argument of the complex number z, $\arg(z)$, where $-\pi < \arg(z) \le \pi$.

double gsl_complex_abs (gsl_complex z)   Function
> This function returns the magnitude of the complex number z, $|z|$.

double gsl_complex_abs2 (gsl_complex z)   Function
> This function returns the squared magnitude of the complex number z, $|z|^2$.

double gsl_complex_logabs (gsl_complex z)   Function
> This function returns the natural logarithm of the magnitude of the complex number z, $\log|z|$. It allows an accurate evaluation of $\log|z|$ when $|z|$ is close to one. The direct evaluation of log(gsl_complex_abs(z)) would lead to a loss of precision in this case.

5.3 Complex arithmetic operators

gsl_complex gsl_complex_add (gsl_complex a,   *Function*
        gsl_complex b)
  This function returns the sum of the complex numbers a and b, $z = a + b$.

gsl_complex gsl_complex_sub (gsl_complex a,   *Function*
        gsl_complex b)
  This function returns the difference of the complex numbers a and b, $z = a - b$.

gsl_complex gsl_complex_mul (gsl_complex a,   *Function*
        gsl_complex b)
  This function returns the product of the complex numbers a and b, $z = ab$.

gsl_complex gsl_complex_div (gsl_complex a,   *Function*
        gsl_complex b)
  This function returns the quotient of the complex numbers a and b, $z = a/b$.

gsl_complex gsl_complex_add_real (gsl_complex a,   *Function*
        double x)
  This function returns the sum of the complex number a and the real number x, $z = a + x$.

gsl_complex gsl_complex_sub_real (gsl_complex a,   *Function*
        double x)
  This function returns the difference of the complex number a and the real number x, $z = a - x$.

gsl_complex gsl_complex_mul_real (gsl_complex a,   *Function*
        double x)
  This function returns the product of the complex number a and the real number x, $z = ax$.

gsl_complex gsl_complex_div_real (gsl_complex a,   *Function*
        double x)
  This function returns the quotient of the complex number a and the real number x, $z = a/x$.

gsl_complex gsl_complex_add_imag (gsl_complex a,   *Function*
        double y)
  This function returns the sum of the complex number a and the imaginary number iy, $z = a + iy$.

gsl_complex gsl_complex_sub_imag (gsl_complex a,   Function
        double y)
This function returns the difference of the complex number a and the
imaginary number iy, $z = a - iy$.

gsl_complex gsl_complex_mul_imag (gsl_complex a,   Function
        double y)
This function returns the product of the complex number a and the
imaginary number iy, $z = a * (iy)$.

gsl_complex gsl_complex_div_imag (gsl_complex a,   Function
        double y)
This function returns the quotient of the complex number a and the
imaginary number iy, $z = a/(iy)$.

gsl_complex gsl_complex_conjugate (gsl_complex z)   Function
This function returns the complex conjugate of the complex number
z, $z^* = x - iy$.

gsl_complex gsl_complex_inverse (gsl_complex z)   Function
This function returns the inverse, or reciprocal, of the complex number
z, $1/z = (x - iy)/(x^2 + y^2)$.

gsl_complex gsl_complex_negative (gsl_complex z)   Function
This function returns the negative of the complex number z, $-z = (-x) + i(-y)$.

5.4 Elementary Complex Functions

gsl_complex gsl_complex_sqrt (gsl_complex z)   Function
This function returns the square root of the complex number z, $\sqrt{z}$.
The branch cut is the negative real axis. The result always lies in the
right half of the complex plane.

gsl_complex gsl_complex_sqrt_real (double x)   Function
This function returns the complex square root of the real number x,
where x may be negative.

gsl_complex gsl_complex_pow (gsl_complex z,   Function
        gsl_complex a)
The function returns the complex number z raised to the complex
power a, z^a. This is computed as $\exp(\log(z) * a)$ using complex logarithms and complex exponentials.

gsl_complex gsl_complex_pow_real (gsl_complex z,   Function
      double x)
  This function returns the complex number z raised to the real power
  x, z^x.

gsl_complex gsl_complex_exp (gsl_complex z)   Function
  This function returns the complex exponential of the complex number
  z, $\exp(z)$.

gsl_complex gsl_complex_log (gsl_complex z)   Function
  This function returns the complex natural logarithm (base e) of the
  complex number z, $\log(z)$. The branch cut is the negative real axis.

gsl_complex gsl_complex_log10 (gsl_complex z)   Function
  This function returns the complex base-10 logarithm of the complex
  number z, $\log_{10}(z)$.

gsl_complex gsl_complex_log_b (gsl_complex z,   Function
      gsl_complex b)
  This function returns the complex base-b logarithm of the complex number z, $\log_b(z)$. This quantity is computed as the ratio
  $\log(z)/\log(b)$.

5.5 Complex Trigonometric Functions

gsl_complex gsl_complex_sin (gsl_complex z)   Function
  This function returns the complex sine of the complex number z,
  $\sin(z) = (\exp(iz) - \exp(-iz))/(2i)$.

gsl_complex gsl_complex_cos (gsl_complex z)   Function
  This function returns the complex cosine of the complex number z,
  $\cos(z) = (\exp(iz) + \exp(-iz))/2$.

gsl_complex gsl_complex_tan (gsl_complex z)   Function
  This function returns the complex tangent of the complex number z,
  $\tan(z) = \sin(z)/\cos(z)$.

gsl_complex gsl_complex_sec (gsl_complex z)   Function
  This function returns the complex secant of the complex number z,
  $\sec(z) = 1/\cos(z)$.

gsl_complex gsl_complex_csc (gsl_complex z)   Function
  This function returns the complex cosecant of the complex number z,
  $\csc(z) = 1/\sin(z)$.

gsl_complex gsl_complex_cot (gsl_complex z)   Function
  This function returns the complex cotangent of the complex number
  z, $\cot(z) = 1/\tan(z)$.

5.6 Inverse Complex Trigonometric Functions

gsl_complex **gsl_complex_arcsin** (gsl_complex z)   *Function*
> This function returns the complex arcsine of the complex number z, $\arcsin(z)$. The branch cuts are on the real axis, less than -1 and greater than 1.

gsl_complex **gsl_complex_arcsin_real** (double z)   *Function*
> This function returns the complex arcsine of the real number z, $\arcsin(z)$. For z between -1 and 1, the function returns a real value in the range $[-\pi/2, \pi/2]$. For z less than -1 the result has a real part of $-\pi/2$ and a positive imaginary part. For z greater than 1 the result has a real part of $\pi/2$ and a negative imaginary part.

gsl_complex **gsl_complex_arccos** (gsl_complex z)   *Function*
> This function returns the complex arccosine of the complex number z, $\arccos(z)$. The branch cuts are on the real axis, less than -1 and greater than 1.

gsl_complex **gsl_complex_arccos_real** (double z)   *Function*
> This function returns the complex arccosine of the real number z, $\arccos(z)$. For z between -1 and 1, the function returns a real value in the range $[0, \pi]$. For z less than -1 the result has a real part of π and a negative imaginary part. For z greater than 1 the result is purely imaginary and positive.

gsl_complex **gsl_complex_arctan** (gsl_complex z)   *Function*
> This function returns the complex arctangent of the complex number z, $\arctan(z)$. The branch cuts are on the imaginary axis, below $-i$ and above i.

gsl_complex **gsl_complex_arcsec** (gsl_complex z)   *Function*
> This function returns the complex arcsecant of the complex number z, $\mathrm{arcsec}(z) = \arccos(1/z)$.

gsl_complex **gsl_complex_arcsec_real** (double z)   *Function*
> This function returns the complex arcsecant of the real number z, $\mathrm{arcsec}(z) = \arccos(1/z)$.

gsl_complex **gsl_complex_arccsc** (gsl_complex z)   *Function*
> This function returns the complex arccosecant of the complex number z, $\mathrm{arccsc}(z) = \arcsin(1/z)$.

`gsl_complex gsl_complex_arccsc_real (double z)`   Function
This function returns the complex arccosecant of the real number z, $\operatorname{arccsc}(z) = \arcsin(1/z)$.

`gsl_complex gsl_complex_arccot (gsl_complex z)`   Function
This function returns the complex arccotangent of the complex number z, $\operatorname{arccot}(z) = \arctan(1/z)$.

5.7 Complex Hyperbolic Functions

`gsl_complex gsl_complex_sinh (gsl_complex z)`   Function
This function returns the complex hyperbolic sine of the complex number z, $\sinh(z) = (\exp(z) - \exp(-z))/2$.

`gsl_complex gsl_complex_cosh (gsl_complex z)`   Function
This function returns the complex hyperbolic cosine of the complex number z, $\cosh(z) = (\exp(z) + \exp(-z))/2$.

`gsl_complex gsl_complex_tanh (gsl_complex z)`   Function
This function returns the complex hyperbolic tangent of the complex number z, $\tanh(z) = \sinh(z)/\cosh(z)$.

`gsl_complex gsl_complex_sech (gsl_complex z)`   Function
This function returns the complex hyperbolic secant of the complex number z, $\operatorname{sech}(z) = 1/\cosh(z)$.

`gsl_complex gsl_complex_csch (gsl_complex z)`   Function
This function returns the complex hyperbolic cosecant of the complex number z, $\operatorname{csch}(z) = 1/\sinh(z)$.

`gsl_complex gsl_complex_coth (gsl_complex z)`   Function
This function returns the complex hyperbolic cotangent of the complex number z, $\coth(z) = 1/\tanh(z)$.

5.8 Inverse Complex Hyperbolic Functions

gsl_complex gsl_complex_arcsinh (gsl_complex z)   Function
  This function returns the complex hyperbolic arcsine of the complex
  number z, arcsinh(z). The branch cuts are on the imaginary axis,
  below $-i$ and above i.

gsl_complex gsl_complex_arccosh (gsl_complex z)   Function
  This function returns the complex hyperbolic arccosine of the complex
  number z, arccosh(z). The branch cut is on the real axis, less than
  1. Note that in this case we use the negative square root in formula
  4.6.21 of Abramowitz & Stegun giving $arccosh(z) = \log(z - \sqrt{z^2 - 1})$.

gsl_complex gsl_complex_arccosh_real (double z)   Function
  This function returns the complex hyperbolic arccosine of the real
  number z, arccosh(z).

gsl_complex gsl_complex_arctanh (gsl_complex z)   Function
  This function returns the complex hyperbolic arctangent of the complex number z, arctanh(z). The branch cuts are on the real axis, less
  than -1 and greater than 1.

gsl_complex gsl_complex_arctanh_real (double z)   Function
  This function returns the complex hyperbolic arctangent of the real
  number z, arctanh(z).

gsl_complex gsl_complex_arcsech (gsl_complex z)   Function
  This function returns the complex hyperbolic arcsecant of the complex
  number z, $arcsech(z) = arccosh(1/z)$.

gsl_complex gsl_complex_arccsch (gsl_complex z)   Function
  This function returns the complex hyperbolic arccosecant of the complex number z, $arccsch(z) = arcsin(1/z)$.

gsl_complex gsl_complex_arccoth (gsl_complex z)   Function
  This function returns the complex hyperbolic arccotangent of the complex number z, $arccoth(z) = arctanh(1/z)$.

5.9 References and Further Reading

The implementations of the elementary and trigonometric functions are based on the following papers,

T. E. Hull, Thomas F. Fairgrieve, Ping Tak Peter Tang, "Implementing Complex Elementary Functions Using Exception Handling", *ACM Transactions on Mathematical Software*, Volume 20 (1994), pp 215–244, Corrigenda, p553

T. E. Hull, Thomas F. Fairgrieve, Ping Tak Peter Tang, "Implementing the complex arcsin and arccosine functions using exception handling", *ACM Transactions on Mathematical Software*, Volume 23 (1997) pp 299–335

The general formulas and details of branch cuts can be found in the following books,

Abramowitz and Stegun, *Handbook of Mathematical Functions*, "Circular Functions in Terms of Real and Imaginary Parts", Formulas 4.3.55–58, "Inverse Circular Functions in Terms of Real and Imaginary Parts", Formulas 4.4.37–39, "Hyperbolic Functions in Terms of Real and Imaginary Parts", Formulas 4.5.49–52, "Inverse Hyperbolic Functions—relation to Inverse Circular Functions", Formulas 4.6.14–19.

Dave Gillespie, *Calc Manual*, Free Software Foundation, ISBN 1-882114-18-3

6 Polynomials

This chapter describes functions for evaluating and solving polynomials. There are routines for finding real and complex roots of quadratic and cubic equations using analytic methods. An iterative polynomial solver is also available for finding the roots of general polynomials with real coefficients (of any order). The functions are declared in the header file `gsl_poly.h`.

6.1 Polynomial Evaluation

`double gsl_poly_eval (const double c[], const int` *len,*   *Function*
`const double` *x*`)`

This function evaluates the polynomial $c[0] + c[1]x + c[2]x^2 + \ldots + c[len-1]x^{len-1}$ using Horner's method for stability. The function is inlined when possible.

6.2 Divided Difference Representation of Polynomials

The functions described here manipulate polynomials stored in Newton's divided-difference representation. The use of divided-differences is described in Abramowitz & Stegun sections 25.1.4 and 25.2.26.

`int gsl_poly_dd_init (double` *dd*`[], const double` *xa*`[],`   *Function*
`const double` *ya*`[], size_t` *size*`)`

This function computes a divided-difference representation of the interpolating polynomial for the points (*xa, ya*) stored in the arrays *xa* and *ya* of length *size*. On output the divided-differences of (*xa,ya*) are stored in the array *dd*, also of length *size*.

`double gsl_poly_dd_eval (const double` *dd*`[], const`   *Function*
`double` *xa*`[], const size_t` *size*`, const double` *x*`)`

This function evaluates the polynomial stored in divided-difference form in the arrays *dd* and *xa* of length *size* at the point *x*.

`int gsl_poly_dd_taylor (double` *c*`[], double` *xp*`, const`   *Function*
`double` *dd*`[], const double` *xa*`[], size_t` *size*`, double` *w*`[])`

This function converts the divided-difference representation of a polynomial to a Taylor expansion. The divided-difference representation is supplied in the arrays *dd* and *xa* of length *size*. On output the Taylor coefficients of the polynomial expanded about the point *xp* are stored in the array *c* also of length *size*. A workspace of length *size* must be provided in the array *w*.

6.3 Quadratic Equations

int gsl_poly_solve_quadratic (double *a*, double *b*,   *Function*
         double *c*, double * *x0*, double * *x1*)
   This function finds the real roots of the quadratic equation,

$$ax^2 + bx + c = 0$$

   The number of real roots (either zero, one or two) is returned, and
   their locations are stored in $x0$ and $x1$. If no real roots are found then
   $x0$ and $x1$ are not modified. If one real root is found (i.e. if $a = 0$)
   then it is stored in $x0$. When two real roots are found they are stored
   in $x0$ and $x1$ in ascending order. The case of coincident roots is not
   considered special. For example $(x-1)^2 = 0$ will have two roots, which
   happen to have exactly equal values.

   The number of roots found depends on the sign of the discriminant
   $b^2 - 4ac$. This will be subject to rounding and cancellation errors when
   computed in double precision, and will also be subject to errors if the
   coefficients of the polynomial are inexact. These errors may cause a
   discrete change in the number of roots. However, for polynomials with
   small integer coefficients the discriminant can always be computed
   exactly.

int gsl_poly_complex_solve_quadratic (double *a*, double   *Function*
         b, double *c*, gsl_complex * *z0*, gsl_complex * *z1*)
   This function finds the complex roots of the quadratic equation,

$$az^2 + bz + c = 0$$

   The number of complex roots is returned (either one or two) and the
   locations of the roots are stored in $z0$ and $z1$. The roots are returned
   in ascending order, sorted first by their real components and then by
   their imaginary components. If only one real root is found (i.e. if
   $a = 0$) then it is stored in $z0$.

6.4 Cubic Equations

int gsl_poly_solve_cubic (double a, double b, double c,   *Function*
     double * $x0$, double * $x1$, double * $x2$)
This function finds the real roots of the cubic equation,

$$x^3 + ax^2 + bx + c = 0$$

with a leading coefficient of unity. The number of real roots (either one or three) is returned, and their locations are stored in $x0$, $x1$ and $x2$. If one real root is found then only $x0$ is modified. When three real roots are found they are stored in $x0$, $x1$ and $x2$ in ascending order. The case of coincident roots is not considered special. For example, the equation $(x - 1)^3 = 0$ will have three roots with exactly equal values.

int gsl_poly_complex_solve_cubic (double a, double b,   *Function*
     double c, gsl_complex * $z0$, gsl_complex * $z1$,
     gsl_complex * $z2$)
This function finds the complex roots of the cubic equation,

$$z^3 + az^2 + bz + c = 0$$

The number of complex roots is returned (always three) and the locations of the roots are stored in $z0$, $z1$ and $z2$. The roots are returned in ascending order, sorted first by their real components and then by their imaginary components.

6.5 General Polynomial Equations

The roots of polynomial equations cannot be found analytically beyond the special cases of the quadratic, cubic and quartic equation. The algorithm described in this section uses an iterative method to find the approximate locations of roots of higher order polynomials.

gsl_poly_complex_workspace *   *Function*
       gsl_poly_complex_workspace_alloc (size_t n)
This function allocates space for a gsl_poly_complex_workspace struct and a workspace suitable for solving a polynomial with n coefficients using the routine gsl_poly_complex_solve.

The function returns a pointer to the newly allocated gsl_poly_complex_workspace if no errors were detected, and a null pointer in the case of error.

void gsl_poly_complex_workspace_free   *Function*
     (gsl_poly_complex_workspace * w)
This function frees all the memory associated with the workspace w.

int gsl_poly_complex_solve (const double * a, size_t n,   Function
        gsl_poly_complex_workspace * w,
        gsl_complex_packed_ptr z)

This function computes the roots of the general polynomial $P(x) = a_0 + a_1 x + a_2 x^2 + ... + a_{n-1} x^{n-1}$ using balanced-QR reduction of the companion matrix. The parameter n specifies the length of the coefficient array. The coefficient of the highest order term must be non-zero. The function requires a workspace w of the appropriate size. The $n-1$ roots are returned in the packed complex array z of length $2(n-1)$, alternating real and imaginary parts.

The function returns GSL_SUCCESS if all the roots are found. If the QR reduction does not converge, the error handler is invoked with an error code of GSL_EFAILED. Note that due to finite precision, roots of higher multiplicity are returned as a cluster of simple roots with reduced accuracy. The solution of polynomials with higher-order roots requires specialized algorithms that take the multiplicity structure into account (see e.g. Z. Zeng, Algorithm 835, ACM Transactions on Mathematical Software, Volume 30, Issue 2 (2004), pp 218–236).

6.6 Examples

To demonstrate the use of the general polynomial solver we will take the polynomial $P(x) = x^5 - 1$ which has the following roots,

$$1, e^{2\pi i/5}, e^{4\pi i/5}, e^{6\pi i/5}, e^{8\pi i/5}$$

The following program will find these roots.

```
#include <stdio.h>
#include <gsl/gsl_poly.h>

int
main (void)
{
  int i;
  /* coefficients of P(x) =  -1 + x^5  */
  double a[6] = { -1, 0, 0, 0, 0, 1 };
  double z[10];

  gsl_poly_complex_workspace * w
      = gsl_poly_complex_workspace_alloc (6);

  gsl_poly_complex_solve (a, 6, w, z);

  gsl_poly_complex_workspace_free (w);
```

```
for (i = 0; i < 5; i++)
  {
    printf ("z%d = %+.18f %+.18f\n",
            i, z[2*i], z[2*i+1]);
  }

  return 0;
}
```

The output of the program is,

```
$ ./a.out
z0 = -0.809016994374947451 +0.587785252292473137
z1 = -0.809016994374947451 -0.587785252292473137
z2 = +0.309016994374947451 +0.951056516295153642
z3 = +0.309016994374947451 -0.951056516295153642
z4 = +1.000000000000000000 +0.000000000000000000
```

which agrees with the analytic result, $z_n = \exp(2\pi n i/5)$.

6.7 References and Further Reading

The balanced-QR method and its error analysis are described in the following papers,

R.S. Martin, G. Peters and J.H. Wilkinson, "The QR Algorithm for Real Hessenberg Matrices", *Numerische Mathematik*, 14 (1970), 219–231.

B.N. Parlett and C. Reinsch, "Balancing a Matrix for Calculation of Eigenvalues and Eigenvectors", *Numerische Mathematik*, 13 (1969), 293–304.

A. Edelman and H. Murakami, "Polynomial roots from companion matrix eigenvalues", *Mathematics of Computation*, Vol. 64, No. 210 (1995), 763–776.

The formulas for divided differences are given in Abramowitz and Stegun,

Abramowitz and Stegun, *Handbook of Mathematical Functions*, Sections 25.1.4 and 25.2.26.

7 Special Functions

This chapter describes the GSL special function library. The library includes routines for calculating the values of Airy functions, Bessel functions, Clausen functions, Coulomb wave functions, Coupling coefficients, the Dawson function, Debye functions, Dilogarithms, Elliptic integrals, Jacobi elliptic functions, Error functions, Exponential integrals, Fermi-Dirac functions, Gamma functions, Gegenbauer functions, Hypergeometric functions, Laguerre functions, Legendre functions and Spherical Harmonics, the Psi (Digamma) Function, Synchrotron functions, Transport functions, Trigonometric functions and Zeta functions. Each routine also computes an estimate of the numerical error in the calculated value of the function.

The functions in this chapter are declared in individual header files, such as 'gsl_sf_airy.h', 'gsl_sf_bessel.h', etc. The complete set of header files can be included using the file 'gsl_sf.h'.

7.1 Usage

The special functions are available in two calling conventions, a *natural form* which returns the numerical value of the function and an *error-handling form* which returns an error code. The two types of function provide alternative ways of accessing the same underlying code.

The *natural form* returns only the value of the function and can be used directly in mathematical expressions. For example, the following function call will compute the value of the Bessel function $J_0(x)$,

```
double y = gsl_sf_bessel_J0 (x);
```

There is no way to access an error code or to estimate the error using this method. To allow access to this information the alternative error-handling form stores the value and error in a modifiable argument,

```
gsl_sf_result result;
int status = gsl_sf_bessel_J0_e (x, &result);
```

The error-handling functions have the suffix _e. The returned status value indicates error conditions such as overflow, underflow or loss of precision. If there are no errors the error-handling functions return GSL_SUCCESS.

7.2 The gsl_sf_result struct

The error handling form of the special functions always calculate an error estimate along with the value of the result. Therefore, structures are provided for amalgamating a value and error estimate. These structures are declared in the header file 'gsl_sf_result.h'.

The gsl_sf_result struct contains value and error fields.

```
typedef struct
{
  double val;
  double err;
} gsl_sf_result;
```

The field *val* contains the value and the field *err* contains an estimate of the absolute error in the value.

In some cases, an overflow or underflow can be detected and handled by a function. In this case, it may be possible to return a scaling exponent as well as an error/value pair in order to save the result from exceeding the dynamic range of the built-in types. The gsl_sf_result_e10 struct contains value and error fields as well as an exponent field such that the actual result is obtained as result * 10^(e10).

```
typedef struct
{
  double val;
  double err;
  int    e10;
} gsl_sf_result_e10;
```

7.3 Modes

The goal of the library is to achieve double precision accuracy wherever possible. However the cost of evaluating some special functions to double precision can be significant, particularly where very high order terms are required. In these cases a mode argument allows the accuracy of the function to be reduced in order to improve performance. The following precision levels are available for the mode argument,

GSL_PREC_DOUBLE

      Double-precision, a relative accuracy of approximately 2×10^{-16}.

GSL_PREC_SINGLE

      Single-precision, a relative accuracy of approximately 1×10^{-7}.

GSL_PREC_APPROX
> Approximate values, a relative accuracy of approximately 5×10^{-4}.

The approximate mode provides the fastest evaluation at the lowest accuracy.

7.4 Airy Functions and Derivatives

The Airy functions $Ai(x)$ and $Bi(x)$ are defined by the integral representations,

$$Ai(x) = \frac{1}{\pi} \int_0^\infty \cos(t^3/3 + xt) \, dt,$$

$$Bi(x) = \frac{1}{\pi} \int_0^\infty (e^{-t^3/3} + \sin(t^3/3 + xt)) \, dt.$$

For further information see Abramowitz & Stegun, Section 10.4. The Airy functions are defined in the header file 'gsl_sf_airy.h'.

7.4.1 Airy Functions

double gsl_sf_airy_Ai (double x, gsl_mode_t *mode*)   Function
int gsl_sf_airy_Ai_e (double x, gsl_mode_t *mode*,   Function
        gsl_sf_result * *result*)
> These routines compute the Airy function $Ai(x)$ with an accuracy specified by *mode*.

double gsl_sf_airy_Bi (double x, gsl_mode_t *mode*)   Function
int gsl_sf_airy_Bi_e (double x, gsl_mode_t *mode*,   Function
        gsl_sf_result * *result*)
> These routines compute the Airy function $Bi(x)$ with an accuracy specified by *mode*.

double gsl_sf_airy_Ai_scaled (double x, gsl_mode_t   Function
        mode)
int gsl_sf_airy_Ai_scaled_e (double x, gsl_mode_t   Function
        mode, gsl_sf_result * *result*)
> These routines compute a scaled version of the Airy function $S_A(x)Ai(x)$. For $x > 0$ the scaling factor $S_A(x)$ is $\exp(+(2/3)x^{3/2})$, and is 1 for $x < 0$.

double `gsl_sf_airy_Bi_scaled` (double *x*, gsl_mode_t   Function
         mode)

int `gsl_sf_airy_Bi_scaled_e` (double *x*, gsl_mode_t   Function
         mode, gsl_sf_result * *result*)

These routines compute a scaled version of the Airy function $S_B(x)Bi(x)$. For $x > 0$ the scaling factor $S_B(x)$ is $\exp(-(2/3)x^{3/2})$, and is 1 for $x < 0$.

7.4.2 Derivatives of Airy Functions

double `gsl_sf_airy_Ai_deriv` (double *x*, gsl_mode_t   Function
         mode)

int `gsl_sf_airy_Ai_deriv_e` (double *x*, gsl_mode_t *mode*,   Function
         gsl_sf_result * *result*)

These routines compute the Airy function derivative $Ai'(x)$ with an accuracy specified by *mode*.

double `gsl_sf_airy_Bi_deriv` (double *x*, gsl_mode_t   Function
         mode)

int `gsl_sf_airy_Bi_deriv_e` (double *x*, gsl_mode_t *mode*,   Function
         gsl_sf_result * *result*)

These routines compute the Airy function derivative $Bi'(x)$ with an accuracy specified by *mode*.

double `gsl_sf_airy_Ai_deriv_scaled` (double *x*,   Function
         gsl_mode_t *mode*)

int `gsl_sf_airy_Ai_deriv_scaled_e` (double *x*,   Function
         gsl_mode_t *mode*, gsl_sf_result * *result*)

These routines compute the scaled Airy function derivative $S_A(x)Ai'(x)$. For $x > 0$ the scaling factor $S_A(x)$ is $\exp(+(2/3)x^{3/2})$, and is 1 for $x < 0$.

double `gsl_sf_airy_Bi_deriv_scaled` (double *x*,   Function
         gsl_mode_t *mode*)

int `gsl_sf_airy_Bi_deriv_scaled_e` (double *x*,   Function
         gsl_mode_t *mode*, gsl_sf_result * *result*)

These routines compute the scaled Airy function derivative $S_B(x)Bi'(x)$. For $x > 0$ the scaling factor $S_B(x)$ is $\exp(-(2/3)x^{3/2})$, and is 1 for $x < 0$.

7.4.3 Zeros of Airy Functions

double gsl_sf_airy_zero_Ai (unsigned int *s*)   Function
int gsl_sf_airy_zero_Ai_e (unsigned int *s*,   Function
          gsl_sf_result * *result*)
> These routines compute the location of the *s*-th zero of the Airy function $Ai(x)$.

double gsl_sf_airy_zero_Bi (unsigned int *s*)   Function
int gsl_sf_airy_zero_Bi_e (unsigned int *s*,   Function
          gsl_sf_result * *result*)
> These routines compute the location of the *s*-th zero of the Airy function $Bi(x)$.

7.4.4 Zeros of Derivatives of Airy Functions

double gsl_sf_airy_zero_Ai_deriv (unsigned int *s*)   Function
int gsl_sf_airy_zero_Ai_deriv_e (unsigned int *s*,   Function
          gsl_sf_result * *result*)
> These routines compute the location of the *s*-th zero of the Airy function derivative $Ai'(x)$.

double gsl_sf_airy_zero_Bi_deriv (unsigned int *s*)   Function
int gsl_sf_airy_zero_Bi_deriv_e (unsigned int *s*,   Function
          gsl_sf_result * *result*)
> These routines compute the location of the *s*-th zero of the Airy function derivative $Bi'(x)$.

7.5 Bessel Functions

The routines described in this section compute the Cylindrical Bessel functions $J_n(x)$, $Y_n(x)$, Modified cylindrical Bessel functions $I_n(x)$, $K_n(x)$, Spherical Bessel functions $j_l(x)$, $y_l(x)$, and Modified Spherical Bessel functions $i_l(x)$, $k_l(x)$. For more information see Abramowitz & Stegun, Chapters 9 and 10. The Bessel functions are defined in the header file 'gsl_sf_bessel.h'.

7.5.1 Regular Cylindrical Bessel Functions

double gsl_sf_bessel_J0 (double x)   *Function*
int gsl_sf_bessel_J0_e (double x, gsl_sf_result *   *Function*
        result)
  These routines compute the regular cylindrical Bessel function of zeroth order, $J_0(x)$.

double gsl_sf_bessel_J1 (double x)   *Function*
int gsl_sf_bessel_J1_e (double x, gsl_sf_result *   *Function*
        result)
  These routines compute the regular cylindrical Bessel function of first
  order, $J_1(x)$.

double gsl_sf_bessel_Jn (int n, double x)   *Function*
int gsl_sf_bessel_Jn_e (int n, double x, gsl_sf_result   *Function*
        * result)
  These routines compute the regular cylindrical Bessel function of order
  n, $J_n(x)$.

int gsl_sf_bessel_Jn_array (int nmin, int nmax, double   *Function*
        x, double result_array[])
  This routine computes the values of the regular cylindrical Bessel functions $J_n(x)$ for n from nmin to nmax inclusive, storing the results in
  the array result_array. The values are computed using recurrence relations for efficiency, and therefore may differ slightly from the exact
  values.

7.5.2 Irregular Cylindrical Bessel Functions

double gsl_sf_bessel_Y0 (double x)   *Function*
int gsl_sf_bessel_Y0_e (double x, gsl_sf_result *   *Function*
        result)
  These routines compute the irregular cylindrical Bessel function of
  zeroth order, $Y_0(x)$, for $x > 0$.

double gsl_sf_bessel_Y1 (double x)   *Function*
int gsl_sf_bessel_Y1_e (double x, gsl_sf_result *   *Function*
        result)
  These routines compute the irregular cylindrical Bessel function of first
  order, $Y_1(x)$, for $x > 0$.

double gsl_sf_bessel_Yn (int *n*,double *x*)   Function
int gsl_sf_bessel_Yn_e (int *n*,double *x*, gsl_sf_result *   Function
        result)

These routines compute the irregular cylindrical Bessel function of order n, $Y_n(x)$, for $x > 0$.

int gsl_sf_bessel_Yn_array (int *nmin*, int *nmax*, double   Function
        x, double *result_array*[])

This routine computes the values of the irregular cylindrical Bessel functions $Y_n(x)$ for n from *nmin* to *nmax* inclusive, storing the results in the array *result_array*. The domain of the function is $x > 0$. The values are computed using recurrence relations for efficiency, and therefore may differ slightly from the exact values.

7.5.3 Regular Modified Cylindrical Bessel Functions

double gsl_sf_bessel_I0 (double *x*)   Function
int gsl_sf_bessel_I0_e (double *x*, gsl_sf_result *   Function
        result)

These routines compute the regular modified cylindrical Bessel function of zeroth order, $I_0(x)$.

double gsl_sf_bessel_I1 (double *x*)   Function
int gsl_sf_bessel_I1_e (double *x*, gsl_sf_result *   Function
        result)

These routines compute the regular modified cylindrical Bessel function of first order, $I_1(x)$.

double gsl_sf_bessel_In (int *n*, double *x*)   Function
int gsl_sf_bessel_In_e (int *n*, double *x*, gsl_sf_result   Function
        * *result*)

These routines compute the regular modified cylindrical Bessel function of order n, $I_n(x)$.

int gsl_sf_bessel_In_array (int *nmin*, int *nmax*, double   Function
        x, double *result_array*[])

This routine computes the values of the regular modified cylindrical Bessel functions $I_n(x)$ for n from *nmin* to *nmax* inclusive, storing the results in the array *result_array*. The start of the range *nmin* must be positive or zero. The values are computed using recurrence relations for efficiency, and therefore may differ slightly from the exact values.

double `gsl_sf_bessel_I0_scaled` (double x)   Function
int `gsl_sf_bessel_I0_scaled_e` (double x, gsl_sf_result   Function
        * *result*)
These routines compute the scaled regular modified cylindrical Bessel
function of zeroth order $\exp(-|x|)I_0(x)$.

double `gsl_sf_bessel_I1_scaled` (double x)   Function
int `gsl_sf_bessel_I1_scaled_e` (double x, gsl_sf_result   Function
        * *result*)
These routines compute the scaled regular modified cylindrical Bessel
function of first order $\exp(-|x|)I_1(x)$.

double `gsl_sf_bessel_In_scaled` (int n, double x)   Function
int `gsl_sf_bessel_In_scaled_e` (int n, double x,   Function
        gsl_sf_result * *result*)
These routines compute the scaled regular modified cylindrical Bessel
function of order n, $\exp(-|x|)I_n(x)$

int `gsl_sf_bessel_In_scaled_array` (int *nmin*, int   Function
        nmax, double x, double *result_array*[])
This routine computes the values of the scaled regular cylindrical
Bessel functions $\exp(-|x|)I_n(x)$ for n from *nmin* to *nmax* inclusive,
storing the results in the array *result_array*. The start of the range
nmin must be positive or zero. The values are computed using recurrence relations for efficiency, and therefore may differ slightly from the
exact values.

7.5.4 Irregular Modified Cylindrical Bessel Functions

double `gsl_sf_bessel_K0` (double x)   Function
int `gsl_sf_bessel_K0_e` (double x, gsl_sf_result *   Function
        result)
These routines compute the irregular modified cylindrical Bessel function of zeroth order, $K_0(x)$, for $x > 0$.

double `gsl_sf_bessel_K1` (double x)   Function
int `gsl_sf_bessel_K1_e` (double x, gsl_sf_result *   Function
        result)
These routines compute the irregular modified cylindrical Bessel function of first order, $K_1(x)$, for $x > 0$.

double gsl_sf_bessel_Kn (int *n*, double *x*)   Function
int gsl_sf_bessel_Kn_e (int *n*, double *x*, gsl_sf_result   Function
        * *result*)

These routines compute the irregular modified cylindrical Bessel function of order n, $K_n(x)$, for $x > 0$.

int gsl_sf_bessel_Kn_array (int *nmin*, int *nmax*, double   Function
        x, double *result_array*[])

This routine computes the values of the irregular modified cylindrical Bessel functions $K_n(x)$ for n from *nmin* to *nmax* inclusive, storing the results in the array *result_array*. The start of the range *nmin* must be positive or zero. The domain of the function is $x > 0$. The values are computed using recurrence relations for efficiency, and therefore may differ slightly from the exact values.

double gsl_sf_bessel_K0_scaled (double *x*)   Function
int gsl_sf_bessel_K0_scaled_e (double *x*, gsl_sf_result   Function
        * *result*)

These routines compute the scaled irregular modified cylindrical Bessel function of zeroth order $\exp(x)K_0(x)$ for $x > 0$.

double gsl_sf_bessel_K1_scaled (double *x*)   Function
int gsl_sf_bessel_K1_scaled_e (double *x*, gsl_sf_result   Function
        * *result*)

These routines compute the scaled irregular modified cylindrical Bessel function of first order $\exp(x)K_1(x)$ for $x > 0$.

double gsl_sf_bessel_Kn_scaled (int *n*, double *x*)   Function
int gsl_sf_bessel_Kn_scaled_e (int *n*, double *x*,   Function
        gsl_sf_result * *result*)

These routines compute the scaled irregular modified cylindrical Bessel function of order n, $\exp(x)K_n(x)$, for $x > 0$.

int gsl_sf_bessel_Kn_scaled_array (int *nmin*, int   Function
        nmax, double *x*, double *result_array*[])

This routine computes the values of the scaled irregular cylindrical Bessel functions $\exp(x)K_n(x)$ for n from *nmin* to *nmax* inclusive, storing the results in the array *result_array*. The start of the range *nmin* must be positive or zero. The domain of the function is $x > 0$. The values are computed using recurrence relations for efficiency, and therefore may differ slightly from the exact values.

7.5.5 Regular Spherical Bessel Functions

double gsl_sf_bessel_j0 (double x)   Function
int gsl_sf_bessel_j0_e (double x, gsl_sf_result *   Function
         result)
   These routines compute the regular spherical Bessel function of zeroth
   order, $j_0(x) = \sin(x)/x$.

double gsl_sf_bessel_j1 (double x)   Function
int gsl_sf_bessel_j1_e (double x, gsl_sf_result *   Function
         result)
   These routines compute the regular spherical Bessel function of first
   order, $j_1(x) = (\sin(x)/x - \cos(x))/x$.

double gsl_sf_bessel_j2 (double x)   Function
int gsl_sf_bessel_j2_e (double x, gsl_sf_result *   Function
         result)
   These routines compute the regular spherical Bessel function of second
   order, $j_2(x) = ((3/x^2 - 1)\sin(x) - 3\cos(x)/x)/x$.

double gsl_sf_bessel_jl (int l, double x)   Function
int gsl_sf_bessel_jl_e (int l, double x, gsl_sf_result   Function
         * result)
   These routines compute the regular spherical Bessel function of order
   l, $j_l(x)$, for $l \geq 0$ and $x \geq 0$.

int gsl_sf_bessel_jl_array (int lmax, double x, double   Function
         result_array[])
   This routine computes the values of the regular spherical Bessel functions $j_l(x)$ for l from 0 to $lmax$ inclusive for $lmax \geq 0$ and $x \geq 0$,
   storing the results in the array result_array. The values are computed using recurrence relations for efficiency, and therefore may differ
   slightly from the exact values.

int gsl_sf_bessel_jl_steed_array (int lmax, double x,   Function
         double * jl_x_array)
   This routine uses Steed's method to compute the values of the regular spherical Bessel functions $j_l(x)$ for l from 0 to $lmax$ inclusive for
   $lmax \geq 0$ and $x \geq 0$, storing the results in the array result_array. The
   Steed/Barnett algorithm is described in Comp. Phys. Comm. 21, 297
   (1981). Steed's method is more stable than the recurrence used in the
   other functions but is also slower.

7.5.6 Irregular Spherical Bessel Functions

double gsl_sf_bessel_y0 (double x)   *Function*
int gsl_sf_bessel_y0_e (double x, gsl_sf_result *   *Function*
      result)

These routines compute the irregular spherical Bessel function of ze-roth order, $y_0(x) = -\cos(x)/x$.

double gsl_sf_bessel_y1 (double x)   *Function*
int gsl_sf_bessel_y1_e (double x, gsl_sf_result *   *Function*
      result)

These routines compute the irregular spherical Bessel function of first order, $y_1(x) = -(\cos(x)/x + \sin(x))/x$.

double gsl_sf_bessel_y2 (double x)   *Function*
int gsl_sf_bessel_y2_e (double x, gsl_sf_result *   *Function*
      result)

These routines compute the irregular spherical Bessel function of sec-ond order, $y_2(x) = (-3/x^3 + 1/x)\cos(x) - (3/x^2)\sin(x)$.

double gsl_sf_bessel_yl (int *l*, double x)   *Function*
int gsl_sf_bessel_yl_e (int *l*, double x, gsl_sf_result   *Function*
      * *result*)

These routines compute the irregular spherical Bessel function of order *l*, $y_l(x)$, for $l \geq 0$.

int gsl_sf_bessel_yl_array (int *lmax*, double x, double   *Function*
      result_array[])

This routine computes the values of the irregular spherical Bessel func-tions $y_l(x)$ for *l* from 0 to *lmax* inclusive for *lmax* ≥ 0, storing the results in the array *result_array*. The values are computed using re-currence relations for efficiency, and therefore may differ slightly from the exact values.

7.5.7 Regular Modified Spherical Bessel Functions

The regular modified spherical Bessel functions $i_l(x)$ are related to the modified Bessel functions of fractional order, $i_l(x) = \sqrt{\pi/(2x)}I_{l+1/2}(x)$

double gsl_sf_bessel_i0_scaled (double x)   *Function*
int gsl_sf_bessel_i0_scaled_e (double x, gsl_sf_result   *Function*
      * *result*)

These routines compute the scaled regular modified spherical Bessel function of zeroth order, $\exp(-|x|)i_0(x)$.

double gsl_sf_bessel_i1_scaled (double x)   Function
int gsl_sf_bessel_i1_scaled_e (double x, gsl_sf_result   Function
            * result)
These routines compute the scaled regular modified spherical Bessel
function of first order, $\exp(-|x|)i_1(x)$.

double gsl_sf_bessel_i2_scaled (double x)   Function
int gsl_sf_bessel_i2_scaled_e (double x, gsl_sf_result   Function
            * result)
These routines compute the scaled regular modified spherical Bessel
function of second order, $\exp(-|x|)i_2(x)$

double gsl_sf_bessel_il_scaled (int l, double x)   Function
int gsl_sf_bessel_il_scaled_e (int l, double x,   Function
            gsl_sf_result * result)
These routines compute the scaled regular modified spherical Bessel
function of order l, $\exp(-|x|)i_l(x)$

int gsl_sf_bessel_il_scaled_array (int lmax, double x,   Function
            double result_array[])
This routine computes the values of the scaled regular modified cylin-
drical Bessel functions $\exp(-|x|)i_l(x)$ for l from 0 to lmax inclusive for
$lmax \geq 0$, storing the results in the array result_array. The values are
computed using recurrence relations for efficiency, and therefore may
differ slightly from the exact values.

7.5.8 Irregular Modified Spherical Bessel Functions

The irregular modified spherical Bessel functions $k_l(x)$ are related
to the irregular modified Bessel functions of fractional order, $k_l(x) = \sqrt{\pi/(2x)}K_{l+1/2}(x)$.

double gsl_sf_bessel_k0_scaled (double x)   Function
int gsl_sf_bessel_k0_scaled_e (double x, gsl_sf_result   Function
            * result)
These routines compute the scaled irregular modified spherical Bessel
function of zeroth order, $\exp(x)k_0(x)$, for $x > 0$.

double gsl_sf_bessel_k1_scaled (double x)   Function
int gsl_sf_bessel_k1_scaled_e (double x, gsl_sf_result   Function
            * result)
These routines compute the scaled irregular modified spherical Bessel
function of first order, $\exp(x)k_1(x)$, for $x > 0$.

```
double gsl_sf_bessel_k2_scaled (double x)                    Function
int gsl_sf_bessel_k2_scaled_e (double x, gsl_sf_result      Function
        * result)
```
These routines compute the scaled irregular modified spherical Bessel function of second order, $\exp(x)k_2(x)$, for $x > 0$.

```
double gsl_sf_bessel_kl_scaled (int l, double x)            Function
int gsl_sf_bessel_kl_scaled_e (int l, double x,             Function
        gsl_sf_result * result)
```
These routines compute the scaled irregular modified spherical Bessel function of order l, $\exp(x)k_l(x)$, for $x > 0$.

```
int gsl_sf_bessel_kl_scaled_array (int lmax, double x,      Function
        double result_array[])
```
This routine computes the values of the scaled irregular modified spherical Bessel functions $\exp(x)k_l(x)$ for l from 0 to $lmax$ inclusive for $lmax \geq 0$ and $x > 0$, storing the results in the array $result\_array$. The values are computed using recurrence relations for efficiency, and therefore may differ slightly from the exact values.

7.5.9 Regular Bessel Function—Fractional Order

```
double gsl_sf_bessel_Jnu (double nu, double x)             Function
int gsl_sf_bessel_Jnu_e (double nu, double x,              Function
        gsl_sf_result * result)
```
These routines compute the regular cylindrical Bessel function of fractional order ν, $J_\nu(x)$.

```
int gsl_sf_bessel_sequence_Jnu_e (double nu,              Function
        gsl_mode_t mode, size_t size, double v[])
```
This function computes the regular cylindrical Bessel function of fractional order ν, $J_\nu(x)$, evaluated at a series of x values. The array v of length $size$ contains the x values. They are assumed to be strictly ordered and positive. The array is over-written with the values of $J_\nu(x_i)$.

7.5.10 Irregular Bessel Functions—Fractional Order

```
double gsl_sf_bessel_Ynu (double nu, double x)            Function
int gsl_sf_bessel_Ynu_e (double nu, double x,             Function
        gsl_sf_result * result)
```
These routines compute the irregular cylindrical Bessel function of fractional order ν, $Y_\nu(x)$.

7.5.11 Regular Modified Bessel Functions— Fractional Order

double gsl_sf_bessel_Inu (double *nu*, double *x*)   Function
int gsl_sf_bessel_Inu_e (double *nu*, double *x*,   Function
   gsl_sf_result * *result*)

These routines compute the regular modified Bessel function of fractional order ν, $I_\nu(x)$ for $x > 0$, $\nu > 0$.

double gsl_sf_bessel_Inu_scaled (double *nu*, double *x*)   Function
int gsl_sf_bessel_Inu_scaled_e (double *nu*, double *x*,   Function
   gsl_sf_result * *result*)

These routines compute the scaled regular modified Bessel function of fractional order ν, $\exp(-|x|)I_\nu(x)$ for $x > 0$, $\nu > 0$.

7.5.12 Irregular Modified Bessel Functions— Fractional Order

double gsl_sf_bessel_Knu (double *nu*, double *x*)   Function
int gsl_sf_bessel_Knu_e (double *nu*, double *x*,   Function
   gsl_sf_result * *result*)

These routines compute the irregular modified Bessel function of fractional order ν, $K_\nu(x)$ for $x > 0$, $\nu > 0$.

double gsl_sf_bessel_lnKnu (double *nu*, double *x*)   Function
int gsl_sf_bessel_lnKnu_e (double *nu*, double *x*,   Function
   gsl_sf_result * *result*)

These routines compute the logarithm of the irregular modified Bessel function of fractional order ν, $\ln(K_\nu(x))$ for $x > 0$, $\nu > 0$.

double gsl_sf_bessel_Knu_scaled (double *nu*, double *x*)   Function
int gsl_sf_bessel_Knu_scaled_e (double *nu*, double *x*,   Function
   gsl_sf_result * *result*)

These routines compute the scaled irregular modified Bessel function of fractional order ν, $\exp(+|x|)K_\nu(x)$ for $x > 0$, $\nu > 0$.

7.5.13 Zeros of Regular Bessel Functions

double gsl_sf_bessel_zero_J0 (unsigned int *s*)   Function
int gsl_sf_bessel_zero_J0_e (unsigned int *s*,   Function
     gsl_sf_result * *result*)
> These routines compute the location of the *s*-th positive zero of the
> Bessel function $J_0(x)$.

double gsl_sf_bessel_zero_J1 (unsigned int *s*)   Function
int gsl_sf_bessel_zero_J1_e (unsigned int *s*,   Function
     gsl_sf_result * *result*)
> These routines compute the location of the *s*-th positive zero of the
> Bessel function $J_1(x)$.

double gsl_sf_bessel_zero_Jnu (double *nu*, unsigned int   Function
     s)
int gsl_sf_bessel_zero_Jnu_e (double *nu*, unsigned int   Function
     s, gsl_sf_result * *result*)
> These routines compute the location of the *s*-th positive zero of the
> Bessel function $J_\nu(x)$. The current implementation does not support
> negative values of *nu*.

7.6 Clausen Functions

The Clausen function is defined by the following integral,

$$Cl_2(x) = -\int_0^x dt \log(2\sin(t/2))$$

It is related to the dilogarithm by $Cl_2(\theta) = \mathrm{Im}(Li_2(e^{i\theta}))$. The Clausen functions are declared in the header file 'gsl_sf_clausen.h'.

double gsl_sf_clausen (double *x*)   Function
int gsl_sf_clausen_e (double *x*, gsl_sf_result * *result*)   Function
> These routines compute the Clausen integral $Cl_2(x)$.

7.7 Coulomb Functions

The prototypes of the Coulomb functions are declared in the header file 'gsl_sf_coulomb.h'. Both bound state and scattering solutions are available.

7.7.1 Normalized Hydrogenic Bound States

double gsl_sf_hydrogenicR_1 (double Z, double r)   Function
int gsl_sf_hydrogenicR_1_e (double Z, double r,   Function
    gsl_sf_result * *result*)
    These routines compute the lowest-order normalized hydrogenic bound state radial wavefunction $R_1 := 2Z\sqrt{Z}\exp(-Zr)$.

double gsl_sf_hydrogenicR (int n, int l, double Z,   Function
    double r)
int gsl_sf_hydrogenicR_e (int n, int l, double Z, double   Function
    r, gsl_sf_result * *result*)
    These routines compute the n-th normalized hydrogenic bound state radial wavefunction,

$$R_n := \frac{2Z^{3/2}}{n^2}\left(\frac{2Zr}{n}\right)^l\sqrt{\frac{(n-l-1)!}{(n+l)!}}\exp(-Zr/n)L^{2l+1}_{n-l-1}(2Zr/n).$$

where $L^a_b(x)$ is the generalized Laguerre polynomial (see Section 7.22 [Laguerre Functions], page 83). The normalization is chosen such that the wavefunction ψ is given by $\psi(n,l,r) = R_n Y_{lm}$.

7.7.2 Coulomb Wave Functions

The Coulomb wave functions $F_L(\eta, x)$, $G_L(\eta, x)$ are described in Abramowitz & Stegun, Chapter 14. Because there can be a large dynamic range of values for these functions, overflows are handled gracefully. If an overflow occurs, GSL_EOVRFLW is signalled and exponent(s) are returned through the modifiable parameters *exp_F*, *exp_G*. The full solution can be reconstructed from the following relations,

$$F_L(\eta, x) = fc[k_L] * \exp(exp_F)$$
$$G_L(\eta, x) = gc[k_L] * \exp(exp_G)$$

$$F'_L(\eta, x) = fcp[k_L] * \exp(exp_F)$$
$$G'_L(\eta, x) = gcp[k_L] * \exp(exp_G)$$

int gsl_sf_coulomb_wave_FG_e (double *eta*, double *x*,   Function
        double *L_F*, int *k*, gsl_sf_result * *F*, gsl_sf_result *
        Fp, gsl_sf_result * *G*, gsl_sf_result * *Gp*, double *
        exp_F, double * *exp_G*)

This function computes the Coulomb wave functions $F_L(\eta, x)$, $G_{L-k}(\eta, x)$ and their derivatives $F'_L(\eta, x)$, $G'_{L-k}(\eta, x)$ with respect to x. The parameters are restricted to $L, L - k > -1/2$, $x > 0$ and integer k. Note that L itself is not restricted to being an integer. The results are stored in the parameters F, G for the function values and Fp, Gp for the derivative values. If an overflow occurs, GSL_EOVRFLW is returned and scaling exponents are stored in the modifiable parameters *exp_F*, *exp_G*.

int gsl_sf_coulomb_wave_F_array (double *L_min*, int   Function
        kmax, double *eta*, double *x*, double *fc_array*[], double *
        F_exponent)

This function computes the Coulomb wave function $F_L(\eta, x)$ for $L = Lmin \ldots Lmin + kmax$, storing the results in *fc_array*. In the case of overflow the exponent is stored in *F_exponent*.

int gsl_sf_coulomb_wave_FG_array (double *L_min*, int   Function
        kmax, double *eta*, double *x*, double *fc_array*[], double
        gc_array[], double * *F_exponent*, double * *G_exponent*)

This function computes the functions $F_L(\eta, x)$, $G_L(\eta, x)$ for $L = Lmin \ldots Lmin + kmax$ storing the results in *fc_array* and *gc_array*. In the case of overflow the exponents are stored in *F_exponent* and *G_exponent*.

int gsl_sf_coulomb_wave_FGp_array (double *L_min*, int   Function
        kmax, double *eta*, double *x*, double *fc_array*[], double
        fcp_array[], double *gc_array*[], double *gcp_array*[], double
        * *F_exponent*, double * *G_exponent*)

This function computes the functions $F_L(\eta, x)$, $G_L(\eta, x)$ and their derivatives $F'_L(\eta, x)$, $G'_L(\eta, x)$ for $L = Lmin \ldots Lmin + kmax$ storing the results in *fc_array*, *gc_array*, *fcp_array* and *gcp_array*. In the case of overflow the exponents are stored in *F_exponent* and *G_exponent*.

int gsl_sf_coulomb_wave_sphF_array (double *L_min*, int   Function
        kmax, double *eta*, double *x*, double *fc_array*[], double
        F_exponent[])

This function computes the Coulomb wave function divided by the argument $F_L(\eta, x)/x$ for $L = Lmin \ldots Lmin + kmax$, storing the results in *fc_array*. In the case of overflow the exponent is stored in *F_exponent*. This function reduces to spherical Bessel functions in the limit $\eta \to 0$.

7.7.3 Coulomb Wave Function Normalization Constant

The Coulomb wave function normalization constant is defined in Abramowitz 14.1.7.

int gsl_sf_coulomb_CL_e (double *L*, double *eta*,   *Function*
        gsl_sf_result * *result*)
  This function computes the Coulomb wave function normalization constant $C_L(\eta)$ for $L > -1$.

int gsl_sf_coulomb_CL_array (double *Lmin*, int *kmax*,   *Function*
        double *eta*, double *cl*[])
  This function computes the Coulomb wave function normalization constant $C_L(\eta)$ for $L = Lmin \ldots Lmin + kmax$, $Lmin > -1$.

7.8 Coupling Coefficients

The Wigner 3-j, 6-j and 9-j symbols give the coupling coefficients for combined angular momentum vectors. Since the arguments of the standard coupling coefficient functions are integer or half-integer, the arguments of the following functions are, by convention, integers equal to twice the actual spin value. For information on the 3-j coefficients see Abramowitz & Stegun, Section 27.9. The functions described in this section are declared in the header file 'gsl_sf_coupling.h'.

7.8.1 3-j Symbols

double gsl_sf_coupling_3j (int *two_ja*, int *two_jb*, int   *Function*
        two_jc, int *two_ma*, int *two_mb*, int *two_mc*)
int gsl_sf_coupling_3j_e (int *two_ja*, int *two_jb*, int   *Function*
        two_jc, int *two_ma*, int *two_mb*, int *two_mc*,
        gsl_sf_result * *result*)
  These routines compute the Wigner 3-j coefficient,

$$\begin{pmatrix} ja & jb & jc \\ ma & mb & mc \end{pmatrix}$$

where the arguments are given in half-integer units, $ja = two\_ja/2$, $ma = two\_ma/2$, etc.

7.8.2 6-j Symbols

double gsl_sf_coupling_6j (int *two_ja*, int *two_jb*, int   Function
        two_jc, int *two_jd*, int *two_je*, int *two_jf*)
int gsl_sf_coupling_6j_e (int *two_ja*, int *two_jb*, int   Function
        two_jc, int *two_jd*, int *two_je*, int *two_jf*,
        gsl_sf_result * *result*)

These routines compute the Wigner 6-j coefficient,

$$\begin{Bmatrix} ja & jb & jc \\ jd & je & jf \end{Bmatrix}$$

where the arguments are given in half-integer units, $ja = two\_ja/2$, $ma = two\_ma/2$, etc.

7.8.3 9-j Symbols

double gsl_sf_coupling_9j (int *two_ja*, int *two_jb*, int   Function
        two_jc, int *two_jd*, int *two_je*, int *two_jf*, int *two_jg*,
        int *two_jh*, int *two_ji*)
int gsl_sf_coupling_9j_e (int *two_ja*, int *two_jb*, int   Function
        two_jc, int *two_jd*, int *two_je*, int *two_jf*, int *two_jg*,
        int *two_jh*, int *two_ji*, gsl_sf_result * *result*)

These routines compute the Wigner 9-j coefficient,

$$\begin{Bmatrix} ja & jb & jc \\ jd & je & jf \\ jg & jh & ji \end{Bmatrix}$$

where the arguments are given in half-integer units, $ja = two\_ja/2$, $ma = two\_ma/2$, etc.

7.9 Dawson Function

The Dawson integral is defined by $\exp(-x^2) \int_0^x dt \exp(t^2)$. A table of Dawson's integral can be found in Abramowitz & Stegun, Table 7.5. The Dawson functions are declared in the header file 'gsl_sf_dawson.h'.

double gsl_sf_dawson (double *x*)   Function
int gsl_sf_dawson_e (double *x*, gsl_sf_result * *result*)   Function

These routines compute the value of Dawson's integral for *x*.

7.10 Debye Functions

The Debye functions $D_n(x)$ are defined by the following integral,

$$D_n(x) = \frac{n}{x^n} \int_0^x dt \frac{t^n}{e^t - 1}$$

For further information see Abramowitz & Stegun, Section 27.1. The Debye functions are declared in the header file 'gsl_sf_debye.h'.

double gsl_sf_debye_1 (double x)   Function
int gsl_sf_debye_1_e (double x, gsl_sf_result * result)   Function
  These routines compute the first-order Debye function $D_1(x) = (1/x) \int_0^x dt(t/(e^t - 1))$.

double gsl_sf_debye_2 (double x)   Function
int gsl_sf_debye_2_e (double x, gsl_sf_result * result)   Function
  These routines compute the second-order Debye function $D_2(x) = (2/x^2) \int_0^x dt(t^2/(e^t - 1))$.

double gsl_sf_debye_3 (double x)   Function
int gsl_sf_debye_3_e (double x, gsl_sf_result * result)   Function
  These routines compute the third-order Debye function $D_3(x) = (3/x^3) \int_0^x dt(t^3/(e^t - 1))$.

double gsl_sf_debye_4 (double x)   Function
int gsl_sf_debye_4_e (double x, gsl_sf_result * result)   Function
  These routines compute the fourth-order Debye function $D_4(x) = (4/x^4) \int_0^x dt(t^4/(e^t - 1))$.

double gsl_sf_debye_5 (double x)   Function
int gsl_sf_debye_5_e (double x, gsl_sf_result * result)   Function
  These routines compute the fifth-order Debye function $D_5(x) = (5/x^5) \int_0^x dt(t^5/(e^t - 1))$.

double gsl_sf_debye_6 (double x)   Function
int gsl_sf_debye_6_e (double x, gsl_sf_result * result)   Function
  These routines compute the fourth-order Debye function $D_6(x) = (6/x^6) \int_0^x dt(t^6/(e^t - 1))$.

7.11 Dilogarithm

The functions described in this section are declared in the header file 'gsl_sf_dilog.h'.

7.11.1 Real Argument

double gsl_sf_dilog (double x)   *Function*
int gsl_sf_dilog_e (double x, gsl_sf_result * *result*)   *Function*
These routines compute the dilogarithm for a real argument. In Lewin's notation this is $Li_2(x)$, the real part of the dilogarithm of a real x. It is defined by the integral representation $Li_2(x) = -\mathrm{Re} \int_0^x ds \log(1 - s)/s$. Note that $\mathrm{Im}(Li_2(x)) = 0$ for $x \leq 1$, and $-\pi \log(x)$ for $x > 1$.

7.11.2 Complex Argument

int gsl_sf_complex_dilog_e (double r, double *theta*,   *Function*
        gsl_sf_result * *result_re*, gsl_sf_result * *result_im*)
This function computes the full complex-valued dilogarithm for the complex argument $z = r \exp(i\theta)$. The real and imaginary parts of the result are returned in *result_re*, *result_im*.

7.12 Elementary Operations

The following functions allow for the propagation of errors when combining quantities by multiplication. The functions are declared in the header file 'gsl_sf_elementary.h'.

int gsl_sf_multiply_e (double x, double y,   *Function*
        gsl_sf_result * *result*)
This function multiplies x and y storing the product and its associated error in *result*.

int gsl_sf_multiply_err_e (double x, double dx, double   *Function*
        y, double dy, gsl_sf_result * *result*)
This function multiplies x and y with associated absolute errors dx and dy. The product $xy \pm xy\sqrt{(dx/x)^2 + (dy/y)^2}$ is stored in *result*.

7.13 Elliptic Integrals

The functions described in this section are declared in the header file 'gsl_sf_ellint.h'.

7.13.1 Definition of Legendre Forms

The Legendre forms of elliptic integrals $F(\phi, k)$, $E(\phi, k)$ and $P(\phi, k, n)$ are defined by,

$$F(\phi, k) = \int_0^\phi dt \frac{1}{\sqrt{(1 - k^2 \sin^2(t))}}$$

$$E(\phi, k) = \int_0^\phi dt \sqrt{(1 - k^2 \sin^2(t))}$$

$$P(\phi, k, n) = \int_0^\phi dt \frac{1}{(1 + n \sin^2(t))\sqrt{1 - k^2 \sin^2(t)}}$$

The complete Legendre forms are denoted by $K(k) = F(\pi/2, k)$ and $E(k) = E(\pi/2, k)$. Further information on the Legendre forms of elliptic integrals can be found in Abramowitz & Stegun, Chapter 17. The notation used here is based on Carlson, *Numerische Mathematik* 33 (1979) 1 and differs slightly from that used by Abramowitz & Stegun.

7.13.2 Definition of Carlson Forms

The Carlson symmetric forms of elliptical integrals $RC(x, y)$, $RD(x, y, z)$, $RF(x, y, z)$ and $RJ(x, y, z, p)$ are defined by,

$$RC(x, y) = 1/2 \int_0^\infty dt (t + x)^{-1/2} (t + y)^{-1}$$

$$RD(x, y, z) = 3/2 \int_0^\infty dt (t + x)^{-1/2} (t + y)^{-1/2} (t + z)^{-3/2}$$

$$RF(x, y, z) = 1/2 \int_0^\infty dt (t + x)^{-1/2} (t + y)^{-1/2} (t + z)^{-1/2}$$

$$RJ(x, y, z, p) = 3/2 \int_0^\infty dt (t + x)^{-1/2} (t + y)^{-1/2} (t + z)^{-1/2} (t + p)^{-1}$$

7.13.3 Legendre Form of Complete Elliptic Integrals

double gsl_sf_ellint_Kcomp (double k, gsl_mode_t *mode*)   Function
int gsl_sf_ellint_Kcomp_e (double k, gsl_mode_t *mode*,   Function
       gsl_sf_result * *result*)
  These routines compute the complete elliptic integral $K(k)$ to the accuracy specified by the mode variable *mode*.

double gsl_sf_ellint_Ecomp (double k, gsl_mode_t *mode*)   Function
int gsl_sf_ellint_Ecomp_e (double k, gsl_mode_t *mode*,   Function
       gsl_sf_result * *result*)
  These routines compute the complete elliptic integral $E(k)$ to the accuracy specified by the mode variable *mode*.

7.13.4 Legendre Form of Incomplete Elliptic Integrals

double gsl_sf_ellint_F (double *phi*, double k,   Function
       gsl_mode_t *mode*)
int gsl_sf_ellint_F_e (double *phi*, double k, gsl_mode_t   Function
       mode, gsl_sf_result * *result*)
  These routines compute the incomplete elliptic integral $F(\phi, k)$ to the accuracy specified by the mode variable *mode*.

double gsl_sf_ellint_E (double *phi*, double k,   Function
       gsl_mode_t *mode*)
int gsl_sf_ellint_E_e (double *phi*, double k, gsl_mode_t   Function
       mode, gsl_sf_result * *result*)
  These routines compute the incomplete elliptic integral $E(\phi, k)$ to the accuracy specified by the mode variable *mode*.

double gsl_sf_ellint_P (double *phi*, double k, double n,   Function
       gsl_mode_t *mode*)
int gsl_sf_ellint_P_e (double *phi*, double k, double n,   Function
       gsl_mode_t *mode*, gsl_sf_result * *result*)
  These routines compute the incomplete elliptic integral $P(\phi, k, n)$ to the accuracy specified by the mode variable *mode*.

double gsl_sf_ellint_D (double *phi*, double *k*, double *n*,   Function
        gsl_mode_t *mode*)
int gsl_sf_ellint_D_e (double *phi*, double *k*, double *n*,   Function
        gsl_mode_t *mode*, gsl_sf_result * *result*)

These functions compute the incomplete elliptic integral $D(\phi, k, n)$ which is defined through the Carlson form $RD(x, y, z)$ by the following relation,

$$D(\phi, k, n) = RD(1 - \sin^2(\phi), 1 - k^2 \sin^2(\phi), 1).$$

7.13.5 Carlson Forms

double gsl_sf_ellint_RC (double *x*, double *y*, gsl_mode_t   Function
        mode)
int gsl_sf_ellint_RC_e (double *x*, double *y*, gsl_mode_t   Function
        mode, gsl_sf_result * *result*)

These routines compute the incomplete elliptic integral $RC(x, y)$ to the accuracy specified by the mode variable *mode*.

double gsl_sf_ellint_RD (double *x*, double *y*, double *z*,   Function
        gsl_mode_t *mode*)
int gsl_sf_ellint_RD_e (double *x*, double *y*, double *z*,   Function
        gsl_mode_t *mode*, gsl_sf_result * *result*)

These routines compute the incomplete elliptic integral $RD(x, y, z)$ to the accuracy specified by the mode variable *mode*.

double gsl_sf_ellint_RF (double *x*, double *y*, double *z*,   Function
        gsl_mode_t *mode*)
int gsl_sf_ellint_RF_e (double *x*, double *y*, double *z*,   Function
        gsl_mode_t *mode*, gsl_sf_result * *result*)

These routines compute the incomplete elliptic integral $RF(x, y, z)$ to the accuracy specified by the mode variable *mode*.

double gsl_sf_ellint_RJ (double *x*, double *y*, double *z*,   Function
        double *p*, gsl_mode_t *mode*)
int gsl_sf_ellint_RJ_e (double *x*, double *y*, double *z*,   Function
        double *p*, gsl_mode_t *mode*, gsl_sf_result * *result*)

These routines compute the incomplete elliptic integral $RJ(x, y, z, p)$ to the accuracy specified by the mode variable *mode*.

7.14 Elliptic Functions (Jacobi)

The Jacobian Elliptic functions are defined in Abramowitz & Stegun, Chapter 16. The functions are declared in the header file 'gsl_sf_elljac.h'.

int gsl_sf_elljac_e (double u, double m, double $*$ sn,   Function
        double $*$ cn, double $*$ dn)
> This function computes the Jacobian elliptic functions $sn(u|m)$, $cn(u|m)$, $dn(u|m)$ by descending Landen transformations.

7.15 Error Functions

The error function is described in Abramowitz & Stegun, Chapter 7. The functions in this section are declared in the header file 'gsl_sf_erf.h'.

7.15.1 Error Function

double gsl_sf_erf (double x)   Function
int gsl_sf_erf_e (double x, gsl_sf_result $*$ $result$)   Function
> These routines compute the error function $\mathrm{erf}(x)$, where $\mathrm{erf}(x) = (2/\sqrt{\pi}) \int_0^x dt \exp(-t^2)$.

7.15.2 Complementary Error Function

double gsl_sf_erfc (double x)   Function
int gsl_sf_erfc_e (double x, gsl_sf_result $*$ $result$)   Function
> These routines compute the complementary error function $\mathrm{erfc}(x) = 1 - \mathrm{erf}(x) = (2/\sqrt{\pi}) \int_x^\infty \exp(-t^2)$.

7.15.3 Log Complementary Error Function

double gsl_sf_log_erfc (double x)   Function
int gsl_sf_log_erfc_e (double x, gsl_sf_result $*$ $result$)   Function
> These routines compute the logarithm of the complementary error function $\log(\mathrm{erfc}(x))$.

7.15.4 Probability functions

The probability functions for the Normal or Gaussian distribution are described in Abramowitz & Stegun, Section 26.2.

double gsl_sf_erf_Z (double x)　　　　　　　　　　　　　Function
int gsl_sf_erf_Z_e (double x, gsl_sf_result * result)　　Function
These routines compute the Gaussian probability density function $Z(x) = (1/\sqrt{2\pi}) \exp(-x^2/2)$.

double gsl_sf_erf_Q (double x)　　　　　　　　　　　　　Function
int gsl_sf_erf_Q_e (double x, gsl_sf_result * result)　　Function
These routines compute the upper tail of the Gaussian probability function $Q(x) = (1/\sqrt{2\pi}) \int_x^\infty dt \exp(-t^2/2)$.

The *hazard function* for the normal distribution, also known as the inverse Mill's ratio, is defined as,

$$h(x) = \frac{Z(x)}{Q(x)} = \sqrt{\frac{2}{\pi}} \frac{\exp(-x^2/2)}{\operatorname{erfc}(x/\sqrt{2})}$$

It decreases rapidly as x approaches $-\infty$ and asymptotes to $h(x) \sim x$ as x approaches $+\infty$.

double gsl_sf_hazard (double x)　　　　　　　　　　　　Function
int gsl_sf_hazard_e (double x, gsl_sf_result * result)　Function
These routines compute the hazard function for the normal distribution.

7.16 Exponential Functions

The functions described in this section are declared in the header file 'gsl_sf_exp.h'.

7.16.1 Exponential Function

double gsl_sf_exp (double x)　　　　　　　　　　　　　　Function
int gsl_sf_exp_e (double x, gsl_sf_result * result)　　Function
These routines provide an exponential function $\exp(x)$ using GSL semantics and error checking.

int gsl_sf_exp_e10_e (double x, gsl_sf_result_e10 *　　Function
　　　result)
This function computes the exponential $\exp(x)$ using the gsl_sf_result_e10 type to return a result with extended range. This function may be useful if the value of $\exp(x)$ would overflow the numeric range of double.

double gsl_sf_exp_mult (double x, double y)   Function
int gsl_sf_exp_mult_e (double x, double y,   Function
          gsl_sf_result * *result*)
These routines exponentiate x and multiply by the factor y to return the product $y\exp(x)$.

int gsl_sf_exp_mult_e10_e (const double x, const double   Function
          y, gsl_sf_result_e10 * *result*)
This function computes the product $y\exp(x)$ using the gsl_sf_result_e10 type to return a result with extended numeric range.

7.16.2 Relative Exponential Functions

double gsl_sf_expm1 (double x)   Function
int gsl_sf_expm1_e (double x, gsl_sf_result * *result*)   Function
These routines compute the quantity $\exp(x) - 1$ using an algorithm that is accurate for small x.

double gsl_sf_exprel (double x)   Function
int gsl_sf_exprel_e (double x, gsl_sf_result * *result*)   Function
These routines compute the quantity $(\exp(x)-1)/x$ using an algorithm that is accurate for small x. For small x the algorithm is based on the expansion $(\exp(x) - 1)/x = 1 + x/2 + x^2/(2*3) + x^3/(2*3*4) + \ldots$.

double gsl_sf_exprel_2 (double x)   Function
int gsl_sf_exprel_2_e (double x, gsl_sf_result * *result*)   Function
These routines compute the quantity $2(\exp(x) - 1 - x)/x^2$ using an algorithm that is accurate for small x. For small x the algorithm is based on the expansion $2(\exp(x) - 1 - x)/x^2 = 1 + x/3 + x^2/(3*4) + x^3/(3*4*5) + \ldots$.

double gsl_sf_exprel_n (int n, double x)   Function
int gsl_sf_exprel_n_e (int n, double x, gsl_sf_result *   Function
          result)
These routines compute the N-relative exponential, which is the n-th generalization of the functions gsl_sf_exprel and gsl_sf_exprel2. The N-relative exponential is given by,

$$\mathrm{exprel}_N(x) = N!/x^N \left(\exp(x) - \sum_{k=0}^{N-1} x^k/k! \right)$$
$$= 1 + x/(N+1) + x^2/((N+1)(N+2)) + \ldots$$
$$= {}_1F_1(1, 1+N, x)$$

7.16.3 Exponentiation With Error Estimate

int gsl_sf_exp_err_e (double x, double dx,   Function
        gsl_sf_result * result)
This function exponentiates x with an associated absolute error dx.

int gsl_sf_exp_err_e10_e (double x, double dx,   Function
        gsl_sf_result_e10 * result)
This function exponentiates a quantity x with an associated absolute
error dx using the gsl_sf_result_e10 type to return a result with
extended range.

int gsl_sf_exp_mult_err_e (double x, double dx, double   Function
        y, double dy, gsl_sf_result * result)
This routine computes the product $y \exp(x)$ for the quantities x, y
with associated absolute errors dx, dy.

int gsl_sf_exp_mult_err_e10_e (double x, double dx,   Function
        double y, double dy, gsl_sf_result_e10 * result)
This routine computes the product $y \exp(x)$ for the quantities x, y
with associated absolute errors dx, dy using the gsl_sf_result_e10
type to return a result with extended range.

7.17 Exponential Integrals

Information on the exponential integrals can be found in Abramowitz
& Stegun, Chapter 5. These functions are declared in the header file
'gsl_sf_expint.h'.

7.17.1 Exponential Integral

double gsl_sf_expint_E1 (double x)   Function
int gsl_sf_expint_E1_e (double x, gsl_sf_result *   Function
        result)
These routines compute the exponential integral $E_1(x)$,

$$E_1(x) := \mathrm{Re} \int_1^\infty dt \exp(-xt)/t.$$

double gsl_sf_expint_E2 (double x)   Function
int gsl_sf_expint_E2_e (double x, gsl_sf_result *   Function
        result)
These routines compute the second-order exponential integral $E_2(x)$,

$$E_2(x) := \mathrm{Re} \int_1^\infty dt \exp(-xt)/t^2.$$

7.17.2 Ei(x)

```
double gsl_sf_expint_Ei (double x)                        Function
int gsl_sf_expint_Ei_e (double x, gsl_sf_result *         Function
     result)
```
These routines compute the exponential integral $Ei(x)$,

$$Ei(x) := -PV \left(\int_{-x}^{\infty} dt \exp(-t)/t \right)$$

where PV denotes the principal value of the integral.

7.17.3 Hyperbolic Integrals

```
double gsl_sf_Shi (double x)                              Function
int gsl_sf_Shi_e (double x, gsl_sf_result * result)      Function
```
These routines compute the integral $Shi(x) = \int_0^x dt \sinh(t)/t$.

```
double gsl_sf_Chi (double x)                              Function
int gsl_sf_Chi_e (double x, gsl_sf_result * result)      Function
```
These routines compute the integral $Chi(x) := \mathrm{Re}[\gamma_E + \log(x) + \int_0^x dt(\cosh[t] - 1)/t]$, where γ_E is the Euler constant (available as the macro M_EULER).

7.17.4 Ei_3(x)

```
double gsl_sf_expint_3 (double x)                         Function
int gsl_sf_expint_3_e (double x, gsl_sf_result * result)  Function
```
These routines compute the third-order exponential integral $Ei_3(x) = \int_0^x dt \exp(-t^3)$ for $x \geq 0$.

7.17.5 Trigonometric Integrals

```
double gsl_sf_Si (const double x)                         Function
int gsl_sf_Si_e (double x, gsl_sf_result * result)       Function
```
These routines compute the Sine integral $Si(x) = \int_0^x dt \sin(t)/t$.

```
double gsl_sf_Ci (const double x)                         Function
int gsl_sf_Ci_e (double x, gsl_sf_result * result)       Function
```
These routines compute the Cosine integral $Ci(x) = - \int_x^{\infty} dt \cos(t)/t$ for $x > 0$.

7.17.6 Arctangent Integral

double gsl_sf_atanint (double x)   Function
int gsl_sf_atanint_e (double x, gsl_sf_result * result)   Function
    These routines compute the Arctangent integral, which is defined as
$AtanInt(x) = \int_0^x dt \arctan(t)/t$.

7.18 Fermi-Dirac Function

    The functions described in this section are declared in the header file
'gsl_sf_fermi_dirac.h'.

7.18.1 Complete Fermi-Dirac Integrals

    The complete Fermi-Dirac integral $F_j(x)$ is given by,

$$F_j(x) := \frac{1}{\Gamma(j+1)} \int_0^\infty dt \frac{t^j}{(\exp(t-x)+1)}$$

double gsl_sf_fermi_dirac_m1 (double x)   Function
int gsl_sf_fermi_dirac_m1_e (double x, gsl_sf_result *   Function
    result)
    These routines compute the complete Fermi-Dirac integral with an
index of -1. This integral is given by $F_{-1}(x) = e^x/(1+e^x)$.

double gsl_sf_fermi_dirac_0 (double x)   Function
int gsl_sf_fermi_dirac_0_e (double x, gsl_sf_result *   Function
    result)
    These routines compute the complete Fermi-Dirac integral with an
index of 0. This integral is given by $F_0(x) = \ln(1+e^x)$.

double gsl_sf_fermi_dirac_1 (double x)   Function
int gsl_sf_fermi_dirac_1_e (double x, gsl_sf_result *   Function
    result)
    These routines compute the complete Fermi-Dirac integral with an
index of 1, $F_1(x) = \int_0^\infty dt(t/(\exp(t-x)+1))$.

double gsl_sf_fermi_dirac_2 (double x)   Function
int gsl_sf_fermi_dirac_2_e (double x, gsl_sf_result *   Function
    result)
    These routines compute the complete Fermi-Dirac integral with an
index of 2, $F_2(x) = (1/2) \int_0^\infty dt(t^2/(\exp(t-x)+1))$.

```
double gsl_sf_fermi_dirac_int (int j, double x)              Function
int gsl_sf_fermi_dirac_int_e (int j, double x,              Function
        gsl_sf_result * result)
```
These routines compute the complete Fermi-Dirac integral with an integer index of j, $F_j(x) = (1/\Gamma(j+1)) \int_0^\infty dt(t^j/(\exp(t-x)+1))$.

```
double gsl_sf_fermi_dirac_mhalf (double x)                  Function
int gsl_sf_fermi_dirac_mhalf_e (double x,                  Function
        gsl_sf_result * result)
```
These routines compute the complete Fermi-Dirac integral $F_{-1/2}(x)$.

```
double gsl_sf_fermi_dirac_half (double x)                  Function
int gsl_sf_fermi_dirac_half_e (double x, gsl_sf_result     Function
        * result)
```
These routines compute the complete Fermi-Dirac integral $F_{1/2}(x)$.

```
double gsl_sf_fermi_dirac_3half (double x)                 Function
int gsl_sf_fermi_dirac_3half_e (double x,                 Function
        gsl_sf_result * result)
```
These routines compute the complete Fermi-Dirac integral $F_{3/2}(x)$.

7.18.2 Incomplete Fermi-Dirac Integrals

The incomplete Fermi-Dirac integral $F_j(x, b)$ is given by,

$$F_j(x,b) := \frac{1}{\Gamma(j+1)} \int_b^\infty dt \frac{t^j}{(\exp(t-x)+1)}$$

```
double gsl_sf_fermi_dirac_inc_0 (double x, double b)        Function
int gsl_sf_fermi_dirac_inc_0_e (double x, double b,        Function
        gsl_sf_result * result)
```
These routines compute the incomplete Fermi-Dirac integral with an index of zero, $F_0(x, b) = \ln(1 + e^{b-x}) - (b - x)$.

7.19 Gamma and Beta Functions

The functions described in this section are declared in the header file 'gsl_sf_gamma.h'.

7.19.1 Gamma Functions

The Gamma function is defined by the following integral,

$$\Gamma(x) = \int_0^\infty dt\, t^{x-1} \exp(-t)$$

It is related to the factorial function by $\Gamma(n) = (n-1)!$ for positive integer n. Further information on the Gamma function can be found in Abramowitz & Stegun, Chapter 6. The functions described in this section are declared in the header file 'gsl_sf_gamma.h'.

double gsl_sf_gamma (double x)   Function
int gsl_sf_gamma_e (double x, gsl_sf_result * *result*)   Function
  These routines compute the Gamma function $\Gamma(x)$, subject to x not being a negative integer. The function is computed using the real Lanczos method. The maximum value of x such that $\Gamma(x)$ is not considered an overflow is given by the macro GSL_SF_GAMMA_XMAX and is 171.0.

double gsl_sf_lngamma (double x)   Function
int gsl_sf_lngamma_e (double x, gsl_sf_result * *result*)   Function
  These routines compute the logarithm of the Gamma function, $\log(\Gamma(x))$, subject to x not a being negative integer. For $x < 0$ the real part of $\log(\Gamma(x))$ is returned, which is equivalent to $\log(|\Gamma(x)|)$. The function is computed using the real Lanczos method.

int gsl_sf_lngamma_sgn_e (double x, gsl_sf_result *   Function
        result_lg, double * *sgn*)
  This routine computes the sign of the gamma function and the logarithm of its magnitude, subject to x not being a negative integer. The function is computed using the real Lanczos method. The value of the gamma function can be reconstructed using the relation $\Gamma(x) = sgn * \exp(resultlg)$.

double gsl_sf_gammastar (double x)   Function
int gsl_sf_gammastar_e (double x, gsl_sf_result *   Function
        result)
  These routines compute the regulated Gamma Function $\Gamma^*(x)$ for $x > 0$. The regulated gamma function is given by,

$$\Gamma^*(x) = \Gamma(x)/(\sqrt{2\pi}x^{(x-1/2)}\exp(-x))$$

$$= \left(1 + \frac{1}{12x} + ...\right) \quad \text{for } x \to \infty$$

and is a useful suggestion of Temme.

double gsl_sf_gammainv (double x)   Function
int gsl_sf_gammainv_e (double x, gsl_sf_result * result)   Function
>   These routines compute the reciprocal of the gamma function, $1/\Gamma(x)$
>   using the real Lanczos method.

int gsl_sf_lngamma_complex_e (double zr, double zi,   Function
>   gsl_sf_result * lnr, gsl_sf_result * arg)
>   This routine computes $\log(\Gamma(z))$ for complex $z = z_r + iz_i$ and z not
>   a negative integer, using the complex Lanczos method. The returned
>   parameters are $lnr = \log|\Gamma(z)|$ and $arg = \arg(\Gamma(z))$ in $(-\pi, \pi]$. Note
>   that the phase part (arg) is not well-determined when $|z|$ is very large,
>   due to inevitable roundoff in restricting to $(-\pi, \pi]$. This will result
>   in a GSL_ELOSS error when it occurs. The absolute value part (lnr),
>   however, never suffers from loss of precision.

7.19.2 Factorials

Although factorials can be computed from the Gamma function, using
the relation $n! = \Gamma(n + 1)$ for non-negative integer n, it is usually more
efficient to call the functions in this section, particularly for small values
of n, whose factorial values are maintained in hardcoded tables.

double gsl_sf_fact (unsigned int n)   Function
int gsl_sf_fact_e (unsigned int n, gsl_sf_result *   Function
>   result)
>   These routines compute the factorial $n!$. The factorial is related to the
>   Gamma function by $n! = \Gamma(n+1)$. The maximum value of n such that
> $n!$ is not considered an overflow is given by the macro GSL_SF_FACT_
>   NMAX and is 170.

double gsl_sf_doublefact (unsigned int n)   Function
int gsl_sf_doublefact_e (unsigned int n, gsl_sf_result   Function
>   * result)
>   These routines compute the double factorial $n!! = n(n-2)(n-4)\ldots$.
>   The maximum value of n such that $n!!$ is not considered an overflow
>   is given by the macro GSL_SF_DOUBLEFACT_NMAX and is 297.

double gsl_sf_lnfact (unsigned int n)   Function
int gsl_sf_lnfact_e (unsigned int n, gsl_sf_result *   Function
>   result)
>   These routines compute the logarithm of the factorial of n, $\log(n!)$. The
>   algorithm is faster than computing $\ln(\Gamma(n + 1))$ via gsl_sf_lngamma
>   for $n < 170$, but defers for larger n.

double `gsl_sf_lndoublefact` (unsigned int *n*)   Function
int `gsl_sf_lndoublefact_e` (unsigned int *n*,   Function
      `gsl_sf_result` * *result*)
    These routines compute the logarithm of the double factorial of *n*,
log(*n*!!).

double `gsl_sf_choose` (unsigned int *n*, unsigned int *m*)   Function
int `gsl_sf_choose_e` (unsigned int *n*, unsigned int *m*,   Function
      `gsl_sf_result` * *result*)
    These routines compute the combinatorial factor n choose m
$= n!/(m!(n - m)!)$

double `gsl_sf_lnchoose` (unsigned int *n*, unsigned int *m*)   Function
int `gsl_sf_lnchoose_e` (unsigned int *n*, unsigned int *m*,   Function
      `gsl_sf_result` * *result*)
    These routines compute the logarithm of n choose m. This is equiva-
lent to the sum $\log(n!) - \log(m!) - \log((n - m)!)$.

double `gsl_sf_taylorcoeff` (int *n*, double *x*)   Function
int `gsl_sf_taylorcoeff_e` (int *n*, double *x*,   Function
      `gsl_sf_result` * *result*)
    These routines compute the Taylor coefficient $x^n/n!$ for $x \geq 0$, $n \geq 0$.

7.19.3 Pochhammer Symbol

double `gsl_sf_poch` (double *a*, double *x*)   Function
int `gsl_sf_poch_e` (double *a*, double *x*, `gsl_sf_result` *   Function
      result)
    These routines compute the Pochhammer symbol $(a)_x = \Gamma(a + x)/\Gamma(a)$, subject to *a* and $a + x$ not being negative integers. The
Pochhammer symbol is also known as the Apell symbol and some-
times written as (a, x).

double `gsl_sf_lnpoch` (double *a*, double *x*)   Function
int `gsl_sf_lnpoch_e` (double *a*, double *x*, `gsl_sf_result`   Function
      * *result*)
    These routines compute the logarithm of the Pochhammer symbol,
$\log((a)_x) = \log(\Gamma(a + x)/\Gamma(a))$ for $a > 0$, $a + x > 0$.

int `gsl_sf_lnpoch_sgn_e` (double *a*, double *x*,   Function
      `gsl_sf_result` * *result*, double * *sgn*)
    These routines compute the sign of the Pochhammer symbol and the
logarithm of its magnitude. The computed parameters are *result* $=$
$\log(|(a)_x|)$ and $sgn = \text{sgn}((a)_x)$ where $(a)_x = \Gamma(a + x)/\Gamma(a)$, subject
to a, $a + x$ not being negative integers.

double gsl_sf_pochrel (double a, double x)   Function
int gsl_sf_pochrel_e (double a, double x, gsl_sf_result   Function
          * result)
These routines compute the relative Pochhammer symbol $((a)_x - 1)/x$
where $(a)_x = \Gamma(a + x)/\Gamma(a)$.

7.19.4 Incomplete Gamma Functions

double gsl_sf_gamma_inc (double a, double x)   Function
int gsl_sf_gamma_inc_e (double a, double x,   Function
          gsl_sf_result * result)
These functions compute the unnormalized incomplete Gamma Function $\Gamma(a, x) = \int_x^\infty dt\, t^{(a-1)} \exp(-t)$ for a real and $x \geq 0$.

double gsl_sf_gamma_inc_Q (double a, double x)   Function
int gsl_sf_gamma_inc_Q_e (double a, double x,   Function
          gsl_sf_result * result)
These routines compute the normalized incomplete Gamma Function $Q(a, x) = 1/\Gamma(a) \int_x^\infty dt\, t^{(a-1)} \exp(-t)$ for $a > 0$, $x \geq 0$.

double gsl_sf_gamma_inc_P (double a, double x)   Function
int gsl_sf_gamma_inc_P_e (double a, double x,   Function
          gsl_sf_result * result)
These routines compute the complementary normalized incomplete Gamma Function $P(a, x) = 1 - Q(a, x) = 1/\Gamma(a) \int_0^x dt\, t^{(a-1)} \exp(-t)$ for $a > 0$, $x \geq 0$.

Note that Abramowitz & Stegun call $P(a, x)$ the incomplete gamma function (section 6.5).

7.19.5 Beta Functions

double gsl_sf_beta (double a, double b)   Function
int gsl_sf_beta_e (double a, double b, gsl_sf_result *   Function
          result)
These routines compute the Beta Function, $B(a, b) = \Gamma(a)\Gamma(b)/\Gamma(a+b)$ for $a > 0$, $b > 0$.

double gsl_sf_lnbeta (double a, double b)   Function
int gsl_sf_lnbeta_e (double a, double b, gsl_sf_result   Function
          * result)
These routines compute the logarithm of the Beta Function, $\log(B(a, b))$ for $a > 0$, $b > 0$.

7.19.6 Incomplete Beta Function

double gsl_sf_beta_inc (double a, double b, double x)   Function
int gsl_sf_beta_inc_e (double a, double b, double x,   Function
      gsl_sf_result * result)

These routines compute the normalized incomplete Beta function
$B_x(a, b)/B(a, b)$ where $B_x(a, b) = \int_0^x t^{a-1}(1 - t)^{b-1}dt$ for $a > 0$, $b > 0$,
and $0 \le x \le 1$.

7.20 Gegenbauer Functions

The Gegenbauer polynomials are defined in Abramowitz & Stegun, Chapter 22, where they are known as Ultraspherical polynomials.
The functions described in this section are declared in the header file
'gsl_sf_gegenbauer.h'.

double gsl_sf_gegenpoly_1 (double lambda, double x)   Function
double gsl_sf_gegenpoly_2 (double lambda, double x)   Function
double gsl_sf_gegenpoly_3 (double lambda, double x)   Function
int gsl_sf_gegenpoly_1_e (double lambda, double x,   Function
      gsl_sf_result * result)
int gsl_sf_gegenpoly_2_e (double lambda, double x,   Function
      gsl_sf_result * result)
int gsl_sf_gegenpoly_3_e (double lambda, double x,   Function
      gsl_sf_result * result)

These functions evaluate the Gegenbauer polynomials $C_n^{(\lambda)}(x)$ using
explicit representations for $n = 1, 2, 3$.

double gsl_sf_gegenpoly_n (int n, double lambda,   Function
      double x)
int gsl_sf_gegenpoly_n_e (int n, double lambda, double   Function
      x, gsl_sf_result * result)

These functions evaluate the Gegenbauer polynomial $C_n^{(\lambda)}(x)$ for a
specific value of n, lambda, x subject to $\lambda > -1/2$, $n \ge 0$.

int gsl_sf_gegenpoly_array (int nmax, double lambda,   Function
      double x, double result_array[])

This function computes an array of Gegenbauer polynomials $C_n^{(\lambda)}(x)$
for $n = 0, 1, 2, \ldots, nmax$, subject to $\lambda > -1/2$, $nmax \ge 0$.

7.21 Hypergeometric Functions

Hypergeometric functions are described in Abramowitz & Stegun, Chapters 13 and 15. These functions are declared in the header file 'gsl_sf_hyperg.h'.

double gsl_sf_hyperg_0F1 (double c, double x)   Function
int gsl_sf_hyperg_0F1_e (double c, double x,   Function
        gsl_sf_result * result)

These routines compute the hypergeometric function $_0F_1(c, x)$.

double gsl_sf_hyperg_1F1_int (int m, int n, double x)   Function
int gsl_sf_hyperg_1F1_int_e (int m, int n, double x,   Function
        gsl_sf_result * result)

These routines compute the confluent hypergeometric function $_1F_1(m, n, x) = M(m, n, x)$ for integer parameters m, n.

double gsl_sf_hyperg_1F1 (double a, double b, double x)   Function
int gsl_sf_hyperg_1F1_e (double a, double b, double x,   Function
        gsl_sf_result * result)

These routines compute the confluent hypergeometric function $_1F_1(a, b, x) = M(a, b, x)$ for general parameters a, b.

double gsl_sf_hyperg_U_int (int m, int n, double x)   Function
int gsl_sf_hyperg_U_int_e (int m, int n, double x,   Function
        gsl_sf_result * result)

These routines compute the confluent hypergeometric function $U(m, n, x)$ for integer parameters m, n.

int gsl_sf_hyperg_U_int_e10_e (int m, int n, double x,   Function
        gsl_sf_result_e10 * result)

This routine computes the confluent hypergeometric function $U(m, n, x)$ for integer parameters m, n using the gsl_sf_result_e10 type to return a result with extended range.

double gsl_sf_hyperg_U (double a, double b, double x)   Function
int gsl_sf_hyperg_U_e (double a, double b, double x,   Function
        gsl_sf_result * result)

These routines compute the confluent hypergeometric function $U(a, b, x)$.

int gsl_sf_hyperg_U_e10_e (double a, double b, double   Function
        x, gsl_sf_result_e10 * result)

This routine computes the confluent hypergeometric function $U(a, b, x)$ using the gsl_sf_result_e10 type to return a result with extended range.

double `gsl_sf_hyperg_2F1` (double a, double b, double c,   Function
        double x)

int `gsl_sf_hyperg_2F1_e` (double a, double b, double c,   Function
        double x, gsl_sf_result * result)

These routines compute the Gauss hypergeometric function $_2F_1(a, b, c, x)$ for $|x| < 1$.

If the arguments (a, b, c, x) are too close to a singularity then the function can return the error code `GSL_EMAXITER` when the series approximation converges too slowly. This occurs in the region of $x = 1$, $c - a - b = m$ for integer m.

double `gsl_sf_hyperg_2F1_conj` (double aR, double aI,   Function
        double c, double x)

int `gsl_sf_hyperg_2F1_conj_e` (double aR, double aI,   Function
        double c, double x, gsl_sf_result * result)

These routines compute the Gauss hypergeometric function $_2F_1(a_R + ia_I, aR - iaI, c, x)$ with complex parameters for $|x| < 1$. exceptions:

double `gsl_sf_hyperg_2F1_renorm` (double a, double b,   Function
        double c, double x)

int `gsl_sf_hyperg_2F1_renorm_e` (double a, double b,   Function
        double c, double x, gsl_sf_result * result)

These routines compute the renormalized Gauss hypergeometric function $_2F_1(a, b, c, x)/\Gamma(c)$ for $|x| < 1$.

double `gsl_sf_hyperg_2F1_conj_renorm` (double aR,   Function
        double aI, double c, double x)

int `gsl_sf_hyperg_2F1_conj_renorm_e` (double aR, double   Function
        aI, double c, double x, gsl_sf_result * result)

These routines compute the renormalized Gauss hypergeometric function $_2F_1(a_R + ia_I, aR - iaI, c, x)/\Gamma(c)$ for $|x| < 1$.

double `gsl_sf_hyperg_2F0` (double a, double b, double x)   Function
int `gsl_sf_hyperg_2F0_e` (double a, double b, double x,   Function
        gsl_sf_result * result)

These routines compute the hypergeometric function $_2F_0(a, b, x)$. The series representation is a divergent hypergeometric series. However, for $x < 0$ we have $_2F_0(a, b, x) = (-1/x)^a U(a, 1 + a - b, -1/x)$

7.22 Laguerre Functions

The generalized Laguerre polynomials are defined in terms of confluent hypergeometric functions as $L_n^a(x) = ((a+1)_n/n!)_1F_1(-n, a+1, x)$, and are sometimes referred to as the associated Laguerre polynomials. They are related to the plain Laguerre polynomials $L_n(x)$ by $L_n^0(x) = L_n(x)$ and $L_n^k(x) = (-1)^k(d^k/dx^k)L_{(n+k)}(x)$. For more information see Abramowitz & Stegun, Chapter 22.

The functions described in this section are declared in the header file 'gsl_sf_laguerre.h'.

double gsl_sf_laguerre_1 (double a, double x)   Function
double gsl_sf_laguerre_2 (double a, double x)   Function
double gsl_sf_laguerre_3 (double a, double x)   Function
int gsl_sf_laguerre_1_e (double a, double x,   Function
        gsl_sf_result * result)
int gsl_sf_laguerre_2_e (double a, double x,   Function
        gsl_sf_result * result)
int gsl_sf_laguerre_3_e (double a, double x,   Function
        gsl_sf_result * result)

These routines evaluate the generalized Laguerre polynomials $L_1^a(x)$, $L_2^a(x)$, $L_3^a(x)$ using explicit representations.

double gsl_sf_laguerre_n (const int n, const double a,   Function
        const double x)
int gsl_sf_laguerre_n_e (int n, double a, double x,   Function
        gsl_sf_result * result)

These routines evaluate the generalized Laguerre polynomials $L_n^a(x)$ for $a > -1$, $n \geq 0$.

7.23 Lambert W Functions

Lambert's W functions, $W(x)$, are defined to be solutions of the equation $W(x) \exp(W(x)) = x$. This function has multiple branches for $x < 0$; however, it has only two real-valued branches. We define $W_0(x)$ to be the principal branch, where $W > -1$ for $x < 0$, and $W_{-1}(x)$ to be the other real branch, where $W < -1$ for $x < 0$. The Lambert functions are declared in the header file 'gsl_sf_lambert.h'.

double gsl_sf_lambert_W0 (double x)   Function
int gsl_sf_lambert_W0_e (double x, gsl_sf_result *   Function
        result)

These compute the principal branch of the Lambert W function, $W_0(x)$.

double gsl_sf_lambert_Wm1 (double x)   Function
int gsl_sf_lambert_Wm1_e (double x, gsl_sf_result *   Function
    result)

These compute the secondary real-valued branch of the Lambert W function, $W_{-1}(x)$.

7.24 Legendre Functions and Spherical Harmonics

The Legendre Functions and Legendre Polynomials are described in Abramowitz & Stegun, Chapter 8. These functions are declared in the header file 'gsl_sf_legendre.h'.

7.24.1 Legendre Polynomials

double gsl_sf_legendre_P1 (double x)   Function
double gsl_sf_legendre_P2 (double x)   Function
double gsl_sf_legendre_P3 (double x)   Function
int gsl_sf_legendre_P1_e (double x, gsl_sf_result *   Function
    result)
int gsl_sf_legendre_P2_e (double x, gsl_sf_result *   Function
    result)
int gsl_sf_legendre_P3_e (double x, gsl_sf_result *   Function
    result)

These functions evaluate the Legendre polynomials $P_l(x)$ using explicit representations for $l = 1, 2, 3$.

double gsl_sf_legendre_Pl (int l, double x)   Function
int gsl_sf_legendre_Pl_e (int l, double x,   Function
    gsl_sf_result * *result*)

These functions evaluate the Legendre polynomial $P_l(x)$ for a specific value of l, x subject to $l \geq 0$, $|x| \leq 1$

int gsl_sf_legendre_Pl_array (int lmax, double x,   Function
    double *result_array*[])
int gsl_sf_legendre_Pl_deriv_array (int lmax, double   Function
    x, double *result_array*[], double *result_deriv_array*[])

These functions compute an array of Legendre polynomials $P_l(x)$, and optionally their derivatives $dP_l(x)/dx$, for $l = 0, \ldots, lmax$, $|x| \leq 1$

double gsl_sf_legendre_Q0 (double x)   Function
int gsl_sf_legendre_Q0_e (double x, gsl_sf_result *   Function
    result)

These routines compute the Legendre function $Q_0(x)$ for $x > -1$, $x \neq 1$.

double gsl_sf_legendre_Q1 (double x)   Function
int gsl_sf_legendre_Q1_e (double x, gsl_sf_result *   Function
      result)
    These routines compute the Legendre function $Q_1(x)$ for $x > -1$, $x \neq 1$.

double gsl_sf_legendre_Ql (int l, double x)   Function
int gsl_sf_legendre_Ql_e (int l, double x,   Function
      gsl_sf_result * *result*)
    These routines compute the Legendre function $Q_l(x)$ for $x > -1$, $x \neq 1$ and $l \geq 0$.

7.24.2 Associated Legendre Polynomials and Spherical Harmonics

The following functions compute the associated Legendre Polynomials $P_l^m(x)$. Note that this function grows combinatorially with l and can overflow for l larger than about 150. There is no trouble for small m, but overflow occurs when m and l are both large. Rather than allow overflows, these functions refuse to calculate $P_l^m(x)$ and return GSL_EOVRFLW when they can sense that l and m are too big.

If you want to calculate a spherical harmonic, then *do not* use these functions. Instead use gsl_sf_legendre_sphPlm below, which uses a similar recursion, but with the normalized functions.

double gsl_sf_legendre_Plm (int l, int m, double x)   Function
int gsl_sf_legendre_Plm_e (int l, int m, double x,   Function
      gsl_sf_result * *result*)
    These routines compute the associated Legendre polynomial $P_l^m(x)$ for $m \geq 0$, $l \geq m$, $|x| \leq 1$.

int gsl_sf_legendre_Plm_array (int lmax, int m, double Function
      x, double *result_array*[])
int gsl_sf_legendre_Plm_deriv_array (int lmax, int m,   Function
      double x, double *result_array*[], double
      result_deriv_array[])
    These functions compute an array of Legendre polynomials $P_l^m(x)$, and optionally their derivatives $dP_l^m(x)/dx$, for $m \geq 0$, $l = |m|, \ldots, lmax$, $|x| \leq 1$.

double gsl_sf_legendre_sphPlm (int l, int m, double x) Function
int gsl_sf_legendre_sphPlm_e (int l, int m, double x,   Function
      gsl_sf_result * *result*)
    These routines compute the normalized associated Legendre polynomial $\sqrt{(2l+1)/(4\pi)}\sqrt{(l-m)!/(l+m)!}P_l^m(x)$ suitable for use in

spherical harmonics. The parameters must satisfy $m \geq 0$, $l \geq m$, $|x| \leq 1$. Theses routines avoid the overflows that occur for the standard normalization of $P_l^m(x)$.

int gsl_sf_legendre_sphPlm_array (int *lmax*, int *m*,   *Function*
      double *x*, double *result_array*[])

int gsl_sf_legendre_sphPlm_deriv_array (int *lmax*, int   *Function*
      m, double *x*, double *result_array*[], double
      result_deriv_array[])

These functions compute an array of normalized associated Legendre functions $\sqrt{(2l+1)/(4\pi)}\sqrt{(l-m)!/(l+m)!}P_l^m(x)$, and optionally their derivatives, for $m \geq 0$, $l = |m|, \ldots, lmax$, $|x| \leq 1$

int gsl_sf_legendre_array_size (const int *lmax*, const   *Function*
      int *m*)

This function returns the size of *result_array*[] needed for the array versions of $P_l^m(x)$, $lmax - m + 1$.

7.24.3 Conical Functions

The Conical Functions $P^{\mu}_{-(1/2)+i\lambda}(x)$ and $Q^{\mu}_{-(1/2)+i\lambda}$ are described in Abramowitz & Stegun, Section 8.12.

double gsl_sf_conicalP_half (double *lambda*, double *x*)   *Function*
int gsl_sf_conicalP_half_e (double *lambda*, double *x*,   *Function*
      gsl_sf_result * *result*)

These routines compute the irregular Spherical Conical Function $P^{1/2}_{-1/2+i\lambda}(x)$ for $x > -1$.

double gsl_sf_conicalP_mhalf (double *lambda*, double *x*)   *Function*
int gsl_sf_conicalP_mhalf_e (double *lambda*, double *x*,   *Function*
      gsl_sf_result * *result*)

These routines compute the regular Spherical Conical Function $P^{-1/2}_{-1/2+i\lambda}(x)$ for $x > -1$.

double gsl_sf_conicalP_0 (double *lambda*, double *x*)   *Function*
int gsl_sf_conicalP_0_e (double *lambda*, double *x*,   *Function*
      gsl_sf_result * *result*)

These routines compute the conical function $P^0_{-1/2+i\lambda}(x)$ for $x > -1$.

double gsl_sf_conicalP_1 (double *lambda*, double *x*)   *Function*
int gsl_sf_conicalP_1_e (double *lambda*, double *x*,   *Function*
      gsl_sf_result * *result*)

These routines compute the conical function $P^1_{-1/2+i\lambda}(x)$ for $x > -1$.

```
double gsl_sf_conicalP_sph_reg (int l, double lambda,        Function
        double x)
int gsl_sf_conicalP_sph_reg_e (int l, double lambda,        Function
        double x, gsl_sf_result * result)
```
These routines compute the Regular Spherical Conical Function
$P^{-1/2-l}_{-1/2+i\lambda}(x)$ for $x > -1$, $l \geq -1$.

```
double gsl_sf_conicalP_cyl_reg (int m, double lambda,       Function
        double x)
int gsl_sf_conicalP_cyl_reg_e (int m, double lambda,        Function
        double x, gsl_sf_result * result)
```
These routines compute the Regular Cylindrical Conical Function
$P^{-m}_{-1/2+i\lambda}(x)$ for $x > -1$, $m \geq -1$.

7.24.4 Radial Functions for Hyperbolic Space

The following spherical functions are specializations of Legendre functions which give the regular eigenfunctions of the Laplacian on a 3-dimensional hyperbolic space $H3d$. Of particular interest is the flat limit, $\lambda \to \infty$, $\eta \to 0$, $\lambda\eta$ fixed.

```
double gsl_sf_legendre_H3d_0 (double lambda, double         Function
        eta)
int gsl_sf_legendre_H3d_0_e (double lambda, double eta,     Function
        gsl_sf_result * result)
```
These routines compute the zeroth radial eigenfunction of the Laplacian on the 3-dimensional hyperbolic space,

$$L_0^{H3d}(\lambda, \eta) := \frac{\sin(\lambda\eta)}{\lambda \sinh(\eta)}$$

for $\eta \geq 0$. In the flat limit this takes the form $L_0^{H3d}(\lambda, \eta) = j_0(\lambda\eta)$.

```
double gsl_sf_legendre_H3d_1 (double lambda, double         Function
        eta)
int gsl_sf_legendre_H3d_1_e (double lambda, double eta,     Function
        gsl_sf_result * result)
```
These routines compute the first radial eigenfunction of the Laplacian on the 3-dimensional hyperbolic space,

$$L_1^{H3d}(\lambda, \eta) := \frac{1}{\sqrt{\lambda^2 + 1}} \left(\frac{\sin(\lambda\eta)}{\lambda \sinh(\eta)} \right) (\coth(\eta) - \lambda \cot(\lambda\eta))$$

for $\eta \geq 0$. In the flat limit this takes the form $L_1^{H3d}(\lambda, \eta) = j_1(\lambda\eta)$.

double gsl_sf_legendre_H3d (int *l*, double *lambda*,   Function
        double *eta*)

int gsl_sf_legendre_H3d_e (int *l*, double *lambda*, double   Function
        eta, gsl_sf_result * *result*)

These routines compute the *l*-th radial eigenfunction of the Laplacian on the 3-dimensional hyperbolic space $\eta \geq 0$, $l \geq 0$. In the flat limit this takes the form $L_l^{H3d}(\lambda, \eta) = j_l(\lambda \eta)$.

int gsl_sf_legendre_H3d_array (int *lmax*, double   Function
        lambda, double *eta*, double *result_array*[])

This function computes an array of radial eigenfunctions $L_l^{H3d}(\lambda, \eta)$ for $0 \leq l \leq lmax$.

7.25 Logarithm and Related Functions

Information on the properties of the Logarithm function can be found in Abramowitz & Stegun, Chapter 4. The functions described in this section are declared in the header file 'gsl_sf_log.h'.

double gsl_sf_log (double *x*)   Function
int gsl_sf_log_e (double *x*, gsl_sf_result * *result*)   Function

These routines compute the logarithm of *x*, $\log(x)$, for $x > 0$.

double gsl_sf_log_abs (double *x*)   Function
int gsl_sf_log_abs_e (double *x*, gsl_sf_result * *result*)   Function

These routines compute the logarithm of the magnitude of *x*, $\log(|x|)$, for $x \neq 0$.

int gsl_sf_complex_log_e (double *zr*, double *zi*,   Function
        gsl_sf_result * *lnr*, gsl_sf_result * *theta*)

This routine computes the complex logarithm of $z = z_r + iz_i$. The results are returned as *lnr*, *theta* such that $\exp(lnr + i\theta) = z_r + iz_i$, where θ lies in the range $[-\pi, \pi]$.

double gsl_sf_log_1plusx (double *x*)   Function
int gsl_sf_log_1plusx_e (double *x*, gsl_sf_result *   Function
        result)

These routines compute $\log(1 + x)$ for $x > -1$ using an algorithm that is accurate for small *x*.

double gsl_sf_log_1plusx_mx (double *x*)   Function
int gsl_sf_log_1plusx_mx_e (double *x*, gsl_sf_result *   Function
        result)

These routines compute $\log(1 + x) - x$ for $x > -1$ using an algorithm that is accurate for small *x*.

7.26 Power Function

The following functions are equivalent to the function `gsl_pow_int` (see Section 4.4 [Small integer powers], page 25) with an error estimate. These functions are declared in the header file 'gsl_sf_pow_int.h'.

double gsl_sf_pow_int (double x, int n) _Function_
int gsl_sf_pow_int_e (double x, int n, gsl_sf_result * _Function_
    result)

These routines compute the power x^n for integer n. The power is computed using the minimum number of multiplications. For example, x^8 is computed as $((x^2)^2)^2$, requiring only 3 multiplications. For reasons of efficiency, these functions do not check for overflow or underflow conditions.

```
#include <gsl/gsl_sf_pow_int.h>
/* compute 3.0**12 */
double y = gsl_sf_pow_int(3.0, 12);
```

7.27 Psi (Digamma) Function

The polygamma functions of order n are defined by

$$\psi^{(n)}(x) = \left(\frac{d}{dx}\right)^n \psi(x) = \left(\frac{d}{dx}\right)^{n+1} \log(\Gamma(x))$$

where $\psi(x) = \Gamma'(x)/\Gamma(x)$ is known as the digamma function. These functions are declared in the header file 'gsl_sf_psi.h'.

7.27.1 Digamma Function

double gsl_sf_psi_int (int n) _Function_
int gsl_sf_psi_int_e (int n, gsl_sf_result * result) _Function_
    These routines compute the digamma function $\psi(n)$ for positive integer
    n. The digamma function is also called the Psi function.

double gsl_sf_psi (double x) _Function_
int gsl_sf_psi_e (double x, gsl_sf_result * result) _Function_
    These routines compute the digamma function $\psi(x)$ for general x,
    $x \neq 0$.

double gsl_sf_psi_1piy (double y) _Function_
int gsl_sf_psi_1piy_e (double y, gsl_sf_result * result) _Function_
    These routines compute the real part of the digamma function on the
    line $1 + iy$, $\mathrm{Re}[\psi(1 + iy)]$.

7.27.2 Trigamma Function

double gsl_sf_psi_1_int (int *n*)   *Function*
int gsl_sf_psi_1_int_e (int *n*, gsl_sf_result * *result*)   *Function*
These routines compute the Trigamma function $\psi'(n)$ for positive integer *n*.

double gsl_sf_psi_1 (double *x*)   *Function*
int gsl_sf_psi_1_e (double *x*, gsl_sf_result * *result*)   *Function*
These routines compute the Trigamma function $\psi'(x)$ for general *x*.

7.27.3 Polygamma Function

double gsl_sf_psi_n (int *n*, double *x*)   *Function*
int gsl_sf_psi_n_e (int *n*, double *x*, gsl_sf_result *   *Function*
        result)
These routines compute the polygamma function $\psi^{(n)}(x)$ for $n \geq 0$, $x > 0$.

7.28 Synchrotron Functions

The functions described in this section are declared in the header file 'gsl_sf_synchrotron.h'.

double gsl_sf_synchrotron_1 (double *x*)   *Function*
int gsl_sf_synchrotron_1_e (double *x*, gsl_sf_result *   *Function*
        result)
These routines compute the first synchrotron function $x \int_x^\infty dt K_{5/3}(t)$ for $x \geq 0$.

double gsl_sf_synchrotron_2 (double *x*)   *Function*
int gsl_sf_synchrotron_2_e (double *x*, gsl_sf_result *   *Function*
        result)
These routines compute the second synchrotron function $x K_{2/3}(x)$ for $x \geq 0$.

7.29 Transport Functions

The transport functions $J(n, x)$ are defined by the integral representations $J(n, x) := \int_0^x dt\, t^n e^t / (e^t - 1)^2$. They are declared in the header file 'gsl_sf_transport.h'.

double gsl_sf_transport_2 (double x)   Function
int gsl_sf_transport_2_e (double x, gsl_sf_result *   Function
    result)
    These routines compute the transport function $J(2, x)$.

double gsl_sf_transport_3 (double x)   Function
int gsl_sf_transport_3_e (double x, gsl_sf_result *   Function
    result)
    These routines compute the transport function $J(3, x)$.

double gsl_sf_transport_4 (double x)   Function
int gsl_sf_transport_4_e (double x, gsl_sf_result *   Function
    result)
    These routines compute the transport function $J(4, x)$.

double gsl_sf_transport_5 (double x)   Function
int gsl_sf_transport_5_e (double x, gsl_sf_result *   Function
    result)
    These routines compute the transport function $J(5, x)$.

7.30 Trigonometric Functions

The library includes its own trigonometric functions in order to provide consistency across platforms and reliable error estimates. These functions are declared in the header file 'gsl_sf_trig.h'.

7.30.1 Circular Trigonometric Functions

double gsl_sf_sin (double x)   Function
int gsl_sf_sin_e (double x, gsl_sf_result * result)   Function
    These routines compute the sine function $\sin(x)$.

double gsl_sf_cos (double x)   Function
int gsl_sf_cos_e (double x, gsl_sf_result * result)   Function
    These routines compute the cosine function $\cos(x)$.

double gsl_sf_hypot (double x, double y)   Function
int gsl_sf_hypot_e (double x, double y, gsl_sf_result *   Function
    result)
    These routines compute the hypotenuse function $\sqrt{x^2 + y^2}$ avoiding overflow and underflow.

double gsl_sf_sinc (double x)   Function
int gsl_sf_sinc_e (double x, gsl_sf_result * result)   Function
   These routines compute $\mathrm{sinc}(x) = \sin(\pi x)/(\pi x)$ for any value of x.

7.30.2 Trigonometric Functions for Complex Arguments

int gsl_sf_complex_sin_e (double zr, double zi,   Function
       gsl_sf_result * szr, gsl_sf_result * szi)
   This function computes the complex sine, $\sin(z_r + iz_i)$ storing the real
and imaginary parts in szr, szi.

int gsl_sf_complex_cos_e (double zr, double zi,   Function
       gsl_sf_result * czr, gsl_sf_result * czi)
   This function computes the complex cosine, $\cos(z_r + iz_i)$ storing the
real and imaginary parts in szr, szi.

int gsl_sf_complex_logsin_e (double zr, double zi,   Function
       gsl_sf_result * lszr, gsl_sf_result * lszi)
   This function computes the logarithm of the complex sine, $\log(\sin(z_r + iz_i))$ storing the real and imaginary parts in szr, szi.

7.30.3 Hyperbolic Trigonometric Functions

double gsl_sf_lnsinh (double x)   Function
int gsl_sf_lnsinh_e (double x, gsl_sf_result * result)   Function
   These routines compute $\log(\sinh(x))$ for $x > 0$.

double gsl_sf_lncosh (double x)   Function
int gsl_sf_lncosh_e (double x, gsl_sf_result * result)   Function
   These routines compute $\log(\cosh(x))$ for any x.

7.30.4 Conversion Functions

int gsl_sf_polar_to_rect (double r, double theta,   Function
       gsl_sf_result * x, gsl_sf_result * y);
   This function converts the polar coordinates (r,theta) to rectilinear
coordinates (x,y), $x = r\cos(\theta)$, $y = r\sin(\theta)$.

int gsl_sf_rect_to_polar (double x, double y,   Function
       gsl_sf_result * r, gsl_sf_result * theta)
   This function converts the rectilinear coordinates (x,y) to polar coordinates (r,theta), such that $x = r\cos(\theta)$, $y = r\sin(\theta)$. The argument theta lies in the range $[-\pi, \pi]$.

7.30.5 Restriction Functions

double gsl_sf_angle_restrict_symm (double *theta*)   Function
int gsl_sf_angle_restrict_symm_e (double * *theta*)   Function
    These routines force the angle *theta* to lie in the range $(-\pi, \pi]$.

double gsl_sf_angle_restrict_pos (double *theta*)   Function
int gsl_sf_angle_restrict_pos_e (double * *theta*)   Function
    These routines force the angle *theta* to lie in the range $[0, 2\pi)$.

7.30.6 Trigonometric Functions With Error Estimates

int gsl_sf_sin_err_e (double *x*, double *dx*,   Function
        gsl_sf_result * *result*)
    This routine computes the sine of an angle *x* with an associated abso-
    lute error *dx*, $\sin(x \pm dx)$. Note that this function is provided in the
    error-handling form only since its purpose is to compute the propa-
    gated error.

int gsl_sf_cos_err_e (double *x*, double *dx*,   Function
        gsl_sf_result * *result*)
    This routine computes the cosine of an angle *x* with an associated
    absolute error *dx*, $\cos(x \pm dx)$. Note that this function is provided
    in the error-handling form only since its purpose is to compute the
    propagated error.

7.31 Zeta Functions

    The Riemann zeta function is defined in Abramowitz & Stegun, Sec-
tion 23.2. The functions described in this section are declared in the
header file 'gsl_sf_zeta.h'.

7.31.1 Riemann Zeta Function

    The Riemann zeta function is defined by the infinite sum $\zeta(s) = \sum_{k=1}^{\infty} k^{-s}$.

double gsl_sf_zeta_int (int *n*)   Function
int gsl_sf_zeta_int_e (int *n*, gsl_sf_result * *result*)   Function
    These routines compute the Riemann zeta function $\zeta(n)$ for integer *n*,
    $n \neq 1$.

double gsl_sf_zeta (double *s*)   Function
int gsl_sf_zeta_e (double *s*, gsl_sf_result * *result*)   Function
    These routines compute the Riemann zeta function $\zeta(s)$ for arbitrary
    $s, s \neq 1$.

7.31.2 Riemann Zeta Function Minus One

For large positive argument, the Riemann zeta function approaches one. In this region the fractional part is interesting, and therefore we need a function to evaluate it explicitly.

double gsl_sf_zetam1_int (int *n*)   Function
int gsl_sf_zetam1_int_e (int *n*, gsl_sf_result * *result*)   Function
    These routines compute $\zeta(n) - 1$ for integer n, $n \neq 1$.

double gsl_sf_zetam1 (double *s*)   Function
int gsl_sf_zetam1_e (double *s*, gsl_sf_result * *result*)   Function
    These routines compute $\zeta(s) - 1$ for arbitrary s, $s \neq 1$.

7.31.3 Hurwitz Zeta Function

The Hurwitz zeta function is defined by $\zeta(s,q) = \sum_0^\infty (k+q)^{-s}$.

double gsl_sf_hzeta (double *s*, double *q*)   Function
int gsl_sf_hzeta_e (double *s*, double *q*, gsl_sf_result *   Function
    result)
    These routines compute the Hurwitz zeta function $\zeta(s,q)$ for $s > 1$, $q > 0$.

7.31.4 Eta Function

The eta function is defined by $\eta(s) = (1 - 2^{1-s})\zeta(s)$.

double gsl_sf_eta_int (int *n*)   Function
int gsl_sf_eta_int_e (int *n*, gsl_sf_result * *result*)   Function
    These routines compute the eta function $\eta(n)$ for integer n.

double gsl_sf_eta (double *s*)   Function
int gsl_sf_eta_e (double *s*, gsl_sf_result * *result*)   Function
    These routines compute the eta function $\eta(s)$ for arbitrary s.

7.32 Examples

The following example demonstrates the use of the error handling form of the special functions, in this case to compute the Bessel function $J_0(5.0)$,

```
#include <stdio.h>
#include <gsl/gsl_errno.h>
#include <gsl/gsl_sf_bessel.h>

int
main (void)
{
  double x = 5.0;
  gsl_sf_result result;

  double expected = -0.17759677131433830434739701;

  int status = gsl_sf_bessel_J0_e (x, &result);

  printf ("status  = %s\n", gsl_strerror(status));
  printf ("J0(5.0) = %.18f\n"
          "        +/- % .18f\n",
          result.val, result.err);
  printf ("exact   = %.18f\n", expected);
  return status;
}
```

Here are the results of running the program,

```
$ ./a.out
status  = success
J0(5.0) = -0.177596771314338292
        +/-  0.000000000000000193
exact   = -0.177596771314338292
```

The next program computes the same quantity using the natural form of the function. In this case the error term *result.err* and return status are not accessible.

```
#include <stdio.h>
#include <gsl/gsl_sf_bessel.h>

int
main (void)
{
  double x = 5.0;
  double expected = -0.17759677131433830434739701;
```

```
double y = gsl_sf_bessel_J0 (x);

printf ("J0(5.0) = %.18f\n", y);
printf ("exact   = %.18f\n", expected);
return 0;
}
```

The results of the function are the same,

```
$ ./a.out
  J0(5.0) = -0.177596771314338292
  exact   = -0.177596771314338292
```

7.33 References and Further Reading

The library follows the conventions of *Abramowitz & Stegun* where possible,

Abramowitz & Stegun (eds.), *Handbook of Mathematical Functions*

The following papers contain information on the algorithms used to compute the special functions,

MISCFUN: A software package to compute uncommon special functions. *ACM Trans. Math. Soft.*, vol. 22, 1996, 288–301

G.N. Watson, A Treatise on the Theory of Bessel Functions, 2nd Edition (Cambridge University Press, 1944).

G. Nemeth, Mathematical Approximations of Special Functions, Nova Science Publishers, ISBN 1-56072-052-2

B.C. Carlson, Special Functions of Applied Mathematics (1977)

W.J. Thompson, Atlas for Computing Mathematical Functions, John Wiley & Sons, New York (1997).

Y.Y. Luke, Algorithms for the Computation of Mathematical Functions, Academic Press, New York (1977).

8 Vectors and Matrices

The functions described in this chapter provide a simple vector and matrix interface to ordinary C arrays. The memory management of these arrays is implemented using a single underlying type, known as a block. By writing your functions in terms of vectors and matrices you can pass a single structure containing both data and dimensions as an argument without needing additional function parameters. The structures are compatible with the vector and matrix formats used by BLAS routines.

8.1 Data types

All the functions are available for each of the standard data-types. The versions for double have the prefix gsl_block, gsl_vector and gsl_matrix. Similarly the versions for single-precision float arrays have the prefix gsl_block_float, gsl_vector_float and gsl_matrix_float. The full list of available types is given below,

gsl_block	double
gsl_block_float	float
gsl_block_long_double	long double
gsl_block_int	int
gsl_block_uint	unsigned int
gsl_block_long	long
gsl_block_ulong	unsigned long
gsl_block_short	short
gsl_block_ushort	unsigned short
gsl_block_char	char
gsl_block_uchar	unsigned char
gsl_block_complex	complex double
gsl_block_complex_float	complex float
gsl_block_complex_long_double	complex long double

Corresponding types exist for the gsl_vector and gsl_matrix functions.

8.2 Blocks

For consistency all memory is allocated through a `gsl_block` structure. The structure contains two components, the size of an area of memory and a pointer to the memory. The `gsl_block` structure looks like this,

```
typedef struct
{
  size_t size;
  double * data;
} gsl_block;
```

Vectors and matrices are made by *slicing* an underlying block. A slice is a set of elements formed from an initial offset and a combination of indices and step-sizes. In the case of a matrix the step-size for the column index represents the row-length. The step-size for a vector is known as the *stride*.

The functions for allocating and deallocating blocks are defined in 'gsl_block.h'

8.2.1 Block allocation

The functions for allocating memory to a block follow the style of `malloc` and `free`. In addition they also perform their own error checking. If there is insufficient memory available to allocate a block then the functions call the GSL error handler (with an error number of `GSL_ENOMEM`) in addition to returning a null pointer. Thus if you use the library error handler to abort your program then it isn't necessary to check every `alloc`.

`gsl_block * gsl_block_alloc (size_t n)`   Function
  This function allocates memory for a block of n double-precision elements, returning a pointer to the block struct. The block is not initialized and so the values of its elements are undefined. Use the function `gsl_block_calloc` if you want to ensure that all the elements are initialized to zero.

  A null pointer is returned if insufficient memory is available to create the block.

`gsl_block * gsl_block_calloc (size_t n)`   Function
  This function allocates memory for a block and initializes all the elements of the block to zero.

void `gsl_block_free` (gsl_block * *b*)   Function

> This function frees the memory used by a block *b* previously allocated
> with `gsl_block_alloc` or `gsl_block_calloc`. The block *b* must be
> a valid block object (a null pointer is not allowed).

8.2.2 Reading and writing blocks

The library provides functions for reading and writing blocks to a file
as binary data or formatted text.

int `gsl_block_fwrite` (FILE * *stream*, const gsl_block *   Function
   b)

> This function writes the elements of the block *b* to the stream *stream*
> in binary format. The return value is 0 for success and `GSL_EFAILED`
> if there was a problem writing to the file. Since the data is written
> in the native binary format it may not be portable between different
> architectures.

int `gsl_block_fread` (FILE * *stream*, gsl_block * *b*)   Function

> This function reads into the block *b* from the open stream *stream* in
> binary format. The block *b* must be preallocated with the correct
> length since the function uses the size of *b* to determine how many
> bytes to read. The return value is 0 for success and `GSL_EFAILED` if
> there was a problem reading from the file. The data is assumed to have
> been written in the native binary format on the same architecture.

int `gsl_block_fprintf` (FILE * *stream*, const gsl_block *   Function
   b, const char * *format*)

> This function writes the elements of the block *b* line-by-line to the
> stream *stream* using the format specifier *format*, which should be one
> of the %g, %e or %f formats for floating point numbers and %d for
> integers. The function returns 0 for success and `GSL_EFAILED` if there
> was a problem writing to the file.

int `gsl_block_fscanf` (FILE * *stream*, gsl_block * *b*)   Function

> This function reads formatted data from the stream *stream* into the
> block *b*. The block *b* must be preallocated with the correct length
> since the function uses the size of *b* to determine how many numbers
> to read. The function returns 0 for success and `GSL_EFAILED` if there
> was a problem reading from the file.

8.2.3 Example programs for blocks

The following program shows how to allocate a block,

```
#include <stdio.h>
#include <gsl/gsl_block.h>

int
main (void)
{
  gsl_block * b = gsl_block_alloc (100);

  printf ("length of block = %u\n", b->size);
  printf ("block data address = %#x\n", b->data);

  gsl_block_free (b);
  return 0;
}
```

Here is the output from the program,

```
length of block = 100
block data address = 0x804b0d8
```

8.3 Vectors

Vectors are defined by a `gsl_vector` structure which describes a slice
of a block. Different vectors can be created which point to the same block.
A vector slice is a set of equally-spaced elements of an area of memory.

The `gsl_vector` structure contains five components, the *size*, the
stride, a pointer to the memory where the elements are stored, *data*, a
pointer to the block owned by the vector, *block*, if any, and an ownership
flag, *owner*. The structure is very simple and looks like this,

```
typedef struct
{
  size_t size;
  size_t stride;
  double * data;
  gsl_block * block;
  int owner;
} gsl_vector;
```

The *size* is simply the number of vector elements. The range of valid
indices runs from 0 to `size-1`. The *stride* is the step-size from one element
to the next in physical memory, measured in units of the appropriate
datatype. The pointer *data* gives the location of the first element of the
vector in memory. The pointer *block* stores the location of the memory

block in which the vector elements are located (if any). If the vector owns this block then the *owner* field is set to one and the block will be deallocated when the vector is freed. If the vector points to a block owned by another object then the *owner* field is zero and any underlying block will not be deallocated with the vector.

The functions for allocating and accessing vectors are defined in 'gsl_vector.h'

8.3.1 Vector allocation

The functions for allocating memory to a vector follow the style of malloc and free. In addition they also perform their own error checking. If there is insufficient memory available to allocate a vector then the functions call the GSL error handler (with an error number of GSL_ENOMEM) in addition to returning a null pointer. Thus if you use the library error handler to abort your program then it isn't necessary to check every alloc.

gsl_vector * gsl_vector_alloc (size_t *n*)   *Function*
     This function creates a vector of length *n*, returning a pointer to a newly initialized vector struct. A new block is allocated for the elements of the vector, and stored in the *block* component of the vector struct. The block is "owned" by the vector, and will be deallocated when the vector is deallocated.

gsl_vector * gsl_vector_calloc (size_t *n*)   *Function*
     This function allocates memory for a vector of length *n* and initializes all the elements of the vector to zero.

void gsl_vector_free (gsl_vector * *v*)   *Function*
     This function frees a previously allocated vector *v*. If the vector was created using gsl_vector_alloc then the block underlying the vector will also be deallocated. If the vector has been created from another object then the memory is still owned by that object and will not be deallocated. The vector *v* must be a valid vector object (a null pointer is not allowed).

8.3.2 Accessing vector elements

Unlike FORTRAN compilers, C compilers do not usually provide support for range checking of vectors and matrices. The functions gsl_vector_get and gsl_vector_set can perform portable range checking for you and report an error if you attempt to access elements outside the allowed range.

The functions for accessing the elements of a vector or matrix are defined in 'gsl_vector.h' and declared extern inline to eliminate function-call overhead. You must compile your program with the macro HAVE_INLINE defined to use these functions.

If necessary you can turn off range checking completely without modifying any source files by recompiling your program with the preprocessor definition GSL_RANGE_CHECK_OFF. Provided your compiler supports inline functions the effect of turning off range checking is to replace calls to gsl_vector_get(v,i) by v->data[i*v->stride] and calls to gsl_vector_set(v,i,x) by v->data[i*v->stride]=x. Thus there should be no performance penalty for using the range checking functions when range checking is turned off.

double gsl_vector_get (const gsl_vector * v, size_t i)   Function
> This function returns the i-th element of a vector v. If i lies outside the allowed range of 0 to $n - 1$ then the error handler is invoked and 0 is returned.

void gsl_vector_set (gsl_vector * v, size_t i, double x)   Function
> This function sets the value of the i-th element of a vector v to x. If i lies outside the allowed range of 0 to $n - 1$ then the error handler is invoked.

double * gsl_vector_ptr (gsl_vector * v, size_t i)   Function
const double * gsl_vector_const_ptr (const gsl_vector   Function
          * v, size_t i)
> These functions return a pointer to the i-th element of a vector v. If i lies outside the allowed range of 0 to $n - 1$ then the error handler is invoked and a null pointer is returned.

8.3.3 Initializing vector elements

void gsl_vector_set_all (gsl_vector * v, double x)   *Function*
    This function sets all the elements of the vector v to the value x.

void gsl_vector_set_zero (gsl_vector * v)   *Function*
    This function sets all the elements of the vector v to zero.

int gsl_vector_set_basis (gsl_vector * v, size_t i)   *Function*
    This function makes a basis vector by setting all the elements of the
    vector v to zero except for the i-th element which is set to one.

8.3.4 Reading and writing vectors

The library provides functions for reading and writing vectors to a file
as binary data or formatted text.

int gsl_vector_fwrite (FILE * stream, const gsl_vector   *Function*
    * v)
    This function writes the elements of the vector v to the stream stream
    in binary format. The return value is 0 for success and GSL_EFAILED
    if there was a problem writing to the file. Since the data is written
    in the native binary format it may not be portable between different
    architectures.

int gsl_vector_fread (FILE * stream, gsl_vector * v)   *Function*
    This function reads into the vector v from the open stream stream in
    binary format. The vector v must be preallocated with the correct
    length since the function uses the size of v to determine how many
    bytes to read. The return value is 0 for success and GSL_EFAILED if
    there was a problem reading from the file. The data is assumed to have
    been written in the native binary format on the same architecture.

int gsl_vector_fprintf (FILE * stream, const gsl_vector   *Function*
    * v, const char * format)
    This function writes the elements of the vector v line-by-line to the
    stream stream using the format specifier format, which should be one
    of the %g, %e or %f formats for floating point numbers and %d for
    integers. The function returns 0 for success and GSL_EFAILED if there
    was a problem writing to the file.

int gsl_vector_fscanf (FILE * stream, gsl_vector * v)   *Function*
    This function reads formatted data from the stream stream into the
    vector v. The vector v must be preallocated with the correct length
    since the function uses the size of v to determine how many numbers
    to read. The function returns 0 for success and GSL_EFAILED if there
    was a problem reading from the file.

8.3.5 Vector views

In addition to creating vectors from slices of blocks it is also possible to slice vectors and create vector views. For example, a subvector of another vector can be described with a view, or two views can be made which provide access to the even and odd elements of a vector.

A vector view is a temporary object, stored on the stack, which can be used to operate on a subset of vector elements. Vector views can be defined for both constant and non-constant vectors, using separate types that preserve constness. A vector view has the type `gsl_vector_view` and a constant vector view has the type `gsl_vector_const_view`. In both cases the elements of the view can be accessed as a `gsl_vector` using the `vector` component of the view object. A pointer to a vector of type `gsl_vector *` or `const gsl_vector *` can be obtained by taking the address of this component with the `&` operator.

When using this pointer it is important to ensure that the view itself remains in scope—the simplest way to do so is by always writing the pointer as `&view.vector`, and never storing this value in another variable.

gsl_vector_view gsl_vector_subvector (gsl_vector * v,   *Function*
          size_t *offset*, size_t *n*)
gsl_vector_const_view gsl_vector_const_subvector   *Function*
          (const gsl_vector * v, size_t *offset*, size_t *n*)
These functions return a vector view of a subvector of another vector *v*. The start of the new vector is offset by *offset* elements from the start of the original vector. The new vector has *n* elements. Mathematically, the *i*-th element of the new vector *v'* is given by,

        v'(i) = v->data[(offset + i)*v->stride]

where the index *i* runs from 0 to n-1.

The data pointer of the returned vector struct is set to null if the combined parameters (*offset*,*n*) overrun the end of the original vector.

The new vector is only a view of the block underlying the original vector, *v*. The block containing the elements of *v* is not owned by the new vector. When the view goes out of scope the original vector *v* and its block will continue to exist. The original memory can only be deallocated by freeing the original vector. Of course, the original vector should not be deallocated while the view is still in use.

The function `gsl_vector_const_subvector` is equivalent to `gsl_vector_subvector` but can be used for vectors which are declared const.

gsl_vector_view gsl_vector_subvector_with_stride   Function
      (gsl_vector * v, size_t *offset*, size_t *stride*, size_t n)
gsl_vector_const_view   Function
        gsl_vector_const_subvector_with_stride (const
      gsl_vector * v, size_t *offset*, size_t *stride*, size_t n)

These functions return a vector view of a subvector of another vector
v with an additional stride argument. The subvector is formed in the
same way as for gsl_vector_subvector but the new vector has n
elements with a step-size of *stride* from one element to the next in the
original vector. Mathematically, the *i*-th element of the new vector v'
is given by,

    v'(i) = v->data[(offset + i*stride)*v->stride]

where the index *i* runs from 0 to n-1.

Note that subvector views give direct access to the underlying elements of the original vector. For example, the following code will zero
the even elements of the vector v of length n, while leaving the odd
elements untouched,

```
gsl_vector_view v_even
  = gsl_vector_subvector_with_stride (v, 0, 2, n/2);
gsl_vector_set_zero (&v_even.vector);
```

A vector view can be passed to any subroutine which takes a vector argument just as a directly allocated vector would be, using
&*view*.vector. For example, the following code computes the norm of
the odd elements of v using the BLAS routine DNRM2,

```
gsl_vector_view v_odd
  = gsl_vector_subvector_with_stride (v, 1, 2, n/2);
double r = gsl_blas_dnrm2 (&v_odd.vector);
```

The function gsl_vector_const_subvector_with_stride is equivalent to gsl_vector_subvector_with_stride but can be used for
vectors which are declared const.

gsl_vector_view gsl_vector_complex_real   Function
      (gsl_vector_complex * v)
gsl_vector_const_view gsl_vector_complex_const_real   Function
      (const gsl_vector_complex * v)

These functions return a vector view of the real parts of the complex
vector *v*.

The function gsl_vector_complex_const_real is equivalent to gsl_
vector_complex_real but can be used for vectors which are declared
const.

`gsl_vector_view gsl_vector_complex_imag`   Function
       `(gsl_vector_complex * v)`
`gsl_vector_const_view gsl_vector_complex_const_imag`   Function
       `(const gsl_vector_complex * v)`

These functions return a vector view of the imaginary parts of the complex vector v.

The function `gsl_vector_complex_const_imag` is equivalent to `gsl_vector_complex_imag` but can be used for vectors which are declared const.

`gsl_vector_view gsl_vector_view_array (double * base,`   Function
       `size_t n)`
`gsl_vector_const_view gsl_vector_const_view_array`   Function
       `(const double * base, size_t n)`

These functions return a vector view of an array. The start of the new vector is given by $base$ and has n elements. Mathematically, the i-th element of the new vector v' is given by,

    `v'(i) = base[i]`

where the index i runs from 0 to n-1.

The array containing the elements of v is not owned by the new vector view. When the view goes out of scope the original array will continue to exist. The original memory can only be deallocated by freeing the original pointer $base$. Of course, the original array should not be deallocated while the view is still in use.

The function `gsl_vector_const_view_array` is equivalent to `gsl_vector_view_array` but can be used for arrays which are declared const.

`gsl_vector_view gsl_vector_view_array_with_stride`   Function
       `(double * base, size_t stride, size_t n)`
`gsl_vector_const_view`   Function
       `gsl_vector_const_view_array_with_stride (const`
       `double * base, size_t stride, size_t n)`

These functions return a vector view of an array $base$ with an additional stride argument. The subvector is formed in the same way as for `gsl_vector_view_array` but the new vector has n elements with a step-size of $stride$ from one element to the next in the original array. Mathematically, the i-th element of the new vector v' is given by,

    `v'(i) = base[i*stride]`

where the index i runs from 0 to n-1.

Note that the view gives direct access to the underlying elements of the original array. A vector view can be passed to any subroutine which takes a vector argument just as a directly allocated vector would be, using &*view*.vector.

The function gsl_vector_const_view_array_with_stride is equivalent to gsl_vector_view_array_with_stride but can be used for arrays which are declared const.

8.3.6 Copying vectors

Common operations on vectors such as addition and multiplication are available in the BLAS part of the library (see Chapter 12 [BLAS Support], page 149). However, it is useful to have a small number of utility functions which do not require the full BLAS code. The following functions fall into this category.

int gsl_vector_memcpy (gsl_vector * *dest*, const   Function
        gsl_vector * *src*)
This function copies the elements of the vector *src* into the vector *dest*. The two vectors must have the same length.

int gsl_vector_swap (gsl_vector * *v*, gsl_vector * *w*)   Function
This function exchanges the elements of the vectors *v* and *w* by copying. The two vectors must have the same length.

8.3.7 Exchanging elements

The following function can be used to exchange, or permute, the elements of a vector.

int gsl_vector_swap_elements (gsl_vector * *v*, size_t *i*,   Function
        size_t *j*)
This function exchanges the *i*-th and *j*-th elements of the vector *v* in-place.

int gsl_vector_reverse (gsl_vector * *v*)   Function
This function reverses the order of the elements of the vector *v*.

8.3.8 Vector operations

The following operations are only defined for real vectors.

int gsl_vector_add (gsl_vector * *a*, const gsl_vector *   Function
        b)
This function adds the elements of vector *b* to the elements of vector *a*, $a_i' = a_i + b_i$. The two vectors must have the same length.

int gsl_vector_sub (gsl_vector * a, const gsl_vector *   Function
            b)

This function subtracts the elements of vector b from the elements of
vector a, $a_i' = a_i - b_i$. The two vectors must have the same length.

int gsl_vector_mul (gsl_vector * a, const gsl_vector *   Function
            b)

This function multiplies the elements of vector a by the elements of
vector b, $a_i' = a_i * b_i$. The two vectors must have the same length.

int gsl_vector_div (gsl_vector * a, const gsl_vector *   Function
            b)

This function divides the elements of vector a by the elements of vector
b, $a_i' = a_i / b_i$. The two vectors must have the same length.

int gsl_vector_scale (gsl_vector * a, const double x)   Function

This function multiplies the elements of vector a by the constant factor
x, $a_i' = x a_i$.

int gsl_vector_add_constant (gsl_vector * a, const   Function
            double x)

This function adds the constant value x to the elements of the vector
a, $a_i' = a_i + x$.

8.3.9 Finding maximum and minimum elements of vectors

double gsl_vector_max (const gsl_vector * v)   Function

This function returns the maximum value in the vector v.

double gsl_vector_min (const gsl_vector * v)   Function

This function returns the minimum value in the vector v.

void gsl_vector_minmax (const gsl_vector * v, double *   Function
            min_out, double * max_out)

This function returns the minimum and maximum values in the vector
v, storing them in min_out and max_out.

size_t gsl_vector_max_index (const gsl_vector * v)   Function

This function returns the index of the maximum value in the vector
v. When there are several equal maximum elements then the lowest
index is returned.

size_t gsl_vector_min_index (const gsl_vector * v)   Function

This function returns the index of the minimum value in the vector v.
When there are several equal minimum elements then the lowest index
is returned.

void gsl_vector_minmax_index (const gsl_vector * v,   Function
        size_t * *imin*, size_t * *imax*)

This function returns the indices of the minimum and maximum values in the vector *v*, storing them in *imin* and *imax*. When there are several equal minimum or maximum elements then the lowest indices are returned.

8.3.10 Vector properties

int gsl_vector_isnull (const gsl_vector * v)   Function

This function returns 1 if all the elements of the vector *v* are zero, and 0 otherwise.

8.3.11 Example programs for vectors

This program shows how to allocate, initialize and read from a vector using the functions gsl_vector_alloc, gsl_vector_set and gsl_vector_get.

```
#include <stdio.h>
#include <gsl/gsl_vector.h>

int
main (void)
{
  int i;
  gsl_vector * v = gsl_vector_alloc (3);

  for (i = 0; i < 3; i++)
    {
      gsl_vector_set (v, i, 1.23 + i);
    }

  for (i = 0; i < 100; i++) /* out of range error */
    {
      printf ("v_%d = %g\n", i, gsl_vector_get (v, i));
    }

  return 0;
}
```

Here is the output from the program. The final loop attempts to read outside the range of the vector v, and the error is trapped by the range-checking code in gsl_vector_get.

```
$ ./a.out
v_0 = 1.23
v_1 = 2.23
v_2 = 3.23
gsl: vector_source.c:12: ERROR: index out of range
Default GSL error handler invoked.
Aborted (core dumped)
```

The next program shows how to write a vector to a file.

```
#include <stdio.h>
#include <gsl/gsl_vector.h>

int
main (void)
{
  int i;
  gsl_vector * v = gsl_vector_alloc (100);

  for (i = 0; i < 100; i++)
    {
      gsl_vector_set (v, i, 1.23 + i);
    }

  {
     FILE * f = fopen ("test.dat", "w");
     gsl_vector_fprintf (f, v, "%.5g");
     fclose (f);
  }
  return 0;
}
```

After running this program the file 'test.dat' should contain the elements of v, written using the format specifier %.5g. The vector could then be read back in using the function gsl_vector_fscanf (f, v) as follows:

```
#include <stdio.h>
#include <gsl/gsl_vector.h>

int
main (void)
{
  int i;
  gsl_vector * v = gsl_vector_alloc (10);

  {
     FILE * f = fopen ("test.dat", "r");
```

```
      gsl_vector_fscanf (f, v);
      fclose (f);
  }

  for (i = 0; i < 10; i++)
    {
      printf ("%g\n", gsl_vector_get(v, i));
    }

  return 0;
}
```

8.4 Matrices

Matrices are defined by a gsl_matrix structure which describes a generalized slice of a block. Like a vector it represents a set of elements in an area of memory, but uses two indices instead of one.

The gsl_matrix structure contains six components, the two dimensions of the matrix, a physical dimension, a pointer to the memory where the elements of the matrix are stored, *data*, a pointer to the block owned by the matrix *block*, if any, and an ownership flag, *owner*. The physical dimension determines the memory layout and can differ from the matrix dimension to allow the use of submatrices. The gsl_matrix structure is very simple and looks like this,

```
typedef struct
{
  size_t size1;
  size_t size2;
  size_t tda;
  double * data;
  gsl_block * block;
  int owner;
} gsl_matrix;
```

Matrices are stored in row-major order, meaning that each row of elements forms a contiguous block in memory. This is the standard "C-language ordering" of two-dimensional arrays. Note that FORTRAN stores arrays in column-major order. The number of rows is *size1*. The range of valid row indices runs from 0 to size1-1. Similarly *size2* is the number of columns. The range of valid column indices runs from 0 to size2-1. The physical row dimension *tda*, or *trailing dimension*, specifies the size of a row of the matrix as laid out in memory.

For example, in the following matrix *size1* is 3, *size2* is 4, and *tda* is 8. The physical memory layout of the matrix begins in the top left hand-corner and proceeds from left to right along each row in turn.

```
00 01 02 03 XX XX XX XX
10 11 12 13 XX XX XX XX
20 21 22 23 XX XX XX XX
```

Each unused memory location is represented by "XX". The pointer *data* gives the location of the first element of the matrix in memory. The pointer *block* stores the location of the memory block in which the elements of the matrix are located (if any). If the matrix owns this block then the *owner* field is set to one and the block will be deallocated when the matrix is freed. If the matrix is only a slice of a block owned by another object then the *owner* field is zero and any underlying block will not be freed.

The functions for allocating and accessing matrices are defined in 'gsl_matrix.h'

8.4.1 Matrix allocation

The functions for allocating memory to a matrix follow the style of malloc and free. They also perform their own error checking. If there is insufficient memory available to allocate a vector then the functions call the GSL error handler (with an error number of GSL_ENOMEM) in addition to returning a null pointer. Thus if you use the library error handler to abort your program then it isn't necessary to check every alloc.

gsl_matrix * gsl_matrix_alloc (size_t *n1*, size_t *n2*)   Function
This function creates a matrix of size *n1* rows by *n2* columns, returning a pointer to a newly initialized matrix struct. A new block is allocated for the elements of the matrix, and stored in the *block* component of the matrix struct. The block is "owned" by the matrix, and will be deallocated when the matrix is deallocated.

gsl_matrix * gsl_matrix_calloc (size_t *n1*, size_t *n2*)   Function
This function allocates memory for a matrix of size *n1* rows by *n2* columns and initializes all the elements of the matrix to zero.

void gsl_matrix_free (gsl_matrix * *m*)   Function
This function frees a previously allocated matrix *m*. If the matrix was created using gsl_matrix_alloc then the block underlying the matrix will also be deallocated. If the matrix has been created from another object then the memory is still owned by that object and will not be deallocated. The matrix *m* must be a valid matrix object (a null pointer is not allowed).

8.4.2 Accessing matrix elements

The functions for accessing the elements of a matrix use the same range checking system as vectors. You can turn off range checking by recompiling your program with the preprocessor definition GSL_RANGE_CHECK_OFF.

The elements of the matrix are stored in "C-order", where the second index moves continuously through memory. More precisely, the element accessed by the functions gsl_matrix_get(m,i,j) and gsl_matrix_set(m,i,j,x) is

    m->data[i * m->tda + j]

where *tda* is the physical row-length of the matrix.

double gsl_matrix_get (const gsl_matrix * m, size_t i,   Function
        size_t j)
   This function returns the (i,j)-th element of a matrix m. If i or j lie outside the allowed range of 0 to $n1 - 1$ and 0 to $n2 - 1$ then the error handler is invoked and 0 is returned.

void gsl_matrix_set (gsl_matrix * m, size_t i, size_t j,   Function
        double x)
   This function sets the value of the (i,j)-th element of a matrix m to x. If i or j lies outside the allowed range of 0 to $n1 - 1$ and 0 to $n2 - 1$ then the error handler is invoked.

double * gsl_matrix_ptr (gsl_matrix * m, size_t i,   Function
        size_t j)
const double * gsl_matrix_const_ptr (const gsl_matrix   Function
        * m, size_t i, size_t j)
   These functions return a pointer to the (i,j)-th element of a matrix m. If i or j lie outside the allowed range of 0 to $n1 - 1$ and 0 to $n2 - 1$ then the error handler is invoked and a null pointer is returned.

8.4.3 Initializing matrix elements

void gsl_matrix_set_all (gsl_matrix * m, double x)   Function
   This function sets all the elements of the matrix m to the value x.

void gsl_matrix_set_zero (gsl_matrix * m)   Function
   This function sets all the elements of the matrix m to zero.

void gsl_matrix_set_identity (gsl_matrix * m)   Function
   This function sets the elements of the matrix m to the corresponding elements of the identity matrix, $m(i,j) = \delta(i,j)$, i.e. a unit diagonal with all off-diagonal elements zero. This applies to both square and rectangular matrices.

8.4.4 Reading and writing matrices

The library provides functions for reading and writing matrices to a file as binary data or formatted text.

int gsl_matrix_fwrite (FILE * *stream*, const gsl_matrix   *Function*
     * *m*)

This function writes the elements of the matrix *m* to the stream *stream* in binary format. The return value is 0 for success and GSL_EFAILED if there was a problem writing to the file. Since the data is written in the native binary format it may not be portable between different architectures.

int gsl_matrix_fread (FILE * *stream*, gsl_matrix * *m*)   *Function*

This function reads into the matrix *m* from the open stream *stream* in binary format. The matrix *m* must be preallocated with the correct dimensions since the function uses the size of *m* to determine how many bytes to read. The return value is 0 for success and GSL_EFAILED if there was a problem reading from the file. The data is assumed to have been written in the native binary format on the same architecture.

int gsl_matrix_fprintf (FILE * *stream*, const gsl_matrix   *Function*
     * *m*, const char * *format*)

This function writes the elements of the matrix *m* line-by-line to the stream *stream* using the format specifier *format*, which should be one of the %g, %e or %f formats for floating point numbers and %d for integers. The function returns 0 for success and GSL_EFAILED if there was a problem writing to the file.

int gsl_matrix_fscanf (FILE * *stream*, gsl_matrix * *m*)   *Function*

This function reads formatted data from the stream *stream* into the matrix *m*. The matrix *m* must be preallocated with the correct dimensions since the function uses the size of *m* to determine how many numbers to read. The function returns 0 for success and GSL_EFAILED if there was a problem reading from the file.

8.4.5 Matrix views

A matrix view is a temporary object, stored on the stack, which can be used to operate on a subset of matrix elements. Matrix views can be defined for both constant and non-constant matrices using separate types that preserve constness. A matrix view has the type gsl_matrix_view and a constant matrix view has the type gsl_matrix_const_view. In both cases the elements of the view can by accessed using the matrix component of the view object. A pointer gsl_matrix * or const gsl_matrix * can be obtained by taking the address of the matrix component with the & operator. In addition to matrix views it is also possible to create vector views of a matrix, such as row or column views.

gsl_matrix_view gsl_matrix_submatrix (gsl_matrix * m,   Function
         size_t k1, size_t k2, size_t n1, size_t n2)
gsl_matrix_const_view gsl_matrix_const_submatrix   Function
         (const gsl_matrix * m, size_t k1, size_t k2, size_t
         n1, size_t n2)
These functions return a matrix view of a submatrix of the matrix m. The upper-left element of the submatrix is the element (k1,k2) of the original matrix. The submatrix has n1 rows and n2 columns. The physical number of columns in memory given by tda is unchanged. Mathematically, the (i,j)-th element of the new matrix is given by,

         m'(i,j) = m->data[(k1*m->tda + k2) + i*m->tda + j]

where the index i runs from 0 to n1-1 and the index j runs from 0 to n2-1.

The data pointer of the returned matrix struct is set to null if the combined parameters (i,j,n1,n2,tda) overrun the ends of the original matrix.

The new matrix view is only a view of the block underlying the existing matrix, m. The block containing the elements of m is not owned by the new matrix view. When the view goes out of scope the original matrix m and its block will continue to exist. The original memory can only be deallocated by freeing the original matrix. Of course, the original matrix should not be deallocated while the view is still in use.

The function gsl_matrix_const_submatrix is equivalent to gsl_matrix_submatrix but can be used for matrices which are declared const.

gsl_matrix_view gsl_matrix_view_array (double * base,   Function
         size_t n1, size_t n2)
gsl_matrix_const_view gsl_matrix_const_view_array   Function
         (const double * base, size_t n1, size_t n2)
These functions return a matrix view of the array base. The matrix has n1 rows and n2 columns. The physical number of columns in memory is also given by n2. Mathematically, the (i,j)-th element of the new matrix is given by,

         m'(i,j) = base[i*n2 + j]

where the index i runs from 0 to n1-1 and the index j runs from 0 to n2-1.

The new matrix is only a view of the array base. When the view goes out of scope the original array base will continue to exist. The original memory can only be deallocated by freeing the original array.

Of course, the original array should not be deallocated while the view is still in use.

The function `gsl_matrix_const_view_array` is equivalent to `gsl_matrix_view_array` but can be used for matrices which are declared `const`.

`gsl_matrix_view gsl_matrix_view_array_with_tda`   Function
      `(double * base, size_t n1, size_t n2, size_t tda)`
`gsl_matrix_const_view`   Function
      `gsl_matrix_const_view_array_with_tda (const double *`
      `base, size_t n1, size_t n2, size_t tda)`

These functions return a matrix view of the array *base* with a physical number of columns *tda* which may differ from the corresponding dimension of the matrix. The matrix has *n1* rows and *n2* columns, and the physical number of columns in memory is given by *tda*. Mathematically, the (i, j)-th element of the new matrix is given by,

      `m'(i,j) = base[i*tda + j]`

where the index i runs from 0 to n1-1 and the index j runs from 0 to n2-1.

The new matrix is only a view of the array *base*. When the view goes out of scope the original array *base* will continue to exist. The original memory can only be deallocated by freeing the original array. Of course, the original array should not be deallocated while the view is still in use.

The function `gsl_matrix_const_view_array_with_tda` is equivalent to `gsl_matrix_view_array_with_tda` but can be used for matrices which are declared `const`.

`gsl_matrix_view gsl_matrix_view_vector (gsl_vector *`   Function
      `v, size_t n1, size_t n2)`
`gsl_matrix_const_view gsl_matrix_const_view_vector`   Function
      `(const gsl_vector * v, size_t n1, size_t n2)`

These functions return a matrix view of the vector *v*. The matrix has *n1* rows and *n2* columns. The vector must have unit stride. The physical number of columns in memory is also given by *n2*. Mathematically, the (i, j)-th element of the new matrix is given by,

      `m'(i,j) = v->data[i*n2 + j]`

where the index i runs from 0 to n1-1 and the index j runs from 0 to n2-1.

The new matrix is only a view of the vector *v*. When the view goes out of scope the original vector *v* will continue to exist. The original memory can only be deallocated by freeing the original vector. Of course, the original vector should not be deallocated while the view is still in use.

The function gsl_matrix_const_view_vector is equivalent to gsl_matrix_view_vector but can be used for matrices which are declared const.

gsl_matrix_view gsl_matrix_view_vector_with_tda   *Function*
      (gsl_vector * v, size_t *n1*, size_t *n2*, size_t *tda*)
gsl_matrix_const_view   *Function*
      gsl_matrix_const_view_vector_with_tda (const
      gsl_vector * v, size_t *n1*, size_t *n2*, size_t *tda*)
These functions return a matrix view of the vector *v* with a physical number of columns *tda* which may differ from the corresponding matrix dimension. The vector must have unit stride. The matrix has *n1* rows and *n2* columns, and the physical number of columns in memory is given by *tda*. Mathematically, the (i, j)-th element of the new matrix is given by,

    m'(i,j) = v->data[i*tda + j]

where the index *i* runs from 0 to n1-1 and the index *j* runs from 0 to n2-1.

The new matrix is only a view of the vector *v*. When the view goes out of scope the original vector *v* will continue to exist. The original memory can only be deallocated by freeing the original vector. Of course, the original vector should not be deallocated while the view is still in use.

The function gsl_matrix_const_view_vector_with_tda is equivalent to gsl_matrix_view_vector_with_tda but can be used for matrices which are declared const.

8.4.6 Creating row and column views

In general there are two ways to access an object, by reference or by copying. The functions described in this section create vector views which allow access to a row or column of a matrix by reference. Modifying elements of the view is equivalent to modifying the matrix, since both the vector view and the matrix point to the same memory block.

gsl_vector_view gsl_matrix_row (gsl_matrix * m, size_t   *Function*
    i)
gsl_vector_const_view gsl_matrix_const_row (const   *Function*
      gsl_matrix * m, size_t *i*)
These functions return a vector view of the *i*-th row of the matrix *m*. The data pointer of the new vector is set to null if *i* is out of range.

The function `gsl_vector_const_row` is equivalent to `gsl_matrix_row` but can be used for matrices which are declared const.

`gsl_vector_view gsl_matrix_column (gsl_matrix * m,`   *Function*
        `size_t j)`
`gsl_vector_const_view gsl_matrix_const_column (const`   *Function*
        `gsl_matrix * m, size_t j)`

These functions return a vector view of the j-th column of the matrix m. The data pointer of the new vector is set to null if j is out of range.

The function `gsl_vector_const_column` is equivalent to `gsl_matrix_column` but can be used for matrices which are declared const.

`gsl_vector_view gsl_matrix_diagonal (gsl_matrix * m)`   *Function*
`gsl_vector_const_view gsl_matrix_const_diagonal`   *Function*
        `(const gsl_matrix * m)`

These functions returns a vector view of the diagonal of the matrix m. The matrix m is not required to be square. For a rectangular matrix the length of the diagonal is the same as the smaller dimension of the matrix.

The function `gsl_matrix_const_diagonal` is equivalent to `gsl_matrix_diagonal` but can be used for matrices which are declared const.

`gsl_vector_view gsl_matrix_subdiagonal (gsl_matrix *`   *Function*
        `m, size_t k)`
`gsl_vector_const_view gsl_matrix_const_subdiagonal`   *Function*
        `(const gsl_matrix * m, size_t k)`

These functions return a vector view of the k-th subdiagonal of the matrix m. The matrix m is not required to be square. The diagonal of the matrix corresponds to $k = 0$.

The function `gsl_matrix_const_subdiagonal` is equivalent to `gsl_matrix_subdiagonal` but can be used for matrices which are declared const.

`gsl_vector_view gsl_matrix_superdiagonal (gsl_matrix *`   *Function*
        `m, size_t k)`
`gsl_vector_const_view gsl_matrix_const_superdiagonal`   *Function*
        `(const gsl_matrix * m, size_t k)`

These functions return a vector view of the k-th superdiagonal of the matrix m. The matrix m is not required to be square. The diagonal of the matrix corresponds to $k = 0$.

The function `gsl_matrix_const_superdiagonal` is equivalent to `gsl_matrix_superdiagonal` but can be used for matrices which are declared const.

8.4.7 Copying matrices

int gsl_matrix_memcpy (gsl_matrix * *dest*, const   Function
      gsl_matrix * *src*)

> This function copies the elements of the matrix *src* into the matrix *dest*. The two matrices must have the same size.

int gsl_matrix_swap (gsl_matrix * *m1*, gsl_matrix * *m2*)   Function

> This function exchanges the elements of the matrices *m1* and *m2* by copying. The two matrices must have the same size.

8.4.8 Copying rows and columns

The functions described in this section copy a row or column of a matrix into a vector. This allows the elements of the vector and the matrix to be modified independently. Note that if the matrix and the vector point to overlapping regions of memory then the result will be undefined. The same effect can be achieved with more generality using gsl_vector_memcpy with vector views of rows and columns.

int gsl_matrix_get_row (gsl_vector * *v*, const   Function
      gsl_matrix * *m*, size_t *i*)

> This function copies the elements of the *i*-th row of the matrix *m* into the vector *v*. The length of the vector must be the same as the length of the row.

int gsl_matrix_get_col (gsl_vector * *v*, const   Function
      gsl_matrix * *m*, size_t *j*)

> This function copies the elements of the *j*-th column of the matrix *m* into the vector *v*. The length of the vector must be the same as the length of the column.

int gsl_matrix_set_row (gsl_matrix * *m*, size_t *i*, const   Function
      gsl_vector * *v*)

> This function copies the elements of the vector *v* into the *i*-th row of the matrix *m*. The length of the vector must be the same as the length of the row.

int gsl_matrix_set_col (gsl_matrix * *m*, size_t *j*, const   Function
      gsl_vector * *v*)

> This function copies the elements of the vector *v* into the *j*-th column of the matrix *m*. The length of the vector must be the same as the length of the column.

8.4.9 Exchanging rows and columns

The following functions can be used to exchange the rows and columns of a matrix.

`int gsl_matrix_swap_rows (gsl_matrix * m, size_t i,`   *Function*
         `size_t j)`

This function exchanges the i-th and j-th rows of the matrix m in-place, i.e. the elements of row i are copied into row j and the elements of row j are copied into row i.

`int gsl_matrix_swap_columns (gsl_matrix * m, size_t i,`   *Function*
         `size_t j)`

This function exchanges the i-th and j-th columns of the matrix m in-place.

`int gsl_matrix_swap_rowcol (gsl_matrix * m, size_t i,`   *Function*
         `size_t j)`

This function exchanges the i-th row and j-th column of the matrix m in-place. The matrix must be square for this operation to be possible.

`int gsl_matrix_transpose_memcpy (gsl_matrix * dest,`   *Function*
         `const gsl_matrix * src)`

This function makes the matrix *dest* the transpose of the matrix *src* by copying the elements of *src* into *dest*. This function works for all matrices provided that the dimensions of the matrix *dest* match the transposed dimensions of the matrix *src*.

`int gsl_matrix_transpose (gsl_matrix * m)`   *Function*

This function replaces the matrix m by its transpose by copying the elements of the matrix in-place. The matrix must be square for this operation to be possible.

8.4.10 Matrix operations

The following operations are defined for real and complex matrices.

`int gsl_matrix_add (gsl_matrix * a, const gsl_matrix *`   *Function*
         `b)`

This function adds the elements of matrix b to the elements of matrix a, $a'(i,j) = a(i,j) + b(i,j)$. The two matrices must have the same dimensions.

`int gsl_matrix_sub (gsl_matrix * a, const gsl_matrix *`   *Function*
         `b)`

This function subtracts the elements of matrix b from the elements of matrix a, $a'(i,j) = a(i,j) - b(i,j)$. The two matrices must have the same dimensions.

int gsl_matrix_mul_elements (gsl_matrix * a, const   *Function*
        gsl_matrix * b)

This function multiplies the elements of matrix a by the elements of matrix b, $a'(i,j) = a(i,j) * b(i,j)$. The two matrices must have the same dimensions.

int gsl_matrix_div_elements (gsl_matrix * a, const   *Function*
        gsl_matrix * b)

This function divides the elements of matrix a by the elements of matrix b, $a'(i,j) = a(i,j)/b(i,j)$. The two matrices must have the same dimensions.

int gsl_matrix_scale (gsl_matrix * a, const double x)   *Function*

This function multiplies the elements of matrix a by the constant factor x, $a'(i,j) = xa(i,j)$.

int gsl_matrix_add_constant (gsl_matrix * a, const   *Function*
        double x)

This function adds the constant value x to the elements of the matrix a, $a'(i,j) = a(i,j) + x$.

8.4.11 Finding maximum and minimum elements of matrices

The following operations are only defined for real matrices.

double gsl_matrix_max (const gsl_matrix * m)   *Function*

This function returns the maximum value in the matrix m.

double gsl_matrix_min (const gsl_matrix * m)   *Function*

This function returns the minimum value in the matrix m.

void gsl_matrix_minmax (const gsl_matrix * m, double *   *Function*
        min_out, double * max_out)

This function returns the minimum and maximum values in the matrix m, storing them in min_out and max_out.

void gsl_matrix_max_index (const gsl_matrix * m,   *Function*
        size_t * imax, size_t * jmax)

This function returns the indices of the maximum value in the matrix m, storing them in imax and jmax. When there are several equal maximum elements then the first element found is returned, searching in row-major order.

void gsl_matrix_min_index (const gsl_matrix * *m*,   Function
          size_t * *imin*, size_t * *jmin*)

This function returns the indices of the minimum value in the matrix
m, storing them in *imin* and *jmin*. When there are several equal minimum elements then the first element found is returned, searching in
row-major order.

void gsl_matrix_minmax_index (const gsl_matrix * *m*,   Function
          size_t * *imin*, size_t * *jmin*, size_t * *imax*, size_t *
          jmax)

This function returns the indices of the minimum and maximum values
in the matrix *m*, storing them in (*imin*,*jmin*) and (*imax*,*jmax*). When
there are several equal minimum or maximum elements then the first
elements found are returned, searching in row-major order.

8.4.12 Matrix properties

int gsl_matrix_isnull (const gsl_matrix * *m*)   Function

This function returns 1 if all the elements of the matrix *m* are zero,
and 0 otherwise.

8.4.13 Example programs for matrices

The program below shows how to allocate, initialize and read from
a matrix using the functions gsl_matrix_alloc, gsl_matrix_set and
gsl_matrix_get.

```
#include <stdio.h>
#include <gsl/gsl_matrix.h>

int
main (void)
{
  int i, j;
  gsl_matrix * m = gsl_matrix_alloc (10, 3);

  for (i = 0; i < 10; i++)
    for (j = 0; j < 3; j++)
      gsl_matrix_set (m, i, j, 0.23 + 100*i + j);

  for (i = 0; i < 100; i++)  /* out of range error */
    for (j = 0; j < 3; j++)
      printf ("m(%d,%d) = %g\n", i, j,
              gsl_matrix_get (m, i, j));
```

```
      return 0;
   }
```

Here is the output from the program. The final loop attempts to read
outside the range of the matrix m, and the error is trapped by the range-
checking code in gsl_matrix_get.

```
$ ./a.out
m(0,0) = 0.23
m(0,1) = 1.23
m(0,2) = 2.23
m(1,0) = 100.23
m(1,1) = 101.23
m(1,2) = 102.23
...
m(9,2) = 902.23
gsl: matrix_source.c:13: ERROR: first index out of range
Default GSL error handler invoked.
Aborted (core dumped)
```

The next program shows how to write a matrix to a file.

```
#include <stdio.h>
#include <gsl/gsl_matrix.h>

int
main (void)
{
  int i, j, k = 0;
  gsl_matrix * m = gsl_matrix_alloc (100, 100);
  gsl_matrix * a = gsl_matrix_alloc (100, 100);

  for (i = 0; i < 100; i++)
    for (j = 0; j < 100; j++)
      gsl_matrix_set (m, i, j, 0.23 + i + j);

  {
    FILE * f = fopen ("test.dat", "wb");
    gsl_matrix_fwrite (f, m);
    fclose (f);
  }

  {
    FILE * f = fopen ("test.dat", "rb");
    gsl_matrix_fread (f, a);
    fclose (f);
  }
```

```
    for (i = 0; i < 100; i++)
      for (j = 0; j < 100; j++)
        {
          double mij = gsl_matrix_get (m, i, j);
          double aij = gsl_matrix_get (a, i, j);
          if (mij != aij) k++;
        }

    printf ("differences = %d (should be zero)\n", k);
    return (k > 0);
  }
```

After running this program the file 'test.dat' should contain the elements of m, written in binary format. The matrix which is read back in using the function gsl_matrix_fread should be exactly equal to the original matrix.

The following program demonstrates the use of vector views. The program computes the column norms of a matrix.

```
#include <math.h>
#include <stdio.h>
#include <gsl/gsl_matrix.h>
#include <gsl/gsl_blas.h>

int
main (void)
{
  size_t i,j;

  gsl_matrix *m = gsl_matrix_alloc (10, 10);

  for (i = 0; i < 10; i++)
    for (j = 0; j < 10; j++)
      gsl_matrix_set (m, i, j, sin (i) + cos (j));

  for (j = 0; j < 10; j++)
    {
      gsl_vector_view column = gsl_matrix_column (m, j);
      double d;

      d = gsl_blas_dnrm2 (&column.vector);

      printf ("matrix column %d, norm = %g\n", j, d);
    }
```

```
    gsl_matrix_free (m);

    return 0;
}
```
Here is the output of the program,
```
$ ./a.out
matrix column 0, norm = 4.31461
matrix column 1, norm = 3.1205
matrix column 2, norm = 2.19316
matrix column 3, norm = 3.26114
matrix column 4, norm = 2.53416
matrix column 5, norm = 2.57281
matrix column 6, norm = 4.20469
matrix column 7, norm = 3.65202
matrix column 8, norm = 2.08524
matrix column 9, norm = 3.07313
```
The results can be confirmed using GNU OCTAVE,
```
$ octave
GNU Octave, version 2.0.16.92
octave> m = sin(0:9)' * ones(1,10)
                 + ones(10,1) * cos(0:9);
octave> sqrt(sum(m.^2))
ans =
   4.3146   3.1205   2.1932   3.2611   2.5342   2.5728
   4.2047   3.6520   2.0852   3.0731
```

8.5 References and Further Reading

The block, vector and matrix objects in GSL follow the valarray model of C++. A description of this model can be found in the following reference,

B. Stroustrup, *The C++ Programming Language* (3rd Ed), Section 22.4 Vector Arithmetic. Addison-Wesley 1997, ISBN 0-201-88954-4.

9 Permutations

This chapter describes functions for creating and manipulating permutations. A permutation p is represented by an array of n integers in the range 0 to $n - 1$, where each integer p_i occurs once and only once. The application of a permutation p to a vector v yields a new vector v' where $v'_i = v_{p_i}$. For example, the array $(0, 1, 3, 2)$ represents a permutation which exchanges the last two elements of a four element vector. The corresponding identity permutation is $(0, 1, 2, 3)$.

Note that the permutations produced by the linear algebra routines correspond to the exchange of matrix columns, and so should be considered as applying to row-vectors in the form $v' = vP$ rather than column-vectors, when permuting the elements of a vector.

The functions described in this chapter are defined in the header file 'gsl_permutation.h'.

9.1 The Permutation struct

A permutation is defined by a structure containing two components, the size of the permutation and a pointer to the permutation array. The elements of the permutation array are all of type size_t. The gsl_permutation structure looks like this,

```
typedef struct
{
  size_t size;
  size_t * data;
} gsl_permutation;
```

9.2 Permutation allocation

gsl_permutation * gsl_permutation_alloc (size_t *n*)   Function
This function allocates memory for a new permutation of size *n*. The permutation is not initialized and its elements are undefined. Use the function gsl_permutation_calloc if you want to create a permutation which is initialized to the identity. A null pointer is returned if insufficient memory is available to create the permutation.

gsl_permutation * gsl_permutation_calloc (size_t *n*)   Function
This function allocates memory for a new permutation of size *n* and initializes it to the identity. A null pointer is returned if insufficient memory is available to create the permutation.

void gsl_permutation_init (gsl_permutation * p)   Function
    This function initializes the permutation p to the identity, i.e.
    $(0, 1, 2, \ldots, n - 1)$.

void gsl_permutation_free (gsl_permutation * p)   Function
    This function frees all the memory used by the permutation p.

int gsl_permutation_memcpy (gsl_permutation * dest,   Function
        const gsl_permutation * src)
    This function copies the elements of the permutation src into the per-
    mutation dest. The two permutations must have the same size.

9.3 Accessing permutation elements

    The following functions can be used to access and manipulate permu-
tations.

size_t gsl_permutation_get (const gsl_permutation * p,   Function
        const size_t i)
    This function returns the value of the i-th element of the permutation
    p. If i lies outside the allowed range of 0 to $n - 1$ then the error handler
    is invoked and 0 is returned.

int gsl_permutation_swap (gsl_permutation * p, const   Function
        size_t i, const size_t j)
    This function exchanges the i-th and j-th elements of the permutation
    p.

9.4 Permutation properties

size_t gsl_permutation_size (const gsl_permutation *   Function
        p)
    This function returns the size of the permutation p.

size_t * gsl_permutation_data (const gsl_permutation *   Function
        p)
    This function returns a pointer to the array of elements in the permu-
    tation p.

int gsl_permutation_valid (gsl_permutation * p)   Function
    This function checks that the permutation p is valid. The n elements
    should contain each of the numbers 0 to $n - 1$ once and only once.

9.5 Permutation functions

void gsl_permutation_reverse (gsl_permutation * p)   Function
    This function reverses the elements of the permutation p.

int gsl_permutation_inverse (gsl_permutation * inv,   Function
        const gsl_permutation * p)
    This function computes the inverse of the permutation p, storing the
    result in inv.

int gsl_permutation_next (gsl_permutation * p)   Function
    This function advances the permutation p to the next permutation in
    lexicographic order and returns GSL_SUCCESS. If no further permuta-
    tions are available it returns GSL_FAILURE and leaves p unmodified.
    Starting with the identity permutation and repeatedly applying this
    function will iterate through all possible permutations of a given order.

int gsl_permutation_prev (gsl_permutation * p)   Function
    This function steps backwards from the permutation p to the previ-
    ous permutation in lexicographic order, returning GSL_SUCCESS. If no
    previous permutation is available it returns GSL_FAILURE and leaves p
    unmodified.

9.6 Applying Permutations

int gsl_permute (const size_t * p, double * data, size_t   Function
        stride, size_t n)
    This function applies the permutation p to the array data of size n
    with stride stride.

int gsl_permute_inverse (const size_t * p, double *   Function
        data, size_t stride, size_t n)
    This function applies the inverse of the permutation p to the array
    data of size n with stride stride.

int gsl_permute_vector (const gsl_permutation * p,   Function
        gsl_vector * v)
    This function applies the permutation p to the elements of the vector
    v, considered as a row-vector acted on by a permutation matrix from
    the right, $v' = vP$. The j-th column of the permutation matrix P is
    given by the p_j-th column of the identity matrix. The permutation p
    and the vector v must have the same length.

int gsl_permute_vector_inverse (const gsl_permutation   *Function*
        * p, gsl_vector * v)

This function applies the inverse of the permutation p to the elements of the vector v, considered as a row-vector acted on by an inverse permutation matrix from the right, $v' = vP^T$. Note that for permutation matrices the inverse is the same as the transpose. The j-th column of the permutation matrix P is given by the p_j-th column of the identity matrix. The permutation p and the vector v must have the same length.

int gsl_permutation_mul (gsl_permutation * p, const   *Function*
        gsl_permutation * pa, const gsl_permutation * pb)

This function combines the two permutations pa and pb into a single permutation p, where $p = pa.pb$. The permutation p is equivalent to applying pb first and then pa.

9.7 Reading and writing permutations

The library provides functions for reading and writing permutations to a file as binary data or formatted text.

int gsl_permutation_fwrite (FILE * stream, const   *Function*
        gsl_permutation * p)

This function writes the elements of the permutation p to the stream stream in binary format. The function returns GSL_EFAILED if there was a problem writing to the file. Since the data is written in the native binary format it may not be portable between different architectures.

int gsl_permutation_fread (FILE * stream,   *Function*
        gsl_permutation * p)

This function reads into the permutation p from the open stream stream in binary format. The permutation p must be preallocated with the correct length since the function uses the size of p to determine how many bytes to read. The function returns GSL_EFAILED if there was a problem reading from the file. The data is assumed to have been written in the native binary format on the same architecture.

int gsl_permutation_fprintf (FILE * stream, const   *Function*
        gsl_permutation * p, const char * format)

This function writes the elements of the permutation p line-by-line to the stream stream using the format specifier format, which should be suitable for a type of size_t. On a GNU system the type modifier Z represents size_t, so "%Zu\n" is a suitable format. The function returns GSL_EFAILED if there was a problem writing to the file.

int gsl_permutation_fscanf (FILE * *stream*,   Function
        gsl_permutation * *p*)

This function reads formatted data from the stream *stream* into the permutation *p*. The permutation *p* must be preallocated with the correct length since the function uses the size of *p* to determine how many numbers to read. The function returns GSL_EFAILED if there was a problem reading from the file.

9.8 Permutations in cyclic form

A permutation can be represented in both *linear* and *cyclic* notations. The functions described in this section convert between the two forms. The linear notation is an index mapping, and has already been described above. The cyclic notation expresses a permutation as a series of circular rearrangements of groups of elements, or *cycles*.

For example, under the cycle (1 2 3), 1 is replaced by 2, 2 is replaced by 3 and 3 is replaced by 1 in a circular fashion. Cycles of different sets of elements can be combined independently, for example (1 2 3) (4 5) combines the cycle (1 2 3) with the cycle (4 5), which is an exchange of elements 4 and 5. A cycle of length one represents an element which is unchanged by the permutation and is referred to as a *singleton*.

It can be shown that every permutation can be decomposed into combinations of cycles. The decomposition is not unique, but can always be rearranged into a standard *canonical form* by a reordering of elements. The library uses the canonical form defined in Knuth's *Art of Computer Programming* (Vol 1, 3rd Ed, 1997) Section 1.3.3, p.178.

The procedure for obtaining the canonical form given by Knuth is,

1. Write all singleton cycles explicitly

2. Within each cycle, put the smallest number first

3. Order the cycles in decreasing order of the first number in the cycle.

For example, the linear representation (2 4 3 0 1) is represented as (1 4) (0 2 3) in canonical form. The permutation corresponds to an exchange of elements 1 and 4, and rotation of elements 0, 2 and 3.

The important property of the canonical form is that it can be reconstructed from the contents of each cycle without the brackets. In addition, by removing the brackets it can be considered as a linear representation of a different permutation. In the example given above the permutation (2 4 3 0 1) would become (1 4 0 2 3). This mapping has many applications in the theory of permutations.

int gsl_permutation_linear_to_canonical   Function
        (gsl_permutation * q, const gsl_permutation * p)
    This function computes the canonical form of the permutation p and
    stores it in the output argument q.

int gsl_permutation_canonical_to_linear   Function
        (gsl_permutation * p, const gsl_permutation * q)
    This function converts a permutation q in canonical form back into
    linear form storing it in the output argument p.

size_t gsl_permutation_inversions (const   Function
        gsl_permutation * p)
    This function counts the number of inversions in the permutation p.
    An inversion is any pair of elements that are not in order. For example,
    the permutation 2031 has three inversions, corresponding to the pairs
    (2,0) (2,1) and (3,1). The identity permutation has no inversions.

size_t gsl_permutation_linear_cycles (const   Function
        gsl_permutation * p)
    This function counts the number of cycles in the permutation p, given
    in linear form.

size_t gsl_permutation_canonical_cycles (const   Function
        gsl_permutation * q)
    This function counts the number of cycles in the permutation q, given
    in canonical form.

9.9 Examples

The example program below creates a random permutation (by shuffling the elements of the identity) and finds its inverse.

```
#include <stdio.h>
#include <gsl/gsl_rng.h>
#include <gsl/gsl_randist.h>
#include <gsl/gsl_permutation.h>

int
main (void)
{
  const size_t N = 10;
  const gsl_rng_type * T;
  gsl_rng * r;

  gsl_permutation * p = gsl_permutation_alloc (N);
  gsl_permutation * q = gsl_permutation_alloc (N);
```

```
        gsl_rng_env_setup();
        T = gsl_rng_default;
        r = gsl_rng_alloc (T);

        printf ("initial permutation:");
        gsl_permutation_init (p);
        gsl_permutation_fprintf (stdout, p, " %u");
        printf ("\n");

        printf (" random permutation:");
        gsl_ran_shuffle (r, p->data, N, sizeof(size_t));
        gsl_permutation_fprintf (stdout, p, " %u");
        printf ("\n");

        printf ("inverse permutation:");
        gsl_permutation_inverse (q, p);
        gsl_permutation_fprintf (stdout, q, " %u");
        printf ("\n");

        return 0;
    }
```

Here is the output from the program,

```
    $ ./a.out
    initial permutation: 0 1 2 3 4 5 6 7 8 9
     random permutation: 1 3 5 2 7 6 0 4 9 8
    inverse permutation: 6 0 3 1 7 2 5 4 9 8
```

The random permutation p[i] and its inverse q[i] are related through the identity p[q[i]] = i, which can be verified from the output.

The next example program steps forward through all possible third-order permutations, starting from the identity,

```
    #include <stdio.h>
    #include <gsl/gsl_permutation.h>

    int
    main (void)
    {
      gsl_permutation * p = gsl_permutation_alloc (3);

      gsl_permutation_init (p);

      do
        {
```

```
            gsl_permutation_fprintf (stdout, p, " %u");
            printf ("\n");
        }
      while (gsl_permutation_next(p) == GSL_SUCCESS);

      return 0;
    }
```

Here is the output from the program,

```
$ ./a.out
  0 1 2
  0 2 1
  1 0 2
  1 2 0
  2 0 1
  2 1 0
```

The permutations are generated in lexicographic order. To reverse the sequence, begin with the final permutation (which is the reverse of the identity) and replace `gsl_permutation_next` with `gsl_permutation_prev`.

9.10 References and Further Reading

The subject of permutations is covered extensively in Knuth's *Sorting and Searching*,

> Donald E. Knuth, *The Art of Computer Programming: Sorting and Searching* (Vol 3, 3rd Ed, 1997), Addison-Wesley, ISBN 0201896850.

For the definition of the *canonical form* see,

> Donald E. Knuth, *The Art of Computer Programming: Fundamental Algorithms* (Vol 1, 3rd Ed, 1997), Addison-Wesley, ISBN 0201896850. Section 1.3.3, *An Unusual Correspondence*, p.178–179.

10 Combinations

This chapter describes functions for creating and manipulating combinations. A combination c is represented by an array of k integers in the range 0 to $n - 1$, where each value c_i occurs at most once. The combination c corresponds to indices of k elements chosen from an n element vector. Combinations are useful for iterating over all k-element subsets of a set.

The functions described in this chapter are defined in the header file 'gsl_combination.h'.

10.1 The Combination struct

A combination is defined by a structure containing three components, the values of n and k, and a pointer to the combination array. The elements of the combination array are all of type size_t, and are stored in increasing order. The gsl_combination structure looks like this,

```
typedef struct
{
  size_t n;
  size_t k;
  size_t *data;
} gsl_combination;
```

10.2 Combination allocation

gsl_combination * gsl_combination_alloc (size_t n,   Function
        size_t k)
This function allocates memory for a new combination with parameters n, k. The combination is not initialized and its elements are undefined. Use the function gsl_combination_calloc if you want to create a combination which is initialized to the lexicographically first combination. A null pointer is returned if insufficient memory is available to create the combination.

gsl_combination * gsl_combination_calloc (size_t n,   Function
        size_t k)
This function allocates memory for a new combination with parameters n, k and initializes it to the lexicographically first combination. A null pointer is returned if insufficient memory is available to create the combination.

void gsl_combination_init_first (gsl_combination * c)   *Function*
>This function initializes the combination c to the lexicographically first combination, i.e. $(0, 1, 2, \ldots, k - 1)$.

void gsl_combination_init_last (gsl_combination * c)   *Function*
>This function initializes the combination c to the lexicographically last combination, i.e. $(n - k, n - k + 1, \ldots, n - 1)$.

void gsl_combination_free (gsl_combination * c)   *Function*
>This function frees all the memory used by the combination c.

int gsl_combination_memcpy (gsl_combination * *dest*,   *Function*
>   const gsl_combination * *src*)
>This function copies the elements of the combination *src* into the combination *dest*. The two combinations must have the same size.

10.3 Accessing combination elements

The following function can be used to access the elements of a combination.

size_t gsl_combination_get (const gsl_combination * c,   *Function*
>   const size_t i)
>This function returns the value of the i-th element of the combination c. If i lies outside the allowed range of 0 to $k - 1$ then the error handler is invoked and 0 is returned.

10.4 Combination properties

size_t gsl_combination_n (const gsl_combination * c)   *Function*
>This function returns the range (n) of the combination c.

size_t gsl_combination_k (const gsl_combination * c)   *Function*
>This function returns the number of elements (k) in the combination c.

size_t * gsl_combination_data (const gsl_combination *   *Function*
>   c)
>This function returns a pointer to the array of elements in the combination c.

int gsl_combination_valid (gsl_combination * c)   *Function*
>This function checks that the combination c is valid. The k elements should lie in the range 0 to $n - 1$, with each value occurring once at most and in increasing order.

10.5 Combination functions

int gsl_combination_next (gsl_combination * c)   Function
  This function advances the combination c to the next combination in
  lexicographic order and returns GSL_SUCCESS. If no further combinations are available it returns GSL_FAILURE and leaves c unmodified.
  Starting with the first combination and repeatedly applying this function will iterate through all possible combinations of a given order.

int gsl_combination_prev (gsl_combination * c)   Function
  This function steps backwards from the combination c to the previous combination in lexicographic order, returning GSL_SUCCESS. If no
  previous combination is available it returns GSL_FAILURE and leaves c
  unmodified.

10.6 Reading and writing combinations

  The library provides functions for reading and writing combinations
  to a file as binary data or formatted text.

int gsl_combination_fwrite (FILE * stream, const   Function
        gsl_combination * c)
  This function writes the elements of the combination c to the stream
  stream in binary format. The function returns GSL_EFAILED if there
  was a problem writing to the file. Since the data is written in the native
  binary format it may not be portable between different architectures.

int gsl_combination_fread (FILE * stream,   Function
        gsl_combination * c)
  This function reads elements from the open stream stream into the
  combination c in binary format. The combination c must be prealло-
  cated with correct values of n and k since the function uses the size
  of c to determine how many bytes to read. The function returns GSL_
  EFAILED if there was a problem reading from the file. The data is
  assumed to have been written in the native binary format on the same
  architecture.

int gsl_combination_fprintf (FILE * stream, const   Function
        gsl_combination * c, const char * format)
  This function writes the elements of the combination c line-by-line to
  the stream stream using the format specifier format, which should be
  suitable for a type of size_t. On a GNU system the type modifier
  Z represents size_t, so "%Zu\n" is a suitable format. The function
  returns GSL_EFAILED if there was a problem writing to the file.

int gsl_combination_fscanf (FILE * *stream*,   Function
          gsl_combination * *c*)

This function reads formatted data from the stream *stream* into the combination *c*. The combination *c* must be preallocated with correct values of n and k since the function uses the size of *c* to determine how many numbers to read. The function returns GSL_EFAILED if there was a problem reading from the file.

10.7 Examples

The example program below prints all subsets of the set $\{0, 1, 2, 3\}$ ordered by size. Subsets of the same size are ordered lexicographically.

```
#include <stdio.h>
#include <gsl/gsl_combination.h>

int
main (void)
{
  gsl_combination * c;
  size_t i;

  printf ("All subsets of {0,1,2,3} by size:\n") ;
  for (i = 0; i <= 4; i++)
    {
      c = gsl_combination_calloc (4, i);
      do
        {
          printf ("{");
          gsl_combination_fprintf (stdout, c, " %u");
          printf (" }\n");
        }
      while (gsl_combination_next (c) == GSL_SUCCESS);
      gsl_combination_free (c);
    }

  return 0;
}
```

Here is the output from the program,

```
$ ./a.out
All subsets of {0,1,2,3} by size:
{ }
{ 0 }
{ 1 }
```

```
{ 2 }
{ 3 }
{ 0 1 }
{ 0 2 }
{ 0 3 }
{ 1 2 }
{ 1 3 }
{ 2 3 }
{ 0 1 2 }
{ 0 1 3 }
{ 0 2 3 }
{ 1 2 3 }
{ 0 1 2 3 }
```

All 16 subsets are generated, and the subsets of each size are sorted lexicographically.

10.8 References and Further Reading

Further information on combinations can be found in,

Donald L. Kreher, Douglas R. Stinson, *Combinatorial Algorithms: Generation, Enumeration and Search*, 1998, CRC Press LLC, ISBN 084933988X

11 Sorting

This chapter describes functions for sorting data, both directly and indirectly (using an index). All the functions use the *heapsort* algorithm. Heapsort is an $O(N \log N)$ algorithm which operates in-place and does not require any additional storage. It also provides consistent performance, the running time for its worst-case (ordered data) being not significantly longer than the average and best cases. Note that the heapsort algorithm does not preserve the relative ordering of equal elements—it is an *unstable* sort. However, the resulting order of equal elements will be consistent across different platforms when using these functions.

11.1 Sorting objects

The following function provides a simple alternative to the standard library function qsort. It is intended for systems lacking qsort, not as a replacement for it. The function qsort should be used whenever possible, as it will be faster and can provide stable ordering of equal elements. Documentation for qsort is available in the *GNU C Library Reference Manual*.

The functions described in this section are defined in the header file 'gsl_heapsort.h'.

void gsl_heapsort (void * *array*, size_t *count*, size_t   Function
          size, gsl_comparison_fn_t *compare*)

This function sorts the *count* elements of the array *array*, each of size *size*, into ascending order using the comparison function *compare*. The type of the comparison function is defined by,

```
int (*gsl_comparison_fn_t) (const void * a,
                            const void * b)
```

A comparison function should return a negative integer if the first argument is less than the second argument, 0 if the two arguments are equal and a positive integer if the first argument is greater than the second argument.

For example, the following function can be used to sort doubles into ascending numerical order.

```
int
compare_doubles (const double * a,
                 const double * b)
{
    if (*a > *b)
        return 1;
```

```
      else if (*a < *b)
         return -1;
      else
         return 0;
   }
```

The appropriate function call to perform the sort is,

```
      gsl_heapsort (array, count, sizeof(double),
                    compare_doubles);
```

Note that unlike qsort the heapsort algorithm cannot be made into a stable sort by pointer arithmetic. The trick of comparing pointers for equal elements in the comparison function does not work for the heapsort algorithm. The heapsort algorithm performs an internal rearrangement of the data which destroys its initial ordering.

int gsl_heapsort_index (size_t * p, const void * array,   Function
       size_t *count*, size_t *size*, gsl_comparison_fn_t
       compare)

This function indirectly sorts the *count* elements of the array *array*, each of size *size*, into ascending order using the comparison function *compare*. The resulting permutation is stored in *p*, an array of length *n*. The elements of *p* give the index of the array element which would have been stored in that position if the array had been sorted in place. The first element of *p* gives the index of the least element in *array*, and the last element of *p* gives the index of the greatest element in *array*. The array itself is not changed.

11.2 Sorting vectors

The following functions will sort the elements of an array or vector, either directly or indirectly. They are defined for all real and integer types using the normal suffix rules. For example, the float versions of the array functions are gsl_sort_float and gsl_sort_float_index. The corresponding vector functions are gsl_sort_vector_float and gsl_sort_vector_float_index. The prototypes are available in the header files 'gsl_sort_float.h' 'gsl_sort_vector_float.h'. The complete set of prototypes can be included using the header files 'gsl_sort.h' and 'gsl_sort_vector.h'.

There are no functions for sorting complex arrays or vectors, since the ordering of complex numbers is not uniquely defined. To sort a complex vector by magnitude compute a real vector containing the magnitudes of the complex elements, and sort this vector indirectly. The resulting index gives the appropriate ordering of the original complex vector.

void gsl_sort (double * *data*, size_t *stride*, size_t *n*)   Function
    This function sorts the *n* elements of the array *data* with stride *stride* into ascending numerical order.

void gsl_sort_vector (gsl_vector * *v*)   Function
    This function sorts the elements of the vector *v* into ascending numerical order.

void gsl_sort_index (size_t * *p*, const double * *data*,   Function
        size_t *stride*, size_t *n*)
    This function indirectly sorts the *n* elements of the array *data* with stride *stride* into ascending order, storing the resulting permutation in *p*. The array *p* must be allocated with a sufficient length to store the *n* elements of the permutation. The elements of *p* give the index of the array element which would have been stored in that position if the array had been sorted in place. The array *data* is not changed.

int gsl_sort_vector_index (gsl_permutation * *p*, const   Function
        gsl_vector * *v*)
    This function indirectly sorts the elements of the vector *v* into ascending order, storing the resulting permutation in *p*. The elements of *p* give the index of the vector element which would have been stored in that position if the vector had been sorted in place. The first element of *p* gives the index of the least element in *v*, and the last element of *p* gives the index of the greatest element in *v*. The vector *v* is not changed.

11.3 Selecting the k smallest or largest elements

    The functions described in this section select the *k* smallest or largest elements of a data set of size N. The routines use an $O(kN)$ direct insertion algorithm which is suited to subsets that are small compared with the total size of the dataset. For example, the routines are useful for selecting the 10 largest values from one million data points, but not for selecting the largest 100,000 values. If the subset is a significant part of the total dataset it may be faster to sort all the elements of the dataset directly with an $O(N \log N)$ algorithm and obtain the smallest or largest values that way.

int gsl_sort_smallest (double * *dest*, size_t *k*, const   Function
        double * *src*, size_t *stride*, size_t *n*)
    This function copies the *k* smallest elements of the array *src*, of size *n* and stride *stride*, in ascending numerical order into the array *dest*. The size *k* of the subset must be less than or equal to *n*. The data *src* is not modified by this operation.

int gsl_sort_largest (double * *dest*, size_t *k*, const   Function
        double * *src*, size_t *stride*, size_t *n*)
This function copies the *k* largest elements of the array *src*, of size *n*
and stride *stride*, in descending numerical order into the array *dest*. *k*
must be less than or equal to *n*. The data *src* is not modified by this
operation.

int gsl_sort_vector_smallest (double * *dest*, size_t *k*,   Function
        const gsl_vector * *v*)
int gsl_sort_vector_largest (double * *dest*, size_t *k*,   Function
        const gsl_vector * *v*)
These functions copy the *k* smallest or largest elements of the vector
v into the array *dest*. *k* must be less than or equal to the length of
the vector *v*.

The following functions find the indices of the *k* smallest or largest
elements of a dataset,

int gsl_sort_smallest_index (size_t * *p*, size_t *k*,   Function
        const double * *src*, size_t *stride*, size_t *n*)
This function stores the indices of the *k* smallest elements of the array
src, of size *n* and stride *stride*, in the array *p*. The indices are chosen so
that the corresponding data is in ascending numerical order. *k* must be
less than or equal to *n*. The data *src* is not modified by this operation.

int gsl_sort_largest_index (size_t * *p*, size_t *k*, const   Function
        double * *src*, size_t *stride*, size_t *n*)
This function stores the indices of the *k* largest elements of the array
src, of size *n* and stride *stride*, in the array *p*. The indices are chosen
so that the corresponding data is in descending numerical order. *k*
must be less than or equal to *n*. The data *src* is not modified by this
operation.

int gsl_sort_vector_smallest_index (size_t * *p*, size_t   Function
        k, const gsl_vector * *v*)
int gsl_sort_vector_largest_index (size_t * *p*, size_t   Function
        k, const gsl_vector * *v*)
These functions store the indices of the *k* smallest or largest elements
of the vector *v* in the array *p*. *k* must be less than or equal to the
length of the vector *v*.

11.4 Computing the rank

The *rank* of an element is its order in the sorted data. The rank is the inverse of the index permutation, *p*. It can be computed using the following algorithm,

```
for (i = 0; i < p->size; i++)
{
    size_t pi = p->data[i];
    rank->data[pi] = i;
}
```

This can be computed directly from the function gsl_permutation_inverse(rank,p).

The following function will print the rank of each element of the vector *v*,

```
void
print_rank (gsl_vector * v)
{
  size_t i;
  size_t n = v->size;
  gsl_permutation * perm = gsl_permutation_alloc(n);
  gsl_permutation * rank = gsl_permutation_alloc(n);

  gsl_sort_vector_index (perm, v);
  gsl_permutation_inverse (rank, perm);

  for (i = 0; i < n; i++)
    {
    double vi = gsl_vector_get(v, i);
    printf ("element = %d, value = %g, rank = %d\n",
            i, vi, rank->data[i]);
    }

  gsl_permutation_free (perm);
  gsl_permutation_free (rank);
}
```

11.5 Examples

The following example shows how to use the permutation p to print the elements of the vector v in ascending order,

```
gsl_sort_vector_index (p, v);

for (i = 0; i < v->size; i++)
{
    double vpi = gsl_vector_get (v, p->data[i]);
    printf ("order = %d, value = %g\n", i, vpi);
}
```

The next example uses the function `gsl_sort_smallest` to select the 5 smallest numbers from 100000 uniform random variates stored in an array,

```
#include <gsl/gsl_rng.h>
#include <gsl/gsl_sort_double.h>

int
main (void)
{
  const gsl_rng_type * T;
  gsl_rng * r;

  size_t i, k = 5, N = 100000;

  double * x = malloc (N * sizeof(double));
  double * small = malloc (k * sizeof(double));

  gsl_rng_env_setup();

  T = gsl_rng_default;
  r = gsl_rng_alloc (T);

  for (i = 0; i < N; i++)
    {
      x[i] = gsl_rng_uniform(r);
    }

  gsl_sort_smallest (small, k, x, 1, N);

  printf ("%d smallest values from %d\n", k, N);

  for (i = 0; i < k; i++)
    {
```

```
        printf ("%d: %.18f\n", i, small[i]);
    }
    return 0;
}
```

The output lists the 5 smallest values, in ascending order,

```
$ ./a.out
5 smallest values from 100000
0: 0.000003489200025797
1: 0.000008199829608202
2: 0.000008953968062997
3: 0.000010712770745158
4: 0.000033531803637743
```

11.6 References and Further Reading

The subject of sorting is covered extensively in Knuth's *Sorting and Searching*,

> Donald E. Knuth, *The Art of Computer Programming: Sorting and Searching* (Vol 3, 3rd Ed, 1997), Addison-Wesley, ISBN 0201896850.

The Heapsort algorithm is described in the following book,

> Robert Sedgewick, *Algorithms in C*, Addison-Wesley, ISBN 0201514257.

12 BLAS Support

The Basic Linear Algebra Subprograms (BLAS) define a set of fundamental operations on vectors and matrices which can be used to create optimized higher-level linear algebra functionality.

The library provides a low-level layer which corresponds directly to the C-language BLAS standard, referred to here as "CBLAS", and a higher-level interface for operations on GSL vectors and matrices. Users who are interested in simple operations on GSL vector and matrix objects should use the high-level layer, which is declared in the file gsl_blas.h. This should satisfy the needs of most users. Note that GSL matrices are implemented using dense-storage so the interface only includes the corresponding dense-storage BLAS functions. The full BLAS functionality for band-format and packed-format matrices is available through the low-level CBLAS interface.

The interface for the gsl_cblas layer is specified in the file gsl_cblas.h. This interface corresponds to the BLAS Technical Forum's draft standard for the C interface to legacy BLAS implementations. Users who have access to other conforming CBLAS implementations can use these in place of the version provided by the library. Note that users who have only a Fortran BLAS library can use a CBLAS conformant wrapper to convert it into a CBLAS library. A reference CBLAS wrapper for legacy Fortran implementations exists as part of the draft CBLAS standard and can be obtained from Netlib. The complete set of CBLAS functions is listed in an appendix (see Appendix D [GSL CBLAS Library], page 541).

There are three levels of BLAS operations,

Level 1   Vector operations, e.g. $y = \alpha x + y$

Level 2   Matrix-vector operations, e.g. $y = \alpha A x + \beta y$

Level 3   Matrix-matrix operations, e.g. $C = \alpha A B + C$

Each routine has a name which specifies the operation, the type of matrices involved and their precisions. Some of the most common operations and their names are given below,

DOT   scalar product, $x^T y$

AXPY   vector sum, $\alpha x + y$

MV   matrix-vector product, Ax

SV   matrix-vector solve, $inv(A)x$

MM   matrix-matrix product, AB

SM   matrix-matrix solve, $inv(A)B$

The types of matrices are,

GE   general

GB   general band

SY   symmetric

SB   symmetric band

SP   symmetric packed

HE   hermitian

HB   hermitian band

HP   hermitian packed

TR   triangular

TB   triangular band

TP   triangular packed

Each operation is defined for four precisions,

S   single real

D   double real

C   single complex

Z   double complex

Thus, for example, the name SGEMM stands for "single-precision general matrix-matrix multiply" and ZGEMM stands for "double-precision complex matrix-matrix multiply".

12.1 GSL BLAS Interface

GSL provides dense vector and matrix objects, based on the relevant built-in types. The library provides an interface to the BLAS operations which apply to these objects. The interface to this functionality is given in the file gsl_blas.h.

12.1.1 Level 1

int gsl_blas_sdsdot (float *alpha*, const   Function
      gsl_vector_float * x, const gsl_vector_float * y,
      float * *result*)
This function computes the sum $\alpha + x^T y$ for the vectors x and y, returning the result in *result*.

int gsl_blas_sdot (const gsl_vector_float * x, const   Function
      gsl_vector_float * y, float * *result*)
int gsl_blas_dsdot (const gsl_vector_float * x, const   Function
      gsl_vector_float * y, double * *result*)
int gsl_blas_ddot (const gsl_vector * x, const   Function
      gsl_vector * y, double * *result*)
These functions compute the scalar product $x^T y$ for the vectors x and y, returning the result in *result*.

int gsl_blas_cdotu (const gsl_vector_complex_float *   Function
      x, const gsl_vector_complex_float * y,
      gsl_complex_float * *dotu*)
int gsl_blas_zdotu (const gsl_vector_complex * x, const   Function
      gsl_vector_complex * y, gsl_complex * *dotu*)
These functions compute the complex scalar product $x^T y$ for the vectors x and y, returning the result in *result*

int gsl_blas_cdotc (const gsl_vector_complex_float *   Function
      x, const gsl_vector_complex_float * y,
      gsl_complex_float * *dotc*)
int gsl_blas_zdotc (const gsl_vector_complex * x, const   Function
      gsl_vector_complex * y, gsl_complex * *dotc*)
These functions compute the complex conjugate scalar product $x^H y$ for the vectors x and y, returning the result in *result*

float gsl_blas_snrm2 (const gsl_vector_float * x)   Function
double gsl_blas_dnrm2 (const gsl_vector * x)   Function
These functions compute the Euclidean norm $||x||_2 = \sqrt{\sum x_i^2}$ of the vector x.

float gsl_blas_scnrm2 (const gsl_vector_complex_float   Function
    * x)
double gsl_blas_dznrm2 (const gsl_vector_complex * x)   Function
    These functions compute the Euclidean norm of the complex vector x,

$$||x||_2 = \sqrt{\sum (\mathrm{Re}(x_i)^2 + \mathrm{Im}(x_i)^2)}.$$

float gsl_blas_sasum (const gsl_vector_float * x)   Function
double gsl_blas_dasum (const gsl_vector * x)   Function
    These functions compute the absolute sum $\sum |x_i|$ of the elements of
    the vector x.

float gsl_blas_scasum (const gsl_vector_complex_float   Function
    * x)
double gsl_blas_dzasum (const gsl_vector_complex * x)   Function
    These functions compute the sum of the magnitudes of the real and
    imaginary parts of the complex vector x, $\sum (|\mathrm{Re}(x_i)| + |\mathrm{Im}(x_i)|)$.

CBLAS_INDEX_t gsl_blas_isamax (const gsl_vector_float   Function
    * x)
CBLAS_INDEX_t gsl_blas_idamax (const gsl_vector * x)   Function
CBLAS_INDEX_t gsl_blas_icamax (const   Function
        gsl_vector_complex_float * x)
CBLAS_INDEX_t gsl_blas_izamax (const   Function
        gsl_vector_complex * x)
    These functions return the index of the largest element of the vector x.
    The largest element is determined by its absolute magnitude for real
    vectors and by the sum of the magnitudes of the real and imaginary
    parts $|\mathrm{Re}(x_i)|+|\mathrm{Im}(x_i)|$ for complex vectors. If the largest value occurs
    several times then the index of the first occurrence is returned.

int gsl_blas_sswap (gsl_vector_float * x,   Function
        gsl_vector_float * y)
int gsl_blas_dswap (gsl_vector * x, gsl_vector * y)   Function
int gsl_blas_cswap (gsl_vector_complex_float * x,   Function
        gsl_vector_complex_float * y)
int gsl_blas_zswap (gsl_vector_complex * x,   Function
        gsl_vector_complex * y)
    These functions exchange the elements of the vectors x and y.

int gsl_blas_scopy (const gsl_vector_float * x,   Function
        gsl_vector_float * y)
int gsl_blas_dcopy (const gsl_vector * x, gsl_vector *   Function
        y)
int gsl_blas_ccopy (const gsl_vector_complex_float *   Function
        x, gsl_vector_complex_float * y)
int gsl_blas_zcopy (const gsl_vector_complex * x,   Function
        gsl_vector_complex * y)
    These functions copy the elements of the vector x into the vector y.

int gsl_blas_saxpy (float alpha, const gsl_vector_float   Function
        * x, gsl_vector_float * y)
int gsl_blas_daxpy (double alpha, const gsl_vector * x,   Function
        gsl_vector * y)
int gsl_blas_caxpy (const gsl_complex_float alpha,   Function
        const gsl_vector_complex_float * x,
        gsl_vector_complex_float * y)
int gsl_blas_zaxpy (const gsl_complex alpha, const   Function
        gsl_vector_complex * x, gsl_vector_complex * y)
    These functions compute the sum $y = \alpha x + y$ for the vectors x and y.

void gsl_blas_sscal (float alpha, gsl_vector_float * x)   Function
void gsl_blas_dscal (double alpha, gsl_vector * x)   Function
void gsl_blas_cscal (const gsl_complex_float alpha,   Function
        gsl_vector_complex_float * x)
void gsl_blas_zscal (const gsl_complex alpha,   Function
        gsl_vector_complex * x)
void gsl_blas_csscal (float alpha,   Function
        gsl_vector_complex_float * x)
void gsl_blas_zdscal (double alpha, gsl_vector_complex   Function
        * x)
    These functions rescale the vector x by the multiplicative factor alpha.

int gsl_blas_srotg (float a[], float b[], float c[], float   Function
        s[])
int gsl_blas_drotg (double a[], double b[], double c[],   Function
        double s[])
    These functions compute a Givens rotation (c, s) which zeroes the vec-
    tor (a, b),

$$\begin{pmatrix} c & s \\ -s & c \end{pmatrix} \begin{pmatrix} a \\ b \end{pmatrix} = \begin{pmatrix} r' \\ 0 \end{pmatrix}$$

The variables a and b are overwritten by the routine.

int gsl_blas_srot (gsl_vector_float * x,   Function
        gsl_vector_float * y, float c, float s)
int gsl_blas_drot (gsl_vector * x, gsl_vector * y,   Function
        const double c, const double s)

These functions apply a Givens rotation $(x', y') = (cx + sy, -sx + cy)$
to the vectors x, y.

int gsl_blas_srotmg (float d1[], float d2[], float b1[],   Function
        float b2, float P[])
int gsl_blas_drotmg (double d1[], double d2[], double   Function
        b1[], double b2, double P[])

These functions compute a modified Givens transformation. The modified Givens transformation is defined in the original Level-1 BLAS specification, given in the references.

int gsl_blas_srotm (gsl_vector_float * x,   Function
        gsl_vector_float * y, const float P[])
int gsl_blas_drotm (gsl_vector * x, gsl_vector * y,   Function
        const double P[])

These functions apply a modified Givens transformation.

12.1.2 Level 2

int gsl_blas_sgemv (CBLAS_TRANSPOSE_t TransA, float   Function
        alpha, const gsl_matrix_float * A, const
        gsl_vector_float * x, float beta, gsl_vector_float *
        y)
int gsl_blas_dgemv (CBLAS_TRANSPOSE_t TransA, double   Function
        alpha, const gsl_matrix * A, const gsl_vector * x,
        double beta, gsl_vector * y)
int gsl_blas_cgemv (CBLAS_TRANSPOSE_t TransA, const   Function
        gsl_complex_float alpha, const
        gsl_matrix_complex_float * A, const
        gsl_vector_complex_float * x, const
        gsl_complex_float beta, gsl_vector_complex_float * y)
int gsl_blas_zgemv (CBLAS_TRANSPOSE_t TransA, const   Function
        gsl_complex alpha, const gsl_matrix_complex * A,
        const gsl_vector_complex * x, const gsl_complex beta,
        gsl_vector_complex * y)

These functions compute the matrix-vector product and sum $y = \alpha op(A)x + \beta y$, where $op(A) = A, A^T, A^H$ for TransA = CblasNoTrans,
CblasTrans, CblasConjTrans.

int gsl_blas_strmv (CBLAS_UPLO_t *Uplo*,   Function
        CBLAS_TRANSPOSE_t *TransA*, CBLAS_DIAG_t *Diag*, const
        gsl_matrix_float * *A*, gsl_vector_float * *x*)

int gsl_blas_dtrmv (CBLAS_UPLO_t *Uplo*,   Function
        CBLAS_TRANSPOSE_t *TransA*, CBLAS_DIAG_t *Diag*, const
        gsl_matrix * *A*, gsl_vector * *x*)

int gsl_blas_ctrmv (CBLAS_UPLO_t *Uplo*,   Function
        CBLAS_TRANSPOSE_t *TransA*, CBLAS_DIAG_t *Diag*, const
        gsl_matrix_complex_float * *A*,
        gsl_vector_complex_float * *x*)

int gsl_blas_ztrmv (CBLAS_UPLO_t *Uplo*,   Function
        CBLAS_TRANSPOSE_t *TransA*, CBLAS_DIAG_t *Diag*, const
        gsl_matrix_complex * *A*, gsl_vector_complex * *x*)

These functions compute the matrix-vector product $x = \alpha op(A)x$
for the triangular matrix A, where $op(A) = A$, A^T, A^H for *TransA*
= CblasNoTrans, CblasTrans, CblasConjTrans. When *Uplo* is
CblasUpper then the upper triangle of A is used, and when *Uplo*
is CblasLower then the lower triangle of A is used. If *Diag* is
CblasNonUnit then the diagonal of the matrix is used, but if *Diag*
is CblasUnit then the diagonal elements of the matrix A are taken as
unity and are not referenced.

int gsl_blas_strsv (CBLAS_UPLO_t *Uplo*,   Function
        CBLAS_TRANSPOSE_t *TransA*, CBLAS_DIAG_t *Diag*, const
        gsl_matrix_float * *A*, gsl_vector_float * *x*)

int gsl_blas_dtrsv (CBLAS_UPLO_t *Uplo*,   Function
        CBLAS_TRANSPOSE_t *TransA*, CBLAS_DIAG_t *Diag*, const
        gsl_matrix * *A*, gsl_vector * *x*)

int gsl_blas_ctrsv (CBLAS_UPLO_t *Uplo*,   Function
        CBLAS_TRANSPOSE_t *TransA*, CBLAS_DIAG_t *Diag*, const
        gsl_matrix_complex_float * *A*,
        gsl_vector_complex_float * *x*)

int gsl_blas_ztrsv (CBLAS_UPLO_t *Uplo*,   Function
        CBLAS_TRANSPOSE_t *TransA*, CBLAS_DIAG_t *Diag*, const
        gsl_matrix_complex * *A*, gsl_vector_complex * *x*)

These functions compute $inv(op(A))x$ for x, where $op(A) = A$, A^T, A^H
for *TransA* = CblasNoTrans, CblasTrans, CblasConjTrans. When
Uplo is CblasUpper then the upper triangle of A is used, and when
Uplo is CblasLower then the lower triangle of A is used. If *Diag* is
CblasNonUnit then the diagonal of the matrix is used, but if *Diag* is
CblasUnit then the diagonal elements of the matrix A are taken as
unity and are not referenced.

int gsl_blas_ssymv (CBLAS_UPLO_t *Uplo*, float *alpha*,   Function
          const gsl_matrix_float * *A*, const gsl_vector_float *
          x, float *beta*, gsl_vector_float * *y*)
int gsl_blas_dsymv (CBLAS_UPLO_t *Uplo*, double *alpha*,   Function
          const gsl_matrix * *A*, const gsl_vector * *x*, double
          beta, gsl_vector * *y*)

These functions compute the matrix-vector product and sum $y = \alpha A x + \beta y$ for the symmetric matrix A. Since the matrix A is symmetric only its upper half or lower half need to be stored. When *Uplo* is CblasUpper then the upper triangle and diagonal of A are used, and when *Uplo* is CblasLower then the lower triangle and diagonal of A are used.

int gsl_blas_chemv (CBLAS_UPLO_t *Uplo*, const   Function
          gsl_complex_float *alpha*, const
          gsl_matrix_complex_float * *A*, const
          gsl_vector_complex_float * *x*, const
          gsl_complex_float *beta*, gsl_vector_complex_float * *y*)
int gsl_blas_zhemv (CBLAS_UPLO_t *Uplo*, const   Function
          gsl_complex *alpha*, const gsl_matrix_complex * *A*,
          const gsl_vector_complex * *x*, const gsl_complex *beta*,
          gsl_vector_complex * *y*)

These functions compute the matrix-vector product and sum $y = \alpha A x + \beta y$ for the hermitian matrix A. Since the matrix A is hermitian only its upper half or lower half need to be stored. When *Uplo* is CblasUpper then the upper triangle and diagonal of A are used, and when *Uplo* is CblasLower then the lower triangle and diagonal of A are used. The imaginary elements of the diagonal are automatically assumed to be zero and are not referenced.

int gsl_blas_sger (float *alpha*, const gsl_vector_float   Function
          * *x*, const gsl_vector_float * *y*, gsl_matrix_float *
          A)
int gsl_blas_dger (double *alpha*, const gsl_vector * *x*,   Function
          const gsl_vector * *y*, gsl_matrix * *A*)
int gsl_blas_cgeru (const gsl_complex_float *alpha*,   Function
          const gsl_vector_complex_float * *x*, const
          gsl_vector_complex_float * *y*,
          gsl_matrix_complex_float * *A*)
int gsl_blas_zgeru (const gsl_complex *alpha*, const   Function
          gsl_vector_complex * *x*, const gsl_vector_complex * *y*,
          gsl_matrix_complex * *A*)

These functions compute the rank-1 update $A = \alpha x y^T + A$ of the matrix A.

int gsl_blas_cgerc (const gsl_complex_float *alpha*,   Function
        const gsl_vector_complex_float * x, const
        gsl_vector_complex_float * y,
        gsl_matrix_complex_float * A)
int gsl_blas_zgerc (const gsl_complex *alpha*, const   Function
        gsl_vector_complex * x, const gsl_vector_complex * y,
        gsl_matrix_complex * A)

These functions compute the conjugate rank-1 update $A = \alpha x y^H + A$ of the matrix A.

int gsl_blas_ssyr (CBLAS_UPLO_t *Uplo*, float *alpha*,   Function
        const gsl_vector_float * x, gsl_matrix_float * A)
int gsl_blas_dsyr (CBLAS_UPLO_t *Uplo*, double *alpha*,   Function
        const gsl_vector * x, gsl_matrix * A)

These functions compute the symmetric rank-1 update $A = \alpha x x^T + A$ of the symmetric matrix A. Since the matrix A is symmetric only its upper half or lower half need to be stored. When *Uplo* is CblasUpper then the upper triangle and diagonal of A are used, and when *Uplo* is CblasLower then the lower triangle and diagonal of A are used.

int gsl_blas_cher (CBLAS_UPLO_t *Uplo*, float *alpha*,   Function
        const gsl_vector_complex_float * x,
        gsl_matrix_complex_float * A)
int gsl_blas_zher (CBLAS_UPLO_t *Uplo*, double *alpha*,   Function
        const gsl_vector_complex * x, gsl_matrix_complex * A)

These functions compute the hermitian rank-1 update $A = \alpha x x^H + A$ of the hermitian matrix A. Since the matrix A is hermitian only its upper half or lower half need to be stored. When *Uplo* is CblasUpper then the upper triangle and diagonal of A are used, and when *Uplo* is CblasLower then the lower triangle and diagonal of A are used. The imaginary elements of the diagonal are automatically set to zero.

int gsl_blas_ssyr2 (CBLAS_UPLO_t *Uplo*, float *alpha*,   Function
        const gsl_vector_float * x, const gsl_vector_float *
        y, gsl_matrix_float * A)
int gsl_blas_dsyr2 (CBLAS_UPLO_t *Uplo*, double *alpha*,   Function
        const gsl_vector * x, const gsl_vector * y, gsl_matrix
        * A)

These functions compute the symmetric rank-2 update $A = \alpha x y^T + \alpha y x^T + A$ of the symmetric matrix A. Since the matrix A is symmetric only its upper half or lower half need to be stored. When *Uplo* is CblasUpper then the upper triangle and diagonal of A are used, and when *Uplo* is CblasLower then the lower triangle and diagonal of A are used.

int gsl_blas_cher2 (CBLAS_UPLO_t *Uplo*, const   Function
       gsl_complex_float *alpha*, const
       gsl_vector_complex_float * *x*, const
       gsl_vector_complex_float * *y*,
       gsl_matrix_complex_float * *A*)

int gsl_blas_zher2 (CBLAS_UPLO_t *Uplo*, const   Function
       gsl_complex *alpha*, const gsl_vector_complex * *x*,
       const gsl_vector_complex * *y*, gsl_matrix_complex * *A*)

These functions compute the hermitian rank-2 update $A = \alpha x y^H + \alpha^* y x^H A$ of the hermitian matrix A. Since the matrix A is hermitian only its upper half or lower half need to be stored. When *Uplo* is CblasUpper then the upper triangle and diagonal of A are used, and when *Uplo* is CblasLower then the lower triangle and diagonal of A are used. The imaginary elements of the diagonal are automatically set to zero.

12.1.3 Level 3

int gsl_blas_sgemm (CBLAS_TRANSPOSE_t *TransA*,   Function
       CBLAS_TRANSPOSE_t *TransB*, float *alpha*, const
       gsl_matrix_float * *A*, const gsl_matrix_float * *B*,
       float *beta*, gsl_matrix_float * *C*)

int gsl_blas_dgemm (CBLAS_TRANSPOSE_t *TransA*,   Function
       CBLAS_TRANSPOSE_t *TransB*, double *alpha*, const
       gsl_matrix * *A*, const gsl_matrix * *B*, double *beta*,
       gsl_matrix * *C*)

int gsl_blas_cgemm (CBLAS_TRANSPOSE_t *TransA*,   Function
       CBLAS_TRANSPOSE_t *TransB*, const gsl_complex_float
       alpha, const gsl_matrix_complex_float * *A*, const
       gsl_matrix_complex_float * *B*, const
       gsl_complex_float *beta*, gsl_matrix_complex_float *
       C)

int gsl_blas_zgemm (CBLAS_TRANSPOSE_t *TransA*,   Function
       CBLAS_TRANSPOSE_t *TransB*, const gsl_complex *alpha*,
       const gsl_matrix_complex * *A*, const
       gsl_matrix_complex * *B*, const gsl_complex *beta*,
       gsl_matrix_complex * *C*)

These functions compute the matrix-matrix product and sum $C = \alpha\, op(A) op(B) + \beta C$ where $op(A) = A$, A^T, A^H for *TransA* = CblasNoTrans, CblasTrans, CblasConjTrans and similarly for the parameter *TransB*.

int gsl_blas_ssymm (CBLAS_SIDE_t *Side*, CBLAS_UPLO_t   Function
    Uplo, float *alpha*, const gsl_matrix_float * *A*, const
    gsl_matrix_float * *B*, float *beta*, gsl_matrix_float *
    C)
int gsl_blas_dsymm (CBLAS_SIDE_t *Side*, CBLAS_UPLO_t   Function
    Uplo, double *alpha*, const gsl_matrix * *A*, const
    gsl_matrix * *B*, double *beta*, gsl_matrix * *C*)
int gsl_blas_csymm (CBLAS_SIDE_t *Side*, CBLAS_UPLO_t   Function
    Uplo, const gsl_complex_float *alpha*, const
    gsl_matrix_complex_float * *A*, const
    gsl_matrix_complex_float * *B*, const
    gsl_complex_float *beta*, gsl_matrix_complex_float *
    C)
int gsl_blas_zsymm (CBLAS_SIDE_t *Side*, CBLAS_UPLO_t   Function
    Uplo, const gsl_complex *alpha*, const
    gsl_matrix_complex * *A*, const gsl_matrix_complex *
    B, const gsl_complex *beta*, gsl_matrix_complex * *C*)

These functions compute the matrix-matrix product and sum $C = \alpha AB + \beta C$ for *Side* is CblasLeft and $C = \alpha BA + \beta C$ for *Side* is CblasRight, where the matrix A is symmetric. When *Uplo* is CblasUpper then the upper triangle and diagonal of A are used, and when *Uplo* is CblasLower then the lower triangle and diagonal of A are used.

int gsl_blas_chemm (CBLAS_SIDE_t *Side*, CBLAS_UPLO_t   Function
    Uplo, const gsl_complex_float *alpha*, const
    gsl_matrix_complex_float * *A*, const
    gsl_matrix_complex_float * *B*, const
    gsl_complex_float *beta*, gsl_matrix_complex_float *
    C)
int gsl_blas_zhemm (CBLAS_SIDE_t *Side*, CBLAS_UPLO_t   Function
    Uplo, const gsl_complex *alpha*, const
    gsl_matrix_complex * *A*, const gsl_matrix_complex *
    B, const gsl_complex *beta*, gsl_matrix_complex * *C*)

These functions compute the matrix-matrix product and sum $C = \alpha AB + \beta C$ for *Side* is CblasLeft and $C = \alpha BA + \beta C$ for *Side* is CblasRight, where the matrix A is hermitian. When *Uplo* is CblasUpper then the upper triangle and diagonal of A are used, and when *Uplo* is CblasLower then the lower triangle and diagonal of A are used. The imaginary elements of the diagonal are automatically set to zero.

int gsl_blas_strmm (CBLAS_SIDE_t *Side*, CBLAS_UPLO_t   Function
          Uplo, CBLAS_TRANSPOSE_t *TransA*, CBLAS_DIAG_t *Diag*,
          float *alpha*, const gsl_matrix_float * *A*,
          gsl_matrix_float * *B*)

int gsl_blas_dtrmm (CBLAS_SIDE_t *Side*, CBLAS_UPLO_t   Function
          Uplo, CBLAS_TRANSPOSE_t *TransA*, CBLAS_DIAG_t *Diag*,
          double *alpha*, const gsl_matrix * *A*, gsl_matrix * *B*)

int gsl_blas_ctrmm (CBLAS_SIDE_t *Side*, CBLAS_UPLO_t   Function
          Uplo, CBLAS_TRANSPOSE_t *TransA*, CBLAS_DIAG_t *Diag*,
          const gsl_complex_float *alpha*, const
          gsl_matrix_complex_float * *A*,
          gsl_matrix_complex_float * *B*)

int gsl_blas_ztrmm (CBLAS_SIDE_t *Side*, CBLAS_UPLO_t   Function
          Uplo, CBLAS_TRANSPOSE_t *TransA*, CBLAS_DIAG_t *Diag*,
          const gsl_complex *alpha*, const gsl_matrix_complex *
          A, gsl_matrix_complex * *B*)

These functions compute the matrix-matrix product $B = \alpha op(A)B$
for *Side* is CblasLeft and $B = \alpha Bop(A)$ for *Side* is CblasRight.
The matrix A is triangular and $op(A) = A$, A^T, A^H for *TransA*
= CblasNoTrans, CblasTrans, CblasConjTrans. When *Uplo* is
CblasUpper then the upper triangle of A is used, and when *Uplo*
is CblasLower then the lower triangle of A is used. If *Diag* is
CblasNonUnit then the diagonal of A is used, but if *Diag* is CblasUnit
then the diagonal elements of the matrix A are taken as unity and are
not referenced.

int gsl_blas_strsm (CBLAS_SIDE_t *Side*, CBLAS_UPLO_t   Function
          Uplo, CBLAS_TRANSPOSE_t *TransA*, CBLAS_DIAG_t *Diag*,
          float *alpha*, const gsl_matrix_float * *A*,
          gsl_matrix_float * *B*)

int gsl_blas_dtrsm (CBLAS_SIDE_t *Side*, CBLAS_UPLO_t   Function
          Uplo, CBLAS_TRANSPOSE_t *TransA*, CBLAS_DIAG_t *Diag*,
          double *alpha*, const gsl_matrix * *A*, gsl_matrix * *B*)

int gsl_blas_ctrsm (CBLAS_SIDE_t *Side*, CBLAS_UPLO_t   Function
          Uplo, CBLAS_TRANSPOSE_t *TransA*, CBLAS_DIAG_t *Diag*,
          const gsl_complex_float *alpha*, const
          gsl_matrix_complex_float * *A*,
          gsl_matrix_complex_float * *B*)

int gsl_blas_ztrsm (CBLAS_SIDE_t *Side*, CBLAS_UPLO_t   Function
          Uplo, CBLAS_TRANSPOSE_t *TransA*, CBLAS_DIAG_t *Diag*,
          const gsl_complex *alpha*, const gsl_matrix_complex *
          A, gsl_matrix_complex * *B*)

These functions compute the inverse-matrix matrix product $B =
\alpha op(inv(A))B$ for *Side* is CblasLeft and $B = \alpha Bop(inv(A))$ for *Side*

is CblasRight. The matrix A is triangular and $op(A) = A$, A^T, A^H for *TransA* = CblasNoTrans, CblasTrans, CblasConjTrans. When *Uplo* is CblasUpper then the upper triangle of A is used, and when *Uplo* is CblasLower then the lower triangle of A is used. If *Diag* is CblasNonUnit then the diagonal of A is used, but if *Diag* is CblasUnit then the diagonal elements of the matrix A are taken as unity and are not referenced.

int gsl_blas_ssyrk (CBLAS_UPLO_t *Uplo*,   *Function*
       CBLAS_TRANSPOSE_t *Trans*, float *alpha*, const
       gsl_matrix_float * A, float *beta*, gsl_matrix_float *
       C)

int gsl_blas_dsyrk (CBLAS_UPLO_t *Uplo*,   *Function*
       CBLAS_TRANSPOSE_t *Trans*, double *alpha*, const
       gsl_matrix * A, double *beta*, gsl_matrix * C)

int gsl_blas_csyrk (CBLAS_UPLO_t *Uplo*,   *Function*
       CBLAS_TRANSPOSE_t *Trans*, const gsl_complex_float
       alpha, const gsl_matrix_complex_float * A, const
       gsl_complex_float *beta*, gsl_matrix_complex_float *
       C)

int gsl_blas_zsyrk (CBLAS_UPLO_t *Uplo*,   *Function*
       CBLAS_TRANSPOSE_t *Trans*, const gsl_complex *alpha*,
       const gsl_matrix_complex * A, const gsl_complex *beta*,
       gsl_matrix_complex * C)

These functions compute a rank-k update of the symmetric matrix C, $C = \alpha AA^T + \beta C$ when *Trans* is CblasNoTrans and $C = \alpha A^T A + \beta C$ when *Trans* is CblasTrans. Since the matrix C is symmetric only its upper half or lower half need to be stored. When *Uplo* is CblasUpper then the upper triangle and diagonal of C are used, and when *Uplo* is CblasLower then the lower triangle and diagonal of C are used.

int gsl_blas_cherk (CBLAS_UPLO_t *Uplo*,   *Function*
       CBLAS_TRANSPOSE_t *Trans*, float *alpha*, const
       gsl_matrix_complex_float * A, float *beta*,
       gsl_matrix_complex_float * C)

int gsl_blas_zherk (CBLAS_UPLO_t *Uplo*,   *Function*
       CBLAS_TRANSPOSE_t *Trans*, double *alpha*, const
       gsl_matrix_complex * A, double *beta*,
       gsl_matrix_complex * C)

These functions compute a rank-k update of the hermitian matrix C, $C = \alpha AA^H + \beta C$ when *Trans* is CblasNoTrans and $C = \alpha A^H A + \beta C$ when *Trans* is CblasTrans. Since the matrix C is hermitian only its upper half or lower half need to be stored. When *Uplo* is CblasUpper then the upper triangle and diagonal of C are used, and when *Uplo* is

CblasLower then the lower triangle and diagonal of C are used. The imaginary elements of the diagonal are automatically set to zero.

int gsl_blas_ssyr2k (CBLAS_UPLO_t *Uplo*,   Function
        CBLAS_TRANSPOSE_t *Trans*, float *alpha*, const
        gsl_matrix_float * A, const gsl_matrix_float * B,
        float *beta*, gsl_matrix_float * C)

int gsl_blas_dsyr2k (CBLAS_UPLO_t *Uplo*,   Function
        CBLAS_TRANSPOSE_t *Trans*, double *alpha*, const
        gsl_matrix * A, const gsl_matrix * B, double *beta*,
        gsl_matrix * C)

int gsl_blas_csyr2k (CBLAS_UPLO_t *Uplo*,   Function
        CBLAS_TRANSPOSE_t *Trans*, const gsl_complex_float
        alpha, const gsl_matrix_complex_float * A, const
        gsl_matrix_complex_float * B, const
        gsl_complex_float *beta*, gsl_matrix_complex_float *
        C)

int gsl_blas_zsyr2k (CBLAS_UPLO_t *Uplo*,   Function
        CBLAS_TRANSPOSE_t *Trans*, const gsl_complex *alpha*,
        const gsl_matrix_complex * A, const
        gsl_matrix_complex * B, const gsl_complex *beta*,
        gsl_matrix_complex * C)

These functions compute a rank-2k update of the symmetric matrix C, $C = \alpha AB^T + \alpha BA^T + \beta C$ when *Trans* is CblasNoTrans and $C = \alpha A^T B + \alpha B^T A + \beta C$ when *Trans* is CblasTrans. Since the matrix C is symmetric only its upper half or lower half need to be stored. When *Uplo* is CblasUpper then the upper triangle and diagonal of C are used, and when *Uplo* is CblasLower then the lower triangle and diagonal of C are used.

int gsl_blas_cher2k (CBLAS_UPLO_t *Uplo*,   Function
        CBLAS_TRANSPOSE_t *Trans*, const gsl_complex_float
        alpha, const gsl_matrix_complex_float * A, const
        gsl_matrix_complex_float * B, float *beta*,
        gsl_matrix_complex_float * C)

int gsl_blas_zher2k (CBLAS_UPLO_t *Uplo*,   Function
        CBLAS_TRANSPOSE_t *Trans*, const gsl_complex *alpha*,
        const gsl_matrix_complex * A, const
        gsl_matrix_complex * B, double *beta*,
        gsl_matrix_complex * C)

These functions compute a rank-2k update of the hermitian matrix C, $C = \alpha AB^H + \alpha^* BA^H + \beta C$ when *Trans* is CblasNoTrans and $C = \alpha A^H B + \alpha^* B^H A + \beta C$ when *Trans* is CblasConjTrans. Since the matrix C is hermitian only its upper half or lower half need to be stored. When *Uplo* is CblasUpper then the upper triangle and diagonal of C are used, and when *Uplo* is CblasLower then the lower triangle and diagonal of C are used. The imaginary elements of the diagonal are automatically set to zero.

12.2 Examples

The following program computes the product of two matrices using the Level-3 BLAS function DGEMM,

$$\begin{pmatrix} 0.11 & 0.12 & 0.13 \\ 0.21 & 0.22 & 0.23 \end{pmatrix} \begin{pmatrix} 1011 & 1012 \\ 1021 & 1022 \\ 1031 & 1031 \end{pmatrix} = \begin{pmatrix} 367.76 & 368.12 \\ 674.06 & 674.72 \end{pmatrix}$$

The matrices are stored in row major order, according to the C convention for arrays.

```c
#include <stdio.h>
#include <gsl/gsl_blas.h>

int
main (void)
{
  double a[] = { 0.11, 0.12, 0.13,
                 0.21, 0.22, 0.23 };

  double b[] = { 1011, 1012,
                 1021, 1022,
                 1031, 1032 };

  double c[] = { 0.00, 0.00,
                 0.00, 0.00 };

  gsl_matrix_view A = gsl_matrix_view_array(a, 2, 3);
  gsl_matrix_view B = gsl_matrix_view_array(b, 3, 2);
  gsl_matrix_view C = gsl_matrix_view_array(c, 2, 2);

  /* Compute C = A B */

  gsl_blas_dgemm (CblasNoTrans, CblasNoTrans,
                  1.0, &A.matrix, &B.matrix,
                  0.0, &C.matrix);

  printf ("[ %g, %g\n", c[0], c[1]);
  printf (" %g, %g ]\n", c[2], c[3]);
```

```
    return 0;
  }
```
Here is the output from the program,
```
  $ ./a.out
  [ 367.76, 368.12
    674.06, 674.72 ]
```

12.3 References and Further Reading

Information on the BLAS standards, including both the legacy and draft interface standards, is available online from the BLAS Homepage and BLAS Technical Forum web-site.

BLAS Homepage
http://www.netlib.org/blas/

BLAS Technical Forum
http://www.netlib.org/cgi-bin/checkout/blast/blast.pl

The following papers contain the specifications for Level 1, Level 2 and Level 3 BLAS.

C. Lawson, R. Hanson, D. Kincaid, F. Krogh, "Basic Linear Algebra Subprograms for Fortran Usage", *ACM Transactions on Mathematical Software*, Vol. 5 (1979), Pages 308–325.

J.J. Dongarra, J. DuCroz, S. Hammarling, R. Hanson, "An Extended Set of Fortran Basic Linear Algebra Subprograms", *ACM Transactions on Mathematical Software*, Vol. 14, No. 1 (1988), Pages 1–32.

J.J. Dongarra, I. Duff, J. DuCroz, S. Hammarling, "A Set of Level 3 Basic Linear Algebra Subprograms", *ACM Transactions on Mathematical Software*, Vol. 16 (1990), Pages 1–28.

Postscript versions of the latter two papers are available from http://www.netlib.org/blas/. A CBLAS wrapper for Fortran BLAS libraries is available from the same location.

13 Linear Algebra

This chapter describes functions for solving linear systems. The library provides linear algebra operations which operate directly on the gsl_vector and gsl_matrix objects. These routines use the standard algorithms from Golub & Van Loan's *Matrix Computations* with Level-1 and Level-2 BLAS calls for efficiency.

The functions described in this chapter are declared in the header file 'gsl_linalg.h'.

13.1 LU Decomposition

A general square matrix A has an LU decomposition into upper and lower triangular matrices,

$$PA = LU$$

where P is a permutation matrix, L is unit lower triangular matrix and U is upper triangular matrix. For square matrices this decomposition can be used to convert the linear system $Ax = b$ into a pair of triangular systems ($Ly = Pb$, $Ux = y$), which can be solved by forward and back-substitution. Note that the LU decomposition is valid for both singular and non-singular matrices.

int gsl_linalg_LU_decomp (gsl_matrix * A,   Function
        gsl_permutation * p, int * *signum*)
int gsl_linalg_complex_LU_decomp (gsl_matrix_complex *   Function
        A, gsl_permutation * p, int * *signum*)

These functions factorize the square matrix A into the LU decomposition $PA = LU$. On output the diagonal and upper triangular part of the input matrix A contain the matrix U. The lower triangular part of the input matrix (excluding the diagonal) contains L. The diagonal elements of L are unity, and are not stored.

The permutation matrix P is encoded in the permutation p. The j-th column of the matrix P is given by the k-th column of the identity matrix, where $k = p_j$ the j-th element of the permutation vector. The sign of the permutation is given by *signum*. It has the value $(-1)^n$, where n is the number of interchanges in the permutation.

The algorithm used in the decomposition is Gaussian Elimination with partial pivoting (Golub & Van Loan, *Matrix Computations*, Algorithm 3.4.1).

int gsl_linalg_LU_solve (const gsl_matrix * *LU*, const   Function
       gsl_permutation * *p*, const gsl_vector * *b*, gsl_vector
       * *x*)

int gsl_linalg_complex_LU_solve (const   Function
       gsl_matrix_complex * *LU*, const gsl_permutation * *p*,
       const gsl_vector_complex * *b*, gsl_vector_complex * *x*)

These functions solve the square system $Ax = b$ using the LU decomposition of A into (LU, p) given by gsl_linalg_LU_decomp or gsl_linalg_complex_LU_decomp.

int gsl_linalg_LU_svx (const gsl_matrix * *LU*, const   Function
       gsl_permutation * *p*, gsl_vector * *x*)

int gsl_linalg_complex_LU_svx (const   Function
       gsl_matrix_complex * *LU*, const gsl_permutation * *p*,
       gsl_vector_complex * *x*)

These functions solve the square system $Ax = b$ in-place using the LU decomposition of A into (LU,p). On input x should contain the right-hand side b, which is replaced by the solution on output.

int gsl_linalg_LU_refine (const gsl_matrix * *A*, const   Function
       gsl_matrix * *LU*, const gsl_permutation * *p*, const
       gsl_vector * *b*, gsl_vector * *x*, gsl_vector * *residual*)

int gsl_linalg_complex_LU_refine (const   Function
       gsl_matrix_complex * *A*, const gsl_matrix_complex *
       LU, const gsl_permutation * *p*, const
       gsl_vector_complex * *b*, gsl_vector_complex * *x*,
       gsl_vector_complex * *residual*)

These functions apply an iterative improvement to x, the solution of $Ax = b$, using the LU decomposition of A into (LU,p). The initial residual $r = Ax - b$ is also computed and stored in *residual*.

int gsl_linalg_LU_invert (const gsl_matrix * *LU*, const   Function
       gsl_permutation * *p*, gsl_matrix * *inverse*)

int gsl_linalg_complex_LU_invert (const   Function
       gsl_matrix_complex * *LU*, const gsl_permutation * *p*,
       gsl_matrix_complex * *inverse*)

These functions compute the inverse of a matrix A from its LU decomposition (LU,p), storing the result in the matrix *inverse*. The inverse is computed by solving the system $Ax = b$ for each column of the identity matrix. It is preferable to avoid direct use of the inverse whenever possible, as the linear solver functions can obtain the same result more efficiently and reliably (consult any introductory textbook on numerical linear algebra for details).

double gsl_linalg_LU_det (gsl_matrix * *LU*, int *signum*)   Function
gsl_complex gsl_linalg_complex_LU_det   Function
        (gsl_matrix_complex * *LU*, int *signum*)
> These functions compute the determinant of a matrix A from its LU
> decomposition, LU. The determinant is computed as the product of the
> diagonal elements of U and the sign of the row permutation *signum*.

double gsl_linalg_LU_lndet (gsl_matrix * *LU*)   Function
double gsl_linalg_complex_LU_lndet   Function
        (gsl_matrix_complex * *LU*)
> These functions compute the logarithm of the absolute value of the
> determinant of a matrix A, $\ln |\det(A)|$, from its LU decomposition,
> LU. This function may be useful if the direct computation of the de-
> terminant would overflow or underflow.

int gsl_linalg_LU_sgndet (gsl_matrix * *LU*, int *signum*)   Function
gsl_complex gsl_linalg_complex_LU_sgndet   Function
        (gsl_matrix_complex * *LU*, int *signum*)
> These functions compute the sign or phase factor of the determinant
> of a matrix A, $\det(A)/|\det(A)|$, from its LU decomposition, LU.

13.2 QR Decomposition

A general rectangular M-by-N matrix A has a QR decomposition into
the product of an orthogonal M-by-M square matrix Q (where $Q^T Q = I$)
and an M-by-N right-triangular matrix R,

$$A = QR$$

This decomposition can be used to convert the linear system $Ax = b$
into the triangular system $Rx = Q^T b$, which can be solved by back-
substitution. Another use of the QR decomposition is to compute an
orthonormal basis for a set of vectors. The first N columns of Q form an
orthonormal basis for the range of A, $ran(A)$, when A has full column
rank.

int gsl_linalg_QR_decomp (gsl_matrix * A, gsl_vector *   Function
        tau)
> This function factorizes the M-by-N matrix A into the QR decom-
> position $A = QR$. On output the diagonal and upper triangular
> part of the input matrix contain the matrix R. The vector *tau*
> and the columns of the lower triangular part of the matrix A con-
> tain the Householder coefficients and Householder vectors which en-
> code the orthogonal matrix Q. The vector *tau* must be of length
> $k = \min(M, N)$. The matrix Q is related to these components by,

$Q = Q_k...Q_2Q_1$ where $Q_i = I - \tau_i v_i v_i^T$ and v_i is the Householder vector $v_i = (0, ..., 1, A(i+1,i), A(i+2,i), ..., A(m,i))$. This is the same storage scheme as used by LAPACK.

The algorithm used to perform the decomposition is Householder QR (Golub & Van Loan, *Matrix Computations*, Algorithm 5.2.1).

int gsl_linalg_QR_solve (const gsl_matrix * QR, const gsl_vector * *tau*, const gsl_vector * *b*, gsl_vector * *x*)   [Function]

This function solves the square system $Ax = b$ using the QR decomposition of A into (QR, *tau*) given by gsl_linalg_QR_decomp. The least-squares solution for rectangular systems can be found using gsl_linalg_QR_lssolve.

int gsl_linalg_QR_svx (const gsl_matrix * QR, const gsl_vector * *tau*, gsl_vector * x)   [Function]

This function solves the square system $Ax = b$ in-place using the QR decomposition of A into (QR,*tau*) given by gsl_linalg_QR_decomp. On input x should contain the right-hand side b, which is replaced by the solution on output.

int gsl_linalg_QR_lssolve (const gsl_matrix * QR, const gsl_vector * *tau*, const gsl_vector * *b*, gsl_vector * *x*, gsl_vector * *residual*)   [Function]

This function finds the least squares solution to the overdetermined system $Ax = b$ where the matrix A has more rows than columns. The least squares solution minimizes the Euclidean norm of the residual, $||Ax - b||$. The routine uses the QR decomposition of A into (QR, *tau*) given by gsl_linalg_QR_decomp. The solution is returned in x. The residual is computed as a by-product and stored in *residual*.

int gsl_linalg_QR_QTvec (const gsl_matrix * QR, const gsl_vector * *tau*, gsl_vector * *v*)   [Function]

This function applies the matrix Q^T encoded in the decomposition (QR,*tau*) to the vector *v*, storing the result $Q^T v$ in *v*. The matrix multiplication is carried out directly using the encoding of the Householder vectors without needing to form the full matrix Q^T.

int gsl_linalg_QR_Qvec (const gsl_matrix * QR, const gsl_vector * *tau*, gsl_vector * *v*)   [Function]

This function applies the matrix Q encoded in the decomposition (QR,*tau*) to the vector *v*, storing the result Qv in *v*. The matrix multiplication is carried out directly using the encoding of the Householder vectors without needing to form the full matrix Q.

int **gsl_linalg_QR_Rsolve** (const gsl_matrix * QR, const   Function
       gsl_vector * b, gsl_vector * x)

This function solves the triangular system $Rx = b$ for x. It may be useful if the product $b' = Q^T b$ has already been computed using gsl_linalg_QR_QTvec.

int **gsl_linalg_QR_Rsvx** (const gsl_matrix * QR,   Function
       gsl_vector * x)

This function solves the triangular system $Rx = b$ for x in-place. On input x should contain the right-hand side b and is replaced by the solution on output. This function may be useful if the product $b' = Q^T b$ has already been computed using gsl_linalg_QR_QTvec.

int **gsl_linalg_QR_unpack** (const gsl_matrix * QR, const   Function
       gsl_vector * tau, gsl_matrix * Q, gsl_matrix * R)

This function unpacks the encoded QR decomposition (QR,tau) into the matrices Q and R, where Q is M-by-M and R is M-by-N.

int **gsl_linalg_QR_QRsolve** (gsl_matrix * Q, gsl_matrix   Function
       * R, const gsl_vector * b, gsl_vector * x)

This function solves the system $Rx = Q^T b$ for x. It can be used when the QR decomposition of a matrix is available in unpacked form as (Q, R).

int **gsl_linalg_QR_update** (gsl_matrix * Q, gsl_matrix *   Function
       R, gsl_vector * w, const gsl_vector * v)

This function performs a rank-1 update wv^T of the QR decomposition (Q, R). The update is given by $Q'R' = QR + wv^T$ where the output matrices Q' and R' are also orthogonal and right triangular. Note that w is destroyed by the update.

int **gsl_linalg_R_solve** (const gsl_matrix * R, const   Function
       gsl_vector * b, gsl_vector * x)

This function solves the triangular system $Rx = b$ for the N-by-N matrix R.

int **gsl_linalg_R_svx** (const gsl_matrix * R, gsl_vector   Function
       * x)

This function solves the triangular system $Rx = b$ in-place. On input x should contain the right-hand side b, which is replaced by the solution on output.

13.3 QR Decomposition with Column Pivoting

The QR decomposition can be extended to the rank deficient case by introducing a column permutation P,

$$AP = QR$$

The first r columns of Q form an orthonormal basis for the range of A for a matrix with column rank r. This decomposition can also be used to convert the linear system $Ax = b$ into the triangular system $Ry = Q^T b$, $x = Py$, which can be solved by back-substitution and permutation. We denote the QR decomposition with column pivoting by QRP^T since $A = QRP^T$.

int gsl_linalg_QRPT_decomp (gsl_matrix * A, gsl_vector   *Function*
        * tau, gsl_permutation * p, int * *signum*, gsl_vector *
        norm)

This function factorizes the M-by-N matrix A into the QRP^T decomposition $A = QRP^T$. On output the diagonal and upper triangular part of the input matrix contain the matrix R. The permutation matrix P is stored in the permutation p. The sign of the permutation is given by *signum*. It has the value $(-1)^n$, where n is the number of interchanges in the permutation. The vector *tau* and the columns of the lower triangular part of the matrix A contain the Householder coefficients and vectors which encode the orthogonal matrix Q. The vector *tau* must be of length $k = \min(M, N)$. The matrix Q is related to these components by, $Q = Q_k...Q_2 Q_1$ where $Q_i = I - \tau_i v_i v_i^T$ and v_i is the Householder vector $v_i = (0, ..., 1, A(i+1, i), A(i+2, i), ..., A(m, i))$. This is the same storage scheme as used by LAPACK. The vector *norm* is a workspace of length N used for column pivoting.

The algorithm used to perform the decomposition is Householder QR with column pivoting (Golub & Van Loan, *Matrix Computations*, Algorithm 5.4.1).

int gsl_linalg_QRPT_decomp2 (const gsl_matrix * A,   *Function*
        gsl_matrix * q, gsl_matrix * r, gsl_vector * *tau*,
        gsl_permutation * p, int * *signum*, gsl_vector * *norm*)

This function factorizes the matrix A into the decomposition $A = QRP^T$ without modifying A itself and storing the output in the separate matrices q and r.

int gsl_linalg_QRPT_solve (const gsl_matrix * QR,   Function
      const gsl_vector * tau, const gsl_permutation * p,
      const gsl_vector * b, gsl_vector * x)

This function solves the square system $Ax = b$ using the QRP^T decomposition of A into (QR, tau, p) given by gsl_linalg_QRPT_decomp.

int gsl_linalg_QRPT_svx (const gsl_matrix * QR, const   Function
      gsl_vector * tau, const gsl_permutation * p,
      gsl_vector * x)

This function solves the square system $Ax = b$ in-place using the QRP^T decomposition of A into (QR,tau,p). On input x should contain the right-hand side b, which is replaced by the solution on output.

int gsl_linalg_QRPT_QRsolve (const gsl_matrix * Q,   Function
      const gsl_matrix * R, const gsl_permutation * p,
      const gsl_vector * b, gsl_vector * x)

This function solves the square system $RP^T x = Q^T b$ for x. It can be used when the QR decomposition of a matrix is available in unpacked form as (Q, R).

int gsl_linalg_QRPT_update (gsl_matrix * Q, gsl_matrix   Function
      * R, const gsl_permutation * p, gsl_vector * u, const
      gsl_vector * v)

This function performs a rank-1 update wv^T of the QRP^T decomposition (Q, R, p). The update is given by $Q'R' = QR + wv^T$ where the output matrices Q' and R' are also orthogonal and right triangular. Note that w is destroyed by the update. The permutation p is not changed.

int gsl_linalg_QRPT_Rsolve (const gsl_matrix * QR,   Function
      const gsl_permutation * p, const gsl_vector * b,
      gsl_vector * x)

This function solves the triangular system $RP^T x = b$ for the N-by-N matrix R contained in QR.

int gsl_linalg_QRPT_Rsvx (const gsl_matrix * QR, const   Function
      gsl_permutation * p, gsl_vector * x)

This function solves the triangular system $RP^T x = b$ in-place for the N-by-N matrix R contained in QR. On input x should contain the right-hand side b, which is replaced by the solution on output.

13.4 Singular Value Decomposition

A general rectangular M-by-N matrix A has a singular value decomposition (SVD) into the product of an M-by-N orthogonal matrix U, an N-by-N diagonal matrix of singular values S and the transpose of an N-by-N orthogonal square matrix V,

$$A = USV^T$$

The singular values $\sigma_i = S_{ii}$ are all non-negative and are generally chosen to form a non-increasing sequence $\sigma_1 \geq \sigma_2 \geq ... \geq \sigma_N \geq 0$.

The singular value decomposition of a matrix has many practical uses. The condition number of the matrix is given by the ratio of the largest singular value to the smallest singular value. The presence of a zero singular value indicates that the matrix is singular. The number of non-zero singular values indicates the rank of the matrix. In practice singular value decomposition of a rank-deficient matrix will not produce exact zeroes for singular values, due to finite numerical precision. Small singular values should be edited by choosing a suitable tolerance.

For a rank-deficient matrix, the null space of A is given by the columns of V corresponding to the zero singular values. Similarly, the range of A is given by columns of U corresponding to the non-zero singular values.

int gsl_linalg_SV_decomp (gsl_matrix * A, gsl_matrix *   Function
        V, gsl_vector * S, gsl_vector * work)
    This function factorizes the M-by-N matrix A into the singular value decomposition $A = USV^T$ for $M \geq N$. On output the matrix A is replaced by U. The diagonal elements of the singular value matrix S are stored in the vector S. The singular values are non-negative and form a non-increasing sequence from S_1 to S_N. The matrix V contains the elements of V in untransposed form. To form the product USV^T it is necessary to take the transpose of V. A workspace of length N is required in work.

    This routine uses the Golub-Reinsch SVD algorithm.

int gsl_linalg_SV_decomp_mod (gsl_matrix * A,   Function
        gsl_matrix * X, gsl_matrix * V, gsl_vector * S,
        gsl_vector * work)
    This function computes the SVD using the modified Golub-Reinsch algorithm, which is faster for $M \gg N$. It requires the vector work of length N and the N-by-N matrix X as additional working space.

int gsl_linalg_SV_decomp_jacobi (gsl_matrix * A,   Function
        gsl_matrix * V, gsl_vector * S)
This function computes the SVD of the M-by-N matrix A using
one-sided Jacobi orthogonalization for M ≥ N. The Jacobi method
can compute singular values to higher relative accuracy than Golub-
Reinsch algorithms (see references for details).

int gsl_linalg_SV_solve (gsl_matrix * U, gsl_matrix *   Function
        V, gsl_vector * S, const gsl_vector * b, gsl_vector *
        x)
This function solves the system $Ax = b$ using the singular value decomposition (U, S, V) of A given by gsl_linalg_SV_decomp.

Only non-zero singular values are used in computing the solution. The
parts of the solution corresponding to singular values of zero are ignored. Other singular values can be edited out by setting them to zero
before calling this function.

In the over-determined case where A has more rows than columns the
system is solved in the least squares sense, returning the solution x
which minimizes $||Ax - b||_2$.

13.5 Cholesky Decomposition

A symmetric, positive definite square matrix A has a Cholesky decomposition into a product of a lower triangular matrix L and its transpose
L^T,

$$A = LL^T$$

This is sometimes referred to as taking the square-root of a matrix. The
Cholesky decomposition can only be carried out when all the eigenvalues
of the matrix are positive. This decomposition can be used to convert the
linear system $Ax = b$ into a pair of triangular systems $(Ly = b, L^Tx = y)$,
which can be solved by forward and back-substitution.

int gsl_linalg_cholesky_decomp (gsl_matrix * A)   Function
This function factorizes the positive-definite symmetric square matrix
A into the Cholesky decomposition $A = LL^T$. On input only the
diagonal and lower-triangular part of the matrix A are needed. On
output the diagonal and lower triangular part of the input matrix A
contain the matrix L. The upper triangular part of the input matrix
contains L^T, the diagonal terms being identical for both L and L^T.
If the matrix is not positive-definite then the decomposition will fail,
returning the error code GSL_EDOM.

int gsl_linalg_cholesky_solve (const gsl_matrix *   Function
        cholesky, const gsl_vector * b, gsl_vector * x)
  This function solves the system $Ax = b$ using the Cholesky decomposition of A into the matrix cholesky given by gsl_linalg_cholesky_
  decomp.

int gsl_linalg_cholesky_svx (const gsl_matrix *   Function
        cholesky, gsl_vector * x)
  This function solves the system $Ax = b$ in-place using the Cholesky
  decomposition of A into the matrix cholesky given by gsl_linalg_
  cholesky_decomp. On input x should contain the right-hand side b,
  which is replaced by the solution on output.

13.6 Tridiagonal Decomposition of Real Symmetric Matrices

A symmetric matrix A can be factorized by similarity transformations
into the form,

$$A = QTQ^T$$

where Q is an orthogonal matrix and T is a symmetric tridiagonal matrix.

int gsl_linalg_symmtd_decomp (gsl_matrix * A,   Function
        gsl_vector * tau)
  This function factorizes the symmetric square matrix A into the symmetric tridiagonal decomposition QTQ^T. On output the diagonal and
  subdiagonal part of the input matrix A contain the tridiagonal matrix
  T. The remaining lower triangular part of the input matrix contains
  the Householder vectors which, together with the Householder coefficients tau, encode the orthogonal matrix Q. This storage scheme is
  the same as used by LAPACK. The upper triangular part of A is not
  referenced.

int gsl_linalg_symmtd_unpack (const gsl_matrix * A,   Function
        const gsl_vector * tau, gsl_matrix * Q, gsl_vector *
        diag, gsl_vector * subdiag)
  This function unpacks the encoded symmetric tridiagonal decomposition (A, tau) obtained from gsl_linalg_symmtd_decomp into the
  orthogonal matrix Q, the vector of diagonal elements diag and the
  vector of subdiagonal elements subdiag.

int gsl_linalg_symmtd_unpack_T (const gsl_matrix * A,   Function
        gsl_vector * $diag$, gsl_vector * $subdiag$)

This function unpacks the diagonal and subdiagonal of the encoded symmetric tridiagonal decomposition (A, tau) obtained from gsl_linalg_symmtd_decomp into the vectors $diag$ and $subdiag$.

13.7 Tridiagonal Decomposition of Hermitian Matrices

A hermitian matrix A can be factorized by similarity transformations into the form,

$$A = UTU^T$$

where U is a unitary matrix and T is a real symmetric tridiagonal matrix.

int gsl_linalg_hermtd_decomp (gsl_matrix_complex * A,   Function
        gsl_vector_complex * tau)

This function factorizes the hermitian matrix A into the symmetric tridiagonal decomposition UTU^T. On output the real parts of the diagonal and subdiagonal part of the input matrix A contain the tridiagonal matrix T. The remaining lower triangular part of the input matrix contains the Householder vectors which, together with the Householder coefficients tau, encode the orthogonal matrix Q. This storage scheme is the same as used by LAPACK. The upper triangular part of A and imaginary parts of the diagonal are not referenced.

int gsl_linalg_hermtd_unpack (const gsl_matrix_complex   Function
        * A, const gsl_vector_complex * tau,
        gsl_matrix_complex * Q, gsl_vector * $diag$, gsl_vector
        * $subdiag$)

This function unpacks the encoded tridiagonal decomposition (A, tau) obtained from gsl_linalg_hermtd_decomp into the unitary matrix U, the real vector of diagonal elements $diag$ and the real vector of subdiagonal elements $subdiag$.

int gsl_linalg_hermtd_unpack_T (const   Function
        gsl_matrix_complex * A, gsl_vector * $diag$, gsl_vector
        * $subdiag$)

This function unpacks the diagonal and subdiagonal of the encoded tridiagonal decomposition (A, tau) obtained from the gsl_linalg_hermtd_decomp into the real vectors $diag$ and $subdiag$.

13.8 Bidiagonalization

A general matrix A can be factorized by similarity transformations into the form,

$$A = UBV^T$$

where U and V are orthogonal matrices and B is a N-by-N bidiagonal matrix with non-zero entries only on the diagonal and superdiagonal. The size of U is M-by-N and the size of V is N-by-N.

int gsl_linalg_bidiag_decomp (gsl_matrix * A,   Function
   gsl_vector * tau_U, gsl_vector * tau_V)

This function factorizes the M-by-N matrix A into bidiagonal form UBV^T. The diagonal and superdiagonal of the matrix B are stored in the diagonal and superdiagonal of A. The orthogonal matrices U and V are stored as compressed Householder vectors in the remaining elements of A. The Householder coefficients are stored in the vectors tau_U and tau_V. The length of tau_U must equal the number of elements in the diagonal of A and the length of tau_V should be one element shorter.

int gsl_linalg_bidiag_unpack (const gsl_matrix * A,   Function
   const gsl_vector * tau_U, gsl_matrix * U, const
   gsl_vector * tau_V, gsl_matrix * V, gsl_vector * diag,
   gsl_vector * superdiag)

This function unpacks the bidiagonal decomposition of A given by gsl_linalg_bidiag_decomp, (A, tau_U, tau_V) into the separate orthogonal matrices U, V and the diagonal vector diag and superdiagonal superdiag. Note that U is stored as a compact M-by-N orthogonal matrix satisfying $U^T U = I$ for efficiency.

int gsl_linalg_bidiag_unpack2 (gsl_matrix * A,   Function
   gsl_vector * tau_U, gsl_vector * tau_V, gsl_matrix *
   V)

This function unpacks the bidiagonal decomposition of A given by gsl_linalg_bidiag_decomp, (A, tau_U, tau_V) into the separate orthogonal matrices U, V and the diagonal vector diag and superdiagonal superdiag. The matrix U is stored in-place in A.

int gsl_linalg_bidiag_unpack_B (const gsl_matrix * A,   Function
   gsl_vector * diag, gsl_vector * superdiag)

This function unpacks the diagonal and superdiagonal of the bidiagonal decomposition of A given by gsl_linalg_bidiag_decomp, into the diagonal vector diag and superdiagonal vector superdiag.

13.9 Householder Transformations

A Householder transformation is a rank-1 modification of the identity matrix which can be used to zero out selected elements of a vector. A Householder matrix P takes the form,

$$P = I - \tau vv^T$$

where v is a vector (called the *Householder vector*) and $\tau = 2/(v^T v)$. The functions described in this section use the rank-1 structure of the Householder matrix to create and apply Householder transformations efficiently.

double gsl_linalg_householder_transform (gsl_vector *   *Function*
        v)
> This function prepares a Householder transformation $P = I - \tau vv^T$ which can be used to zero all the elements of the input vector except the first. On output the transformation is stored in the vector v and the scalar τ is returned.

int gsl_linalg_householder_hm (double tau, const   *Function*
        gsl_vector * v, gsl_matrix * A)
> This function applies the Householder matrix P defined by the scalar *tau* and the vector v to the left-hand side of the matrix A. On output the result PA is stored in A.

int gsl_linalg_householder_mh (double tau, const   *Function*
        gsl_vector * v, gsl_matrix * A)
> This function applies the Householder matrix P defined by the scalar *tau* and the vector v to the right-hand side of the matrix A. On output the result AP is stored in A.

int gsl_linalg_householder_hv (double tau, const   *Function*
        gsl_vector * v, gsl_vector * w)
> This function applies the Householder transformation P defined by the scalar *tau* and the vector v to the vector w. On output the result Pw is stored in w.

13.10 Householder solver for linear systems

int gsl_linalg_HH_solve (gsl_matrix * A, const   *Function*
        gsl_vector * b, gsl_vector * x)
This function solves the system $Ax = b$ directly using Householder
transformations. On output the solution is stored in x and b is not
modified. The matrix A is destroyed by the Householder transformations.

int gsl_linalg_HH_svx (gsl_matrix * A, gsl_vector * x)   *Function*
This function solves the system $Ax = b$ in-place using Householder
transformations. On input x should contain the right-hand side b,
which is replaced by the solution on output. The matrix A is destroyed
by the Householder transformations.

13.11 Tridiagonal Systems

int gsl_linalg_solve_tridiag (const gsl_vector * diag,   *Function*
        const gsl_vector * e, const gsl_vector * f, const
        gsl_vector * b, gsl_vector * x)
This function solves the general N-by-N system $Ax = b$ where A is
tridiagonal ($N \geq 2$). The super-diagonal and sub-diagonal vectors e
and f must be one element shorter than the diagonal vector diag. The
form of A for the 4-by-4 case is shown below,

$$A = \begin{pmatrix} d_0 & e_0 & 0 & 0 \\ f_0 & d_1 & e_1 & 0 \\ 0 & f_1 & d_2 & e_2 \\ 0 & 0 & f_2 & d_3 \end{pmatrix}$$

int gsl_linalg_solve_symm_tridiag (const gsl_vector *   *Function*
        diag, const gsl_vector * e, const gsl_vector * b,
        gsl_vector * x)
This function solves the general N-by-N system $Ax = b$ where A is
symmetric tridiagonal ($N \geq 2$). The off-diagonal vector e must be one
element shorter than the diagonal vector diag. The form of A for the
4-by-4 case is shown below,

$$A = \begin{pmatrix} d_0 & e_0 & 0 & 0 \\ e_0 & d_1 & e_1 & 0 \\ 0 & e_1 & d_2 & e_2 \\ 0 & 0 & e_2 & d_3 \end{pmatrix}$$

The current implementation uses a variant of Cholesky decomposition
which can cause division by zero if the matrix is not positive definite.

int gsl_linalg_solve_cyc_tridiag (const gsl_vector *   Function
        diag, const gsl_vector * e, const gsl_vector * f, const
        gsl_vector * b, gsl_vector * x)

This function solves the general N-by-N system $Ax = b$ where A is
cyclic tridiagonal ($N \geq 3$). The cyclic super-diagonal and sub-diagonal
vectors e and f must have the same number of elements as the diagonal
vector *diag*. The form of A for the 4-by-4 case is shown below,

$$A = \begin{pmatrix} d_0 & e_0 & 0 & f_3 \\ f_0 & d_1 & e_1 & 0 \\ 0 & f_1 & d_2 & e_2 \\ e_3 & 0 & f_2 & d_3 \end{pmatrix}$$

int gsl_linalg_solve_symm_cyc_tridiag (const   Function
        gsl_vector * *diag*, const gsl_vector * e, const
        gsl_vector * b, gsl_vector * x)

This function solves the general N-by-N system $Ax = b$ where A is
symmetric cyclic tridiagonal ($N \geq 3$). The cyclic off-diagonal vector e
must have the same number of elements as the diagonal vector *diag*.
The form of A for the 4-by-4 case is shown below,

$$A = \begin{pmatrix} d_0 & e_0 & 0 & e_3 \\ e_0 & d_1 & e_1 & 0 \\ 0 & e_1 & d_2 & e_2 \\ e_3 & 0 & e_2 & d_3 \end{pmatrix}$$

13.12 Examples

The following program solves the linear system $Ax = b$. The system
to be solved is,

$$\begin{pmatrix} 0.18 & 0.60 & 0.57 & 0.96 \\ 0.41 & 0.24 & 0.99 & 0.58 \\ 0.14 & 0.30 & 0.97 & 0.66 \\ 0.51 & 0.13 & 0.19 & 0.85 \end{pmatrix} \begin{pmatrix} x_0 \\ x_1 \\ x_2 \\ x_3 \end{pmatrix} = \begin{pmatrix} 1.0 \\ 2.0 \\ 3.0 \\ 4.0 \end{pmatrix}$$

and the solution is found using LU decomposition of the matrix A.

```
#include <stdio.h>
#include <gsl/gsl_linalg.h>

int
main (void)
{
    double a_data[] = { 0.18, 0.60, 0.57, 0.96,
                        0.41, 0.24, 0.99, 0.58,
                        0.14, 0.30, 0.97, 0.66,
```

```
                              0.51, 0.13, 0.19, 0.85 };

     double b_data[] = { 1.0, 2.0, 3.0, 4.0 };

     gsl_matrix_view m
       = gsl_matrix_view_array (a_data, 4, 4);

     gsl_vector_view b
       = gsl_vector_view_array (b_data, 4);

     gsl_vector *x = gsl_vector_alloc (4);

     int s;

     gsl_permutation * p = gsl_permutation_alloc (4);

     gsl_linalg_LU_decomp (&m.matrix, p, &s);

     gsl_linalg_LU_solve (&m.matrix, p, &b.vector, x);

     printf ("x = \n");
     gsl_vector_fprintf (stdout, x, "%g");

     gsl_permutation_free (p);
     return 0;
   }
```

Here is the output from the program,

```
   x = -4.05205
   -12.6056
   1.66091
   8.69377
```

This can be verified by multiplying the solution x by the original matrix A using GNU OCTAVE,

```
   octave> A = [ 0.18, 0.60, 0.57, 0.96;
                 0.41, 0.24, 0.99, 0.58;
                 0.14, 0.30, 0.97, 0.66;
                 0.51, 0.13, 0.19, 0.85 ];

   octave> x = [ -4.05205; -12.6056; 1.66091; 8.69377];

   octave> A * x
   ans =
     1.0000
```

```
2.0000
3.0000
4.0000
```

This reproduces the original right-hand side vector, b, in accordance with the equation $Ax = b$.

13.13 References and Further Reading

Further information on the algorithms described in this section can be found in the following book,

G. H. Golub, C. F. Van Loan, *Matrix Computations* (3rd Ed, 1996), Johns Hopkins University Press, ISBN 0-8018-5414-8.

The Modified Golub-Reinsch algorithm is described in the following paper,

T.F. Chan, "An Improved Algorithm for Computing the Singular Value Decomposition", *ACM Transactions on Mathematical Software*, 8 (1982), pp 72–83.

The Jacobi algorithm for singular value decomposition is described in the following papers,

J.C. Nash, "A one-sided transformation method for the singular value decomposition and algebraic eigenproblem", *Computer Journal*, Volume 18, Number 1 (1973), p 74–76

James Demmel, Kresimir Veselic, "Jacobi's Method is more accurate than QR", *Lapack Working Note 15* (LAWN-15), October 1989. Available from netlib, http://www.netlib.org/lapack/ in the lawns or lawnspdf directories.

14 Eigensystems

This chapter describes functions for computing eigenvalues and eigenvectors of matrices. There are routines for real symmetric and complex hermitian matrices, and eigenvalues can be computed with or without eigenvectors. The algorithms used are symmetric bidiagonalization followed by QR reduction.

The functions described in this chapter are declared in the header file 'gsl_eigen.h'.

14.1 Overview

The eigensystems routines can compute eigenvalues with and without eigenvectors, for symmetric and hermitian matrices. The following table shows the naming convention of the routines:

gsl_eigen_symm
> symmetric matrix, eigenvalues only

gsl_eigen_symmv
> symmetric matrix, eigenvalues and eigenvectors

gsl_eigen_herm
> hermitian matrix, eigenvalues only

gsl_eigen_hermv
> hermitian matrix, eigenvalues and eigenvectors

The computed results are real, except for the eigenvectors of a hermitian matrix which are complex,

All the routines require a workspace. This must be allocated for the specific size of the system, and can be reused for other problems of the same size. Different workspaces are used for each type of system.

14.2 Real Symmetric Matrices

The following routines compute the eigenvalues of a real symmetric matrix. The eigenvalues are all real.

gsl_eigen_symm_workspace * gsl_eigen_symm_alloc   *Function*
(const size_t n)

This function allocates a workspace for computing eigenvalues of n-by-n real symmetric matrices. The size of the workspace is $O(2n)$.

void gsl_eigen_symm_free (gsl_eigen_symm_workspace *   *Function*
w)

This function frees the memory associated with the workspace w.

int gsl_eigen_symm (gsl_matrix * A, gsl_vector * eval,   *Function*
gsl_eigen_symm_workspace * w)

This function computes the eigenvalues of the real symmetric matrix A. Additional workspace of the appropriate size must be provided in w. The diagonal and lower triangular part of A are destroyed during the computation, but the strict upper triangular part is not referenced. The eigenvalues are stored in the vector eval and are unordered.

The following routines compute the eigenvalues and eigenvectors of a real symmetric matrix. The eigenvalues and eigenvectors are all real.

gsl_eigen_symmv_workspace * gsl_eigen_symmv_alloc   *Function*
(const size_t n)

This function allocates a workspace for computing eigenvalues and eigenvectors of n-by-n real symmetric matrices. The size of the workspace is $O(4n)$.

void gsl_eigen_symmv_free (gsl_eigen_symmv_workspace *   *Function*
w)

This function frees the memory associated with the workspace w.

int gsl_eigen_symmv (gsl_matrix * A, gsl_vector * eval,   *Function*
gsl_matrix * evec, gsl_eigen_symmv_workspace * w)

This function computes the eigenvalues and eigenvectors of the real symmetric matrix A. Additional workspace of the appropriate size must be provided in w. The diagonal and lower triangular part of A are destroyed during the computation, but the strict upper triangular part is not referenced. The eigenvalues are stored in the vector eval and are unordered. The corresponding eigenvectors are stored in the columns of the matrix evec. For example, the eigenvector in the first column corresponds to the first eigenvalue. The eigenvectors are guaranteed to be mutually orthogonal and normalised to unit magnitude.

14.3 Complex Hermitian Matrices

The following routines compute the eigenvalues of a hermitian matrix.
The eigenvalues are all real.

gsl_eigen_herm_workspace * gsl_eigen_herm_alloc   *Function*
    (const size_t *n*)

This function allocates a workspace for computing eigenvalues of *n*-by-
n complex hermitian matrices. The size of the workspace is $O(3n)$.

void gsl_eigen_herm_free (gsl_eigen_herm_workspace *   *Function*
    w)

This function frees the memory associated with the workspace *w*.

int gsl_eigen_herm (gsl_matrix_complex * *A*, gsl_vector   *Function*
    * *eval*, gsl_eigen_herm_workspace * *w*)

This function computes the eigenvalues of the complex hermitian matrix *A*. Additional workspace of the appropriate size must be provided
in *w*. The diagonal and lower triangular part of *A* are destroyed during
the computation, but the strict upper triangular part is not referenced.
The imaginary parts of the diagonal are assumed to be zero and are
not referenced. The eigenvalues are stored in the vector *eval* and are
unordered.

The following routines compute the eigenvalues and eigenvectors of
a hermitian matrix. The eigenvalues are real and the eigenvectors are
complex.

gsl_eigen_hermv_workspace * gsl_eigen_hermv_alloc   *Function*
    (const size_t *n*)

This function allocates a workspace for computing eigenvalues and
eigenvectors of *n*-by-*n* complex hermitian matrices. The size of the
workspace is $O(5n)$.

void gsl_eigen_hermv_free (gsl_eigen_hermv_workspace *   *Function*
    w)

This function frees the memory associated with the workspace *w*.

int gsl_eigen_hermv (gsl_matrix_complex * *A*,   *Function*
    gsl_vector * *eval*, gsl_matrix_complex * *evec*,
    gsl_eigen_hermv_workspace * *w*)

This function computes the eigenvalues and eigenvectors of the complex hermitian matrix *A*. Additional workspace of the appropriate size
must be provided in *w*. The diagonal and lower triangular part of *A* are
destroyed during the computation, but the strict upper triangular part
is not referenced. The imaginary parts of the diagonal are assumed

to be zero and are not referenced. The eigenvalues are stored in the vector *eval* and are unordered. The corresponding complex eigenvectors are stored in the columns of the matrix *evec*. For example, the eigenvector in the first column corresponds to the first eigenvalue. The eigenvectors are guaranteed to be mutually orthogonal and normalised to unit magnitude.

14.4 Sorting Eigenvalues and Eigenvectors

The routines in this section can be used to sort eigenvalues and their corresponding eigenvectors.

int gsl_eigen_symmv_sort (gsl_vector * *eval*, gsl_matrix   Function
        * *evec*, gsl_eigen_sort_t *sort_type*)
This function simultaneously sorts the eigenvalues stored in the vector *eval* and the corresponding real eigenvectors stored in the columns of the matrix *evec* into ascending or descending order according to the value of the parameter *sort_type*,

GSL_EIGEN_SORT_VAL_ASC
        ascending order in numerical value

GSL_EIGEN_SORT_VAL_DESC
        descending order in numerical value

GSL_EIGEN_SORT_ABS_ASC
        ascending order in magnitude

GSL_EIGEN_SORT_ABS_DESC
        descending order in magnitude

int gsl_eigen_hermv_sort (gsl_vector * *eval*,   Function
        gsl_matrix_complex * *evec*, gsl_eigen_sort_t *sort_type*)
This function simultaneously sorts the eigenvalues stored in the vector *eval* and the corresponding complex eigenvectors stored in the columns of the matrix *evec* into ascending or descending order according to the value of the parameter *sort_type* as shown above.

14.5 Examples

The following program computes the eigenvalues and eigenvectors of the 4-th order Hilbert matrix, $H(i,j) = 1/(i+j+1)$.

```c
#include <stdio.h>
#include <gsl/gsl_math.h>
#include <gsl/gsl_eigen.h>

int
main (void)
{
  double data[] = { 1.0  , 1/2.0, 1/3.0, 1/4.0,
                    1/2.0, 1/3.0, 1/4.0, 1/5.0,
                    1/3.0, 1/4.0, 1/5.0, 1/6.0,
                    1/4.0, 1/5.0, 1/6.0, 1/7.0 };

  gsl_matrix_view m
    = gsl_matrix_view_array (data, 4, 4);

  gsl_vector *eval = gsl_vector_alloc (4);
  gsl_matrix *evec = gsl_matrix_alloc (4, 4);

  gsl_eigen_symmv_workspace * w =
    gsl_eigen_symmv_alloc (4);

  gsl_eigen_symmv (&m.matrix, eval, evec, w);

  gsl_eigen_symmv_free (w);

  gsl_eigen_symmv_sort (eval, evec,
                        GSL_EIGEN_SORT_ABS_ASC);

  {
    int i;

    for (i = 0; i < 4; i++)
      {
        double eval_i
          = gsl_vector_get (eval, i);
        gsl_vector_view evec_i
          = gsl_matrix_column (evec, i);

        printf ("eigenvalue = %g\n", eval_i);
        printf ("eigenvector = \n");
```

```
                    gsl_vector_fprintf (stdout,
                                     &evec_i.vector, "%g");
        }
    }

    return 0;
}
```

Here is the beginning of the output from the program,

```
$ ./a.out
eigenvalue = 9.67023e-05
eigenvector =
-0.0291933
0.328712
-0.791411
0.514553
...
```

This can be compared with the corresponding output from GNU OCTAVE,

```
octave> [v,d] = eig(hilb(4));
octave> diag(d)
ans =

    9.6702e-05
    6.7383e-03
    1.6914e-01
    1.5002e+00

octave> v
v =

    0.029193    0.179186   -0.582076    0.792608
   -0.328712   -0.741918    0.370502    0.451923
    0.791411    0.100228    0.509579    0.322416
   -0.514553    0.638283    0.514048    0.252161
```

Note that the eigenvectors can differ by a change of sign, since the sign of an eigenvector is arbitrary.

14.6 References and Further Reading

Further information on the algorithms described in this section can be found in the following book,

G. H. Golub, C. F. Van Loan, *Matrix Computations* (3rd Ed, 1996), Johns Hopkins University Press, ISBN 0-8018-5414-8.

15 Fast Fourier Transforms (FFTs)

This chapter describes functions for performing Fast Fourier Transforms (FFTs). The library includes radix-2 routines (for lengths which are a power of two) and mixed-radix routines (which work for any length). For efficiency there are separate versions of these routines for real data and complex data.

The mixed-radix routines are a reimplementation of the FFTPACK library of Paul Swarztrauber. Fortran code for FFTPACK is available on Netlib (FFTPACK also includes some routines for sine and cosine transforms but these are currently not available in GSL).

For details and derivations of the underlying algorithms consult the document *GSL FFT Algorithms* (see Section 15.8 [FFT References and Further Reading], page 208).

15.1 Mathematical Definitions

Fast Fourier Transforms are efficient algorithms for calculating the discrete fourier transform (DFT),

$$x_j = \sum_{k=0}^{N-1} z_k \exp(-2\pi ijk/N)$$

The DFT usually arises as an approximation to the continuous fourier transform when functions are sampled at discrete intervals in space or time. The naive evaluation of the discrete fourier transform is a matrix-vector multiplication $W\vec{z}$ and a general matrix-vector multiplication, such as this, takes $O(N^2)$ operations for N data-points.

Fast fourier transform algorithms use a divide-and-conquer strategy to factorize the matrix W into smaller sub-matrices, corresponding to the integer factors of the length N. If N can be factorized into a product of integers $f_1 f_2 \ldots f_n$ then the DFT can be computed in $O(N \sum f_i)$ operations. For a radix-2 FFT this gives an operation count of $O(N \log_2 N)$.

All the FFT functions offer three types of transform: forwards, inverse and backwards, based on the same mathematical definitions. The definition of the *forward fourier transform*, $x = \text{FFT}(z)$, is,

$$x_j = \sum_{k=0}^{N-1} z_k \exp(-2\pi ijk/N)$$

and the definition of the *inverse fourier transform*, $x = \text{IFFT}(z)$, is,

$$z_j = \frac{1}{N} \sum_{k=0}^{N-1} x_k \exp(2\pi ijk/N).$$

The factor of $1/N$ makes this a true inverse. For example, a call to gsl_fft_complex_forward followed by a call to gsl_fft_complex_inverse should return the original data (within numerical errors).

In general there are two possible choices for the sign of the exponential in the transform/ inverse-transform pair. GSL follows the same convention as FFTPACK, using a negative exponential for the forward transform. The advantage of this convention is that the inverse transform recreates the original function with simple fourier synthesis. Numerical Recipes uses the opposite convention, a positive exponential in the forward transform.

The *backwards FFT* is simply our terminology for an unscaled version of the inverse FFT,

$$z_j^{backwards} = \sum_{k=0}^{N-1} x_k \exp(2\pi ijk/N).$$

When the overall scale of the result is unimportant it is often convenient to use the backwards FFT instead of the inverse to save unnecessary divisions.

15.2   Overview of complex data FFTs

The inputs and outputs for the complex FFT routines are *packed arrays* of floating point numbers. In a packed array the real and imaginary parts of each complex number are placed in alternate neighboring elements. The gsl_complex_packed_array type is used to refer to such arrays and is simply defined as a double * pointer in 'gsl_complex.h'.

For example, the following definition of a packed array of length 6,

```
double x[3*2];
gsl_complex_packed_array data = x;
```

can be used to hold an array of three complex numbers, z[3], in the following way,

```
data[0] = Re(z[0])
data[1] = Im(z[0])
data[2] = Re(z[1])
data[3] = Im(z[1])
data[4] = Re(z[2])
data[5] = Im(z[2])
```

The array indices for the data have the same ordering as those in the definition of the DFT—i.e. there are no index transformations or permutations of the data.

A *stride* parameter allows the user to perform transforms on the elements z[stride*i] instead of z[i]. A stride greater than 1 can be used to take an in-place FFT of the column of a matrix. A stride of 1 accesses the array without any additional spacing between elements.

To perform an FFT on a vector argument, such as gsl_vector_complex * v, use the following definitions (or their equivalents) when calling the functions described in this chapter:

```
gsl_complex_packed_array data = v->data;
size_t stride = v->stride;
size_t n = v->size;
```

For physical applications it is important to remember that the index appearing in the DFT does not correspond directly to a physical frequency. If the time-step of the DFT is Δ then the frequency-domain includes both positive and negative frequencies, ranging from $-1/(2\Delta)$ through 0 to $+1/(2\Delta)$. The positive frequencies are stored from the beginning of the array up to the middle, and the negative frequencies are stored backwards from the end of the array.

Here is a table which shows the layout of the array *data*, and the correspondence between the time-domain data z, and the frequency-domain data x:

index	z	x = FFT(z)
0	z(t = 0)	x(f = 0)
1	z(t = 1)	x(f = 1/(N Delta))
2	z(t = 2)	x(f = 2/(N Delta))
.	. . . .	. . . .
N/2	z(t = N/2)	x(f = +1/(2 Delta), -1/(2 Delta))
.	. . . .	. . . .
N-3	z(t = N-3)	x(f = -3/(N Delta))
N-2	z(t = N-2)	x(f = -2/(N Delta))
N-1	z(t = N-1)	x(f = -1/(N Delta))

When N is even, the location $N/2$ contains the most positive and negative frequencies $(+1/(2\Delta), -1/(2\Delta))$ which are equivalent. If N is odd then the general structure of the table above still applies, but $N/2$ does not appear.

15.3 Radix-2 FFT routines for complex data

The radix-2 algorithms described below are simple and compact, although not necessarily the most efficient. They use the Cooley-Tukey algorithm to compute in-place complex FFTs for lengths which are a power of 2—no additional storage is required. The corresponding self-sorting mixed-radix routines offer better performance at the expense of requiring additional working space.

All the functions described in this section are declared in the header file 'gsl_fft_complex.h'.

int gsl_fft_complex_radix2_forward   Function
        (gsl_complex_packed_array *data*, size_t *stride*, size_t
        n)
int gsl_fft_complex_radix2_backward   Function
        (gsl_complex_packed_array *data*, size_t *stride*, size_t
        n)
int gsl_fft_complex_radix2_inverse   Function
        (gsl_complex_packed_array *data*, size_t *stride*, size_t
        n)
int gsl_fft_complex_radix2_transform   Function
        (gsl_complex_packed_array *data*, size_t *stride*, size_t
        n, gsl_fft_direction *sign*)

These functions compute forward, backward and inverse FFTs of length n with stride *stride*, on the packed complex array *data* using an in-place radix-2 decimation-in-time algorithm. The length of the transform n is restricted to powers of two. For the transform version of the function the *sign* argument can be either gsl_fft_forward (-1) or gsl_fft_backward $(+1)$.

The functions return a value of GSL_SUCCESS if no errors were detected, or GSL_EDOM if the length of the data n is not a power of two.

```
int gsl_fft_complex_radix2_dif_forward                    Function
        (gsl_complex_packed_array data, size_t stride, size_t
        n)
int gsl_fft_complex_radix2_dif_backward                   Function
        (gsl_complex_packed_array data, size_t stride, size_t
        n)
int gsl_fft_complex_radix2_dif_inverse                    Function
        (gsl_complex_packed_array data, size_t stride, size_t
        n)
int gsl_fft_complex_radix2_dif_transform                  Function
        (gsl_complex_packed_array data, size_t stride, size_t
        n, gsl_fft_direction sign)
```

These are decimation-in-frequency versions of the radix-2 FFT functions.

Here is an example program which computes the FFT of a short pulse in a sample of length 128. To make the resulting fourier transform real the pulse is defined for equal positive and negative times $(-10 \ldots 10)$, where the negative times wrap around the end of the array.

```
#include <stdio.h>
#include <math.h>
#include <gsl/gsl_errno.h>
#include <gsl/gsl_fft_complex.h>

#define REAL(z,i) ((z)[2*(i)])
#define IMAG(z,i) ((z)[2*(i)+1])

int
main (void)
{
   int i; double data[2*128];

   for (i = 0; i < 128; i++)
     {
        REAL(data,i) = 0.0; IMAG(data,i) = 0.0;
     }

   REAL(data,0) = 1.0;

   for (i = 1; i <= 10; i++)
     {
        REAL(data,i) = REAL(data,128-i) = 1.0;
     }
```

```
for (i = 0; i < 128; i++)
  {
    printf ("%d %e %e\n", i,
            REAL(data,i), IMAG(data,i));
  }
printf ("\n");

gsl_fft_complex_radix2_forward (data, 1, 128);

for (i = 0; i < 128; i++)
  {
    printf ("%d %e %e\n", i,
            REAL(data,i)/sqrt(128),
            IMAG(data,i)/sqrt(128));
  }

return 0;
}
```

Note that we have assumed that the program is using the default error
handler (which calls abort for any errors). If you are not using a safe error
handler you would need to check the return status of gsl_fft_complex_radix2_forward.

The transformed data is rescaled by $1/\sqrt{N}$ so that it fits on the same
plot as the input. Only the real part is shown, by the choice of the input
data the imaginary part is zero. Allowing for the wrap-around of negative
times at $t = 128$, and working in units of k/N, the DFT approximates
the continuum fourier transform, giving a modulated sine function.

$$\int_{-a}^{+a} e^{-2\pi i k x} dx = \frac{\sin(2\pi ka)}{\pi k}$$

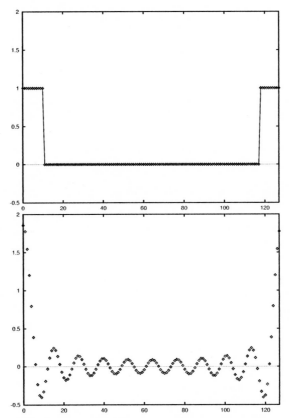

A pulse and its discrete fourier transform, output from the example program.

15.4 Mixed-radix FFT routines for complex data

This section describes mixed-radix FFT algorithms for complex data. The mixed-radix functions work for FFTs of any length. They are a reimplementation of Paul Swarztrauber's Fortran FFTPACK library. The theory is explained in the review article *Self-sorting Mixed-radix FFTs* by Clive Temperton. The routines here use the same indexing scheme and basic algorithms as FFTPACK.

The mixed-radix algorithm is based on sub-transform modules—highly optimized small length FFTs which are combined to create larger FFTs. There are efficient modules for factors of 2, 3, 4, 5, 6 and 7. The modules for the composite factors of 4 and 6 are faster than combining the modules for 2 ∗ 2 and 2 ∗ 3. The factors and their trigonometric lookup tables are stored in a *wavetable*, which must precomputed for transforms of a given length.

For factors which are not implemented as modules there is a fall-back to a general length-n module which uses Singleton's method for efficiently computing a DFT. This module is $O(n^2)$, and slower than a dedicated module would be but works for any length n. Of course, lengths which use the general length-n module will still be factorized as much as possible. For example, a length of 143 will be factorized into $11 * 13$. Large prime factors are the worst case scenario, e.g. as found in $n = 2 * 3 * 99991$, and should be avoided because their $O(n^2)$ scaling will dominate the run-time (consult the document *GSL FFT Algorithms* included in the GSL distribution if you encounter this problem).

The mixed-radix wavetable initialization function returns the list of factors chosen by the library for a given length N. It can be used to check how well the length has been factorized, and estimate the run-time. To a first approximation the run-time scales as $N \sum f_i$, where the f_i are the factors of N. For programs under user control you may wish to issue a warning that the transform will be slow when the length is poorly factorized. If you frequently encounter data lengths which cannot be factorized using the existing small-prime modules consult *GSL FFT Algorithms* for details on adding support for other factors.

All the functions described in this section are declared in the header file 'gsl_fft_complex.h'.

gsl_fft_complex_wavetable *   Function
        gsl_fft_complex_wavetable_alloc (size_t n)
This function prepares a trigonometric lookup table for a complex FFT of length n. The function returns a pointer to the newly allocated gsl_fft_complex_wavetable if no errors were detected, and a null pointer in the case of error. The length n is factorized into a product of subtransforms, and the factors and their trigonometric coefficients are stored in the wavetable. The trigonometric coefficients are computed using direct calls to sin and cos, for accuracy. Recursion relations could be used to compute the lookup table faster, but if an application performs many FFTs of the same length then this computation is a one-off overhead which does not affect the final throughput.

The wavetable structure can be used repeatedly for any transform of the same length. The table is not modified by calls to any of the other FFT functions. The same wavetable can be used for both forward and backward (or inverse) transforms of a given length.

void gsl_fft_complex_wavetable_free   Function
     (gsl_fft_complex_wavetable * *wavetable*)
    This function frees the memory associated with the wavetable
    wavetable. The wavetable can be freed if no further FFTs of the same
    length will be needed.

The gsl_fft_complex_wavetable structure contains internal parameters
for the FFT. It is not necessary to set any of the components directly but
it can sometimes be useful to examine them. For example, the chosen
factorization of the FFT length is given and can be used to provide an
estimate of the run-time or numerical error. The wavetable structure is
declared in the header file 'gsl_fft_complex.h'.

gsl_fft_complex_wavetable   Data Type
    This is a structure that holds the factorization and trigonometric
    lookup tables for the mixed-radix fft algorithm. It has the following
    components:

    size_t n   This is the number of complex data points

    size_t nf   This is the number of factors that the length n was de-
        composed into.

    size_t factor[64]
        This is the array of factors. Only the first nf elements
        are used.

    gsl_complex * trig
        This is a pointer to a preallocated trigonometric lookup
        table of n complex elements.

    gsl_complex * twiddle[64]
        This is an array of pointers into trig, giving the twiddle
        factors for each pass.

The mixed radix algorithms require additional working space to hold the
intermediate steps of the transform.

gsl_fft_complex_workspace *   Function
     gsl_fft_complex_workspace_alloc (size_t *n*)
    This function allocates a workspace for a complex transform of length
    n.

void gsl_fft_complex_workspace_free   Function
     (gsl_fft_complex_workspace * *workspace*)
    This function frees the memory associated with the workspace
    workspace. The workspace can be freed if no further FFTs of the
    same length will be needed.

The following functions compute the transform,

int gsl_fft_complex_forward (gsl_complex_packed_array   *Function*
   data, size_t *stride*, size_t *n*, const
   gsl_fft_complex_wavetable * *wavetable*,
   gsl_fft_complex_workspace * *work*)

int gsl_fft_complex_backward   *Function*
   (gsl_complex_packed_array *data*, size_t *stride*, size_t
   n, const gsl_fft_complex_wavetable * *wavetable*,
   gsl_fft_complex_workspace * *work*)

int gsl_fft_complex_inverse (gsl_complex_packed_array   *Function*
   data, size_t *stride*, size_t *n*, const
   gsl_fft_complex_wavetable * *wavetable*,
   gsl_fft_complex_workspace * *work*)

int gsl_fft_complex_transform   *Function*
   (gsl_complex_packed_array *data*, size_t *stride*, size_t
   n, const gsl_fft_complex_wavetable * *wavetable*,
   gsl_fft_complex_workspace * *work*, gsl_fft_direction
   sign)

These functions compute forward, backward and inverse FFTs of length n with stride *stride*, on the packed complex array *data*, using a mixed radix decimation-in-frequency algorithm. There is no restriction on the length n. Efficient modules are provided for subtransforms of length 2, 3, 4, 5, 6 and 7. Any remaining factors are computed with a general $O(n^2)$ module. The caller must supply a *wavetable* containing the trigonometric lookup tables and a workspace *work*. For the transform version of the function the *sign* argument can be either gsl_fft_forward (-1) or gsl_fft_backward ($+1$).

The functions return a value of 0 if no errors were detected. The following gsl_errno conditions are defined for these functions:

GSL_EDOM The length of the data n is not a positive integer (i.e. n is zero).

GSL_EINVAL

   The length of the data n and the length used to compute the given *wavetable* do not match.

Here is an example program which computes the FFT of a short pulse in a sample of length 630 ($= 2*3*3*5*7$) using the mixed-radix algorithm.

```
#include <stdio.h>
#include <math.h>
#include <gsl/gsl_errno.h>
#include <gsl/gsl_fft_complex.h>
```

```
#define REAL(z,i) ((z)[2*(i)])
#define IMAG(z,i) ((z)[2*(i)+1])

int
main (void)
{
  int i;
  const int n = 630;
  double data[2*n];

  gsl_fft_complex_wavetable * wavetable;
  gsl_fft_complex_workspace * workspace;

  for (i = 0; i < n; i++)
    {
      REAL(data,i) = 0.0;
      IMAG(data,i) = 0.0;
    }

  data[0] = 1.0;

  for (i = 1; i <= 10; i++)
    {
      REAL(data,i) = REAL(data,n-i) = 1.0;
    }

  for (i = 0; i < n; i++)
    {
      printf ("%d: %e %e\n", i, REAL(data,i),
                                IMAG(data,i));
    }
  printf ("\n");

  wavetable = gsl_fft_complex_wavetable_alloc (n);
  workspace = gsl_fft_complex_workspace_alloc (n);

  for (i = 0; i < wavetable->nf; i++)
    {
      printf ("# factor %d: %d\n", i,
              wavetable->factor[i]);
    }

  gsl_fft_complex_forward (data, 1, n,
```

```
                              wavetable, workspace);

    for (i = 0; i < n; i++)
      {
        printf ("%d: %e %e\n", i, REAL(data,i),
                                   IMAG(data,i));
      }

    gsl_fft_complex_wavetable_free (wavetable);
    gsl_fft_complex_workspace_free (workspace);
    return 0;
  }
```

Note that we have assumed that the program is using the default gsl error handler (which calls abort for any errors). If you are not using a safe error handler you would need to check the return status of all the gsl routines.

15.5 Overview of real data FFTs

The functions for real data are similar to those for complex data. However, there is an important difference between forward and inverse transforms. The fourier transform of a real sequence is not real. It is a complex sequence with a special symmetry:

$$z_k = z_{N-k}^*$$

A sequence with this symmetry is called *conjugate-complex* or *half-complex*. This different structure requires different storage layouts for the forward transform (from real to half-complex) and inverse transform (from half-complex back to real). As a consequence the routines are divided into two sets: functions in gsl_fft_real which operate on real sequences and functions in gsl_fft_halfcomplex which operate on half-complex sequences.

Functions in gsl_fft_real compute the frequency coefficients of a real sequence. The half-complex coefficients c_k of a real sequence x_j are given by fourier analysis,

$$c_k = \sum_{j=0}^{N-1} x_j \exp(-2\pi i jk/N)$$

Functions in gsl_fft_halfcomplex compute inverse or backwards transforms. They reconstruct real sequences by fourier synthesis from their half-complex frequency coefficients, c_k,

$$x_j = \frac{1}{N} \sum_{k=0}^{N-1} c_k \exp(2\pi i j k / N)$$

The symmetry of the half-complex sequence implies that only half of the complex numbers in the output need to be stored. The remaining half can be reconstructed using the half-complex symmetry condition. This works for all lengths, even and odd—when the length is even, the middle coefficient $k = N/2$ is also real. Thus only N real numbers are required to store the half-complex sequence, and the transform of a real sequence can be stored in the same size array as the original data.

The precise storage arrangements depend on the algorithm, and are different for radix-2 and mixed-radix routines. The radix-2 function operates in-place, which constrains the locations where each element can be stored. The restriction forces real and imaginary parts to be stored far apart. The mixed-radix algorithm does not have this restriction, and it stores the real and imaginary parts of a given term in neighboring locations (which is desirable for better locality of memory accesses).

15.6 Radix-2 FFT routines for real data

This section describes radix-2 FFT algorithms for real data. They use the Cooley-Tukey algorithm to compute in-place FFTs for lengths which are a power of 2.

The radix-2 FFT functions for real data are declared in the header files 'gsl_fft_real.h'

int gsl_fft_real_radix2_transform (double *data[]*,   Function
        size_t *stride*, size_t *n*)

This function computes an in-place radix-2 FFT of length n and stride *stride* on the real array *data*. The output is a half-complex sequence, which is stored in-place. The arrangement of the half-complex terms uses the following scheme: for $k < N/2$ the real part of the k-th term is stored in location k, and the corresponding imaginary part is stored in location $N - k$. Terms with $k > N/2$ can be reconstructed using the symmetry $z_k = z^*_{N-k}$. The terms for $k = 0$ and $k = N/2$ are both purely real, and count as a special case. Their real parts are stored in locations 0 and $N/2$ respectively, while their imaginary parts (which are zero) are not stored.

The following table shows the correspondence between the output *data* and the equivalent results obtained by considering the input data as a complex sequence with zero imaginary part,

```
complex[0].real    =    data[0]
complex[0].imag    =    0
complex[1].real    =    data[1]
complex[1].imag    =    data[N-1]
..............          ................
complex[k].real    =    data[k]
complex[k].imag    =    data[N-k]
..............          ................
complex[N/2].real  =    data[N/2]
complex[N/2].imag  =    0
..............          ................
complex[k'].real   =    data[k]        k' = N - k
complex[k'].imag   =    -data[N-k]
..............          ................
complex[N-1].real  =    data[1]
complex[N-1].imag  =    -data[N-1]
```

The radix-2 FFT functions for half-complex data are declared in the header file 'gsl_fft_halfcomplex.h'.

int gsl_fft_halfcomplex_radix2_inverse (double *data*[],   Function
       size_t *stride*, size_t *n*)

int gsl_fft_halfcomplex_radix2_backward (double *data*[],   Function
       size_t *stride*, size_t *n*)

These functions compute the inverse or backwards in-place radix-2 FFT of length *n* and stride *stride* on the half-complex sequence *data* stored according the output scheme used by gsl_fft_real_radix2. The result is a real array stored in natural order.

15.7 Mixed-radix FFT routines for real data

This section describes mixed-radix FFT algorithms for real data. The mixed-radix functions work for FFTs of any length. They are a reimplementation of the real-FFT routines in the Fortran FFTPACK library by Paul Swarztrauber. The theory behind the algorithm is explained in the article *Fast Mixed-Radix Real Fourier Transforms* by Clive Temperton. The routines here use the same indexing scheme and basic algorithms as FFTPACK.

The functions use the FFTPACK storage convention for half-complex sequences. In this convention the half-complex transform of a real sequence is stored with frequencies in increasing order, starting at zero, with the real and imaginary parts of each frequency in neighboring locations. When a value is known to be real the imaginary part is not stored. The imaginary part of the zero-frequency component is never stored. It is known to be zero (since the zero frequency component is simply the sum of the input data, all real). For a sequence of even length the imaginary part of the frequency $n/2$ is not stored either, since the symmetry $z_k = z^*_{N-k}$ implies that this is purely real too.

The storage scheme is best shown by some examples. The table below shows the output for an odd-length sequence, $n = 5$. The two columns give the correspondence between the 5 values in the half-complex sequence returned by `gsl_fft_real_transform`, *halfcomplex*[] and the values *complex*[] that would be returned if the same real input sequence were passed to `gsl_fft_complex_backward` as a complex sequence (with imaginary parts set to 0),

```
complex[0].real  =   halfcomplex[0]
complex[0].imag  =   0
complex[1].real  =   halfcomplex[1]
complex[1].imag  =   halfcomplex[2]
complex[2].real  =   halfcomplex[3]
complex[2].imag  =   halfcomplex[4]
complex[3].real  =   halfcomplex[3]
complex[3].imag  =  -halfcomplex[4]
complex[4].real  =   halfcomplex[1]
complex[4].imag  =  -halfcomplex[2]
```

The upper elements of the *complex* array, complex[3] and complex[4] are filled in using the symmetry condition. The imaginary part of the zero-frequency term complex[0].imag is known to be zero by the symmetry.

The next table shows the output for an even-length sequence, $n = 6$ In the even case there are two values which are purely real,

```
complex[0].real  =   halfcomplex[0]
complex[0].imag  =   0
complex[1].real  =   halfcomplex[1]
complex[1].imag  =   halfcomplex[2]
complex[2].real  =   halfcomplex[3]
complex[2].imag  =   halfcomplex[4]
complex[3].real  =   halfcomplex[5]
complex[3].imag  =   0
complex[4].real  =   halfcomplex[3]
complex[4].imag  =  -halfcomplex[4]
complex[5].real  =   halfcomplex[1]
complex[5].imag  =  -halfcomplex[2]
```

The upper elements of the *complex* array, complex[4] and complex[5] are filled in using the symmetry condition. Both complex[0].imag and complex[3].imag are known to be zero.

All these functions are declared in the header files 'gsl_fft_real.h' and 'gsl_fft_halfcomplex.h'.

gsl_fft_real_wavetable * gsl_fft_real_wavetable_alloc   Function
        (size_t *n*)
gsl_fft_halfcomplex_wavetable *   Function
        gsl_fft_halfcomplex_wavetable_alloc (size_t *n*)

These functions prepare trigonometric lookup tables for an FFT of size *n* real elements. The functions return a pointer to the newly allocated struct if no errors were detected, and a null pointer in the case of error. The length *n* is factorized into a product of subtransforms, and the factors and their trigonometric coefficients are stored in the wavetable. The trigonometric coefficients are computed using direct calls to sin and cos, for accuracy. Recursion relations could be used to compute the lookup table faster, but if an application performs many FFTs of the same length then computing the wavetable is a one-off overhead which does not affect the final throughput.

The wavetable structure can be used repeatedly for any transform of the same length. The table is not modified by calls to any of the other FFT functions. The appropriate type of wavetable must be used for forward real or inverse half-complex transforms.

void gsl_fft_real_wavetable_free   Function
        (gsl_fft_real_wavetable * *wavetable*)
void gsl_fft_halfcomplex_wavetable_free   Function
        (gsl_fft_halfcomplex_wavetable * *wavetable*)

These functions free the memory associated with the wavetable *wavetable*. The wavetable can be freed if no further FFTs of the same length will be needed.

The mixed radix algorithms require additional working space to hold the intermediate steps of the transform,

gsl_fft_real_workspace * gsl_fft_real_workspace_alloc   Function
        (size_t *n*)

This function allocates a workspace for a real transform of length *n*. The same workspace can be used for both forward real and inverse halfcomplex transforms.

void gsl_fft_real_workspace_free   Function
        (gsl_fft_real_workspace * *workspace*)

This function frees the memory associated with the workspace *workspace*. The workspace can be freed if no further FFTs of the same length will be needed.

The following functions compute the transforms of real and half-complex data,

int gsl_fft_real_transform (double *data*[], size_t *stride,*   Function
        size_t *n*, const gsl_fft_real_wavetable * *wavetable,*
        gsl_fft_real_workspace * *work*)

int gsl_fft_halfcomplex_transform (double *data*[],   Function
        size_t *stride*, size_t *n*, const
        gsl_fft_halfcomplex_wavetable * *wavetable,*
        gsl_fft_real_workspace * *work*)

These functions compute the FFT of *data*, a real or half-complex array
of length *n*, using a mixed radix decimation-in-frequency algorithm.
For gsl_fft_real_transform *data* is an array of time-ordered real
data. For gsl_fft_halfcomplex_transform *data* contains fourier coefficients in the half-complex ordering described above. There is no
restriction on the length *n*. Efficient modules are provided for subtransforms of length 2, 3, 4 and 5. Any remaining factors are computed
with a general $O(n^2)$ module. The caller must supply a *wavetable* containing trigonometric lookup tables and a workspace *work*.

int gsl_fft_real_unpack (const double *real_coefficient*[],   Function
        gsl_complex_packed_array *complex_coefficient*, size_t
        stride, size_t *n*)

This function converts a single real array, *real_coefficient* into an equivalent complex array, *complex_coefficient*, (with imaginary part set to
zero), suitable for gsl_fft_complex routines. The algorithm for the
conversion is simply,

```
for (i = 0; i < n; i++)
  {
    complex_coefficient[i].real
      = real_coefficient[i];
    complex_coefficient[i].imag
      = 0.0;
  }
```

int gsl_fft_halfcomplex_unpack (const double   Function
        halfcomplex_coefficient[], gsl_complex_packed_array
        complex_coefficient, size_t *stride*, size_t *n*)

This function converts *halfcomplex_coefficient*, an array of half-
complex coefficients as returned by gsl_fft_real_transform, into
an ordinary complex array, *complex_coefficient*. It fills in the complex
array using the symmetry $z_k = z_{N-k}^*$ to reconstruct the redundant
elements. The algorithm for the conversion is,

```
complex_coefficient[0].real
  = halfcomplex_coefficient[0];
complex_coefficient[0].imag
  = 0.0;

for (i = 1; i < n - i; i++)
  {
    double hc_real
      = halfcomplex_coefficient[2 * i - 1];
    double hc_imag
      = halfcomplex_coefficient[2 * i];
    complex_coefficient[i].real = hc_real;
    complex_coefficient[i].imag = hc_imag;
    complex_coefficient[n - i].real = hc_real;
    complex_coefficient[n - i].imag = -hc_imag;
  }

if (i == n - i)
  {
    complex_coefficient[i].real
      = halfcomplex_coefficient[n - 1];
    complex_coefficient[i].imag
      = 0.0;
  }
```

Here is an example program using gsl_fft_real_transform and gsl_fft_halfcomplex_inverse. It generates a real signal in the shape of a square pulse. The pulse is fourier transformed to frequency space, and all but the lowest ten frequency components are removed from the array of fourier coefficients returned by gsl_fft_real_transform.

The remaining fourier coefficients are transformed back to the time-domain, to give a filtered version of the square pulse. Since fourier coefficients are stored using the half-complex symmetry both positive and negative frequencies are removed and the final filtered signal is also real.

```
#include <stdio.h>
#include <math.h>
#include <gsl/gsl_errno.h>
#include <gsl/gsl_fft_real.h>
#include <gsl/gsl_fft_halfcomplex.h>

int
main (void)
{
```

```
int i, n = 100;
double data[n];

gsl_fft_real_wavetable * real;
gsl_fft_halfcomplex_wavetable * hc;
gsl_fft_real_workspace * work;

for (i = 0; i < n; i++)
  {
    data[i] = 0.0;
  }

for (i = n / 3; i < 2 * n / 3; i++)
  {
    data[i] = 1.0;
  }

for (i = 0; i < n; i++)
  {
    printf ("%d: %e\n", i, data[i]);
  }
printf ("\n");

work = gsl_fft_real_workspace_alloc (n);
real = gsl_fft_real_wavetable_alloc (n);

gsl_fft_real_transform (data, 1, n,
                        real, work);

gsl_fft_real_wavetable_free (real);

for (i = 11; i < n; i++)
  {
    data[i] = 0;
  }

hc = gsl_fft_halfcomplex_wavetable_alloc (n);

gsl_fft_halfcomplex_inverse (data, 1, n,
                             hc, work);
gsl_fft_halfcomplex_wavetable_free (hc);

for (i = 0; i < n; i++)
```

```
    {
        printf ("%d: %e\n", i, data[i]);
    }

  gsl_fft_real_workspace_free (work);
  return 0;
}
```

Low-pass filtered version of a real pulse,
output from the example program.

15.8 References and Further Reading

A good starting point for learning more about the FFT is the review article *Fast Fourier Transforms: A Tutorial Review and A State of the Art* by Duhamel and Vetterli,

> P. Duhamel and M. Vetterli. Fast fourier transforms: A tutorial review and a state of the art. *Signal Processing*, 19:259–299, 1990.

To find out about the algorithms used in the GSL routines you may want to consult the document *GSL FFT Algorithms* (it is included in GSL, as 'doc/fftalgorithms.tex'). This has general information on FFTs and explicit derivations of the implementation for each routine. There are also references to the relevant literature. For convenience some of the more important references are reproduced below.

There are several introductory books on the FFT with example programs, such as *The Fast Fourier Transform* by Brigham and *DFT/FFT and Convolution Algorithms* by Burrus and Parks,

E. Oran Brigham. *The Fast Fourier Transform*. Prentice Hall, 1974.

C. S. Burrus and T. W. Parks. *DFT/FFT and Convolution Algorithms*. Wiley, 1984.

Both these introductory books cover the radix-2 FFT in some detail. The mixed-radix algorithm at the heart of the FFTPACK routines is reviewed in Clive Temperton's paper,

Clive Temperton. Self-sorting mixed-radix fast fourier transforms. *Journal of Computational Physics*, 52(1):1–23, 1983.

The derivation of FFTs for real-valued data is explained in the following two articles,

Henrik V. Sorenson, Douglas L. Jones, Michael T. Heideman, and C. Sidney Burrus. Real-valued fast fourier transform algorithms. *IEEE Transactions on Acoustics, Speech, and Signal Processing*, ASSP-35(6):849–863, 1987.

Clive Temperton. Fast mixed-radix real fourier transforms. *Journal of Computational Physics*, 52:340–350, 1983.

In 1979 the IEEE published a compendium of carefully-reviewed Fortran FFT programs in *Programs for Digital Signal Processing*. It is a useful reference for implementations of many different FFT algorithms,

Digital Signal Processing Committee and IEEE Acoustics, Speech, and Signal Processing Committee, editors. *Programs for Digital Signal Processing*. IEEE Press, 1979.

For large-scale FFT work we recommend the use of the dedicated FFTW library by Frigo and Johnson. The FFTW library is self-optimizing—it automatically tunes itself for each hardware platform in order to achieve maximum performance. It is available under the GNU GPL.

FFTW Website, http://www.fftw.org/

The source code for FFTPACK is available from Netlib,

FFTPACK, http://www.netlib.org/fftpack/

16 Numerical Integration

This chapter describes routines for performing numerical integration (quadrature) of a function in one dimension. There are routines for adaptive and non-adaptive integration of general functions, with specialised routines for specific cases. These include integration over infinite and semi-infinite ranges, singular integrals, including logarithmic singularities, computation of Cauchy principal values and oscillatory integrals. The library reimplements the algorithms used in QUADPACK, a numerical integration package written by Piessens, Doncker-Kapenga, Uberhuber and Kahaner. Fortran code for QUADPACK is available on Netlib.

The functions described in this chapter are declared in the header file 'gsl_integration.h'.

16.1 Introduction

Each algorithm computes an approximation to a definite integral of the form,

$$I = \int_a^b f(x)w(x)\,dx$$

where $w(x)$ is a weight function (for general integrands $w(x) = 1$). The user provides absolute and relative error bounds (*epsabs*, *epsrel*) which specify the following accuracy requirement,

$$|RESULT - I| \le \max(epsabs, epsrel\,|I|)$$

where $RESULT$ is the numerical approximation obtained by the algorithm. The algorithms attempt to estimate the absolute error $ABSERR = |RESULT - I|$ in such a way that the following inequality holds,

$$|RESULT - I| \le ABSERR \le \max(epsabs, epsrel\,|I|)$$

The routines will fail to converge if the error bounds are too stringent, but always return the best approximation obtained up to that stage.

The algorithms in QUADPACK use a naming convention based on the following letters,

Q - quadrature routine

N - non-adaptive integrator
A - adaptive integrator

G - general integrand (user-defined)

W - weight function with integrand

S - singularities can be more readily integrated
P - points of special difficulty can be supplied
I - infinite range of integration
O - oscillatory weight function, cos or sin
F - Fourier integral
C - Cauchy principal value

The algorithms are built on pairs of quadrature rules, a higher order rule and a lower order rule. The higher order rule is used to compute the best approximation to an integral over a small range. The difference between the results of the higher order rule and the lower order rule gives an estimate of the error in the approximation.

16.1.1 Integrands without weight functions

The algorithms for general functions (without a weight function) are based on Gauss-Kronrod rules.

A Gauss-Kronrod rule begins with a classical Gaussian quadrature rule of order m. This is extended with additional points between each of the abscissae to give a higher order Kronrod rule of order $2m + 1$. The Kronrod rule is efficient because it reuses existing function evaluations from the Gaussian rule.

The higher order Kronrod rule is used as the best approximation to the integral, and the difference between the two rules is used as an estimate of the error in the approximation.

16.1.2 Integrands with weight functions

For integrands with weight functions the algorithms use Clenshaw-Curtis quadrature rules.

A Clenshaw-Curtis rule begins with an n-th order Chebyshev polynomial approximation to the integrand. This polynomial can be integrated exactly to give an approximation to the integral of the original function. The Chebyshev expansion can be extended to higher orders to improve the approximation and provide an estimate of the error.

16.1.3 Integrands with singular weight functions

The presence of singularities (or other behavior) in the integrand can cause slow convergence in the Chebyshev approximation. The modified Clenshaw-Curtis rules used in QUADPACK separate out several common weight functions which cause slow convergence.

These weight functions are integrated analytically against the Chebyshev polynomials to precompute *modified Chebyshev moments*. Combining the moments with the Chebyshev approximation to the function gives the desired integral. The use of analytic integration for the singular part of the function allows exact cancellations and substantially improves the overall convergence behavior of the integration.

16.2 QNG non-adaptive Gauss-Kronrod integration

The QNG algorithm is a non-adaptive procedure which uses fixed Gauss-Kronrod abscissae to evaluate the integrand at up to 87 sample points. It is provided for fast integration of smooth functions.

int gsl_integration_qng (const gsl_function * f, double   Function
        a, double b, double epsabs, double epsrel, double *
        result, double * abserr, size_t * neval)

This function applies the Gauss-Kronrod 10-point, 21-point, 43-point and 87-point integration rules in succession until an estimate of the integral of f over (a, b) is achieved within the desired absolute and relative error limits, *epsabs* and *epsrel*. The function returns the final approximation, *result*, an estimate of the absolute error, *abserr* and the number of function evaluations used, *neval*. The Gauss-Kronrod rules are designed in such a way that each rule uses all the results of its predecessors, in order to minimize the total number of function evaluations.

16.3 QAG adaptive integration

The QAG algorithm is a simple adaptive integration procedure. The integration region is divided into subintervals, and on each iteration the subinterval with the largest estimated error is bisected. This reduces the overall error rapidly, as the subintervals become concentrated around local difficulties in the integrand. These subintervals are managed by a gsl_integration_workspace struct, which handles the memory for the subinterval ranges, results and error estimates.

gsl_integration_workspace *   Function
      gsl_integration_workspace_alloc (size_t n)

This function allocates a workspace sufficient to hold n double precision intervals, their integration results and error estimates.

void gsl_integration_workspace_free   Function
      (gsl_integration_workspace * w)

This function frees the memory associated with the workspace w.

int gsl_integration_qag (const gsl_function * f, double   Function
      a, double b, double *epsabs*, double *epsrel*, size_t *limit*,
      int *key*, gsl_integration_workspace * *workspace*,
      double * *result*, double * *abserr*)

This function applies an integration rule adaptively until an estimate of the integral of f over (a, b) is achieved within the desired absolute and relative error limits, *epsabs* and *epsrel*. The function returns the final approximation, *result*, and an estimate of the absolute error, *abserr*. The integration rule is determined by the value of *key*, which should be chosen from the following symbolic names,

    GSL_INTEG_GAUSS15   (key = 1)
    GSL_INTEG_GAUSS21   (key = 2)
    GSL_INTEG_GAUSS31   (key = 3)
    GSL_INTEG_GAUSS41   (key = 4)
    GSL_INTEG_GAUSS51   (key = 5)
    GSL_INTEG_GAUSS61   (key = 6)

corresponding to the 15, 21, 31, 41, 51 and 61 point Gauss-Kronrod rules. The higher-order rules give better accuracy for smooth functions, while lower-order rules save time when the function contains local difficulties, such as discontinuities.

On each iteration the adaptive integration strategy bisects the interval with the largest error estimate. The subintervals and their results are stored in the memory provided by *workspace*. The maximum number of subintervals is given by *limit*, which may not exceed the allocated size of the workspace.

16.4 QAGS adaptive integration with singularities

The presence of an integrable singularity in the integration region causes an adaptive routine to concentrate new subintervals around the singularity. As the subintervals decrease in size the successive approximations to the integral converge in a limiting fashion. This approach to the limit can be accelerated using an extrapolation procedure. The QAGS algorithm combines adaptive bisection with the Wynn epsilon-algorithm to speed up the integration of many types of integrable singularities.

int gsl_integration_qags (const gsl_function * f,   Function
        double a, double b, double epsabs, double epsrel,
        size_t limit, gsl_integration_workspace * workspace,
        double * result, double * abserr)

This function applies the Gauss-Kronrod 21-point integration rule adaptively until an estimate of the integral of f over (a, b) is achieved within the desired absolute and relative error limits, epsabs and epsrel. The results are extrapolated using the epsilon-algorithm, which accelerates the convergence of the integral in the presence of discontinuities and integrable singularities. The function returns the final approximation from the extrapolation, result, and an estimate of the absolute error, abserr. The subintervals and their results are stored in the memory provided by workspace. The maximum number of subintervals is given by limit, which may not exceed the allocated size of the workspace.

16.5 QAGP adaptive integration with known singular points

int gsl_integration_qagp (const gsl_function * f,   Function
        double * pts, size_t npts, double epsabs, double epsrel,
        size_t limit, gsl_integration_workspace * workspace,
        double * result, double * abserr)

This function applies the adaptive integration algorithm QAGS taking account of the user-supplied locations of singular points. The array pts of length npts should contain the endpoints of the integration ranges defined by the integration region and locations of the singularities. For example, to integrate over the region (a, b) with break-points at x_1, x_2, x_3 (where $a < x_1 < x_2 < x_3 < b$) the following pts array should be used

```
pts[0] = a
pts[1] = x1
pts[2] = x2
pts[3] = x3
pts[4] = b
```

with $npts = 5$.

If the locations of the singular points in the integration region are known then this routine will be significantly faster than QAGS.

16.6 QAGI adaptive integration on infinite intervals

int gsl_integration_qagi (gsl_function * f, double   *Function*
       epsabs, double epsrel, size_t limit,
       gsl_integration_workspace * workspace, double *
       result, double * abserr)

This function computes the integral of the function f over the infinite interval $(-\infty, +\infty)$. The integral is mapped onto the semi-open interval $(0, 1]$ using the transformation $x = (1 - t)/t$,

$$\int_{-\infty}^{+\infty} dx\, f(x) = \int_{0}^{1} dt\, (f((1-t)/t) + f(-(1-t)/t))/t^2.$$

It is then integrated using the QAGS algorithm. The normal 21-point Gauss-Kronrod rule of QAGS is replaced by a 15-point rule, because the transformation can generate an integrable singularity at the origin. In this case a lower-order rule is more efficient.

int gsl_integration_qagiu (gsl_function * f, double a,   *Function*
       double epsabs, double epsrel, size_t limit,
       gsl_integration_workspace * workspace, double *
       result, double * abserr)

This function computes the integral of the function f over the semi-infinite interval $(a, +\infty)$. The integral is mapped onto the semi-open interval $(0, 1]$ using the transformation $x = a + (1 - t)/t$,

$$\int_{a}^{+\infty} dx\, f(x) = \int_{0}^{1} dt\, f(a + (1-t)/t)/t^2$$

and then integrated using the QAGS algorithm.

int gsl_integration_qagil (gsl_function * f, double b,   Function
        double epsabs, double epsrel, size_t limit,
        gsl_integration_workspace * workspace, double *
        result, double * abserr)

This function computes the integral of the function f over the semi-infinite interval $(-\infty, b)$. The integral is mapped onto the semi-open interval $(0, 1]$ using the transformation $x = b - (1 - t)/t$,

$$\int_{-\infty}^{b} dx\, f(x) = \int_{0}^{1} dt\, f(b - (1 - t)/t)/t^2$$

and then integrated using the QAGS algorithm.

16.7 QAWC adaptive integration for Cauchy principal values

int gsl_integration_qawc (gsl_function * f, double a,   Function
        double b, double c, double epsabs, double epsrel,
        size_t limit, gsl_integration_workspace * workspace,
        double * result, double * abserr)

This function computes the Cauchy principal value of the integral of f over (a, b), with a singularity at c,

$$I = \int_{a}^{b} dx\, \frac{f(x)}{x - c} = \lim_{\epsilon \to 0} \left\{ \int_{a}^{c-\epsilon} dx\, \frac{f(x)}{x - c} + \int_{c+\epsilon}^{b} dx\, \frac{f(x)}{x - c} \right\}$$

The adaptive bisection algorithm of QAG is used, with modifications to ensure that subdivisions do not occur at the singular point $x = c$. When a subinterval contains the point $x = c$ or is close to it then a special 25-point modified Clenshaw-Curtis rule is used to control the singularity. Further away from the singularity the algorithm uses an ordinary 15-point Gauss-Kronrod integration rule.

16.8 QAWS adaptive integration for singular functions

The QAWS algorithm is designed for integrands with algebraic-logarithmic singularities at the end-points of an integration region. In order to work efficiently the algorithm requires a precomputed table of Chebyshev moments.

gsl_integration_qaws_table *   Function
        gsl_integration_qaws_table_alloc (double alpha,
        double beta, int mu, int nu)

This function allocates space for a gsl_integration_qaws_table struct and its associated workspace describing a singular weight function $W(x)$ with the parameters $(\alpha, \beta, \mu, \nu)$,

$$W(x) = (x - a)^{\alpha}(b - x)^{\beta} \log^{\mu}(x - a) \log^{\nu}(b - x)$$

where $\alpha > -1$, $\beta > -1$, and $\mu = 0, 1$, $\nu = 0, 1$. The weight function can take four different forms depending on the values of μ and ν,

$$
\begin{aligned}
W(x) &= (x - a)^{\alpha}(b - x)^{\beta} & (\mu = 0, \nu = 0) \\
W(x) &= (x - a)^{\alpha}(b - x)^{\beta} \log(x - a) & (\mu = 1, \nu = 0) \\
W(x) &= (x - a)^{\alpha}(b - x)^{\beta} \log(b - x) & (\mu = 0, \nu = 1) \\
W(x) &= (x - a)^{\alpha}(b - x)^{\beta} \log(x - a) \log(b - x) & (\mu = 1, \nu = 1)
\end{aligned}
$$

The singular points (a, b) do not have to be specified until the integral is computed, where they are the endpoints of the integration range.

The function returns a pointer to the newly allocated table gsl_integration_qaws_table if no errors were detected, and a null pointer in the case of error.

int gsl_integration_qaws_table_set   Function
        (gsl_integration_qaws_table * t, double alpha, double
        beta, int mu, int nu)

This function modifies the parameters $(\alpha, \beta, \mu, \nu)$ of an existing gsl_integration_qaws_table struct t, updating the precomputed Chebyshev moments.

void gsl_integration_qaws_table_free   Function
        (gsl_integration_qaws_table * t)

This function frees all the memory associated with the gsl_integration_qaws_table struct t.

int gsl_integration_qaws (gsl_function * f, const   Function
        double a, const double b, gsl_integration_qaws_table
        * t, const double *epsabs*, const double *epsrel*, const
        size_t *limit*, gsl_integration_workspace * *workspace*,
        double * *result*, double * *abserr*)

This function computes the integral of the function $f(x)$ over the interval (a, b) with the singular weight function $(x - a)^\alpha (b - x)^\beta \log^\mu (x - a) \log^\nu (b - x)$. The parameters of the weight function $(\alpha, \beta, \mu, \nu)$ are taken from the table t. The integral is,

$$I = \int_a^b dx \, f(x)(x - a)^\alpha (b - x)^\beta \log^\mu (x - a) \log^\nu (b - x).$$

The adaptive bisection algorithm of QAG is used. When a subinterval contains one of the endpoints then a special 25-point modified Clenshaw-Curtis rule is used to control the singularities. For subintervals which do not include the endpoints an ordinary 15-point Gauss-Kronrod integration rule is used.

16.9 QAWO adaptive integration for oscillatory functions

The QAWO algorithm is designed for integrands with an oscillatory factor, $\sin(\omega x)$ or $\cos(\omega x)$. In order to work efficiently the algorithm requires a table of Chebyshev moments which must be pre-computed with calls to the functions below.

gsl_integration_qawo_table *   Function
        gsl_integration_qawo_table_alloc (double *omega*,
        double L, enum gsl_integration_qawo_enum *sine*, size_t
        n)

This function allocates space for a gsl_integration_qawo_table struct, and its associated workspace describing a sine or cosine weight function $W(x)$ with the parameters (ω, L),

$$W(x) = \left\{ \begin{array}{c} \sin(\omega x) \\ \cos(\omega x) \end{array} \right\}$$

The parameter L must be the length of the interval over which the function will be integrated $L = b - a$. The choice of sine or cosine is made with the parameter *sine* which should be chosen from one of the two following symbolic values:

```
GSL_INTEG_COSINE
GSL_INTEG_SINE
```

The `gsl_integration_qawo_table` is a table of the trigonometric co-efficients required in the integration process. The parameter n determines the number of levels of coefficients that are computed. Each level corresponds to one bisection of the interval L, so that n levels are sufficient for subintervals down to the length $L/2^n$. The integration routine `gsl_integration_qawo` returns the error `GSL_ETABLE` if the number of levels is insufficient for the requested accuracy.

int gsl_integration_qawo_table_set   Function
      (gsl_integration_qawo_table * t, double omega, double
      L, enum gsl_integration_qawo_enum sine)
This function changes the parameters omega, L and sine of the existing workspace t, updating the table of Chebyshev moments.

int gsl_integration_qawo_table_set_length   Function
      (gsl_integration_qawo_table * t, double L)
This function allows the length parameter L of the workspace t to be changed, updating the table of Chebyshev moments.

void gsl_integration_qawo_table_free   Function
      (gsl_integration_qawo_table * t)
This function frees all the memory associated with the workspace t.

int gsl_integration_qawo (gsl_function * f, const   Function
      double a, const double epsabs, const double epsrel,
      const size_t limit, gsl_integration_workspace *
      workspace, gsl_integration_qawo_table * wf, double *
      result, double * abserr)
This function uses an adaptive algorithm to compute the integral of f over (a, b) with the weight function $\sin(\omega x)$ or $\cos(\omega x)$,

$$I = \int_a^b dx\, f(x) \left\{ \begin{array}{l} \sin(\omega x) \\ \cos(\omega x) \end{array} \right\}$$

The choice of weight function is specified by the parameters used when setting up the precomputed table wf. The results are extrapolated using the epsilon-algorithm to accelerate the convergence of the integral. The function returns the final approximation from the extrapolation, result, and an estimate of the absolute error, abserr. The subintervals and their results are stored in the memory provided by workspace. The maximum number of subintervals is given by limit, which may not exceed the allocated size of the workspace.

Those subintervals with "large" widths d where $d\omega > 4$ are computed using a 25-point Clenshaw-Curtis integration rule, which handles the oscillatory behavior. Subintervals with a "small" widths where $d\omega < 4$ are computed using a 15-point Gauss-Kronrod integration.

16.10 QAWF adaptive integration for Fourier integrals

int gsl_integration_qawf (gsl_function * f, const $\qquad$ *Function*
    double a, const double *epsabs*, const size_t *limit*,
    gsl_integration_workspace * *workspace*,
    gsl_integration_workspace * *cycle_workspace*,
    gsl_integration_qawo_table * *wf*, double * *result*,
    double * *abserr*)

This function attempts to compute a Fourier integral of the function f over the semi-infinite interval $[a, +\infty)$.

$$I = \int_a^{+\infty} dx\, f(x) \left\{ \begin{array}{c} \sin(\omega x) \\ \cos(\omega x) \end{array} \right\}$$

The parameter ω and choice of sin or cos is taken from the table *wf* (the length L can take any value, since it is overridden by this function to a value appropriate for the fourier integration). The integral is computed using the QAWO algorithm over each of the subintervals,

$$C_1 = [a, a + c]$$
$$C_2 = [a + c, a + 2c]$$
$$\ldots = \ldots$$
$$C_k = [a + (k-1)c, a + kc]$$

where $c = (2\,\text{floor}(|\omega|) + 1)\pi/|\omega|$. The width c is chosen to cover an odd number of periods so that the contributions from the intervals alternate in sign and are monotonically decreasing when f is positive and monotonically decreasing. The sum of this sequence of contributions is accelerated using the epsilon-algorithm.

This function works to an overall absolute tolerance of *abserr*. The following strategy is used: on each interval C_k the algorithm tries to achieve the tolerance

$$TOL_k = u_k\, abserr$$

where $u_k = (1-p)p^{k-1}$ and $p = 9/10$. The sum of the geometric series of contributions from each interval gives an overall tolerance of *abserr*.

If the integration of a subinterval leads to difficulties then the accuracy requirement for subsequent intervals is relaxed,

$$TOL_k = u_k \max(abserr, \max_{i<k}\{E_i\})$$

where E_k is the estimated error on the interval C_k.

The subintervals and their results are stored in the memory provided by *workspace*. The maximum number of subintervals is given by *limit*, which may not exceed the allocated size of the workspace. The integration over each subinterval uses the memory provided by *cycle_workspace* as workspace for the QAWO algorithm.

16.11 Error codes

In addition to the standard error codes for invalid arguments the functions can return the following values,

GSL_EMAXITER
> the maximum number of subdivisions was exceeded.

GSL_EROUND
> cannot reach tolerance because of roundoff error, or roundoff error was detected in the extrapolation table.

GSL_ESING   a non-integrable singularity or other bad integrand behavior was found in the integration interval.

GSL_EDIVERGE
> the integral is divergent, or too slowly convergent to be integrated numerically.

16.12 Examples

The integrator QAGS will handle a large class of definite integrals. For example, consider the following integral, which has a algebraic-logarithmic singularity at the origin,

$$\int_0^1 x^{-1/2} \log(x)\,dx = -4$$

The program below computes this integral with a relative accuracy bound of 1e-7.

```
#include <stdio.h>
#include <math.h>
#include <gsl/gsl_integration.h>

double f (double x, void * params) {
  double alpha = *(double *) params;
  double f = log(alpha*x) / sqrt(x);
  return f;
}

int
main (void)
{
  gsl_integration_workspace * w
    = gsl_integration_workspace_alloc (1000);

  double result, error;
  double expected = -4.0;
  double alpha = 1.0;

  gsl_function F;
  F.function = &f;
  F.params = &alpha;

  gsl_integration_qags (&F, 0, 1, 0, 1e-7, 1000,
                        w, &result, &error);

  printf ("result          = % .18f\n", result);
  printf ("exact result    = % .18f\n", expected);
  printf ("estimated error = % .18f\n", error);
  printf ("actual error    = % .18f\n", result - expected);
  printf ("intervals =  %d\n", w->size);

  return 0;
}
```

The results below show that the desired accuracy is achieved after 8 sub-divisions.

```
$ ./a.out
result          = -3.999999999999973799
exact result    = -4.000000000000000000
estimated error =  0.000000000000246025
actual error    =  0.000000000000026201
intervals =  8
```

In fact, the extrapolation procedure used by QAGS produces an accuracy of almost twice as many digits. The error estimate returned by the extrapolation procedure is larger than the actual error, giving a margin of safety of one order of magnitude.

16.13 References and Further Reading

The following book is the definitive reference for QUADPACK, and was written by the original authors. It provides descriptions of the algorithms, program listings, test programs and examples. It also includes useful advice on numerical integration and many references to the numerical integration literature used in developing QUADPACK.

R. Piessens, E. de Doncker-Kapenga, C.W. Uberhuber, D.K. Kahaner. QUADPACK *A subroutine package for automatic integration* Springer Verlag, 1983.

17 Random Number Generation

The library provides a large collection of random number generators which can be accessed through a uniform interface. Environment variables allow you to select different generators and seeds at runtime, so that you can easily switch between generators without needing to recompile your program. Each instance of a generator keeps track of its own state, allowing the generators to be used in multi-threaded programs. Additional functions are available for transforming uniform random numbers into samples from continuous or discrete probability distributions such as the Gaussian, log-normal or Poisson distributions.

These functions are declared in the header file 'gsl_rng.h'.

17.1 General comments on random numbers

In 1988, Park and Miller wrote a paper entitled "Random number generators: good ones are hard to find." [Commun. ACM, 31, 1192–1201]. Fortunately, some excellent random number generators are available, though poor ones are still in common use. You may be happy with the system-supplied random number generator on your computer, but you should be aware that as computers get faster, requirements on random number generators increase. Nowadays, a simulation that calls a random number generator millions of times can often finish before you can make it down the hall to the coffee machine and back.

A very nice review of random number generators was written by Pierre L'Ecuyer, as Chapter 4 of the book: Handbook on Simulation, Jerry Banks, ed. (Wiley, 1997). The chapter is available in postscript from L'Ecuyer's ftp site (see references). Knuth's volume on Seminumerical Algorithms (originally published in 1968) devotes 170 pages to random number generators, and has recently been updated in its 3rd edition (1997). It is brilliant, a classic. If you don't own it, you should stop reading right now, run to the nearest bookstore, and buy it.

A good random number generator will satisfy both theoretical and statistical properties. Theoretical properties are often hard to obtain (they require real math!), but one prefers a random number generator with a long period, low serial correlation, and a tendency *not* to "fall mainly on the planes." Statistical tests are performed with numerical simulations. Generally, a random number generator is used to estimate some quantity for which the theory of probability provides an exact answer. Comparison to this exact answer provides a measure of "randomness".

17.2 The Random Number Generator Interface

It is important to remember that a random number generator is not a "real" function like sine or cosine. Unlike real functions, successive calls to a random number generator yield different return values. Of course that is just what you want for a random number generator, but to achieve this effect, the generator must keep track of some kind of "state" variable. Sometimes this state is just an integer (sometimes just the value of the previously generated random number), but often it is more complicated than that and may involve a whole array of numbers, possibly with some indices thrown in. To use the random number generators, you do not need to know the details of what comprises the state, and besides that varies from algorithm to algorithm.

The random number generator library uses two special structs, gsl_rng_type which holds static information about each type of generator and gsl_rng which describes an instance of a generator created from a given gsl_rng_type.

The functions described in this section are declared in the header file 'gsl_rng.h'.

17.3 Random number generator initialization

gsl_rng * gsl_rng_alloc (const gsl_rng_type * T)   Function
    This function returns a pointer to a newly-created instance of a random number generator of type T. For example, the following code creates an instance of the Tausworthe generator,

        gsl_rng * r = gsl_rng_alloc (gsl_rng_taus);

    If there is insufficient memory to create the generator then the function returns a null pointer and the error handler is invoked with an error code of GSL_ENOMEM.

    The generator is automatically initialized with the default seed, gsl_rng_default_seed. This is zero by default but can be changed either directly or by using the environment variable GSL_RNG_SEED (see Section 17.6 [Random number environment variables], page 229).

    The details of the available generator types are described later in this chapter.

void gsl_rng_set (const gsl_rng * r, unsigned long int *Function*
s)

> This function initializes (or 'seeds') the random number generator. If the generator is seeded with the same value of *s* on two different runs, the same stream of random numbers will be generated by successive calls to the routines below. If different values of *s* are supplied, then the generated streams of random numbers should be completely different. If the seed *s* is zero then the standard seed from the original implementation is used instead. For example, the original Fortran source code for the ranlux generator used a seed of 314159265, and so choosing *s* equal to zero reproduces this when using gsl_rng_ranlux.

void gsl_rng_free (gsl_rng * r) *Function*

> This function frees all the memory associated with the generator *r*.

17.4 Sampling from a random number generator

The following functions return uniformly distributed random numbers, either as integers or double precision floating point numbers. To obtain non-uniform distributions see Chapter 19 [Random Number Distributions], page 249.

unsigned long int gsl_rng_get (const gsl_rng * r) *Function*

> This function returns a random integer from the generator *r*. The minimum and maximum values depend on the algorithm used, but all integers in the range [*min*,*max*] are equally likely. The values of *min* and *max* can determined using the auxiliary functions gsl_rng_max (r) and gsl_rng_min (r).

double gsl_rng_uniform (const gsl_rng * r) *Function*

> This function returns a double precision floating point number uniformly distributed in the range [0,1). The range includes 0.0 but excludes 1.0. The value is typically obtained by dividing the result of gsl_rng_get(r) by gsl_rng_max(r) + 1.0 in double precision. Some generators compute this ratio internally so that they can provide floating point numbers with more than 32 bits of randomness (the maximum number of bits that can be portably represented in a single unsigned long int).

double gsl_rng_uniform_pos (const gsl_rng * r) *Function*

> This function returns a positive double precision floating point number uniformly distributed in the range (0,1), excluding both 0.0 and 1.0. The number is obtained by sampling the generator with the algorithm of gsl_rng_uniform until a non-zero value is obtained. You can use this function if you need to avoid a singularity at 0.0.

unsigned long int gsl_rng_uniform_int (const gsl_rng *   Function
       r, unsigned long int n)

This function returns a random integer from 0 to $n - 1$ inclusive by
scaling down and/or discarding samples from the generator r. All
integers in the range $[0, n - 1]$ are produced with equal probability.
For generators with a non-zero minimum value an offset is applied so
that zero is returned with the correct probability.

Note that this function is designed for sampling from ranges smaller
than the range of the underlying generator. The parameter n must be
less than or equal to the range of the generator r. If n is larger than
the range of the generator then the function calls the error handler
with an error code of GSL_EINVAL and returns zero.

In particular, this function is not intended for generating the full range
of unsigned integer values $[0, 2^{32} - 1]$. Instead choose a generator with
the maximal integer range and zero mimimum value, such as gsl_rng_
ranlxd1, gsl_rng_mt19937 or gsl_rng_taus, and sample it directly
using gsl_rng_get. The range of each generator can be found using
the auxiliary functions described in the next section.

17.5 Auxiliary random number generator functions

The following functions provide information about an existing generator. You should use them in preference to hard-coding the generator
parameters into your own code.

const char * gsl_rng_name (const gsl_rng * r)   Function

This function returns a pointer to the name of the generator. For
example,

        printf ("r is a '%s' generator\n",
                gsl_rng_name (r));

would print something like r is a 'taus' generator.

unsigned long int gsl_rng_max (const gsl_rng * r)   Function

gsl_rng_max returns the largest value that gsl_rng_get can return.

unsigned long int gsl_rng_min (const gsl_rng * r)   Function

gsl_rng_min returns the smallest value that gsl_rng_get can return.
Usually this value is zero. There are some generators with algorithms
that cannot return zero, and for these generators the minimum value
is 1.

void * gsl_rng_state (const gsl_rng * r)	Function
size_t gsl_rng_size (const gsl_rng * r)	Function

These functions return a pointer to the state of generator r and its size. You can use this information to access the state directly. For example, the following code will write the state of a generator to a stream,

```
void * state = gsl_rng_state (r);
size_t n = gsl_rng_size (r);
fwrite (state, n, 1, stream);
```

const gsl_rng_type ** gsl_rng_types_setup (void)	Function

This function returns a pointer to an array of all the available generator types, terminated by a null pointer. The function should be called once at the start of the program, if needed. The following code fragment shows how to iterate over the array of generator types to print the names of the available algorithms,

```
const gsl_rng_type **t, **t0;

t0 = gsl_rng_types_setup ();

printf ("Available generators:\n");

for (t = t0; *t != 0; t++)
  {
    printf ("%s\n", (*t)->name);
  }
```

17.6 Random number environment variables

The library allows you to choose a default generator and seed from the environment variables GSL_RNG_TYPE and GSL_RNG_SEED and the function gsl_rng_env_setup. This makes it easy try out different generators and seeds without having to recompile your program.

const gsl_rng_type * gsl_rng_env_setup (void)	Function

This function reads the environment variables GSL_RNG_TYPE and GSL_RNG_SEED and uses their values to set the corresponding library variables gsl_rng_default and gsl_rng_default_seed. These global variables are defined as follows,

```
extern const gsl_rng_type *gsl_rng_default
extern unsigned long int gsl_rng_default_seed
```

The environment variable GSL_RNG_TYPE should be the name of a generator, such as taus or mt19937. The environment variable GSL_RNG_SEED should contain the desired seed value. It is converted to an unsigned long int using the C library function strtoul.

If you don't specify a generator for GSL_RNG_TYPE then gsl_rng_mt19937 is used as the default. The initial value of gsl_rng_default_seed is zero.

Here is a short program which shows how to create a global generator using the environment variables GSL_RNG_TYPE and GSL_RNG_SEED,

```
#include <stdio.h>
#include <gsl/gsl_rng.h>

gsl_rng * r;  /* global generator */

int
main (void)
{
  const gsl_rng_type * T;

  gsl_rng_env_setup();

  T = gsl_rng_default;
  r = gsl_rng_alloc (T);

  printf ("generator type: %s\n", gsl_rng_name (r));
  printf ("seed = %lu\n", gsl_rng_default_seed);
  printf ("first value = %lu\n", gsl_rng_get (r));
  return 0;
}
```

Running the program without any environment variables uses the initial defaults, an mt19937 generator with a seed of 0,

```
$ ./a.out
  generator type: mt19937
  seed = 0
  first value = 4293858116
```

By setting the two variables on the command line we can change the default generator and the seed,

```
$ GSL_RNG_TYPE="taus" GSL_RNG_SEED=123 ./a.out
GSL_RNG_TYPE=taus
GSL_RNG_SEED=123
generator type: taus
seed = 123
```

```
first value = 2720986350
```

17.7 Copying random number generator state

The above methods do not expose the random number 'state' which changes from call to call. It is often useful to be able to save and restore the state. To permit these practices, a few somewhat more advanced functions are supplied. These include:

int gsl_rng_memcpy (gsl_rng * *dest*, const gsl_rng * *src*)   Function
  This function copies the random number generator *src* into the pre-existing generator *dest*, making *dest* into an exact copy of *src*. The two generators must be of the same type.

gsl_rng * gsl_rng_clone (const gsl_rng * *r*)   Function
  This function returns a pointer to a newly created generator which is an exact copy of the generator *r*.

17.8 Reading and writing random number generator state

The library provides functions for reading and writing the random number state to a file as binary data.

int gsl_rng_fwrite (FILE * *stream*, const gsl_rng * *r*)   Function
  This function writes the random number state of the random number generator *r* to the stream *stream* in binary format. The return value is 0 for success and GSL_EFAILED if there was a problem writing to the file. Since the data is written in the native binary format it may not be portable between different architectures.

int gsl_rng_fread (FILE * *stream*, gsl_rng * *r*)   Function
  This function reads the random number state into the random number generator *r* from the open stream *stream* in binary format. The random number generator *r* must be preinitialized with the correct random number generator type since type information is not saved. The return value is 0 for success and GSL_EFAILED if there was a problem reading from the file. The data is assumed to have been written in the native binary format on the same architecture.

17.9 Random number generator algorithms

The functions described above make no reference to the actual algorithm used. This is deliberate so that you can switch algorithms without having to change any of your application source code. The library provides a large number of generators of different types, including simulation quality generators, generators provided for compatibility with other libraries and historical generators from the past.

The following generators are recommended for use in simulation. They have extremely long periods, low correlation and pass most statistical tests.

gsl_rng_mt19937   Generator

The MT19937 generator of Makoto Matsumoto and Takuji Nishimura is a variant of the twisted generalized feedback shift-register algorithm, and is known as the "Mersenne Twister" generator. It has a Mersenne prime period of $2^{19937} - 1$ (about 10^{6000}) and is equi-distributed in 623 dimensions. It has passed the DIEHARD statistical tests. It uses 624 words of state per generator and is comparable in speed to the other generators. The original generator used a default seed of 4357 and choosing s equal to zero in gsl_rng_set reproduces this.

For more information see,

> Makoto Matsumoto and Takuji Nishimura, "Mersenne Twister: A 623-dimensionally equidistributed uniform pseudorandom number generator". *ACM Transactions on Modeling and Computer Simulation*, Vol. 8, No. 1 (Jan. 1998), Pages 3–30

The generator gsl_rng_mt19937 uses the second revision of the seeding procedure published by the two authors above in 2002. The original seeding procedures could cause spurious artifacts for some seed values. They are still available through the alternative generators gsl_rng_mt19937_1999 and gsl_rng_mt19937_1998.

gsl_rng_ranlxs0   Generator
gsl_rng_ranlxs1   Generator
gsl_rng_ranlxs2   Generator

The generator ranlxs0 is a second-generation version of the RANLUX algorithm of Lüscher, which produces "luxury random numbers". This generator provides single precision output (24 bits) at three luxury levels ranlxs0, ranlxs1 and ranlxs2. It uses double-precision floating point arithmetic internally and can be significantly faster than the integer version of ranlux, particularly on 64-bit architectures. The period of the generator is about 10^{171}. The algorithm has mathematically proven properties and can provide truly decorrelated numbers at a known level of randomness. The higher luxury levels provide increased decorrelation between samples as an additional safety margin.

gsl_rng_ranlxd1   Generator
gsl_rng_ranlxd2   Generator
These generators produce double precision output (48 bits) from the RANLXS generator. The library provides two luxury levels ranlxd1 and ranlxd2.

gsl_rng_ranlux   Generator
gsl_rng_ranlux389   Generator
The ranlux generator is an implementation of the original algorithm developed by Lüscher. It uses a lagged-fibonacci-with-skipping algorithm to produce "luxury random numbers". It is a 24-bit generator, originally designed for single-precision IEEE floating point numbers. This implementation is based on integer arithmetic, while the second-generation versions RANLXS and RANLXD described above provide floating-point implementations which will be faster on many platforms. The period of the generator is about 10^{171}. The algorithm has mathematically proven properties and it can provide truly decorrelated numbers at a known level of randomness. The default level of decorrelation recommended by Lüscher is provided by gsl_rng_ranlux, while gsl_rng_ranlux389 gives the highest level of randomness, with all 24 bits decorrelated. Both types of generator use 24 words of state per generator.

For more information see,

> M. Lüscher, "A portable high-quality random number generator for lattice field theory calculations", *Computer Physics Communications*, 79 (1994) 100–110.

> F. James, "RANLUX: A Fortran implementation of the high-quality pseudo-random number generator of Lüscher", *Computer Physics Communications*, 79 (1994) 111–114

gsl_rng_cmrg   Generator
This is a combined multiple recursive generator by L'Ecuyer. Its sequence is,

$$z_n = (x_n - y_n) \bmod m_1$$

where the two underlying generators x_n and y_n are,

$$x_n = (a_1 x_{n-1} + a_2 x_{n-2} + a_3 x_{n-3}) \bmod m_1$$
$$y_n = (b_1 y_{n-1} + b_2 y_{n-2} + b_3 y_{n-3}) \bmod m_2$$

with coefficients $a_1 = 0$, $a_2 = 63308$, $a_3 = -183326$, $b_1 = 86098$, $b_2 = 0$, $b_3 = -539608$, and moduli $m_1 = 2^{31} - 1 = 2147483647$ and $m_2 = 2145483479$.

The period of this generator is $\mathrm{lcm}(m_1^3 - 1, m_2^3 - 1)$, which is approximately 2^{185} (about 10^{56}). It uses 6 words of state per generator. For more information see,

> P. L'Ecuyer, "Combined Multiple Recursive Random Number Generators", *Operations Research*, 44, 5 (1996), 816–822.

`gsl_rng_mrg`   Generator

This is a fifth-order multiple recursive generator by L'Ecuyer, Blouin and Coutre. Its sequence is,

$$x_n = (a_1 x_{n-1} + a_5 x_{n-5}) \bmod m$$

with $a_1 = 107374182$, $a_2 = a_3 = a_4 = 0$, $a_5 = 104480$ and $m = 2^{31} - 1$. The period of this generator is about 10^{46}. It uses 5 words of state per generator. More information can be found in the following paper,

> P. L'Ecuyer, F. Blouin, and R. Coutre, "A search for good multiple recursive random number generators", *ACM Transactions on Modeling and Computer Simulation* 3, 87–98 (1993).

`gsl_rng_taus`   Generator
`gsl_rng_taus2`   Generator

This is a maximally equidistributed combined Tausworthe generator by L'Ecuyer. The sequence is,

$$x_n = (s_n^1 \oplus s_n^2 \oplus s_n^3)$$

where,

$$s_{n+1}^1 = (((s_n^1 \,\&\, 4294967294) \ll 12) \oplus (((s_n^1 \ll 13) \oplus s_n^1) \gg 19))$$
$$s_{n+1}^2 = (((s_n^2 \,\&\, 4294967288) \ll 4) \oplus (((s_n^2 \ll 2) \oplus s_n^2) \gg 25))$$
$$s_{n+1}^3 = (((s_n^3 \,\&\, 4294967280) \ll 17) \oplus (((s_n^3 \ll 3) \oplus s_n^3) \gg 11))$$

computed modulo 2^{32}. In the formulas above $\oplus$ denotes "exclusive-or". Note that the algorithm relies on the properties of 32-bit unsigned integers and has been implemented using a bitmask of 0xFFFFFFFF to make it work on 64 bit machines.

The period of this generator is 2^{88} (about 10^{26}). It uses 3 words of state per generator. For more information see,

> P. L'Ecuyer, "Maximally Equidistributed Combined Tausworthe Generators", *Mathematics of Computation*, 65, 213 (1996), 203–213.

The generator `gsl_rng_taus2` uses the same algorithm as `gsl_rng_taus` but with an improved seeding procedure described in the paper,

> P. L'Ecuyer, "Tables of Maximally Equidistributed Combined LFSR Generators", *Mathematics of Computation*, 68, 225 (1999), 261–269

The generator `gsl_rng_taus2` should now be used in preference to `gsl_rng_taus`.

`gsl_rng_gfsr4`   Generator

The `gfsr4` generator is like a lagged-fibonacci generator, and produces each number as an xor'd sum of four previous values.

$$r_n = r_{n-A} \oplus r_{n-B} \oplus r_{n-C} \oplus r_{n-D}$$

Ziff (ref below) notes that "it is now widely known" that two-tap registers (such as R250, which is described below) have serious flaws, the most obvious one being the three-point correlation that comes from the definition of the generator. Nice mathematical properties can be derived for GFSR's, and numerics bears out the claim that 4-tap GFSR's with appropriately chosen offsets are as random as can be measured, using the author's test.

This implementation uses the values suggested the example on p392 of Ziff's article: $A = 471$, $B = 1586$, $C = 6988$, $D = 9689$.

If the offsets are appropriately chosen (such as the one ones in this implementation), then the sequence is said to be maximal; that means that the period is $2^D - 1$, where D is the longest lag. (It is one less than 2^D because it is not permitted to have all zeros in the `ra[]` array.) For this implementation with $D = 9689$ that works out to about 10^{2917}.

Note that the implementation of this generator using a 32-bit integer amounts to 32 parallel implementations of one-bit generators. One consequence of this is that the period of this 32-bit generator is the same as for the one-bit generator. Moreover, this independence means that all 32-bit patterns are equally likely, and in particular that 0 is an allowed random value. (We are grateful to Heiko Bauke for clarifying for us these properties of GFSR random number generators.)

For more information see,

> Robert M. Ziff, "Four-tap shift-register-sequence random-number generators", *Computers in Physics*, 12(4), Jul/Aug 1998, pp 385–392.

17.10 Unix random number generators

The standard Unix random number generators rand, random and rand48 are provided as part of GSL. Although these generators are widely available individually often they aren't all available on the same platform. This makes it difficult to write portable code using them and so we have included the complete set of Unix generators in GSL for convenience. Note that these generators don't produce high-quality randomness and aren't suitable for work requiring accurate statistics. However, if you won't be measuring statistical quantities and just want to introduce some variation into your program then these generators are quite acceptable.

gsl_rng_rand   Generator

This is the BSD rand generator. Its sequence is

$$x_{n+1} = (ax_n + c) \bmod m$$

with $a = 1103515245$, $c = 12345$ and $m = 2^{31}$. The seed specifies the initial value, x_1. The period of this generator is 2^{31}, and it uses 1 word of storage per generator.

gsl_rng_random_bsd   Generator
gsl_rng_random_libc5   Generator
gsl_rng_random_glibc2   Generator

These generators implement the random family of functions, a set of linear feedback shift register generators originally used in BSD Unix. There are several versions of random in use today: the original BSD version (e.g. on SunOS4), a libc5 version (found on older GNU/Linux systems) and a glibc2 version. Each version uses a different seeding procedure, and thus produces different sequences.

The original BSD routines accepted a variable length buffer for the generator state, with longer buffers providing higher-quality randomness. The random function implemented algorithms for buffer lengths of 8, 32, 64, 128 and 256 bytes, and the algorithm with the largest length that would fit into the user-supplied buffer was used. To support these algorithms additional generators are available with the following names,

    gsl_rng_random8_bsd
    gsl_rng_random32_bsd
    gsl_rng_random64_bsd
    gsl_rng_random128_bsd
    gsl_rng_random256_bsd

where the numeric suffix indicates the buffer length. The original BSD random function used a 128-byte default buffer and so gsl_rng_random_bsd has been made equivalent to gsl_rng_random128_bsd. Corresponding versions of the libc5 and glibc2 generators are also available, with the names gsl_rng_random8_libc5, gsl_rng_random8_glibc2, etc.

gsl_rng_rand48   Generator

This is the Unix rand48 generator. Its sequence is

$$x_{n+1} = (ax_n + c) \bmod m$$

defined on 48-bit unsigned integers with $a = 25214903917$, $c = 11$ and $m = 2^{48}$. The seed specifies the upper 32 bits of the initial value, x_1, with the lower 16 bits set to 0x330E. The function gsl_rng_get returns the upper 32 bits from each term of the sequence. This does not have a direct parallel in the original rand48 functions, but forcing the result to type long int reproduces the output of mrand48. The function gsl_rng_uniform uses the full 48 bits of internal state to return the double precision number x_n/m, which is equivalent to the function drand48. Note that some old versions of the GNU C Library contained a bug in mrand48 which caused it to produce different results (only the lower 16-bits of the return value were set).

17.11 Other random number generators

The generators in this section are provided for compatibility with existing libraries. If you are converting an existing program to use GSL then you can select these generators to check your new implementation against the original one, using the same random number generator. After verifying that your new program reproduces the original results you can then switch to a higher-quality generator.

Note that most of the generators in this section are based on single linear congruence relations, which are the least sophisticated type of generator. In particular, linear congruences have poor properties when used with a non-prime modulus, as several of these routines do (e.g. with a power of two modulus, 2^{31} or 2^{32}). This leads to periodicity in the least significant bits of each number, with only the higher bits having any randomness. Thus if you want to produce a random bitstream it is best to avoid using the least significant bits.

gsl_rng_ranf   Generator

This is the CRAY random number generator RANF. Its sequence is

$$x_{n+1} = (ax_n) \bmod m$$

defined on 48-bit unsigned integers with $a = 44485709377909$ and $m = 2^{48}$. The seed specifies the lower 32 bits of the initial value, x_1, with the lowest bit set to prevent the seed taking an even value. The upper 16 bits of x_1 are set to 0. A consequence of this procedure is that the pairs of seeds 2 and 3, 4 and 5, etc produce the same sequences.

The generator compatible with the CRAY MATHLIB routine RANF. It produces double precision floating point numbers which should be identical to those from the original RANF.

There is a subtlety in the implementation of the seeding. The initial state is reversed through one step, by multiplying by the modular inverse of $a \bmod m$. This is done for compatibility with the original CRAY implementation.

Note that you can only seed the generator with integers up to 2^{32}, while the original CRAY implementation uses non-portable wide integers which can cover all 2^{48} states of the generator.

The function gsl_rng_get returns the upper 32 bits from each term of the sequence. The function gsl_rng_uniform uses the full 48 bits to return the double precision number x_n/m.

The period of this generator is 2^{46}.

gsl_rng_ranmar   Generator

This is the RANMAR lagged-fibonacci generator of Marsaglia, Zaman and Tsang. It is a 24-bit generator, originally designed for single-precision IEEE floating point numbers. It was included in the CERN-LIB high-energy physics library.

gsl_rng_r250   Generator

This is the shift-register generator of Kirkpatrick and Stoll. The sequence is based on the recurrence

$$x_n = x_{n-103} \oplus x_{n-250}$$

where $\oplus$ denotes "exclusive-or", defined on 32-bit words. The period of this generator is about 2^{250} and it uses 250 words of state per generator.

For more information see,

> S. Kirkpatrick and E. Stoll, "A very fast shift-register sequence random number generator", *Journal of Computational Physics*, 40, 517–526 (1981)

gsl_rng_tt800   Generator

This is an earlier version of the twisted generalized feedback shift-register generator, and has been superseded by the development of MT19937. However, it is still an acceptable generator in its own right. It has a period of 2^{800} and uses 33 words of storage per generator.

For more information see,

> Makoto Matsumoto and Yoshiharu Kurita, "Twisted GFSR Generators II", *ACM Transactions on Modelling and Computer Simulation*, Vol. 4, No. 3, 1994, pages 254–266.

gsl_rng_vax   Generator

This is the VAX generator MTH$RANDOM. Its sequence is,

$$x_{n+1} = (ax_n + c) \bmod m$$

with $a = 69069$, $c = 1$ and $m = 2^{32}$. The seed specifies the initial value, x_1. The period of this generator is 2^{32} and it uses 1 word of storage per generator.

gsl_rng_transputer   Generator

This is the random number generator from the INMOS Transputer Development system. Its sequence is,

$$x_{n+1} = (ax_n) \bmod m$$

with $a = 1664525$ and $m = 2^{32}$. The seed specifies the initial value, x_1.

gsl_rng_randu   Generator

This is the IBM RANDU generator. Its sequence is

$$x_{n+1} = (ax_n) \bmod m$$

with $a = 65539$ and $m = 2^{31}$. The seed specifies the initial value, x_1. The period of this generator was only 2^{29}. It has become a textbook example of a poor generator.

gsl_rng_minstd   Generator

This is Park and Miller's "minimal standard" MINSTD generator, a simple linear congruence which takes care to avoid the major pitfalls of such algorithms. Its sequence is,

$$x_{n+1} = (ax_n) \bmod m$$

with $a = 16807$ and $m = 2^{31} - 1 = 2147483647$. The seed specifies the initial value, x_1. The period of this generator is about 2^{31}.

This generator is used in the IMSL Library (subroutine RNUN) and in MATLAB (the RAND function). It is also sometimes known by the acronym "GGL" (I'm not sure what that stands for).

For more information see,

> Park and Miller, "Random Number Generators: Good ones are hard to find", *Communications of the ACM*, October 1988, Volume 31, No 10, pages 1192–1201.

gsl_rng_uni   Generator
gsl_rng_uni32   Generator
This is a reimplementation of the 16-bit SLATEC random number generator RUNIF. A generalization of the generator to 32 bits is provided by `gsl_rng_uni32`. The original source code is available from NETLIB.

gsl_rng_slatec   Generator
This is the SLATEC random number generator RAND. It is ancient. The original source code is available from NETLIB.

gsl_rng_zuf   Generator
This is the ZUFALL lagged Fibonacci series generator of Peterson. Its sequence is,

$$t = u_{n-273} + u_{n-607}$$
$$u_n = t - \mathrm{floor}(t)$$

The original source code is available from NETLIB. For more information see,

> W. Petersen, "Lagged Fibonacci Random Number Generators for the NEC SX-3", *International Journal of High Speed Computing* (1994).

gsl_rng_knuthran2   Generator
This is a second-order multiple recursive generator described by Knuth in *Seminumerical Algorithms*, 3rd Ed., page 108. Its sequence is,

$$x_n = (a_1 x_{n-1} + a_2 x_{n-2}) \bmod m$$

with $a_1 = 271828183$, $a_2 = 314159269$, and $m = 2^{31} - 1$.

gsl_rng_knuthran   Generator
This is a second-order multiple recursive generator described by Knuth in *Seminumerical Algorithms*, 3rd Ed., Section 3.6. Knuth provides its C code.

gsl_rng_borosh13   Generator
gsl_rng_fishman18   Generator
gsl_rng_fishman20   Generator
gsl_rng_lecuyer21   Generator
gsl_rng_waterman14   Generator

These multiplicative generators are taken from Knuth's *Seminumerical Algorithms*, 3rd Ed., pages 106–108. Their sequence is,

$$x_{n+1} = (ax_n) \bmod m$$

where the seed specifies the initial value, x_1. The parameters a and m are as follows, Borosh-Niederreiter: $a = 1812433253$, $m = 2^{32}$, Fishman18: $a = 62089911$, $m = 2^{31} - 1$, Fishman20: $a = 48271$, $m = 2^{31} - 1$, L'Ecuyer: $a = 40692$, $m = 2^{31} - 249$, Waterman: $a = 1566083941$, $m = 2^{32}$.

gsl_rng_fishman2x   Generator

This is the L'Ecuyer–Fishman random number generator. It is taken from Knuth's *Seminumerical Algorithms*, 3rd Ed., page 108. Its sequence is,

$$z_{n+1} = (x_n - y_n) \bmod m$$

with $m = 2^{31} - 1$. x_n and y_n are given by the fishman20 and lecuyer21 algorithms. The seed specifies the initial value, x_1.

gsl_rng_coveyou   Generator

This is the Coveyou random number generator. It is taken from Knuth's *Seminumerical Algorithms*, 3rd Ed., Section 3.2.2. Its sequence is,

$$x_{n+1} = (x_n(x_n + 1)) \bmod m$$

with $m = 2^{32}$. The seed specifies the initial value, x_1.

17.12 Performance

The following table shows the relative performance of a selection the available random number generators. The fastest simulation quality generators are taus, gfsr4 and mt19937. The generators which offer the best mathematically-proven quality are those based on the RANLUX algorithm.

```
1754 k ints/sec,     870 k doubles/sec, taus
1613 k ints/sec,     855 k doubles/sec, gfsr4
1370 k ints/sec,     769 k doubles/sec, mt19937
 565 k ints/sec,     571 k doubles/sec, ranlxs0
 400 k ints/sec,     405 k doubles/sec, ranlxs1
 490 k ints/sec,     389 k doubles/sec, mrg
 407 k ints/sec,     297 k doubles/sec, ranlux
 243 k ints/sec,     254 k doubles/sec, ranlxd1
 251 k ints/sec,     253 k doubles/sec, ranlxs2
 238 k ints/sec,     215 k doubles/sec, cmrg
 247 k ints/sec,     198 k doubles/sec, ranlux389
 141 k ints/sec,     140 k doubles/sec, ranlxd2

1852 k ints/sec,     935 k doubles/sec, ran3
 813 k ints/sec,     575 k doubles/sec, ran0
 787 k ints/sec,     476 k doubles/sec, ran1
 379 k ints/sec,     292 k doubles/sec, ran2
```

17.13 Examples

The following program demonstrates the use of a random number generator to produce uniform random numbers in the range [0.0, 1.0),

```c
#include <stdio.h>
#include <gsl/gsl_rng.h>

int
main (void)
{
  const gsl_rng_type * T;
  gsl_rng * r;

  int i, n = 10;

  gsl_rng_env_setup();

  T = gsl_rng_default;
  r = gsl_rng_alloc (T);
```

```
for (i = 0; i < n; i++)
  {
    double u = gsl_rng_uniform (r);
    printf ("%.5f\n", u);
  }

gsl_rng_free (r);

return 0;
}
```

Here is the output of the program,

```
$ ./a.out
0.99974
0.16291
0.28262
0.94720
0.23166
0.48497
0.95748
0.74431
0.54004
0.73995
```

The numbers depend on the seed used by the generator. The default seed can be changed with the GSL_RNG_SEED environment variable to produce a different stream of numbers. The generator itself can be changed using the environment variable GSL_RNG_TYPE. Here is the output of the program using a seed value of 123 and the multiple-recursive generator mrg,

```
$ GSL_RNG_SEED=123 GSL_RNG_TYPE=mrg ./a.out
GSL_RNG_TYPE=mrg
GSL_RNG_SEED=123
0.33050
0.86631
0.32982
0.67620
0.53391
0.06457
0.16847
0.70229
0.04371
0.86374
```

17.14 References and Further Reading

The subject of random number generation and testing is reviewed extensively in Knuth's *Seminumerical Algorithms*.

> Donald E. Knuth, *The Art of Computer Programming: Seminumerical Algorithms* (Vol 2, 3rd Ed, 1997), Addison-Wesley, ISBN 0201896842.

Further information is available in the review paper written by Pierre L'Ecuyer,

> P. L'Ecuyer, "Random Number Generation", Chapter 4 of the Handbook on Simulation, Jerry Banks Ed., Wiley, 1998, 93–137.
>
> `http://www.iro.umontreal.ca/~lecuyer/papers.html` in the file 'handsim.ps'.

The source code for the DIEHARD random number generator tests is also available online,

> *DIEHARD source code* G. Marsaglia,
>
> `http://stat.fsu.edu/pub/diehard/`

A comprehensive set of random number generator tests is available from NIST,

> NIST Special Publication 800-22, "A Statistical Test Suite for the Validation of Random Number Generators and Pseudo Random Number Generators for Cryptographic Applications".
>
> `http://csrc.nist.gov/rng/`

17.15 Acknowledgements

Thanks to Makoto Matsumoto, Takuji Nishimura and Yoshiharu Kurita for making the source code to their generators (MT19937, MM&TN; TT800, MM&YK) available under the GNU General Public License. Thanks to Martin Lüscher for providing notes and source code for the RANLXS and RANLXD generators.

18 Quasi-Random Sequences

This chapter describes functions for generating quasi-random sequences in arbitrary dimensions. A quasi-random sequence progressively covers a d-dimensional space with a set of points that are uniformly distributed. Quasi-random sequences are also known as low-discrepancy sequences. The quasi-random sequence generators use an interface that is similar to the interface for random number generators, except that seeding is not required—each generator produces a single sequence.

The functions described in this section are declared in the header file 'gsl_qrng.h'.

18.1 Quasi-random number generator initialization

gsl_qrng * gsl_qrng_alloc (const gsl_qrng_type * T,   Function
  unsigned int d)
This function returns a pointer to a newly-created instance of a quasi-random sequence generator of type T and dimension d. If there is insufficient memory to create the generator then the function returns a null pointer and the error handler is invoked with an error code of GSL_ENOMEM.

void gsl_qrng_free (gsl_qrng * q)   Function
This function frees all the memory associated with the generator q.

void gsl_qrng_init (gsl_qrng * q)   Function
This function reinitializes the generator q to its starting point. Note that quasi-random sequences do not use a seed and always produce the same set of values.

18.2 Sampling from a quasi-random number generator

int gsl_qrng_get (const gsl_qrng * q, double x[])   Function
This function stores the next point from the sequence generator q in the array x. The space available for x must match the dimension of the generator. The point x will lie in the range $0 < x_i < 1$ for each x_i.

18.3 Auxiliary quasi-random number generator functions

const char * gsl_qrng_name (const gsl_qrng * q)   *Function*
    This function returns a pointer to the name of the generator.

size_t gsl_qrng_size (const gsl_qrng * q)   *Function*
void * gsl_qrng_state (const gsl_qrng * q)   *Function*
    These functions return a pointer to the state of generator r and its
    size. You can use this information to access the state directly. For
    example, the following code will write the state of a generator to a
    stream,

```
void * state = gsl_qrng_state (q);
size_t n = gsl_qrng_size (q);
fwrite (state, n, 1, stream);
```

18.4 Saving and resorting quasi-random number generator state

int gsl_qrng_memcpy (gsl_qrng * *dest*, const gsl_qrng *   *Function*
        src)
    This function copies the quasi-random sequence generator *src* into the
    pre-existing generator *dest*, making *dest* into an exact copy of *src*. The
    two generators must be of the same type.

gsl_qrng * gsl_qrng_clone (const gsl_qrng * q)   *Function*
    This function returns a pointer to a newly created generator which is
    an exact copy of the generator q.

18.5 Quasi-random number generator algorithms

The following quasi-random sequence algorithms are available,

gsl_qrng_niederreiter_2   *Generator*
    This generator uses the algorithm described in Bratley, Fox, Niederre-
    iter, *ACM Trans. Model. Comp. Sim.* 2, 195 (1992). It is valid up to
    12 dimensions.

gsl_qrng_sobol   *Generator*
    This generator uses the Sobol sequence described in Antonov, Saleev,
    USSR Comput. Maths. Math. Phys. 19, 252 (1980). It is valid up to
    40 dimensions.

18.6 Examples

The following program prints the first 1024 points of the 2-dimensional Sobol sequence.

```
#include <stdio.h>
#include <gsl/gsl_qrng.h>

int
main (void)
{
  int i;
  gsl_qrng * q = gsl_qrng_alloc (gsl_qrng_sobol, 2);

  for (i = 0; i < 1024; i++)
    {
      double v[2];
      gsl_qrng_get (q, v);
      printf ("%.5f %.5f\n", v[0], v[1]);
    }

  gsl_qrng_free (q);
  return 0;
}
```

Here is the output from the program,

```
$ ./a.out
0.50000 0.50000
0.75000 0.25000
0.25000 0.75000
0.37500 0.37500
0.87500 0.87500
0.62500 0.12500
0.12500 0.62500
....
```

It can be seen that successive points progressively fill-in the spaces between previous points.

The following plot shows the distribution in the x-y plane of the first 1024 points from the Sobol sequence,

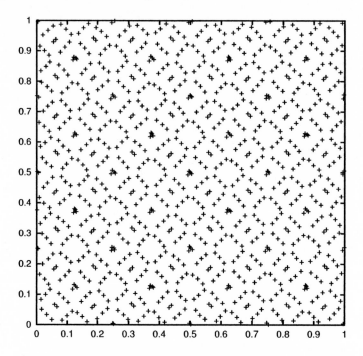

Distribution of the first 1024 points
from the quasi-random Sobol sequence

18.7 References

The implementations of the quasi-random sequence routines are based on the algorithms described in the following paper,

P. Bratley and B.L. Fox and H. Niederreiter, "Algorithm 738: Programs to Generate Niederreiter's Low-discrepancy Sequences", *ACM Transactions on Mathematical Software*, Vol. 20, No. 4, December, 1994, p. 494–495.

19 Random Number Distributions

This chapter describes functions for generating random variates and computing their probability distributions. Samples from the distributions described in this chapter can be obtained using any of the random number generators in the library as an underlying source of randomness.

In the simplest cases a non-uniform distribution can be obtained analytically from the uniform distribution of a random number generator by applying an appropriate transformation. This method uses one call to the random number generator. More complicated distributions are created by the *acceptance-rejection* method, which compares the desired distribution against a distribution which is similar and known analytically. This usually requires several samples from the generator.

The library also provides cumulative distribution functions and inverse cumulative distribution functions, sometimes referred to as quantile functions. The cumulative distribution functions and their inverses are computed separately for the upper and lower tails of the distribution, allowing full accuracy to be retained for small results.

The functions for random variates and probability density functions described in this section are declared in 'gsl_randist.h'. The corresponding cumulative distribution functions are declared in 'gsl_cdf.h'.

Note that the discrete random variate functions always return a value of type unsigned int, and on most platforms this has a maximum value of $2^{32} - 1 \approx 4.29 \times 10^9$. To prevent incorrect results due to overflow, they should only be called with parameters where there is a negligible probability of a variate exceeding this limit.

19.1 Introduction

Continuous random number distributions are defined by a probability density function, $p(x)$, such that the probability of x occurring in the infinitesimal range x to $x + dx$ is $p\,dx$.

The cumulative distribution function for the lower tail $P(x)$ is defined by the integral,

$$P(x) = \int_{-\infty}^{x} dx' p(x')$$

and gives the probability of a variate taking a value less than x. The cumulative distribution function for the upper tail $Q(x)$ is defined by the integral,

$$Q(x) = \int_x^{+\infty} dx' p(x')$$

and gives the probability of a variate taking a value greater than x. The upper and lower cumulative distribution functions are related by $P(x) + Q(x) = 1$ and satisfy $0 \leq P(x) \leq 1$, $0 \leq Q(x) \leq 1$.

The inverse cumulative distributions, $x = P^{-1}(P)$ and $x = Q^{-1}(Q)$ give the values of x which correspond to a specific value of P or Q. They can be used to find confidence limits from probability values.

For discrete distributions the probability of sampling the integer value k is given by $p(k)$, where $\sum_k p(k) = 1$. The cumulative distribution for the lower tail $P(k)$ of a discrete distribution is defined as,

$$P(k) = \sum_{i \leq k} p(i)$$

where the sum is over the allowed range of the distribution less than or equal to k. The cumulative distribution for the upper tail of a discrete distribution $Q(k)$ is defined as,

$$Q(k) = \sum_{i > k} p(i)$$

giving the sum of probabilities for all values greater than k. These two definitions satisfy the identity $P(k) + Q(k) = 1$. If the range of the distribution is 1 to n inclusive then $P(n) = 1$, $Q(n) = 0$ while $P(1) = p(1)$, $Q(1) = 1 - p(1)$.

19.2 The Gaussian Distribution

double gsl_ran_gaussian (const gsl_rng * r, double   *Function*
      sigma)

This function returns a Gaussian random variate, with mean zero and standard deviation *sigma*. The probability distribution for Gaussian random variates is,

$$p(x)dx = \frac{1}{\sqrt{2\pi\sigma^2}} \exp(-x^2/2\sigma^2)dx$$

for x in the range $-\infty$ to $+\infty$. Use the transformation $z = \mu + x$ on the numbers returned by gsl_ran_gaussian to obtain a Gaussian distribution with mean μ. This function uses the Box-Mueller algorithm which requires two calls to the random number generator r.

double gsl_ran_gaussian_pdf (double x, double *sigma*)   *Function*

This function computes the probability density $p(x)$ at x for a Gaussian distribution with standard deviation *sigma*, using the formula given above.

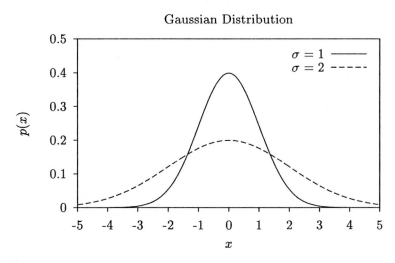

Gaussian Distribution

double gsl_ran_gaussian_ziggurat (const gsl_rng * r,   *Function*
      double *sigma*)

double gsl_ran_gaussian_ratio_method (const gsl_rng *   *Function*
      r, double *sigma*)

This function computes a Gaussian random variate using the alternative Marsaglia-Tsang ziggurat and Kinderman-Monahan-Leva ratio methods. The Ziggurat algorithm is the fastest available algorithm in most cases.

double gsl_ran_ugaussian (const gsl_rng * r)   Function
double gsl_ran_ugaussian_pdf (double x)   Function
double gsl_ran_ugaussian_ratio_method (const gsl_rng *   Function
        r)

These functions compute results for the unit Gaussian distribution. They are equivalent to the functions above with a standard deviation of one, *sigma* = 1.

double gsl_cdf_gaussian_P (double x, double *sigma*)   Function
double gsl_cdf_gaussian_Q (double x, double *sigma*)   Function
double gsl_cdf_gaussian_Pinv (double P, double *sigma*)   Function
double gsl_cdf_gaussian_Qinv (double Q, double *sigma*)   Function

These functions compute the cumulative distribution functions $P(x)$, $Q(x)$ and their inverses for the Gaussian distribution with standard deviation *sigma*.

double gsl_cdf_ugaussian_P (double x)   Function
double gsl_cdf_ugaussian_Q (double x)   Function
double gsl_cdf_ugaussian_Pinv (double P)   Function
double gsl_cdf_ugaussian_Qinv (double Q)   Function

These functions compute the cumulative distribution functions $P(x)$, $Q(x)$ and their inverses for the unit Gaussian distribution.

19.3 The Gaussian Tail Distribution

double gsl_ran_gaussian_tail (const gsl_rng * r, double   Function
      a, double *sigma*)

This function provides random variates from the upper tail of a Gaussian distribution with standard deviation *sigma*. The values returned are larger than the lower limit a, which must be positive. The method is based on Marsaglia's famous rectangle-wedge-tail algorithm (Ann. Math. Stat. 32, 894–899 (1961)), with this aspect explained in Knuth, v2, 3rd ed, p139,586 (exercise 11).

The probability distribution for Gaussian tail random variates is,

$$p(x)dx = \frac{1}{N(a;\sigma)\sqrt{2\pi\sigma^2}} \exp(-x^2/2\sigma^2)dx$$

for $x > a$ where $N(a;\sigma)$ is the normalization constant,

$$N(a;\sigma) = \frac{1}{2}\mathrm{erfc}\left(\frac{a}{\sqrt{2\sigma^2}}\right).$$

double gsl_ran_gaussian_tail_pdf (double x, double a,   Function
      double *sigma*)

This function computes the probability density $p(x)$ at x for a Gaussian tail distribution with standard deviation *sigma* and lower limit a, using the formula given above.

Gaussian Tail Distribution

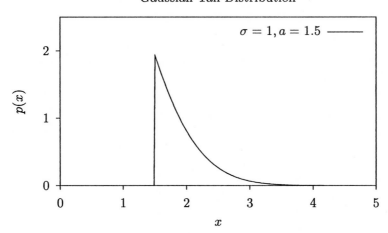

double gsl_ran_ugaussian_tail (const gsl_rng * r,   Function
       double a)

double gsl_ran_ugaussian_tail_pdf (double x, double a)   Function

These functions compute results for the tail of a unit Gaussian distribution. They are equivalent to the functions above with a standard deviation of one, *sigma* = 1.

19.4 The Bivariate Gaussian Distribution

void gsl_ran_bivariate_gaussian (const gsl_rng * r,   Function
        double *sigma_x*, double *sigma_y*, double *rho*, double * x,
        double * y)

This function generates a pair of correlated Gaussian variates, with mean zero, correlation coefficient *rho* and standard deviations *sigma_x* and *sigma_y* in the x and y directions. The probability distribution for bivariate Gaussian random variates is,

$$p(x,y)dxdy = \frac{1}{2\pi\sigma_x\sigma_y\sqrt{1-\rho^2}}\exp\left(-\frac{(x^2/\sigma_x^2 + y^2/\sigma_y^2 - 2\rho xy/(\sigma_x\sigma_y))}{2(1-\rho^2)}\right)dxdy$$

for x, y in the range $-\infty$ to $+\infty$. The correlation coefficient *rho* should lie between 1 and -1.

double gsl_ran_bivariate_gaussian_pdf (double x,   Function
        double y, double *sigma_x*, double *sigma_y*, double *rho*)

This function computes the probability density $p(x,y)$ at (x,y) for a bivariate Gaussian distribution with standard deviations *sigma_x*, *sigma_y* and correlation coefficient *rho*, using the formula given above.

Bivariate Gaussian Distribution

$$\sigma_x = 1, \sigma_y = 1, \rho = 0.9 \quad\text{———}$$

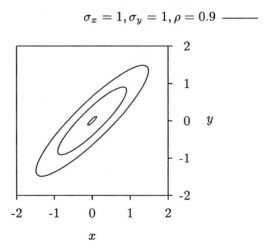

19.5 The Exponential Distribution

double gsl_ran_exponential (const gsl_rng * r, double   Function
        mu)
This function returns a random variate from the exponential distribution with mean *mu*. The distribution is,

$$p(x)dx = \frac{1}{\mu} \exp(-x/\mu)dx$$

for $x \geq 0$.

double gsl_ran_exponential_pdf (double x, double mu)   Function
This function computes the probability density $p(x)$ at x for an exponential distribution with mean *mu*, using the formula given above.

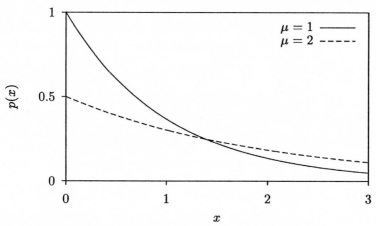

Exponential Distribution

double gsl_cdf_exponential_P (double x, double mu)   Function
double gsl_cdf_exponential_Q (double x, double mu)   Function
double gsl_cdf_exponential_Pinv (double P, double mu)   Function
double gsl_cdf_exponential_Qinv (double Q, double mu)   Function
These functions compute the cumulative distribution functions $P(x)$, $Q(x)$ and their inverses for the exponential distribution with mean *mu*.

19.6 The Laplace Distribution

double gsl_ran_laplace (const gsl_rng * r, double a)   Function
  This function returns a random variate from the Laplace distribution
  with width a. The distribution is,

$$p(x)dx = \frac{1}{2a}\exp(-|x/a|)dx$$

  for $-\infty < x < \infty$.

double gsl_ran_laplace_pdf (double x, double a)   Function
  This function computes the probability density $p(x)$ at x for a Laplace
  distribution with width a, using the formula given above.

Laplace Distribution (Two-sided Exponential)

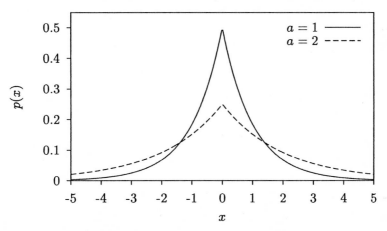

double gsl_cdf_laplace_P (double x, double a)   Function
double gsl_cdf_laplace_Q (double x, double a)   Function
double gsl_cdf_laplace_Pinv (double P, double a)   Function
double gsl_cdf_laplace_Qinv (double Q, double a)   Function
  These functions compute the cumulative distribution functions $P(x)$,
  $Q(x)$ and their inverses for the Laplace distribution with width a.

19.7 The Exponential Power Distribution

double gsl_ran_exppow (const gsl_rng * r, double a,   Function
        double b)
This function returns a random variate from the exponential power
distribution with scale parameter a and exponent b. The distribution
is,

$$p(x)dx = \frac{1}{2a\Gamma(1 + 1/b)} \exp(-|x/a|^b)dx$$

for $x \geq 0$. For $b = 1$ this reduces to the Laplace distribution. For $b = 2$
it has the same form as a gaussian distribution, but with $a = \sqrt{2}\sigma$.

double gsl_ran_exppow_pdf (double x, double a, double   Function
        b)
This function computes the probability density $p(x)$ at x for an exponential power distribution with scale parameter a and exponent b,
using the formula given above.

double gsl_cdf_exppow_P (double x, double a, double b)   Function
double gsl_cdf_exppow_Q (double x, double a, double b)   Function
    These functions compute the cumulative distribution functions $P(x)$,
    $Q(x)$ for the exponential power distribution with parameters a and b.

19.8 The Cauchy Distribution

double gsl_ran_cauchy (const gsl_rng * r, double a)   Function
   This function returns a random variate from the Cauchy distribution
   with scale parameter a. The probability distribution for Cauchy random variates is,

$$p(x)dx = \frac{1}{a\pi(1 + (x/a)^2)}dx$$

   for x in the range $-\infty$ to $+\infty$. The Cauchy distribution is also known
   as the Lorentz distribution.

double gsl_ran_cauchy_pdf (double x, double a)   Function
   This function computes the probability density $p(x)$ at x for a Cauchy
   distribution with scale parameter a, using the formula given above.

Cauchy Distribution

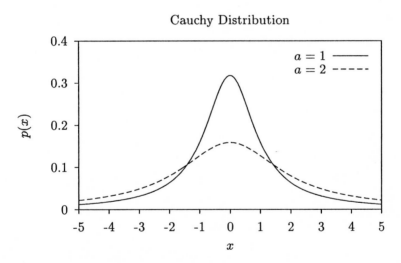

double gsl_cdf_cauchy_P (double x, double a)   Function
double gsl_cdf_cauchy_Q (double x, double a)   Function
double gsl_cdf_cauchy_Pinv (double P, double a)   Function
double gsl_cdf_cauchy_Qinv (double Q, double a)   Function
   These functions compute the cumulative distribution functions $P(x)$,
   $Q(x)$ and their inverses for the Cauchy distribution with scale parameter a.

19.9 The Rayleigh Distribution

double gsl_ran_rayleigh (const gsl_rng * r, double   Function
      sigma)

This function returns a random variate from the Rayleigh distribution
with scale parameter sigma. The distribution is,

$$p(x)dx = \frac{x}{\sigma^2} \exp(-x^2/(2\sigma^2))dx$$

for $x > 0$.

double gsl_ran_rayleigh_pdf (double x, double sigma)   Function

This function computes the probability density $p(x)$ at x for a Rayleigh
distribution with scale parameter sigma, using the formula given
above.

Rayleigh Distribution

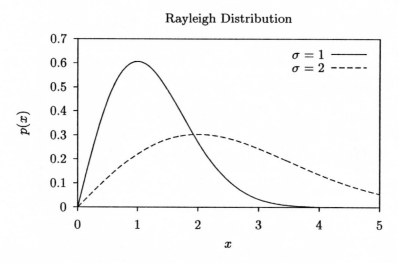

double gsl_cdf_rayleigh_P (double x, double sigma)   Function
double gsl_cdf_rayleigh_Q (double x, double sigma)   Function
double gsl_cdf_rayleigh_Pinv (double P, double sigma)   Function
double gsl_cdf_rayleigh_Qinv (double Q, double sigma)   Function

These functions compute the cumulative distribution functions $P(x)$,
$Q(x)$ and their inverses for the Rayleigh distribution with scale parameter sigma.

19.10 The Rayleigh Tail Distribution

double gsl_ran_rayleigh_tail (const gsl_rng * r, double   Function
    a, double *sigma*)
    This function returns a random variate from the tail of the Rayleigh
    distribution with scale parameter *sigma* and a lower limit of a. The
    distribution is,

$$p(x)dx = \frac{x}{\sigma^2} \exp((a^2 - x^2)/(2\sigma^2))dx$$

for $x > a$.

double gsl_ran_rayleigh_tail_pdf (double x, double a,   Function
    double *sigma*)
    This function computes the probability density $p(x)$ at x for a Rayleigh
    tail distribution with scale parameter *sigma* and lower limit a, using
    the formula given above.

Rayleigh Tail Distribution

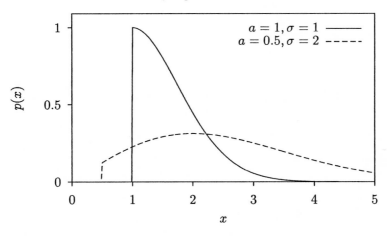

19.11 The Landau Distribution

double gsl_ran_landau (const gsl_rng * r)   *Function*
  This function returns a random variate from the Landau distribution.
  The probability distribution for Landau random variates is defined
  analytically by the complex integral,

$$p(x) = \frac{1}{2\pi i} \int_{c-i\infty}^{c+i\infty} ds \, \exp(s \log(s) + xs)$$

  For numerical purposes it is more convenient to use the following equivalent form of the integral,

$$p(x) = (1/\pi) \int_0^\infty dt \, \exp(-t \log(t) - xt) \sin(\pi t).$$

double gsl_ran_landau_pdf (double x)   *Function*
  This function computes the probability density $p(x)$ at x for the Landau distribution using an approximation to the formula given above.

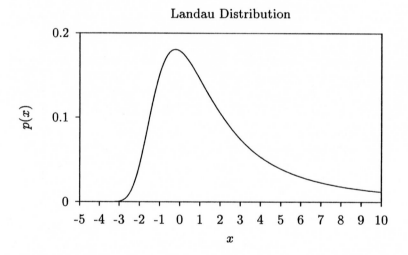

19.12 The Levy alpha-Stable Distributions

double gsl_ran_levy (const gsl_rng * r, double c, double   Function
       alpha)

This function returns a random variate from the Levy symmetric stable distribution with scale c and exponent $alpha$. The symmetric stable probability distribution is defined by a fourier transform,

$$p(x) = \frac{1}{2\pi} \int_{-\infty}^{+\infty} dt \exp(-itx - |ct|^{\alpha})$$

There is no explicit solution for the form of $p(x)$ and the library does not define a corresponding pdf function. For $\alpha = 1$ the distribution reduces to the Cauchy distribution. For $\alpha = 2$ it is a Gaussian distribution with $\sigma = \sqrt{2}c$. For $\alpha < 1$ the tails of the distribution become extremely wide.

The algorithm only works for $0 < \alpha \leq 2$.

Levy Distribution

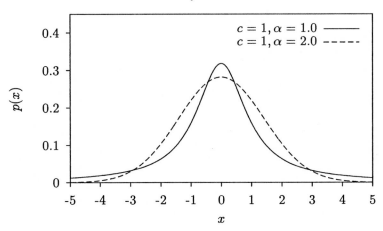

19.13 The Levy skew alpha-Stable Distribution

double gsl_ran_levy_skew (const gsl_rng * r, double c,   Function
        double *alpha*, double *beta*)

This function returns a random variate from the Levy skew stable distribution with scale c, exponent *alpha* and skewness parameter *beta*. The skewness parameter must lie in the range $[-1, 1]$. The Levy skew stable probability distribution is defined by a fourier transform,

$$p(x) = \frac{1}{2\pi} \int_{-\infty}^{+\infty} dt \exp(-itx - |ct|^\alpha (1 - i\beta \text{sign}(t) \tan(\pi\alpha/2)))$$

When $\alpha = 1$ the term $\tan(\pi\alpha/2)$ is replaced by $-(2/\pi) \log|t|$. There is no explicit solution for the form of $p(x)$ and the library does not define a corresponding pdf function. For $\alpha = 2$ the distribution reduces to a Gaussian distribution with $\sigma = \sqrt{2}c$ and the skewness parameter has no effect. For $\alpha < 1$ the tails of the distribution become extremely wide. The symmetric distribution corresponds to $\beta = 0$.

The algorithm only works for $0 < \alpha \le 2$.

The Levy alpha-stable distributions have the property that if N alpha-stable variates are drawn from the distribution $p(c, \alpha, \beta)$ then the sum $Y = X_1 + X_2 + \ldots + X_N$ will also be distributed as an alpha-stable variate, $p(N^{1/\alpha}c, \alpha, \beta)$.

Levy Skew Distribution

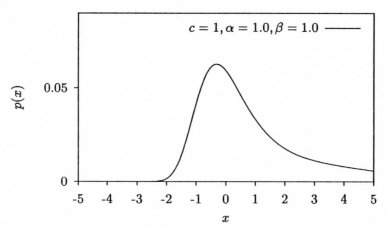

19.14 The Gamma Distribution

double gsl_ran_gamma (const gsl_rng * r, double a,   Function
      double b)

This function returns a random variate from the gamma distribution.
The distribution function is,

$$p(x)dx = \frac{1}{\Gamma(a)b^a} x^{a-1} e^{-x/b} dx$$

for $x > 0$. The gamma distribution with an integer parameter a is
known as the Erlang distribution. The variates are computed using
the algorithms from Knuth (vol 2).

double gsl_ran_gamma_mt (const gsl_rng * r, double a,   Function
      double b)

This function returns a gamma variate using the Marsaglia-Tsang fast
gamma method.

double gsl_ran_gamma_pdf (double x, double a, double b)   Function

This function computes the probability density $p(x)$ at x for a gamma
distribution with parameters a and b, using the formula given above.

Gamma Distribution

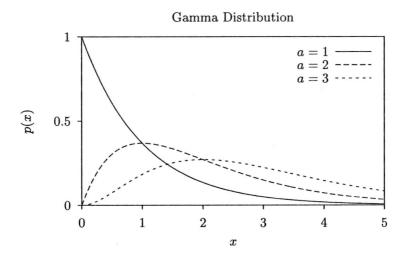

double `gsl_cdf_gamma_P` (double x, double a, double b)   Function
double `gsl_cdf_gamma_Q` (double x, double a, double b)   Function
double `gsl_cdf_gamma_Pinv` (double P, double a, double   Function
    b)
double `gsl_cdf_gamma_Qinv` (double Q, double a, double   Function
    b)

These functions compute the cumulative distribution functions $P(x)$, $Q(x)$ and their inverses for the gamma distribution with parameters a and b.

19.15 The Flat (Uniform) Distribution

double gsl_ran_flat (const gsl_rng * r, double a, double   Function
    b)
This function returns a random variate from the flat (uniform) distribution from a to b. The distribution is,

$$p(x)dx = \frac{1}{(b-a)}dx$$

if $a \le x < b$ and 0 otherwise.

double gsl_ran_flat_pdf (double x, double a, double b)   Function
This function computes the probability density $p(x)$ at x for a uniform
distribution from a to b, using the formula given above.

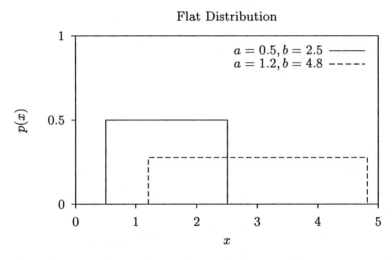

double gsl_cdf_flat_P (double x, double a, double b)   Function
double gsl_cdf_flat_Q (double x, double a, double b)   Function
double gsl_cdf_flat_Pinv (double P, double a, double b)   Function
double gsl_cdf_flat_Qinv (double Q, double a, double b)   Function
These functions compute the cumulative distribution functions $P(x)$,
$Q(x)$ and their inverses for a uniform distribution from a to b.

19.16 The Lognormal Distribution

double gsl_ran_lognormal (const gsl_rng * r, double   *Function*
      zeta, double *sigma*)

This function returns a random variate from the lognormal distribution. The distribution function is,

$$p(x)dx = \frac{1}{x\sqrt{2\pi\sigma^2}}\exp(-(\ln(x)-\zeta)^2/2\sigma^2)dx$$

for $x > 0$.

double gsl_ran_lognormal_pdf (double *x*, double *zeta*,   *Function*
      double *sigma*)

This function computes the probability density $p(x)$ at x for a lognormal distribution with parameters *zeta* and *sigma*, using the formula given above.

Lognormal Distribution

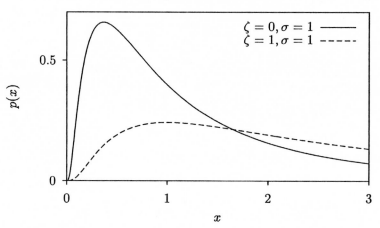

double `gsl_cdf_lognormal_P` (double *x*, double *zeta*,   Function
        double *sigma*)

double `gsl_cdf_lognormal_Q` (double *x*, double *zeta*,   Function
        double *sigma*)

double `gsl_cdf_lognormal_Pinv` (double *P*, double *zeta*, Function
        double *sigma*)

double `gsl_cdf_lognormal_Qinv` (double *Q*, double *zeta*, Function
        double *sigma*)

These functions compute the cumulative distribution functions $P(x)$, $Q(x)$ and their inverses for the lognormal distribution with parameters *zeta* and *sigma*.

19.17 The Chi-squared Distribution

The chi-squared distribution arises in statistics. If Y_i are n independent gaussian random variates with unit variance then the sum-of-squares,

$$X_i = \sum_i Y_i^2$$

has a chi-squared distribution with n degrees of freedom.

double gsl_ran_chisq (const gsl_rng * r, double *nu*)   *Function*
    This function returns a random variate from the chi-squared distribution with *nu* degrees of freedom. The distribution function is,

$$p(x)dx = \frac{1}{2\Gamma(\nu/2)}(x/2)^{\nu/2-1}\exp(-x/2)dx$$

for $x \geq 0$.

double gsl_ran_chisq_pdf (double *x*, double *nu*)   *Function*
    This function computes the probability density $p(x)$ at x for a chi-squared distribution with *nu* degrees of freedom, using the formula given above.

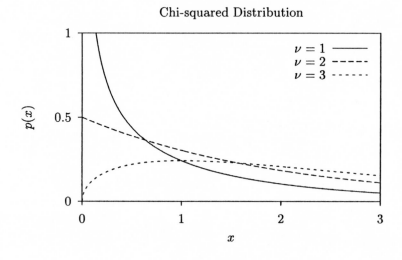

Chi-squared Distribution

double `gsl_cdf_chisq_P` (double *x*, double *nu*)   Function
double `gsl_cdf_chisq_Q` (double *x*, double *nu*)   Function
double `gsl_cdf_chisq_Pinv` (double *P*, double *nu*)   Function
double `gsl_cdf_chisq_Qinv` (double *Q*, double *nu*)   Function

These functions compute the cumulative distribution functions $P(x)$, $Q(x)$ and their inverses for the chi-squared distribution with *nu* degrees of freedom.

19.18 The F-distribution

The F-distribution arises in statistics. If Y_1 and Y_2 are chi-squared deviates with ν_1 and ν_2 degrees of freedom then the ratio,

$$X = \frac{(Y_1/\nu_1)}{(Y_2/\nu_2)}$$

has an F-distribution $F(x; \nu_1, \nu_2)$.

double **gsl_ran_fdist** (const gsl_rng * r, double *nu1*,   Function
         double *nu2*)

This function returns a random variate from the F-distribution with degrees of freedom *nu1* and *nu2*. The distribution function is,

$$p(x)dx = \frac{\Gamma((\nu_1 + \nu_2)/2)}{\Gamma(\nu_1/2)\Gamma(\nu_2/2)} \nu_1^{\nu_1/2} \nu_2^{\nu_2/2} x^{\nu_1/2-1} (\nu_2 + \nu_1 x)^{-\nu_1/2-\nu_2/2}$$

for $x \geq 0$.

double **gsl_ran_fdist_pdf** (double x, double *nu1*, double   Function
         nu2)

This function computes the probability density $p(x)$ at x for an F-distribution with *nu1* and *nu2* degrees of freedom, using the formula given above.

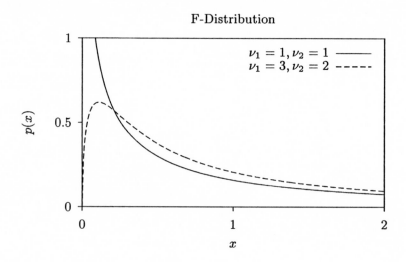

F-Distribution

double gsl_cdf_fdist_P (double x, double *nu1*, double   Function
    nu2)

double gsl_cdf_fdist_Q (double x, double *nu1*, double   Function
    nu2)

double gsl_cdf_fdist_Pinv (double P, double *nu1*,   Function
    double *nu2*)

double gsl_cdf_fdist_Qinv (double Q, double *nu1*,   Function
    double *nu2*)

These functions compute the cumulative distribution functions $P(x)$, $Q(x)$ and their inverses for the F-distribution with *nu1* and *nu2* degrees of freedom.

19.19 The t-distribution

The t-distribution, also known as Student's t distribution, arises in statistics. If Y_1 has a normal distribution and Y_2 has a chi-squared distribution with ν degrees of freedom then the ratio,

$$X = \frac{Y_1}{\sqrt{Y_2/\nu}}$$

has a t-distribution $t(x;\nu)$ with ν degrees of freedom.

double gsl_ran_tdist (const gsl_rng * r, double nu)   Function
This function returns a random variate from the t-distribution. The distribution function is,

$$p(x)dx = \frac{\Gamma((\nu+1)/2)}{\sqrt{\pi\nu}\Gamma(\nu/2)}(1+x^2/\nu)^{-(\nu+1)/2}dx$$

for $-\infty < x < +\infty$.

double gsl_ran_tdist_pdf (double x, double nu)   Function
This function computes the probability density $p(x)$ at x for a t-distribution with nu degrees of freedom, using the formula given above.

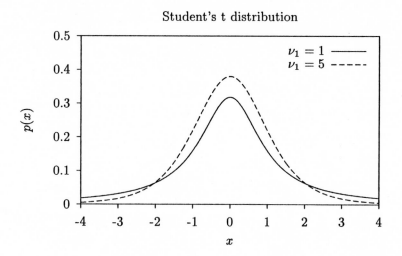

Student's t distribution

double `gsl_cdf_tdist_P` (double x, double *nu*)   Function
double `gsl_cdf_tdist_Q` (double x, double *nu*)   Function
double `gsl_cdf_tdist_Pinv` (double P, double *nu*)   Function
double `gsl_cdf_tdist_Qinv` (double Q, double *nu*)   Function

These functions compute the cumulative distribution functions $P(x)$, $Q(x)$ and their inverses for the t-distribution with *nu* degrees of freedom.

19.20 The Beta Distribution

double gsl_ran_beta (const gsl_rng * r, double a, double   *Function*
    b)
This function returns a random variate from the beta distribution.
The distribution function is,

$$p(x)dx = \frac{\Gamma(a+b)}{\Gamma(a)\Gamma(b)} x^{a-1}(1-x)^{b-1}dx$$

for $0 \le x \le 1$.

double gsl_ran_beta_pdf (double x, double a, double b)   *Function*
This function computes the probability density $p(x)$ at x for a beta
distribution with parameters a and b, using the formula given above.

Beta Distribution

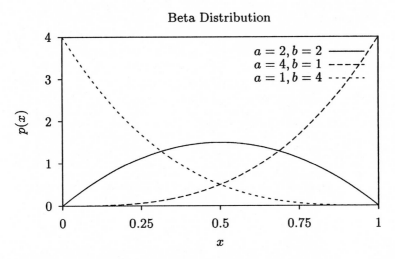

double gsl_cdf_beta_P (double x, double a, double b)   *Function*
double gsl_cdf_beta_Q (double x, double a, double b)   *Function*
double gsl_cdf_beta_Pinv (double P, double a, double b)   *Function*
double gsl_cdf_beta_Qinv (double Q, double a, double b)   *Function*
These functions compute the cumulative distribution functions $P(x)$,
$Q(x)$ and their inverses for the beta distribution with parameters a
and b.

19.21 The Logistic Distribution

double gsl_ran_logistic (const gsl_rng * r, double a)   Function
     This function returns a random variate from the logistic distribution.
     The distribution function is,

$$p(x)dx = \frac{\exp(-x/a)}{a(1 + \exp(-x/a))^2}dx$$

     for $-\infty < x < +\infty$.

double gsl_ran_logistic_pdf (double x, double a)   Function
     This function computes the probability density $p(x)$ at x for a logistic
     distribution with scale parameter a, using the formula given above.

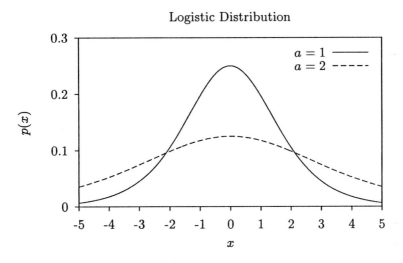

double gsl_cdf_logistic_P (double x, double a)   Function
double gsl_cdf_logistic_Q (double x, double a)   Function
double gsl_cdf_logistic_Pinv (double P, double a)   Function
double gsl_cdf_logistic_Qinv (double Q, double a)   Function
     These functions compute the cumulative distribution functions $P(x)$,
     $Q(x)$ and their inverses for the logistic distribution with scale param-
     eter a.

19.22 The Pareto Distribution

double gsl_ran_pareto (const gsl_rng * r, double a,   Function
      double b)

This function returns a random variate from the Pareto distribution of order a. The distribution function is,

$$p(x)dx = (a/b)/(x/b)^{a+1}dx$$

for $x \geq b$.

double gsl_ran_pareto_pdf (double x, double a, double   Function
      b)

This function computes the probability density $p(x)$ at x for a Pareto distribution with exponent a and scale b, using the formula given above.

Pareto Distribution

double gsl_cdf_pareto_P (double x, double a, double b)   Function
double gsl_cdf_pareto_Q (double x, double a, double b)   Function
double gsl_cdf_pareto_Pinv (double P, double a, double   Function
      b)
double gsl_cdf_pareto_Qinv (double Q, double a, double   Function
      b)

These functions compute the cumulative distribution functions $P(x)$, $Q(x)$ and their inverses for the Pareto distribution with exponent a and scale b.

19.23 Spherical Vector Distributions

The spherical distributions generate random vectors, located on a spherical surface. They can be used as random directions, for example in the steps of a random walk.

void gsl_ran_dir_2d (const gsl_rng * r, double * x,   *Function*
         double * y)

void gsl_ran_dir_2d_trig_method (const gsl_rng * r,   *Function*
         double * x, double * y)

This function returns a random direction vector $v = (x, y)$ in two dimensions. The vector is normalized such that $|v|^2 = x^2 + y^2 = 1$. The obvious way to do this is to take a uniform random number between 0 and 2π and let x and y be the sine and cosine respectively. Two trig functions would have been expensive in the old days, but with modern hardware implementations, this is sometimes the fastest way to go. This is the case for the Pentium (but not the case for the Sun Sparcstation). One can avoid the trig evaluations by choosing x and y in the interior of a unit circle (choose them at random from the interior of the enclosing square, and then reject those that are outside the unit circle), and then dividing by $\sqrt{x^2 + y^2}$. A much cleverer approach, attributed to von Neumann (See Knuth, v2, 3rd ed, p140, exercise 23), requires neither trig nor a square root. In this approach, u and v are chosen at random from the interior of a unit circle, and then $x = (u^2 - v^2)/(u^2 + v^2)$ and $y = 2uv/(u^2 + v^2)$.

void gsl_ran_dir_3d (const gsl_rng * r, double * x,   *Function*
         double * y, double * z)

This function returns a random direction vector $v = (x, y, z)$ in three dimensions. The vector is normalized such that $|v|^2 = x^2 + y^2 + z^2 = 1$. The method employed is due to Robert E. Knop (CACM 13, 326 (1970)), and explained in Knuth, v2, 3rd ed, p136. It uses the surprising fact that the distribution projected along any axis is actually uniform (this is only true for 3 dimensions).

void gsl_ran_dir_nd (const gsl_rng * r, size_t n, double   *Function*
         * x)

This function returns a random direction vector $v = (x_1, x_2, \ldots, x_n)$ in n dimensions. The vector is normalized such that $|v|^2 = x_1^2 + x_2^2 + \cdots + x_n^2 = 1$. The method uses the fact that a multivariate gaussian distribution is spherically symmetric. Each component is generated to have a gaussian distribution, and then the components are normalized. The method is described by Knuth, v2, 3rd ed, p135–136, and attributed to G. W. Brown, Modern Mathematics for the Engineer (1956).

19.24 The Weibull Distribution

double gsl_ran_weibull (const gsl_rng * r, double a,   Function
      double b)
    This function returns a random variate from the Weibull distribution.
    The distribution function is,

$$p(x)dx = \frac{b}{a^b} x^{b-1} \exp(-(x/a)^b)dx$$

    for $x \geq 0$.

double gsl_ran_weibull_pdf (double x, double a, double   Function
      b)
    This function computes the probability density $p(x)$ at x for a Weibull
    distribution with scale a and exponent b, using the formula given
    above.

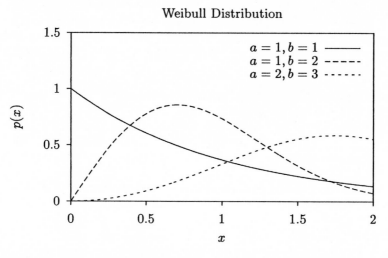

double gsl_cdf_weibull_P (double x, double a, double b)   Function
double gsl_cdf_weibull_Q (double x, double a, double b)   Function
double gsl_cdf_weibull_Pinv (double P, double a,   Function
      double b)
double gsl_cdf_weibull_Qinv (double Q, double a,   Function
      double b)
    These functions compute the cumulative distribution functions $P(x)$,
    $Q(x)$ and their inverses for the Weibull distribution with scale a and
    exponent b.

19.25 The Type-1 Gumbel Distribution

double gsl_ran_gumbel1 (const gsl_rng * r, double a,   Function
        double b)

This function returns a random variate from the Type-1 Gumbel distribution. The Type-1 Gumbel distribution function is,

$$p(x)dx = ab \exp(-(b \exp(-ax) + ax))dx$$

for $-\infty < x < \infty$.

double gsl_ran_gumbel1_pdf (double x, double a, double   Function
        b)

This function computes the probability density $p(x)$ at x for a Type-1 Gumbel distribution with parameters a and b, using the formula given above.

Type 1 Gumbel Distribution

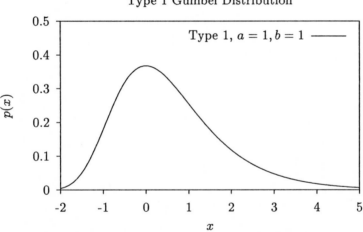

double gsl_cdf_gumbel1_P (double x, double a, double b)   Function
double gsl_cdf_gumbel1_Q (double x, double a, double b)   Function
double gsl_cdf_gumbel1_Pinv (double P, double a,   Function
        double b)
double gsl_cdf_gumbel1_Qinv (double Q, double a,   Function
        double b)

These functions compute the cumulative distribution functions $P(x)$, $Q(x)$ and their inverses for the Type-1 Gumbel distribution with parameters a and b.

19.26 The Type-2 Gumbel Distribution

double gsl_ran_gumbel2 (const gsl_rng * r, double a,   *Function*
        double b)

This function returns a random variate from the Type-2 Gumbel distribution. The Type-2 Gumbel distribution function is,

$$p(x)dx = abx^{-a-1}\exp(-bx^{-a})dx$$

for $0 < x < \infty$.

double gsl_ran_gumbel2_pdf (double x, double a, double   *Function*
        b)

This function computes the probability density $p(x)$ at x for a Type-2 Gumbel distribution with parameters a and b, using the formula given above.

Type 2 Gumbel Distribution

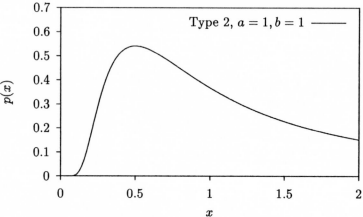

double gsl_cdf_gumbel2_P (double x, double a, double b)   *Function*
double gsl_cdf_gumbel2_Q (double x, double a, double b)   *Function*
double gsl_cdf_gumbel2_Pinv (double P, double a,   *Function*
        double b)
double gsl_cdf_gumbel2_Qinv (double Q, double a,   *Function*
        double b)

These functions compute the cumulative distribution functions $P(x)$, $Q(x)$ and their inverses for the Type-2 Gumbel distribution with parameters a and b.

19.27 The Dirichlet Distribution

void gsl_ran_dirichlet (const gsl_rng * r, size_t K,   Function
    const double alpha[], double theta[])

This function returns an array of K random variates from a Dirichlet distribution of order $K - 1$. The distribution function is

$$p(\theta_1, \ldots, \theta_K) \, d\theta_1 \cdots d\theta_K = \frac{1}{Z} \prod_{i=1}^{K} \theta_i^{\alpha_i - 1} \, \delta(1 - \sum_{i=1}^{K} \theta_i) d\theta_1 \cdots d\theta_K$$

for $\theta_i \geq 0$ and $\alpha_i \geq 0$. The delta function ensures that $\sum \theta_i = 1$. The normalization factor Z is

$$Z = \frac{\prod_{i=1}^{K} \Gamma(\alpha_i)}{\Gamma(\sum_{i=1}^{K} \alpha_i)}$$

The random variates are generated by sampling K values from gamma distributions with parameters $a = \alpha_i$, $b = 1$, and renormalizing. See A.M. Law, W.D. Kelton, *Simulation Modeling and Analysis* (1991).

double gsl_ran_dirichlet_pdf (size_t K, const double   Function
    alpha[], const double theta[])

This function computes the probability density $p(\theta_1, \ldots, \theta_K)$ at theta[K] for a Dirichlet distribution with parameters alpha[K], using the formula given above.

double gsl_ran_dirichlet_lnpdf (size_t K, const double   Function
    alpha[], const double theta[])

This function computes the logarithm of the probability density $p(\theta_1, \ldots, \theta_K)$ for a Dirichlet distribution with parameters alpha[K].

19.28   General Discrete Distributions

Given K discrete events with different probabilities $P[k]$, produce a random value k consistent with its probability.

The obvious way to do this is to preprocess the probability list by generating a cumulative probability array with $K + 1$ elements:

$$C[0] = 0$$
$$C[k + 1] = C[k] + P[k].$$

Note that this construction produces $C[K] = 1$. Now choose a uniform deviate u between 0 and 1, and find the value of k such that $C[k] \leq u < C[k + 1]$. Although this in principle requires of order $\log K$ steps per random number generation, they are fast steps, and if you use something like $\lfloor uK \rfloor$ as a starting point, you can often do pretty well.

But faster methods have been devised. Again, the idea is to preprocess the probability list, and save the result in some form of lookup table; then the individual calls for a random discrete event can go rapidly. An approach invented by G. Marsaglia (Generating discrete random numbers in a computer, Comm ACM 6, 37–38 (1963)) is very clever, and readers interested in examples of good algorithm design are directed to this short and well-written paper. Unfortunately, for large K, Marsaglia's lookup table can be quite large.

A much better approach is due to Alastair J. Walker (An efficient method for generating discrete random variables with general distributions, ACM Trans on Mathematical Software 3, 253–256 (1977); see also Knuth, v2, 3rd ed, p120–121,139). This requires two lookup tables, one floating point and one integer, but both only of size K. After preprocessing, the random numbers are generated in O(1) time, even for large K. The preprocessing suggested by Walker requires $O(K^2)$ effort, but that is not actually necessary, and the implementation provided here only takes $O(K)$ effort. In general, more preprocessing leads to faster generation of the individual random numbers, but a diminishing return is reached pretty early. Knuth points out that the optimal preprocessing is combinatorially difficult for large K.

This method can be used to speed up some of the discrete random number generators below, such as the binomial distribution. To use it for something like the Poisson Distribution, a modification would have to be made, since it only takes a finite set of K outcomes.

`gsl_ran_discrete_t * gsl_ran_discrete_preproc (size_t`   *Function*
     K, `const double * ` P)

This function returns a pointer to a structure that contains the lookup table for the discrete random number generator. The array $P[]$ contains the probabilities of the discrete events; these array elements must all be positive, but they needn't add up to one (so you can think of them more generally as "weights")—the preprocessor will normalize appropriately. This return value is used as an argument for the `gsl_ran_discrete` function below.

`size_t gsl_ran_discrete (const gsl_rng * r, const`   *Function*
     `gsl_ran_discrete_t * ` g)

After the preprocessor, above, has been called, you use this function to get the discrete random numbers.

`double gsl_ran_discrete_pdf (size_t ` k`, const`   *Function*
     `gsl_ran_discrete_t * ` g)

Returns the probability $P[k]$ of observing the variable k. Since $P[k]$ is not stored as part of the lookup table, it must be recomputed; this computation takes $O(K)$, so if K is large and you care about the original array $P[k]$ used to create the lookup table, then you should just keep this original array $P[k]$ around.

`void gsl_ran_discrete_free (gsl_ran_discrete_t * ` g)   *Function*

De-allocates the lookup table pointed to by g.

19.29 The Poisson Distribution

unsigned int gsl_ran_poisson (const gsl_rng * r, double   Function
      mu)
  This function returns a random integer from the Poisson distribution
  with mean mu. The probability distribution for Poisson variates is,

$$p(k) = \frac{\mu^k}{k!} \exp(-\mu)$$

  for $k \geq 0$.

double gsl_ran_poisson_pdf (unsigned int k, double mu)   Function
  This function computes the probability $p(k)$ of obtaining k from a
  Poisson distribution with mean mu, using the formula given above.

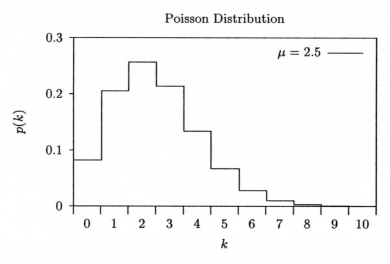

double gsl_cdf_poisson_P (unsigned int k, double mu)   Function
double gsl_cdf_poisson_Q (unsigned int k, double mu)   Function
  These functions compute the cumulative distribution functions $P(k)$,
  $Q(k)$ for the Poisson distribution with parameter mu.

19.30 The Bernoulli Distribution

unsigned int gsl_ran_bernoulli (const gsl_rng * r,   Function
      double p)
   This function returns either 0 or 1, the result of a Bernoulli trial with
   probability p. The probability distribution for a Bernoulli trial is,

$$p(0) = 1 - p$$
$$p(1) = p$$

double gsl_ran_bernoulli_pdf (unsigned int k, double p)   Function
   This function computes the probability $p(k)$ of obtaining k from a
   Bernoulli distribution with probability parameter p, using the formula
   given above.

19.31 The Binomial Distribution

unsigned int gsl_ran_binomial (const gsl_rng * r,   *Function*
        double p, unsigned int n)

This function returns a random integer from the binomial distribution,
the number of successes in n independent trials with probability p. The
probability distribution for binomial variates is,

$$p(k) = \frac{n!}{k!(n-k)!}p^k(1-p)^{n-k}$$

for $0 \le k \le n$.

double gsl_ran_binomial_pdf (unsigned int k, double p,   *Function*
        unsigned int n)

This function computes the probability $p(k)$ of obtaining k from a
binomial distribution with parameters p and n, using the formula given
above.

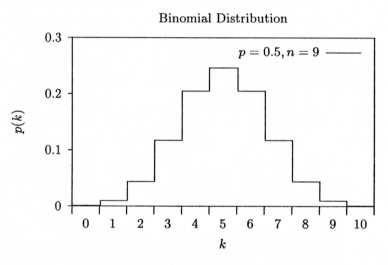

double gsl_cdf_binomial_P (unsigned int k, double p,   *Function*
        unsigned int n)
double gsl_cdf_binomial_Q (unsigned int k, double p,   *Function*
        unsigned int n)

These functions compute the cumulative distribution functions $P(k)$,
$Q(k)$ for the binomial distribution with parameters p and n.

19.32 The Multinomial Distribution

void gsl_ran_multinomial (const gsl_rng * r, size_t K,   Function
          unsigned int N, const double $p[]$, unsigned int $n[]$)
This function computes a random sample $n[]$ from the multinomial
distribution formed by N trials from an underlying distribution $p[K]$.
The distribution function for the array $n[]$ is,

$$P(n_1, n_2, \cdots, n_K) = \frac{N!}{n_1! n_2! \cdots n_K!} \, p_1^{n_1} p_2^{n_2} \cdots p_K^{n_K}$$

where $(n_1, n_2, \ldots, n_K)$ are nonnegative integers with $\sum_{k=1}^{K} n_k = N$,
and $(p_1, p_2, \ldots, p_K)$ is a probability distribution with $\sum p_i = 1$. If the
array $p[K]$ is not normalized then its entries will be treated as weights
and normalized appropriately. The arrays $n[]$ and $p[]$ must both be of
length K.

Random variates are generated using the conditional binomial method
(see C.S. David, *The computer generation of multinomial random variates*, Comp. Stat. Data Anal. 16 (1993) 205–217 for details).

double gsl_ran_multinomial_pdf (size_t K, const double   Function
          $p[]$, const unsigned int $n[]$)
This function computes the probability $P(n_1, n_2, \ldots, n_K)$ of sampling
$n[K]$ from a multinomial distribution with parameters $p[K]$, using the
formula given above.

double gsl_ran_multinomial_lnpdf (size_t K, const   Function
          double $p[]$, const unsigned int $n[]$)
This function returns the logarithm of the probability for the multinomial distribution $P(n_1, n_2, \ldots, n_K)$ with parameters $p[K]$.

19.33 The Negative Binomial Distribution

unsigned int gsl_ran_negative_binomial (const gsl_rng   Function
        * r, double p, double n)

This function returns a random integer from the negative binomial distribution. The probability distribution for negative binomial variates is,

$$p(k) = \frac{\Gamma(n+k)}{\Gamma(k+1)\Gamma(n)} p^n (1-p)^k$$

Note that n is not required to be an integer and generalises the Pascal distribution.

double gsl_ran_negative_binomial_pdf (unsigned int k,   Function
        double p, double n)

This function computes the probability $p(k)$ of obtaining k from a negative binomial distribution with parameters p and n, using the formula given above.

double gsl_cdf_negative_binomial_P (unsigned int k,   Function
        double p, double n)

double gsl_cdf_negative_binomial_Q (unsigned int k,   Function
        double p, double n)

These functions compute the cumulative distribution functions $P(k)$, $Q(k)$ for the negative binomial distribution with parameters p and n.

19.34 The Pascal Distribution

unsigned int gsl_ran_pascal (const gsl_rng * r, double   Function
      p, unsigned int n)

This function returns a random integer from the Pascal distribution,
the number of failures occurring before n successes in independent
trials with probability p of success. The Pascal distribution is simply
a negative binomial distribution with an integer value of n.

$$p(k) = \frac{(n + k - 1)!}{k!(n - 1)!}p^n(1 - p)^k$$

for $k \geq 0$

double gsl_ran_pascal_pdf (unsigned int k, double p,   Function
      unsigned int n)

This function computes the probability $p(k)$ of obtaining k from a
Pascal distribution with parameters p and n, using the formula given
above.

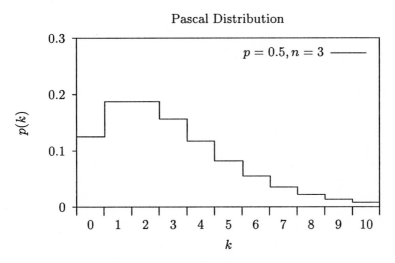

double gsl_cdf_pascal_P (unsigned int k, double p,   Function
      unsigned int n)
double gsl_cdf_pascal_Q (unsigned int k, double p,   Function
      unsigned int n)

These functions compute the cumulative distribution functions $P(k)$,
$Q(k)$ for the Pascal distribution with parameters p and n.

19.35 The Geometric Distribution

unsigned int gsl_ran_geometric (const gsl_rng * r,   *Function*
        double p)
This function returns a random integer from the geometric distribution, the number of independent trials with probability p until the first success. The probability distribution for geometric variates is,

$$p(k) = p(1-p)^{k-1}$$

for $k \geq 1$. Note that the distribution begins with $k = 1$ with this definition. There is another convention in which the exponent $k - 1$ is replaced by k.

double gsl_ran_geometric_pdf (unsigned int k, double p)   *Function*
This function computes the probability $p(k)$ of obtaining k from a geometric distribution with probability parameter p, using the formula given above.

double gsl_cdf_geometric_P (unsigned int k, double p)   *Function*
double gsl_cdf_geometric_Q (unsigned int k, double p)   *Function*
These functions compute the cumulative distribution functions $P(k)$, $Q(k)$ for the geometric distribution with parameter p.

19.36 The Hypergeometric Distribution

unsigned int gsl_ran_hypergeometric (const gsl_rng * r,   Function
        unsigned int n1, unsigned int n2, unsigned int t)
  This function returns a random integer from the hypergeometric distribution. The probability distribution for hypergeometric random variates is,

$$p(k) = C(n_1, k)C(n_2, t - k)/C(n_1 + n_2, t)$$

where $C(a, b) = a!/(b!(a - b)!)$ and $t \leq n_1 + n_2$. The domain of k is $\max(0, t - n_2), \ldots, \min(t, n_1)$.

If a population contains n_1 elements of "type 1" and n_2 elements of "type 2" then the hypergeometric distribution gives the probability of obtaining k elements of "type 1" in t samples from the population without replacement.

double gsl_ran_hypergeometric_pdf (unsigned int k,   Function
        unsigned int n1, unsigned int n2, unsigned int t)
  This function computes the probability $p(k)$ of obtaining k from a hypergeometric distribution with parameters n1, n2, t, using the formula given above.

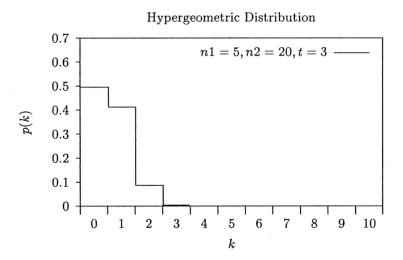

double gsl_cdf_hypergeometric_P (unsigned int k,   Function
        unsigned int $n1$, unsigned int $n2$, unsigned int t)
double gsl_cdf_hypergeometric_Q (unsigned int k,   Function
        unsigned int $n1$, unsigned int $n2$, unsigned int t)
    These functions compute the cumulative distribution functions $P(k)$,
    $Q(k)$ for the hypergeometric distribution with parameters $n1$, $n2$ and
    t.

19.37 The Logarithmic Distribution

unsigned int gsl_ran_logarithmic (const gsl_rng * r,   *Function*
        double p)

This function returns a random integer from the logarithmic distribution. The probability distribution for logarithmic random variates is,

$$p(k) = \frac{-1}{\log(1-p)}\left(\frac{p^k}{k}\right)$$

for $k \geq 1$.

double gsl_ran_logarithmic_pdf (unsigned int k, double   *Function*
        p)

This function computes the probability $p(k)$ of obtaining k from a logarithmic distribution with probability parameter p, using the formula given above.

Logarithmic Distribution

19.38 Shuffling and Sampling

The following functions allow the shuffling and sampling of a set of objects. The algorithms rely on a random number generator as a source of randomness and a poor quality generator can lead to correlations in the output. In particular it is important to avoid generators with a short period. For more information see Knuth, v2, 3rd ed, Section 3.4.2, "Random Sampling and Shuffling".

void gsl_ran_shuffle (const gsl_rng * r, void * *base*,   Function
        size_t *n*, size_t *size*)

This function randomly shuffles the order of *n* objects, each of size *size*, stored in the array *base*[]. The output of the random number generator *r* is used to produce the permutation. The algorithm generates all possible *n*! permutations with equal probability, assuming a perfect source of random numbers.

The following code shows how to shuffle the numbers from 0 to 51,

```
int a[52];

for (i = 0; i < 52; i++)
  {
    a[i] = i;
  }


gsl_ran_shuffle (r, a, 52, sizeof (int));
```

int gsl_ran_choose (const gsl_rng * r, void * *dest*,   Function
        size_t *k*, void * *src*, size_t *n*, size_t *size*)

This function fills the first *k* elements of the array *dest*[] with objects taken randomly from the first *n* elements of the array *src*[]. The objects are each of size *size*. The output of the random number generator *r* is used to make the selection. The algorithm ensures all possible samples are equally likely, assuming a perfect source of randomness.

The objects are sampled *without* replacement, thus each object can only appear once in *dest*[]. It is required that *k* be less than or equal to n. The objects in *dest* will be in the same relative order as those in *src*. You will need to call gsl_ran_shuffle(r, dest, n, size) if you want to randomize the order.

The following code shows how to select a random sample of three unique numbers from the set 0 to 99,

```
double a[3], b[100];

for (i = 0; i < 100; i++)
  {
    b[i] = (double) i;
  }

gsl_ran_choose (r, a, 3, b, 100, sizeof (double));
```

void gsl_ran_sample (const gsl_rng * r, void * *dest*,   *Function*
      size_t *k*, void * *src*, size_t *n*, size_t *size*)

This function is like gsl_ran_choose but samples *k* items from the original array of *n* items *src* with replacement, so the same object can appear more than once in the output sequence *dest*. There is no requirement that *k* be less than *n* in this case.

19.39 Examples

The following program demonstrates the use of a random number generator to produce variates from a distribution. It prints 10 samples from the Poisson distribution with a mean of 3.

```
#include <stdio.h>
#include <gsl/gsl_rng.h>
#include <gsl/gsl_randist.h>

int
main (void)
{
  const gsl_rng_type * T;
  gsl_rng * r;

  int i, n = 10;
  double mu = 3.0;

  /* create a generator chosen by the
     environment variable GSL_RNG_TYPE */

  gsl_rng_env_setup();

  T = gsl_rng_default;
  r = gsl_rng_alloc (T);

  /* print n random variates chosen from
     the poisson distribution with mean
```

```
      parameter mu */

  for (i = 0; i < n; i++)
    {
      unsigned int k = gsl_ran_poisson (r, mu);
      printf (" %u", k);
    }

  printf ("\n");
  return 0;
}
```

If the library and header files are installed under '/usr/local' (the default
location) then the program can be compiled with these options,

```
$ gcc -Wall demo.c -lgsl -lgslcblas -lm
```

Here is the output of the program,

```
$ ./a.out
 2 5 5 2 1 0 3 4 1 1
```

The variates depend on the seed used by the generator. The seed for the
default generator type gsl_rng_default can be changed with the GSL_
RNG_SEED environment variable to produce a different stream of variates,

```
$ GSL_RNG_SEED=123 ./a.out
GSL_RNG_SEED=123
 4 5 6 3 3 1 4 2 5 5
```

The following program generates a random walk in two dimensions.

```
#include <stdio.h>
#include <gsl/gsl_rng.h>
#include <gsl/gsl_randist.h>

int
main (void)
{
  int i;
  double x = 0, y = 0, dx, dy;

  const gsl_rng_type * T;
  gsl_rng * r;

  gsl_rng_env_setup();
  T = gsl_rng_default;
  r = gsl_rng_alloc (T);

  printf ("%g %g\n", x, y);
```

```
for (i = 0; i < 10; i++)
  {
    gsl_ran_dir_2d (r, &dx, &dy);
    x += dx; y += dy;
    printf ("%g %g\n", x, y);
  }
return 0;
}
```

Here is the output from the program, three 10-step random walks from the origin,

Random walk

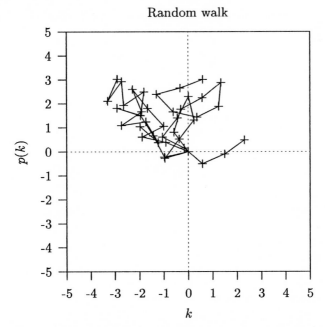

The following program computes the upper and lower cumulative distribution functions for the standard normal distribution at $x = 2$.

```
#include <stdio.h>
#include <gsl/gsl_cdf.h>

int
main (void)
{
  double P, Q;
  double x = 2.0;
```

```
P = gsl_cdf_ugaussian_P (x);
printf ("prob(x < %f) = %f\n", x, P);

Q = gsl_cdf_ugaussian_Q (x);
printf ("prob(x > %f) = %f\n", x, Q);

x = gsl_cdf_ugaussian_Pinv (P);
printf ("Pinv(%f) = %f\n", P, x);

x = gsl_cdf_ugaussian_Qinv (Q);
printf ("Qinv(%f) = %f\n", Q, x);

    return 0;
}
```

Here is the output of the program,

```
prob(x < 2.000000) = 0.977250
prob(x > 2.000000) = 0.022750
Pinv(0.977250) = 2.000000
Qinv(0.022750) = 2.000000
```

19.40 References and Further Reading

For encyclopaedic coverage of random variates readers are advised to consult the book *Non-Uniform Random Variate Generation* by Luc Devroye. It covers every imaginable distribution and provides hundreds of algorithms.

Luc Devroye, *Non-Uniform Random Variate Generation*, Springer-Verlag, ISBN 0-387-96305-7.

The subject of random variate generation is also reviewed by Knuth, who describes algorithms for all the major distributions.

Donald E. Knuth, *The Art of Computer Programming: Seminumerical Algorithms* (Vol 2, 3rd Ed, 1997), Addison-Wesley, ISBN 0201896842.

The Particle Data Group provides a short review of techniques for generating distributions of random numbers in the "Monte Carlo" section of its Annual Review of Particle Physics.

Review of Particle Properties R.M. Barnett et al., Physical Review D54, 1 (1996) http://pdg.lbl.gov/.

The Review of Particle Physics is available online in postscript and pdf format.

An overview of methods used to compute cumulative distribution functions can be found in *Statistical Computing* by W.J. Kennedy and J.E. Gentle. Another general reference is *Elements of Statistical Computing* by R.A. Thisted.

> William E. Kennedy and James E. Gentle, *Statistical Computing* (1980), Marcel Dekker, ISBN 0-8247-6898-1.

> Ronald A. Thisted, *Elements of Statistical Computing* (1988), Chapman & Hall, ISBN 0-412-01371-1.

The cumulative distribution functions for the Gaussian distribution are based on the following papers,

> *Rational Chebyshev Approximations Using Linear Equations*, W.J. Cody, W. Fraser, J.F. Hart. Numerische Mathematik 12, 242–251 (1968).

> *Rational Chebyshev Approximations for the Error Function*, W.J. Cody. Mathematics of Computation 23, n107, 631–637 (July 1969).

20 Statistics

This chapter describes the statistical functions in the library. The basic statistical functions include routines to compute the mean, variance and standard deviation. More advanced functions allow you to calculate absolute deviations, skewness, and kurtosis as well as the median and arbitrary percentiles. The algorithms use recurrence relations to compute average quantities in a stable way, without large intermediate values that might overflow or cause spurious cancellation errors.

The functions are available in versions for datasets in the standard floating-point and integer types. The versions for double precision floating-point data have the prefix gsl_stats and are declared in the header file 'gsl_statistics_double.h'. The versions for integer data have the prefix gsl_stats_int and are declared in the header file 'gsl_statistics_int.h'. Other types are declared in corresponding header files according to the standard GSL naming conventions (see Section 2.9 [Support for different numeric types], page 14).

20.1 Mean, Standard Deviation and Variance

double gsl_stats_mean (const double *data[]*, size_t   Function
     stride, size_t *n*)
This function returns the arithmetic mean of *data*, a dataset of length *n* with stride *stride*. The arithmetic mean, or *sample mean*, is denoted by $\hat{\mu}$ and defined as,

$$\hat{\mu} = \frac{1}{N} \sum x_i$$

where x_i are the elements of the dataset *data*. For samples drawn from a gaussian distribution the variance of $\hat{\mu}$ is σ^2/N.

double gsl_stats_variance (const double *data[]*, size_t   Function
     stride, size_t *n*)
This function returns the estimated, or *sample*, variance of *data*, a dataset of length *n* with stride *stride*. The estimated variance is denoted by $\hat{\sigma}^2$ and is defined by,

$$\hat{\sigma}^2 = \frac{1}{(N-1)} \sum (x_i - \hat{\mu})^2$$

where x_i are the elements of the dataset *data*. Note that the normalization factor of $1/(N-1)$ results from the derivation of $\hat{\sigma}^2$ as an unbiased estimator of the population variance σ^2. For samples drawn from a gaussian distribution the variance of $\hat{\sigma}^2$ itself is $2\sigma^4/N$.

This function computes the mean via a call to `gsl_stats_mean`. If you have already computed the mean then you can pass it directly to `gsl_stats_variance_m`.

double `gsl_stats_variance_m` (const double *data*[], size_t   Function
        stride, size_t *n*, double *mean*)
This function returns the sample variance of *data* relative to the given value of *mean*. The function is computed with $\hat{\mu}$ replaced by the value of *mean* that you supply,

$$\hat{\sigma}^2 = \frac{1}{(N-1)} \sum (x_i - mean)^2$$

double `gsl_stats_sd` (const double *data*[], size_t *stride*,   Function
        size_t *n*)
double `gsl_stats_sd_m` (const double *data*[], size_t   Function
        stride, size_t *n*, double *mean*)
The standard deviation is defined as the square root of the variance. These functions return the square root of the corresponding variance functions above.

double `gsl_stats_variance_with_fixed_mean` (const   Function
        double *data*[], size_t *stride*, size_t *n*, double *mean*)
This function computes an unbiased estimate of the variance of *data* when the population mean *mean* of the underlying distribution is known *a priori*. In this case the estimator for the variance uses the factor $1/N$ and the sample mean $\hat{\mu}$ is replaced by the known population mean μ,

$$\hat{\sigma}^2 = \frac{1}{N} \sum (x_i - \mu)^2$$

double `gsl_stats_sd_with_fixed_mean` (const double   Function
        data[], size_t *stride*, size_t *n*, double *mean*)
This function calculates the standard deviation of *data* for a fixed population mean *mean*. The result is the square root of the corresponding variance function.

20.2 Absolute deviation

double gsl_stats_absdev (const double *data*[], size_t   Function
        stride, size_t *n*)

This function computes the absolute deviation from the mean of *data*,
a dataset of length *n* with stride *stride*. The absolute deviation from
the mean is defined as,

$$absdev = \frac{1}{N} \sum |x_i - \hat{\mu}|$$

where x_i are the elements of the dataset *data*. The absolute deviation
from the mean provides a more robust measure of the width of a distribution than the variance. This function computes the mean of *data*
via a call to gsl_stats_mean.

double gsl_stats_absdev_m (const double *data*[], size_t   Function
        stride, size_t *n*, double *mean*)

This function computes the absolute deviation of the dataset *data*
relative to the given value of *mean*,

$$absdev = \frac{1}{N} \sum |x_i - mean|$$

This function is useful if you have already computed the mean of *data*
(and want to avoid recomputing it), or wish to calculate the absolute
deviation relative to another value (such as zero, or the median).

20.3 Higher moments (skewness and kurtosis)

double gsl_stats_skew (const double *data*[], size_t   Function
        stride, size_t *n*)

This function computes the skewness of *data*, a dataset of length *n*
with stride *stride*. The skewness is defined as,

$$skew = \frac{1}{N} \sum \left(\frac{x_i - \hat{\mu}}{\hat{\sigma}} \right)^3$$

where x_i are the elements of the dataset *data*. The skewness measures
the asymmetry of the tails of a distribution.

The function computes the mean and estimated standard deviation of
data via calls to gsl_stats_mean and gsl_stats_sd.

double `gsl_stats_skew_m_sd` (const double *data*[], size_t   *Function*
        stride, size_t *n*, double *mean*, double *sd*)

This function computes the skewness of the dataset *data* using the
given values of the mean *mean* and standard deviation *sd*,

$$skew = \frac{1}{N} \sum \left(\frac{x_i - mean}{sd} \right)^3$$

These functions are useful if you have already computed the mean and
standard deviation of *data* and want to avoid recomputing them.

double `gsl_stats_kurtosis` (const double *data*[], size_t   *Function*
        stride, size_t *n*)

This function computes the kurtosis of *data*, a dataset of length n with
stride *stride*. The kurtosis is defined as,

$$kurtosis = \left(\frac{1}{N} \sum \left(\frac{x_i - \hat{\mu}}{\hat{\sigma}} \right)^4 \right) - 3$$

The kurtosis measures how sharply peaked a distribution is, relative
to its width. The kurtosis is normalized to zero for a gaussian distribution.

double `gsl_stats_kurtosis_m_sd` (const double *data*[],   *Function*
        size_t *stride*, size_t *n*, double *mean*, double *sd*)

This function computes the kurtosis of the dataset *data* using the given
values of the mean *mean* and standard deviation *sd*,

$$kurtosis = \frac{1}{N} \left(\sum \left(\frac{x_i - mean}{sd} \right)^4 \right) - 3$$

This function is useful if you have already computed the mean and
standard deviation of *data* and want to avoid recomputing them.

20.4 Autocorrelation

double gsl_stats_lag1_autocorrelation (const double   *Function*
    data[], const size_t *stride*, const size_t *n*)
This function computes the lag-1 autocorrelation of the dataset *data*.

$$a_1 = \frac{\sum_{i=1}^{n}(x_i - \hat{\mu})(x_{i-1} - \hat{\mu})}{\sum_{i=1}^{n}(x_i - \hat{\mu})(x_i - \hat{\mu})}$$

double gsl_stats_lag1_autocorrelation_m (const double   *Function*
    data[], const size_t *stride*, const size_t *n*, const
    double *mean*)
This function computes the lag-1 autocorrelation of the dataset *data*
using the given value of the mean *mean*.

20.5 Covariance

double gsl_stats_covariance (const double *data1*[],   *Function*
    const size_t *stride1*, const double *data2*[], const size_t
    stride2, const size_t *n*)
This function computes the covariance of the datasets *data1* and *data2*
which must both be of the same length *n*.

$$covar = \frac{1}{(n-1)} \sum_{i=1}^{n}(x_i - \hat{x})(y_i - \hat{y})$$

double gsl_stats_covariance_m (const double *data1*[],   *Function*
    const size_t *stride1*, const double *data2*[], const size_t
    stride2, const size_t *n*, const double *mean1*, const
    double *mean2*)
This function computes the covariance of the datasets *data1* and *data2*
using the given values of the means, *mean1* and *mean2*. This is useful
if you have already computed the means of *data1* and *data2* and want
to avoid recomputing them.

20.6 Weighted Samples

The functions described in this section allow the computation of statistics for weighted samples. The functions accept an array of samples, x_i, with associated weights, w_i. Each sample x_i is considered as having been drawn from a Gaussian distribution with variance σ_i^2, and the sample weight w_i is defined as the reciprocal of this variance, $w_i = 1/\sigma_i^2$. Setting a weight to zero corresponds to removing a sample from a dataset. Any datapoints with negative (unphysical) weights are automatically excluded from the calculations.

double gsl_stats_wmean (const double w[], size_t   Function
        wstride, const double data[], size_t stride, size_t n)

This function returns the weighted mean of the dataset data with stride stride and length n, using the set of weights w with stride wstride and length n. The weighted mean is defined as,

$$\hat{\mu} = \frac{\sum w_i x_i}{\sum w_i}$$

double gsl_stats_wvariance (const double w[], size_t   Function
        wstride, const double data[], size_t stride, size_t n)

This function returns the estimated variance of the dataset data with stride stride and length n, using the set of weights w with stride wstride and length n. The estimated variance of a weighted dataset is defined as,

$$\hat{\sigma}^2 = \frac{\sum w_i}{(\sum w_i)^2 - \sum(w_i^2)} \sum w_i (x_i - \hat{\mu})^2$$

Note that this expression reduces to an unweighted variance with the familiar $1/(N-1)$ factor when there are N equal non-zero weights.

double gsl_stats_wvariance_m (const double w[], size_t   Function
        wstride, const double data[], size_t stride, size_t n,
        double wmean)

This function returns the estimated variance of the weighted dataset data using the given weighted mean wmean.

double gsl_stats_wsd (const double w[], size_t wstride,   Function
        const double data[], size_t stride, size_t n)

The standard deviation is defined as the square root of the variance. This function returns the square root of the corresponding variance function gsl_stats_wvariance above.

double gsl_stats_wsd_m (const double w[], size_t   Function
        wstride, const double data[], size_t stride, size_t n,
        double wmean)

This function returns the square root of the corresponding variance
function gsl_stats_wvariance_m above.

double gsl_stats_wvariance_with_fixed_mean (const   Function
        double w[], size_t wstride, const double data[], size_t
        stride, size_t n, const double mean)

This function computes an unbiased estimate of the variance of
weighted dataset data when the population mean mean of the underlying distribution is known a priori. In this case the estimator for the
variance replaces the sample mean $\hat{\mu}$ by the known population mean
μ,

$$\hat{\sigma}^2 = \frac{\sum w_i(x_i - \mu)^2}{\sum w_i}$$

double gsl_stats_wsd_with_fixed_mean (const double   Function
        w[], size_t wstride, const double data[], size_t stride,
        size_t n, const double mean)

The standard deviation is defined as the square root of the variance.
This function returns the square root of the corresponding variance
function above.

double gsl_stats_wabsdev (const double w[], size_t   Function
        wstride, const double data[], size_t stride, size_t n)

This function computes the weighted absolute deviation from the
weighted mean of data. The absolute deviation from the mean is defined as,

$$absdev = \frac{\sum w_i|x_i - \hat{\mu}|}{\sum w_i}$$

double gsl_stats_wabsdev_m (const double w[], size_t   Function
        wstride, const double data[], size_t stride, size_t n,
        double wmean)

This function computes the absolute deviation of the weighted dataset
data about the given weighted mean wmean.

double gsl_stats_wskew (const double w[], size_t   Function
        wstride, const double data[], size_t stride, size_t n)

This function computes the weighted skewness of the dataset data.

$$skew = \frac{\sum w_i((x_i - \hat{\mu})/\sigma)^3}{\sum w_i}$$

double gsl_stats_wskew_m_sd (const double w[], size_t   Function
        wstride, const double data[], size_t stride, size_t n,
        double wmean, double wsd)

This function computes the weighted skewness of the dataset data
using the given values of the weighted mean and weighted standard
deviation, wmean and wsd.

double gsl_stats_wkurtosis (const double w[], size_t   Function
        wstride, const double data[], size_t stride, size_t n)

This function computes the weighted kurtosis of the dataset data.

$$kurtosis = \frac{\sum w_i((x_i - \hat{\mu})/\hat{\sigma})^4}{\sum w_i} - 3$$

double gsl_stats_wkurtosis_m_sd (const double w[],   Function
        size_t wstride, const double data[], size_t stride,
        size_t n, double wmean, double wsd)

This function computes the weighted kurtosis of the dataset data using
the given values of the weighted mean and weighted standard deviation, wmean and wsd.

20.7 Maximum and Minimum values

The following functions find the maximum and minimum values of
a dataset (or their indices). If the data contains NaNs then a NaN will
be returned, since the maximum or minimum value is undefined. For
functions which return an index, the location of the first NaN in the array
is returned.

double gsl_stats_max (const double data[], size_t stride,   Function
        size_t n)

This function returns the maximum value in data, a dataset of length
n with stride stride. The maximum value is defined as the value of the
element x_i which satisfies $x_i \geq x_j$ for all j.

If you want instead to find the element with the largest absolute magnitude you will need to apply fabs or abs to your data before calling
this function.

double gsl_stats_min (const double data[], size_t stride,   Function
        size_t n)

This function returns the minimum value in data, a dataset of length
n with stride stride. The minimum value is defined as the value of the
element x_i which satisfies $x_i \leq x_j$ for all j.

If you want instead to find the element with the smallest absolute
magnitude you will need to apply fabs or abs to your data before
calling this function.

void gsl_stats_minmax (double * *min*, double * *max*,   Function
        const double *data*[], size_t *stride*, size_t *n*)
This function finds both the minimum and maximum values *min*, *max*
in *data* in a single pass.

size_t gsl_stats_max_index (const double *data*[], size_t   Function
        stride, size_t *n*)
This function returns the index of the maximum value in *data*, a
dataset of length *n* with stride *stride*. The maximum value is defined as the value of the element x_i which satisfies $x_i \geq x_j$ for all j.
When there are several equal maximum elements then the first one is
chosen.

size_t gsl_stats_min_index (const double *data*[], size_t   Function
        stride, size_t *n*)
This function returns the index of the minimum value in *data*, a dataset
of length *n* with stride *stride*. The minimum value is defined as the
value of the element x_i which satisfies $x_i \geq x_j$ for all j. When there
are several equal minimum elements then the first one is chosen.

void gsl_stats_minmax_index (size_t * *min_index*, size_t   Function
        * *max_index*, const double *data*[], size_t *stride*, size_t
        n)
This function returns the indexes *min_index*, *max_index* of the minimum and maximum values in *data* in a single pass.

20.8 Median and Percentiles

The median and percentile functions described in this section operate
on sorted data. For convenience the functions use *quantiles*, measured on
a scale of 0 to 1, instead of percentiles (which use a scale of 0 to 100).

double gsl_stats_median_from_sorted_data (const double   Function
        sorted_data[], size_t *stride*, size_t *n*)
This function returns the median value of *sorted_data*, a dataset of
length *n* with stride *stride*. The elements of the array must be in
ascending numerical order. There are no checks to see whether the
data are sorted, so the function gsl_sort should always be used first.
When the dataset has an odd number of elements the median is the
value of element $(n-1)/2$. When the dataset has an even number
of elements the median is the mean of the two nearest middle values,
elements $(n-1)/2$ and $n/2$. Since the algorithm for computing the
median involves interpolation this function always returns a floating-
point number, even for integer data types.

double gsl_stats_quantile_from_sorted_data (const   *Function*
        double *sorted_data*[], size_t *stride*, size_t *n*, double *f*)

This function returns a quantile value of *sorted_data*, a double-precision array of length *n* with stride *stride*. The elements of the array must be in ascending numerical order. The quantile is determined by the *f*, a fraction between 0 and 1. For example, to compute the value of the 75th percentile *f* should have the value 0.75.

There are no checks to see whether the data are sorted, so the function gsl_sort should always be used first.

The quantile is found by interpolation, using the formula

$$\text{quantile} = (1 - \delta)x_i + \delta x_{i+1}$$

where i is floor($(n-1)f$) and δ is $(n-1)f - i$.

Thus the minimum value of the array (data[0*stride]) is given by *f* equal to zero, the maximum value (data[(n-1)*stride]) is given by *f* equal to one and the median value is given by *f* equal to 0.5. Since the algorithm for computing quantiles involves interpolation this function always returns a floating-point number, even for integer data types.

20.9 Examples

Here is a basic example of how to use the statistical functions:

```
#include <stdio.h>
#include <gsl/gsl_statistics.h>

int
main(void)
{
  double data[5] = {17.2, 18.1, 16.5, 18.3, 12.6};
  double mean, variance, largest, smallest;

  mean     = gsl_stats_mean(data, 1, 5);
  variance = gsl_stats_variance(data, 1, 5);
  largest  = gsl_stats_max(data, 1, 5);
  smallest = gsl_stats_min(data, 1, 5);

  printf ("The dataset is %g, %g, %g, %g, %g\n",
          data[0], data[1], data[2], data[3], data[4]);

  printf ("The sample mean is %g\n", mean);
  printf ("The estimated variance is %g\n", variance);
  printf ("The largest value is %g\n", largest);
  printf ("The smallest value is %g\n", smallest);
```

```
        return 0;
    }
```

The program should produce the following output,

```
The dataset is 17.2, 18.1, 16.5, 18.3, 12.6
The sample mean is 16.54
The estimated variance is 4.2984
The largest value is 18.3
The smallest value is 12.6
```

Here is an example using sorted data,

```
#include <stdio.h>
#include <gsl/gsl_sort.h>
#include <gsl/gsl_statistics.h>

int
main(void)
{
    double data[5] = {17.2, 18.1, 16.5, 18.3, 12.6};
    double median, upperq, lowerq;

    printf ("Original dataset:  %g, %g, %g, %g, %g\n",
            data[0], data[1], data[2], data[3], data[4]);

    gsl_sort (data, 1, 5);

    printf ("Sorted dataset: %g, %g, %g, %g, %g\n",
            data[0], data[1], data[2], data[3], data[4]);

    median
      = gsl_stats_median_from_sorted_data (data,
                                            1, 5);

    upperq
      = gsl_stats_quantile_from_sorted_data (data,
                                            1, 5,
                                            0.75);
    lowerq
      = gsl_stats_quantile_from_sorted_data (data,
                                            1, 5,
                                            0.25);

    printf ("The median is %g\n", median);
    printf ("The upper quartile is %g\n", upperq);
    printf ("The lower quartile is %g\n", lowerq);
```

```
   return 0;
}
```

This program should produce the following output,

```
Original dataset: 17.2, 18.1, 16.5, 18.3, 12.6
Sorted dataset: 12.6, 16.5, 17.2, 18.1, 18.3
The median is 17.2
The upper quartile is 18.1
The lower quartile is 16.5
```

20.10   References and Further Reading

The standard reference for almost any topic in statistics is the multi-volume *Advanced Theory of Statistics* by Kendall and Stuart.

> Maurice Kendall, Alan Stuart, and J. Keith Ord. *The Advanced Theory of Statistics* (multiple volumes) reprinted as *Kendall's Advanced Theory of Statistics*. Wiley, ISBN 047023380X.

Many statistical concepts can be more easily understood by a Bayesian approach. The following book by Gelman, Carlin, Stern and Rubin gives a comprehensive coverage of the subject.

> Andrew Gelman, John B. Carlin, Hal S. Stern, Donald B. Rubin. *Bayesian Data Analysis* (2nd Ed). Chapman & Hall, ISBN 158488388X.

For physicists the Particle Data Group provides useful reviews of Probability and Statistics in the "Mathematical Tools" section of its Annual Review of Particle Physics.

> *Review of Particle Properties* R.M. Barnett et al., Physical Review D54, 1 (1996)

The Review of Particle Physics is available online at the website http://pdg.lbl.gov/.

21 Histograms

This chapter describes functions for creating histograms. Histograms provide a convenient way of summarizing the distribution of a set of data. A histogram consists of a set of *bins* which count the number of events falling into a given range of a continuous variable, x. The bins contain floating-point numbers, so they can be used to record both integer and non-integer distributions. The histogram bins can have user-defined ranges (uniformly spaced bins are the default). Both one and two-dimensional histograms are supported.

Once a histogram has been created it can also be converted into a probability distribution function. The library provides efficient routines for selecting random samples from probability distributions. This can be useful for generating simulations based on real data.

The functions are declared in the header files 'gsl_histogram.h' and 'gsl_histogram2d.h'.

21.1 The histogram struct

A histogram is defined by the following struct,

`gsl_histogram`   *Data Type*

   `size_t n`   This is the number of histogram bins

   `double * range`
                  The ranges of the bins are stored in an array of $n + 1$ elements pointed to by *range*.

   `double * bin`
                  The counts for each bin are stored in an array of n elements pointed to by *bin*. The bins are floating-point numbers, so you can increment them by non-integer values if necessary.

The range for *bin*[i] is given by *range*[i] to *range*[i+1]. For n bins there are $n + 1$ entries in the array *range*. Each bin is inclusive at the lower end and exclusive at the upper end. Mathematically this means that the bins are defined by the following inequality,

$$\text{bin[i] corresponds to range[i]} \leq x < \text{range[i+1]}$$

Here is a diagram of the correspondence between ranges and bins on the number-line for x,

```
[ bin[0] )[ bin[1] )[ bin[2] )[ bin[3] )[ bin[4] )
---|---------|---------|---------|---------|---------|---   x
  r[0]      r[1]      r[2]      r[3]      r[4]      r[5]
```

In this picture the values of the *range* array are denoted by r. On the left-hand side of each bin the square bracket '[' denotes an inclusive lower bound ($r \leq x$), and the round parentheses ')' on the right-hand side denote an exclusive upper bound ($x < r$). Thus any samples which fall on the upper end of the histogram are excluded. If you want to include this value for the last bin you will need to add an extra bin to your histogram.

The gsl_histogram struct and its associated functions are defined in the header file 'gsl_histogram.h'.

21.2 Histogram allocation

The functions for allocating memory to a histogram follow the style of malloc and free. In addition they also perform their own error checking. If there is insufficient memory available to allocate a histogram then the functions call the error handler (with an error number of GSL_ENOMEM) in addition to returning a null pointer. Thus if you use the library error handler to abort your program then it isn't necessary to check every histogram alloc.

gsl_histogram * gsl_histogram_alloc (size_t *n*)   Function
This function allocates memory for a histogram with *n* bins, and returns a pointer to a newly created gsl_histogram struct. If insufficient memory is available a null pointer is returned and the error handler is invoked with an error code of GSL_ENOMEM. The bins and ranges are not initialized, and should be prepared using one of the range-setting functions below in order to make the histogram ready for use.

int gsl_histogram_set_ranges (gsl_histogram * *h*, const   Function
          double *range*[], size_t *size*)
This function sets the ranges of the existing histogram *h* using the array *range* of size *size*. The values of the histogram bins are reset to zero. The range array should contain the desired bin limits. The ranges can be arbitrary, subject to the restriction that they are monotonically increasing.

The following example shows how to create a histogram with logarithmic bins with ranges [1,10), [10,100) and [100,1000).

```
gsl_histogram * h = gsl_histogram_alloc (3);

/* bin[0] covers the range 1 <= x < 10 */
/* bin[1] covers the range 10 <= x < 100 */
/* bin[2] covers the range 100 <= x < 1000 */

double range[4] = { 1.0, 10.0, 100.0, 1000.0 };

gsl_histogram_set_ranges (h, range, 4);
```
Note that the size of the *range* array should be defined to be one element bigger than the number of bins. The additional element is required for the upper value of the final bin.

int gsl_histogram_set_ranges_uniform (gsl_histogram *   Function
      h, double *xmin*, double *xmax*)
This function sets the ranges of the existing histogram *h* to cover the range *xmin* to *xmax* uniformly. The values of the histogram bins are reset to zero. The bin ranges are shown in the table below,

$$\begin{aligned} \text{bin}[0] &\Leftarrow & xmin \leq x < xmin + d \\ \text{bin}[1] &\Leftarrow & xmin + d \leq x < xmin + 2d \\ \ldots\,\ldots & & \ldots\quad\ldots\quad\ldots \\ \text{bin}[n\text{-}1] &\Leftarrow & xmin + (n-1)d \leq x < xmax \end{aligned}$$

where d is the bin spacing, $d = (xmax - xmin)/n$.

void gsl_histogram_free (gsl_histogram * *h*)   Function
This function frees the histogram *h* and all of the memory associated with it.

21.3 Copying Histograms

int gsl_histogram_memcpy (gsl_histogram * *dest*, const   Function
      gsl_histogram * *src*)
This function copies the histogram *src* into the pre-existing histogram *dest*, making *dest* into an exact copy of *src*. The two histograms must be of the same size.

gsl_histogram * gsl_histogram_clone (const   Function
      gsl_histogram * *src*)
This function returns a pointer to a newly created histogram which is an exact copy of the histogram *src*.

21.4 Updating and accessing histogram elements

There are two ways to access histogram bins, either by specifying an x coordinate or by using the bin-index directly. The functions for accessing the histogram through x coordinates use a binary search to identify the bin which covers the appropriate range.

int gsl_histogram_increment (gsl_histogram * h, double   Function
       x)
This function updates the histogram h by adding one (1.0) to the bin whose range contains the coordinate x.

If x lies in the valid range of the histogram then the function returns zero to indicate success. If x is less than the lower limit of the histogram then the function returns GSL_EDOM, and none of bins are modified. Similarly, if the value of x is greater than or equal to the upper limit of the histogram then the function returns GSL_EDOM, and none of the bins are modified. The error handler is not called, however, since it is often necessary to compute histograms for a small range of a larger dataset, ignoring the values outside the range of interest.

int gsl_histogram_accumulate (gsl_histogram * h,   Function
       double x, double weight)
This function is similar to gsl_histogram_increment but increases the value of the appropriate bin in the histogram h by the floating-point number weight.

double gsl_histogram_get (const gsl_histogram * h,   Function
       size_t i)
This function returns the contents of the i-th bin of the histogram h. If i lies outside the valid range of indices for the histogram then the error handler is called with an error code of GSL_EDOM and the function returns 0.

int gsl_histogram_get_range (const gsl_histogram * h,   Function
       size_t i, double * lower, double * upper)
This function finds the upper and lower range limits of the i-th bin of the histogram h. If the index i is valid then the corresponding range limits are stored in lower and upper. The lower limit is inclusive (i.e. events with this coordinate are included in the bin) and the upper limit is exclusive (i.e. events with the coordinate of the upper limit are excluded and fall in the neighboring higher bin, if it exists). The function returns 0 to indicate success. If i lies outside the valid range of indices for the histogram then the error handler is called and the function returns an error code of GSL_EDOM.

double gsl_histogram_max (const gsl_histogram * h)   Function
double gsl_histogram_min (const gsl_histogram * h)   Function
size_t gsl_histogram_bins (const gsl_histogram * h)   Function
> These functions return the maximum upper and minimum lower range limits and the number of bins of the histogram h. They provide a way of determining these values without accessing the gsl_histogram struct directly.

void gsl_histogram_reset (gsl_histogram * h)   Function
> This function resets all the bins in the histogram h to zero.

21.5 Searching histogram ranges

The following functions are used by the access and update routines to locate the bin which corresponds to a given x coordinate.

int gsl_histogram_find (const gsl_histogram * h, double   Function
     x, size_t * i)
> This function finds and sets the index i to the bin number which covers the coordinate x in the histogram h. The bin is located using a binary search. The search includes an optimization for histograms with uniform range, and will return the correct bin immediately in this case. If x is found in the range of the histogram then the function sets the index i and returns GSL_SUCCESS. If x lies outside the valid range of the histogram then the function returns GSL_EDOM and the error handler is invoked.

21.6 Histogram Statistics

double gsl_histogram_max_val (const gsl_histogram * h)   Function
> This function returns the maximum value contained in the histogram bins.

size_t gsl_histogram_max_bin (const gsl_histogram * h)   Function
> This function returns the index of the bin containing the maximum value. In the case where several bins contain the same maximum value the smallest index is returned.

double gsl_histogram_min_val (const gsl_histogram * h)   Function
> This function returns the minimum value contained in the histogram bins.

size_t gsl_histogram_min_bin (const gsl_histogram * h)   Function
> This function returns the index of the bin containing the minimum value. In the case where several bins contain the same minimum value the smallest index is returned.

double `gsl_histogram_mean` (const `gsl_histogram` * *h*)   Function
> This function returns the mean of the histogrammed variable, where the histogram is regarded as a probability distribution. Negative bin values are ignored for the purposes of this calculation. The accuracy of the result is limited by the bin width.

double `gsl_histogram_sigma` (const `gsl_histogram` * *h*)   Function
> This function returns the standard deviation of the histogrammed variable, where the histogram is regarded as a probability distribution. Negative bin values are ignored for the purposes of this calculation. The accuracy of the result is limited by the bin width.

double `gsl_histogram_sum` (const `gsl_histogram` * *h*)   Function
> This function returns the sum of all bin values. Negative bin values are included in the sum.

21.7 Histogram Operations

int `gsl_histogram_equal_bins_p` (const `gsl_histogram` *   Function
> *h1*, const `gsl_histogram` * *h2*)
> This function returns 1 if the all of the individual bin ranges of the two histograms are identical, and 0 otherwise.

int `gsl_histogram_add` (`gsl_histogram` * *h1*, const   Function
> `gsl_histogram` * *h2*)
> This function adds the contents of the bins in histogram *h2* to the corresponding bins of histogram *h1*, i.e. $h'_1(i) = h_1(i) + h_2(i)$. The two histograms must have identical bin ranges.

int `gsl_histogram_sub` (`gsl_histogram` * *h1*, const   Function
> `gsl_histogram` * *h2*)
> This function subtracts the contents of the bins in histogram *h2* from the corresponding bins of histogram *h1*, i.e. $h'_1(i) = h_1(i) - h_2(i)$. The two histograms must have identical bin ranges.

int `gsl_histogram_mul` (`gsl_histogram` * *h1*, const   Function
> `gsl_histogram` * *h2*)
> This function multiplies the contents of the bins of histogram *h1* by the contents of the corresponding bins in histogram *h2*, i.e. $h'_1(i) = h_1(i) * h_2(i)$. The two histograms must have identical bin ranges.

int `gsl_histogram_div` (`gsl_histogram` * *h1*, const   Function
> `gsl_histogram` * *h2*)
> This function divides the contents of the bins of histogram *h1* by the contents of the corresponding bins in histogram *h2*, i.e. $h'_1(i) = h_1(i)/h_2(i)$. The two histograms must have identical bin ranges.

int gsl_histogram_scale (gsl_histogram * h, double   Function
         scale)

This function multiplies the contents of the bins of histogram h by the constant scale, i.e. $h_1'(i) = h_1(i) * scale$.

int gsl_histogram_shift (gsl_histogram * h, double   Function
         offset)

This function shifts the contents of the bins of histogram h by the constant offset, i.e. $h_1'(i) = h_1(i) + offset$.

21.8 Reading and writing histograms

The library provides functions for reading and writing histograms to a file as binary data or formatted text.

int gsl_histogram_fwrite (FILE * stream, const   Function
         gsl_histogram * h)

This function writes the ranges and bins of the histogram h to the stream stream in binary format. The return value is 0 for success and GSL_EFAILED if there was a problem writing to the file. Since the data is written in the native binary format it may not be portable between different architectures.

int gsl_histogram_fread (FILE * stream, gsl_histogram *   Function
         h)

This function reads into the histogram h from the open stream stream in binary format. The histogram h must be preallocated with the correct size since the function uses the number of bins in h to determine how many bytes to read. The return value is 0 for success and GSL_EFAILED if there was a problem reading from the file. The data is assumed to have been written in the native binary format on the same architecture.

int gsl_histogram_fprintf (FILE * stream, const   Function
         gsl_histogram * h, const char * range_format, const
         char * bin_format)

This function writes the ranges and bins of the histogram h line-by-line to the stream stream using the format specifiers range_format and bin_format. These should be one of the %g, %e or %f formats for floating point numbers. The function returns 0 for success and GSL_EFAILED if there was a problem writing to the file. The histogram output is formatted in three columns, and the columns are separated by spaces, like this,

```
range[0] range[1] bin[0]
range[1] range[2] bin[1]
range[2] range[3] bin[2]
....
range[n-1] range[n] bin[n-1]
```

The values of the ranges are formatted using *range_format* and the
value of the bins are formatted using *bin_format*. Each line contains
the lower and upper limit of the range of the bins and the value of the
bin itself. Since the upper limit of one bin is the lower limit of the
next there is duplication of these values between lines but this allows
the histogram to be manipulated with line-oriented tools.

int gsl_histogram_fscanf (FILE * *stream*, gsl_histogram   Function
    * *h*)

This function reads formatted data from the stream *stream* into the
histogram *h*. The data is assumed to be in the three-column format
used by gsl_histogram_fprintf. The histogram *h* must be preallocated with the correct length since the function uses the size of *h*
to determine how many numbers to read. The function returns 0 for
success and GSL_EFAILED if there was a problem reading from the file.

21.9 Resampling from histograms

A histogram made by counting events can be regarded as a measurement of a probability distribution. Allowing for statistical error, the height
of each bin represents the probability of an event where the value of x
falls in the range of that bin. The probability distribution function has
the one-dimensional form $p(x)dx$ where,

$$p(x) = n_i/(Nw_i)$$

In this equation n_i is the number of events in the bin which contains x,
w_i is the width of the bin and N is the total number of events. The
distribution of events within each bin is assumed to be uniform.

21.10 The histogram probability distribution struct

The probability distribution function for a histogram consists of a set of *bins* which measure the probability of an event falling into a given range of a continuous variable x. A probability distribution function is defined by the following struct, which actually stores the cumulative probability distribution function. This is the natural quantity for generating samples via the inverse transform method, because there is a one-to-one mapping between the cumulative probability distribution and the range [0,1]. It can be shown that by taking a uniform random number in this range and finding its corresponding coordinate in the cumulative probability distribution we obtain samples with the desired probability distribution. If an even faster lookup is required, see the alternative preprocessing method described in Section 19.28 [General Discrete Distributions], page 284.

`gsl_histogram_pdf`   Data Type

> `size_t n`   This is the number of bins used to approximate the probability distribution function.
>
> `double * range`
> > The ranges of the bins are stored in an array of $n + 1$ elements pointed to by *range*.
>
> `double * sum`
> > The cumulative probability for the bins is stored in an array of n elements pointed to by *sum*.

The following functions allow you to create a `gsl_histogram_pdf` struct which represents this probability distribution and generate random samples from it.

`gsl_histogram_pdf * gsl_histogram_pdf_alloc (size_t n)`   Function
> This function allocates memory for a probability distribution with n bins and returns a pointer to a newly initialized `gsl_histogram_pdf` struct. If insufficient memory is available a null pointer is returned and the error handler is invoked with an error code of `GSL_ENOMEM`.

`int gsl_histogram_pdf_init (gsl_histogram_pdf * p,`   Function
`        const gsl_histogram * h)`
> This function initializes the probability distribution p with the contents of the histogram h. If any of the bins of h are negative then the error handler is invoked with an error code of `GSL_EDOM` because a probability distribution cannot contain negative values.

void gsl_histogram_pdf_free (gsl_histogram_pdf * p)   Function
    This function frees the probability distribution function p and all of
the memory associated with it.

double gsl_histogram_pdf_sample (const   Function
        gsl_histogram_pdf * p, double r)
    This function uses r, a uniform random number between zero and one,
to compute a single random sample from the probability distribution p.
The algorithm used to compute the sample s is given by the following
formula,

$$s = \text{range}[i] + \delta * (\text{range}[i+1] - \text{range}[i])$$

where i is the index which satisfies $sum[i] \leq r < sum[i+1]$ and *delta*
is $(r - sum[i])/(sum[i+1] - sum[i])$.

21.11 Example programs for histograms

    The following program shows how to make a simple histogram of a
column of numerical data supplied on stdin. The program takes three
arguments, specifying the upper and lower bounds of the histogram and
the number of bins. It then reads numbers from stdin, one line at a time,
and adds them to the histogram. When there is no more data to read it
prints out the accumulated histogram using gsl_histogram_fprintf.

```
#include <stdio.h>
#include <stdlib.h>
#include <gsl/gsl_histogram.h>

int
main (int argc, char **argv)
{
  double a, b;
  size_t n;

  if (argc != 4)
    {
      printf ("Usage: gsl-histogram xmin xmax n\n"
              "Computes a histogram of the data "
              "on stdin using n bins from xmin "
              "to xmax\n");
      exit (0);
    }

  a = atof (argv[1]);
  b = atof (argv[2]);
```

```
n = atoi (argv[3]);

{
  double x;
  gsl_histogram * h = gsl_histogram_alloc (n);
  gsl_histogram_set_ranges_uniform (h, a, b);

  while (fscanf (stdin, "%lg", &x) == 1)
    {
      gsl_histogram_increment (h, x);
    }
  gsl_histogram_fprintf (stdout, h, "%g", "%g");
  gsl_histogram_free (h);
}
exit (0);
}
```

Here is an example of the program in use. We generate 10000 random samples from a Cauchy distribution with a width of 30 and histogram them over the range -100 to 100, using 200 bins.

```
$ gsl-randist 0 10000 cauchy 30
  | gsl-histogram -100 100 200 > histogram.dat
```

A plot of the resulting histogram shows the familiar shape of the Cauchy distribution and the fluctuations caused by the finite sample size.

```
$ awk '{print $1, $3 ; print $2, $3}' histogram.dat
  | graph -T X
```

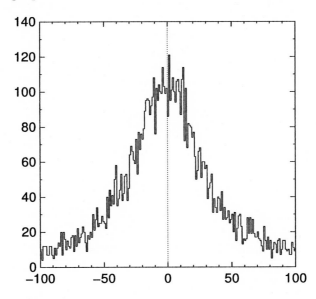

21.12 Two dimensional histograms

A two dimensional histogram consists of a set of *bins* which count the number of events falling in a given area of the (x, y) plane. The simplest way to use a two dimensional histogram is to record two-dimensional position information, $n(x, y)$. Another possibility is to form a *joint distribution* by recording related variables. For example a detector might record both the position of an event (x) and the amount of energy it deposited E. These could be histogrammed as the joint distribution $n(x, E)$.

21.13 The 2D histogram struct

Two dimensional histograms are defined by the following struct,

`gsl_histogram2d`   Data Type

    `size_t nx, ny`
> This is the number of histogram bins in the x and y directions.

    `double * xrange`
> The ranges of the bins in the x-direction are stored in an array of *nx* + 1 elements pointed to by *xrange*.

    `double * yrange`
> The ranges of the bins in the y-direction are stored in an array of *ny* + 1 elements pointed to by *yrange*.

    `double * bin`
> The counts for each bin are stored in an array pointed to by *bin*. The bins are floating-point numbers, so you can increment them by non-integer values if necessary. The array *bin* stores the two dimensional array of bins in a single block of memory according to the mapping `bin(i,j) = bin[i * ny + j]`.

The range for `bin(i,j)` is given by `xrange[i]` to `xrange[i+1]` in the x-direction and `yrange[j]` to `yrange[j+1]` in the y-direction. Each bin is inclusive at the lower end and exclusive at the upper end. Mathematically this means that the bins are defined by the following inequality,

$$\text{bin(i,j) corresponds to} \quad xrange[i] \le x < xrange[i+1]$$
$$\text{and} \quad yrange[j] \le y < yrange[j+1]$$

Note that any samples which fall on the upper sides of the histogram are excluded. If you want to include these values for the side bins you will need to add an extra row or column to your histogram.

The `gsl_histogram2d` struct and its associated functions are defined in the header file 'gsl_histogram2d.h'.

21.14 2D Histogram allocation

The functions for allocating memory to a 2D histogram follow the
style of malloc and free. In addition they also perform their own error
checking. If there is insufficient memory available to allocate a histogram
then the functions call the error handler (with an error number of GSL_
ENOMEM) in addition to returning a null pointer. Thus if you use the library
error handler to abort your program then it isn't necessary to check every
2D histogram alloc.

gsl_histogram2d * gsl_histogram2d_alloc (size_t nx,   Function
        size_t ny)
This function allocates memory for a two-dimensional histogram with
nx bins in the x direction and ny bins in the y direction. The function
returns a pointer to a newly created gsl_histogram2d struct. If insufficient memory is available a null pointer is returned and the error
handler is invoked with an error code of GSL_ENOMEM. The bins and
ranges must be initialized with one of the functions below before the
histogram is ready for use.

int gsl_histogram2d_set_ranges (gsl_histogram2d * h,   Function
        const double xrange[], size_t xsize, const double
        yrange[], size_t ysize)
This function sets the ranges of the existing histogram h using the
arrays xrange and yrange of size xsize and ysize respectively. The
values of the histogram bins are reset to zero.

int gsl_histogram2d_set_ranges_uniform   Function
        (gsl_histogram2d * h, double xmin, double xmax,
        double ymin, double ymax)
This function sets the ranges of the existing histogram h to cover the
ranges xmin to xmax and ymin to ymax uniformly. The values of the
histogram bins are reset to zero.

void gsl_histogram2d_free (gsl_histogram2d * h)   Function
This function frees the 2D histogram h and all of the memory associated with it.

21.15 Copying 2D Histograms

int gsl_histogram2d_memcpy (gsl_histogram2d * *dest*,   Function
        const gsl_histogram2d * *src*)
   This function copies the histogram *src* into the pre-existing histogram
   dest, making *dest* into an exact copy of *src*. The two histograms must
   be of the same size.

gsl_histogram2d * gsl_histogram2d_clone (const   Function
        gsl_histogram2d * *src*)
   This function returns a pointer to a newly created histogram which is
   an exact copy of the histogram *src*.

21.16 Updating and accessing 2D histogram elements

   You can access the bins of a two-dimensional histogram either by specifying a pair of (x, y) coordinates or by using the bin indices (i, j) directly.
The functions for accessing the histogram through (x, y) coordinates use
binary searches in the x and y directions to identify the bin which covers
the appropriate range.

int gsl_histogram2d_increment (gsl_histogram2d * *h*,   Function
        double *x*, double *y*)
   This function updates the histogram *h* by adding one (1.0) to the bin
   whose x and y ranges contain the coordinates (x, y).

   If the point (x, y) lies inside the valid ranges of the histogram then
   the function returns zero to indicate success. If (x, y) lies outside the
   limits of the histogram then the function returns GSL_EDOM, and none
   of the bins are modified. The error handler is not called, since it is
   often necessary to compute histograms for a small range of a larger
   dataset, ignoring any coordinates outside the range of interest.

int gsl_histogram2d_accumulate (gsl_histogram2d * *h*,   Function
        double *x*, double *y*, double *weight*)
   This function is similar to gsl_histogram2d_increment but increases
   the value of the appropriate bin in the histogram *h* by the floating-
   point number *weight*.

double gsl_histogram2d_get (const gsl_histogram2d * *h*,   Function
        size_t *i*, size_t *j*)
   This function returns the contents of the (i, j)-th bin of the histogram
   h. If (i, j) lies outside the valid range of indices for the histogram then
   the error handler is called with an error code of GSL_EDOM and the
   function returns 0.

int gsl_histogram2d_get_xrange (const gsl_histogram2d   Function
        * h, size_t i, double * xlower, double * xupper)
int gsl_histogram2d_get_yrange (const gsl_histogram2d   Function
        * h, size_t j, double * ylower, double * yupper)
These functions find the upper and lower range limits of the i-th and j-th bins in the x and y directions of the histogram h. The range limits are stored in xlower and xupper or ylower and yupper. The lower limits are inclusive (i.e. events with these coordinates are included in the bin) and the upper limits are exclusive (i.e. events with the value of the upper limit are not included and fall in the neighboring higher bin, if it exists). The functions return 0 to indicate success. If i or j lies outside the valid range of indices for the histogram then the error handler is called with an error code of GSL_EDOM.

double gsl_histogram2d_xmax (const gsl_histogram2d *   Function
        h)
double gsl_histogram2d_xmin (const gsl_histogram2d *   Function
        h)
size_t gsl_histogram2d_nx (const gsl_histogram2d * h)   Function
double gsl_histogram2d_ymax (const gsl_histogram2d *   Function
        h)
double gsl_histogram2d_ymin (const gsl_histogram2d *   Function
        h)
size_t gsl_histogram2d_ny (const gsl_histogram2d * h)   Function
These functions return the maximum upper and minimum lower range limits and the number of bins for the x and y directions of the histogram h. They provide a way of determining these values without accessing the gsl_histogram2d struct directly.

void gsl_histogram2d_reset (gsl_histogram2d * h)   Function
This function resets all the bins of the histogram h to zero.

21.17 Searching 2D histogram ranges

The following functions are used by the access and update routines to locate the bin which corresponds to a given (x, y) coordinate.

int gsl_histogram2d_find (const gsl_histogram2d * h,   Function
        double x, double y, size_t * i, size_t * j)
This function finds and sets the indices i and j to the to the bin which covers the coordinates (x, y). The bin is located using a binary search. The search includes an optimization for histograms with uniform ranges, and will return the correct bin immediately in this case. If (x, y) is found then the function sets the indices (i, j) and

returns GSL_SUCCESS. If (x, y) lies outside the valid range of the histogram then the function returns GSL_EDOM and the error handler is invoked.

21.18 2D Histogram Statistics

double gsl_histogram2d_max_val (const gsl_histogram2d   Function
        * h)

This function returns the maximum value contained in the histogram bins.

void gsl_histogram2d_max_bin (const gsl_histogram2d *   Function
        h, size_t * i, size_t * j)

This function finds the indices of the bin containing the maximum value in the histogram h and stores the result in (i, j). In the case where several bins contain the same maximum value the first bin found is returned.

double gsl_histogram2d_min_val (const gsl_histogram2d   Function
        * h)

This function returns the minimum value contained in the histogram bins.

void gsl_histogram2d_min_bin (const gsl_histogram2d *   Function
        h, size_t * i, size_t * j)

This function finds the indices of the bin containing the minimum value in the histogram h and stores the result in (i, j). In the case where several bins contain the same maximum value the first bin found is returned.

double gsl_histogram2d_xmean (const gsl_histogram2d *   Function
        h)

This function returns the mean of the histogrammed x variable, where the histogram is regarded as a probability distribution. Negative bin values are ignored for the purposes of this calculation.

double gsl_histogram2d_ymean (const gsl_histogram2d *   Function
        h)

This function returns the mean of the histogrammed y variable, where the histogram is regarded as a probability distribution. Negative bin values are ignored for the purposes of this calculation.

double gsl_histogram2d_xsigma (const gsl_histogram2d *   Function
     h)
    This function returns the standard deviation of the histogrammed x
    variable, where the histogram is regarded as a probability distribution.
    Negative bin values are ignored for the purposes of this calculation.

double gsl_histogram2d_ysigma (const gsl_histogram2d *   Function
     h)
    This function returns the standard deviation of the histogrammed y
    variable, where the histogram is regarded as a probability distribution.
    Negative bin values are ignored for the purposes of this calculation.

double gsl_histogram2d_cov (const gsl_histogram2d * h)   Function
    This function returns the covariance of the histogrammed x and y
    variables, where the histogram is regarded as a probability distribution.
    Negative bin values are ignored for the purposes of this calculation.

double gsl_histogram2d_sum (const gsl_histogram2d * h)   Function
    This function returns the sum of all bin values. Negative bin values
    are included in the sum.

21.19 2D Histogram Operations

int gsl_histogram2d_equal_bins_p (const   Function
     gsl_histogram2d * h1, const gsl_histogram2d * h2)
    This function returns 1 if all the individual bin ranges of the two
    histograms are identical, and 0 otherwise.

int gsl_histogram2d_add (gsl_histogram2d * h1, const   Function
     gsl_histogram2d * h2)
    This function adds the contents of the bins in histogram h2 to the
    corresponding bins of histogram h1, i.e. $h_1'(i,j) = h_1(i,j) + h_2(i,j)$.
    The two histograms must have identical bin ranges.

int gsl_histogram2d_sub (gsl_histogram2d * h1, const   Function
     gsl_histogram2d * h2)
    This function subtracts the contents of the bins in histogram h2 from
    the corresponding bins of histogram h1, i.e. $h_1'(i,j) = h_1(i,j) - h_2(i,j)$.
    The two histograms must have identical bin ranges.

int gsl_histogram2d_mul (gsl_histogram2d * h1, const   Function
     gsl_histogram2d * h2)
    This function multiplies the contents of the bins of histogram h1 by
    the contents of the corresponding bins in histogram h2, i.e. $h_1'(i,j) = h_1(i,j) * h_2(i,j)$. The two histograms must have identical bin ranges.

int gsl_histogram2d_div (gsl_histogram2d * *h1*, const   Function
          gsl_histogram2d * *h2*)

This function divides the contents of the bins of histogram *h1* by the contents of the corresponding bins in histogram *h2*, i.e. $h_1'(i,j) = h_1(i,j)/h_2(i,j)$. The two histograms must have identical bin ranges.

int gsl_histogram2d_scale (gsl_histogram2d * *h*, double   Function
          scale)

This function multiplies the contents of the bins of histogram *h* by the constant *scale*, i.e. $h_1'(i,j) = h_1(i,j) * scale$.

int gsl_histogram2d_shift (gsl_histogram2d * *h*, double   Function
          offset)

This function shifts the contents of the bins of histogram *h* by the constant *offset*, i.e. $h_1'(i,j) = h_1(i,j) + offset$.

21.20 Reading and writing 2D histograms

The library provides functions for reading and writing two dimensional histograms to a file as binary data or formatted text.

int gsl_histogram2d_fwrite (FILE * *stream*, const   Function
          gsl_histogram2d * *h*)

This function writes the ranges and bins of the histogram *h* to the stream *stream* in binary format. The return value is 0 for success and GSL_EFAILED if there was a problem writing to the file. Since the data is written in the native binary format it may not be portable between different architectures.

int gsl_histogram2d_fread (FILE * *stream*,   Function
          gsl_histogram2d * *h*)

This function reads into the histogram *h* from the stream *stream* in binary format. The histogram *h* must be preallocated with the correct size since the function uses the number of x and y bins in *h* to determine how many bytes to read. The return value is 0 for success and GSL_EFAILED if there was a problem reading from the file. The data is assumed to have been written in the native binary format on the same architecture.

int gsl_histogram2d_fprintf (FILE * *stream*, const   Function
          gsl_histogram2d * *h*, const char * *range_format*, const
          char * *bin_format*)

This function writes the ranges and bins of the histogram *h* line-by-line to the stream *stream* using the format specifiers *range_format* and *bin_format*. These should be one of the %g, %e or %f formats for floating

point numbers. The function returns 0 for success and `GSL_EFAILED`
if there was a problem writing to the file. The histogram output is
formatted in five columns, and the columns are separated by spaces,
like this,

```
xrange[0] xrange[1] yrange[0] yrange[1] bin(0,0)
xrange[0] xrange[1] yrange[1] yrange[2] bin(0,1)
xrange[0] xrange[1] yrange[2] yrange[3] bin(0,2)
....
xrange[0] xrange[1] yrange[ny-1] yrange[ny] bin(0,ny-1)

xrange[1] xrange[2] yrange[0] yrange[1] bin(1,0)
xrange[1] xrange[2] yrange[1] yrange[2] bin(1,1)
xrange[1] xrange[2] yrange[1] yrange[2] bin(1,2)
....
xrange[1] xrange[2] yrange[ny-1] yrange[ny] bin(1,ny-1)


....


xrange[nx-1] xrange[nx] yrange[0] yrange[1] bin(nx-1,0)
xrange[nx-1] xrange[nx] yrange[1] yrange[2] bin(nx-1,1)
xrange[nx-1] xrange[nx] yrange[1] yrange[2] bin(nx-1,2)
....
xrange[nx-1] xrange[nx] yrange[ny-1] yrange[ny] bin(nx-1,ny-
1)
```

Each line contains the lower and upper limits of the bin and the contents of the bin. Since the upper limits of the each bin are the lower
limits of the neighboring bins there is duplication of these values but
this allows the histogram to be manipulated with line-oriented tools.

`int gsl_histogram2d_fscanf (FILE * stream,`   Function
    `gsl_histogram2d * h)`

This function reads formatted data from the stream *stream* into the
histogram *h*. The data is assumed to be in the five-column format used
by `gsl_histogram_fprintf`. The histogram *h* must be preallocated
with the correct lengths since the function uses the sizes of *h* to determine how many numbers to read. The function returns 0 for success
and `GSL_EFAILED` if there was a problem reading from the file.

21.21 Resampling from 2D histograms

As in the one-dimensional case, a two-dimensional histogram made by counting events can be regarded as a measurement of a probability distribution. Allowing for statistical error, the height of each bin represents the probability of an event where (x,y) falls in the range of that bin. For a two-dimensional histogram the probability distribution takes the form $p(x, y)dxdy$ where,

$$p(x,y) = n_{ij}/(NA_{ij})$$

In this equation n_{ij} is the number of events in the bin which contains (x, y), A_{ij} is the area of the bin and N is the total number of events. The distribution of events within each bin is assumed to be uniform.

gsl_histogram2d_pdf   Data Type

>   size_t nx, ny
>> This is the number of histogram bins used to approximate the probability distribution function in the x and y directions.

>   double * xrange
>> The ranges of the bins in the x-direction are stored in an array of $nx + 1$ elements pointed to by *xrange*.

>   double * yrange
>> The ranges of the bins in the y-direction are stored in an array of $ny + 1$ pointed to by *yrange*.

>   double * sum
>> The cumulative probability for the bins is stored in an array of $nx*ny$ elements pointed to by *sum*.

The following functions allow you to create a gsl_histogram2d_pdf struct which represents a two dimensional probability distribution and generate random samples from it.

gsl_histogram2d_pdf * gsl_histogram2d_pdf_alloc   Function
>   (size_t nx, size_t ny)
This function allocates memory for a two-dimensional probability distribution of size *nx*-by-*ny* and returns a pointer to a newly initialized gsl_histogram2d_pdf struct. If insufficient memory is available a null pointer is returned and the error handler is invoked with an error code of GSL_ENOMEM.

int gsl_histogram2d_pdf_init (gsl_histogram2d_pdf * p, *Function* **const gsl_histogram2d * h)**

This function initializes the two-dimensional probability distribution calculated p from the histogram h. If any of the bins of h are negative then the error handler is invoked with an error code of GSL_EDOM because a probability distribution cannot contain negative values.

void gsl_histogram2d_pdf_free (gsl_histogram2d_pdf * p) *Function*

This function frees the two-dimensional probability distribution function p and all of the memory associated with it.

int gsl_histogram2d_pdf_sample (const *Function* **gsl_histogram2d_pdf * p, double r1, double r2, double * x, double * y)**

This function uses two uniform random numbers between zero and one, r1 and r2, to compute a single random sample from the two-dimensional probability distribution p.

21.22 Example programs for 2D histograms

This program demonstrates two features of two-dimensional histograms. First a 10-by-10 two-dimensional histogram is created with x and y running from 0 to 1. Then a few sample points are added to the histogram, at (0.3,0.3) with a height of 1, at (0.8,0.1) with a height of 5 and at (0.7,0.9) with a height of 0.5. This histogram with three events is used to generate a random sample of 1000 simulated events, which are printed out.

```
#include <stdio.h>
#include <gsl/gsl_rng.h>
#include <gsl/gsl_histogram2d.h>

int
main (void)
{
  const gsl_rng_type * T;
  gsl_rng * r;

  gsl_histogram2d * h = gsl_histogram2d_alloc (10, 10);

  gsl_histogram2d_set_ranges_uniform (h,
                                      0.0, 1.0,
                                      0.0, 1.0);

  gsl_histogram2d_accumulate (h, 0.3, 0.3, 1);
  gsl_histogram2d_accumulate (h, 0.8, 0.1, 5);
  gsl_histogram2d_accumulate (h, 0.7, 0.9, 0.5);

  gsl_rng_env_setup ();

  T = gsl_rng_default;
  r = gsl_rng_alloc (T);

  {
    int i;
    gsl_histogram2d_pdf * p
      = gsl_histogram2d_pdf_alloc (h->nx, h->ny);

    gsl_histogram2d_pdf_init (p, h);

    for (i = 0; i < 1000; i++) {
      double x, y;
      double u = gsl_rng_uniform (r);
```

```
        double v = gsl_rng_uniform (r);

        gsl_histogram2d_pdf_sample (p, u, v, &x, &y);

        printf ("%g %g\n", x, y);
     }
  }

  return 0;
}
```

The following plot shows the distribution of the simulated events. Using a higher resolution grid we can see the original underlying histogram and also the statistical fluctuations caused by the events being uniformly distributed over the area of the original bins.

22 N-tuples

This chapter describes functions for creating and manipulating *ntuples*, sets of values associated with events. The ntuples are stored in files. Their values can be extracted in any combination and *booked* in a histogram using a selection function.

The values to be stored are held in a user-defined data structure, and an ntuple is created associating this data structure with a file. The values are then written to the file (normally inside a loop) using the ntuple functions described below.

A histogram can be created from ntuple data by providing a selection function and a value function. The selection function specifies whether an event should be included in the subset to be analyzed or not. The value function computes the entry to be added to the histogram for each event.

All the ntuple functions are defined in the header file 'gsl_ntuple.h'

22.1 The ntuple struct

Ntuples are manipulated using the gsl_ntuple struct. This struct contains information on the file where the ntuple data is stored, a pointer to the current ntuple data row and the size of the user-defined ntuple data struct.

```
typedef struct {
    FILE * file;
    void * ntuple_data;
    size_t size;
} gsl_ntuple;
```

22.2 Creating ntuples

gsl_ntuple * gsl_ntuple_create (char * *filename*, void *   Function
        ntuple_data, size_t *size*)
This function creates a new write-only ntuple file *filename* for ntuples of size *size* and returns a pointer to the newly created ntuple struct. Any existing file with the same name is truncated to zero length and overwritten. A pointer to memory for the current ntuple row *ntuple_data* must be supplied—this is used to copy ntuples in and out of the file.

22.3 Opening an existing ntuple file

`gsl_ntuple * gsl_ntuple_open` (`char *` *filename*, `void *`   Function
       ntuple_data, `size_t` *size*)

This function opens an existing ntuple file *filename* for reading and
returns a pointer to a corresponding ntuple struct. The ntuples in the
file must have size *size*. A pointer to memory for the current ntuple
row *ntuple_data* must be supplied—this is used to copy ntuples in and
out of the file.

22.4 Writing ntuples

`int gsl_ntuple_write` (`gsl_ntuple *` *ntuple*)   Function

This function writes the current ntuple *ntuple->ntuple_data* of size
ntuple->size to the corresponding file.

`int gsl_ntuple_bookdata` (`gsl_ntuple *` *ntuple*)   Function

This function is a synonym for `gsl_ntuple_write`.

22.5 Reading ntuples

`int gsl_ntuple_read` (`gsl_ntuple *` *ntuple*)   Function

This function reads the current row of the ntuple file for *ntuple* and
stores the values in *ntuple->data*.

22.6 Closing an ntuple file

`int gsl_ntuple_close` (`gsl_ntuple *` *ntuple*)   Function

This function closes the ntuple file *ntuple* and frees its associated allocated memory.

22.7 Histogramming ntuple values

Once an ntuple has been created its contents can be histogrammed in various ways using the function `gsl_ntuple_project`. Two user-defined functions must be provided, a function to select events and a function to compute scalar values. The selection function and the value function both accept the ntuple row as a first argument and other parameters as a second argument.

The *selection function* determines which ntuple rows are selected for histogramming. It is defined by the following struct,

```
typedef struct {
  int (* function) (void * ntuple_data, void * params);
  void * params;
} gsl_ntuple_select_fn;
```

The struct component *function* should return a non-zero value for each ntuple row that is to be included in the histogram.

The *value function* computes scalar values for those ntuple rows selected by the selection function,

```
typedef struct {
  double (* function) (void * ntuple_data, void * params);
  void * params;
} gsl_ntuple_value_fn;
```

In this case the struct component *function* should return the value to be added to the histogram for the ntuple row.

int gsl_ntuple_project (gsl_histogram * *h*, gsl_ntuple *   Function
        ntuple, gsl_ntuple_value_fn * *value_func*,
        gsl_ntuple_select_fn * *select_func*)

This function updates the histogram *h* from the ntuple *ntuple* using the functions *value_func* and *select_func*. For each ntuple row where the selection function *select_func* is non-zero the corresponding value of that row is computed using the function *value_func* and added to the histogram. Those ntuple rows where *select_func* returns zero are ignored. New entries are added to the histogram, so subsequent calls can be used to accumulate further data in the same histogram.

22.8 Examples

The following example programs demonstrate the use of ntuples in managing a large dataset. The first program creates a set of 10,000 simulated "events", each with 3 associated values (x, y, z). These are generated from a gaussian distribution with unit variance, for demonstration purposes, and written to the ntuple file 'test.dat'.

```
#include <gsl/gsl_ntuple.h>
#include <gsl/gsl_rng.h>
#include <gsl/gsl_randist.h>

struct data
{
  double x;
  double y;
  double z;
};

int
main (void)
{
  const gsl_rng_type * T;
  gsl_rng * r;

  struct data ntuple_row;
  int i;

  gsl_ntuple *ntuple
    = gsl_ntuple_create ("test.dat", &ntuple_row,
                         sizeof (ntuple_row));

  gsl_rng_env_setup ();

  T = gsl_rng_default;
  r = gsl_rng_alloc (T);

  for (i = 0; i < 10000; i++)
    {
      ntuple_row.x = gsl_ran_ugaussian (r);
      ntuple_row.y = gsl_ran_ugaussian (r);
      ntuple_row.z = gsl_ran_ugaussian (r);

      gsl_ntuple_write (ntuple);
    }
```

```
      gsl_ntuple_close (ntuple);
      return 0;
    }
```

The next program analyses the ntuple data in the file 'test.dat'. The analysis procedure is to compute the squared-magnitude of each event, $E^2 = x^2 + y^2 + z^2$, and select only those which exceed a lower limit of 1.5. The selected events are then histogrammed using their E^2 values.

```
    #include <math.h>
    #include <gsl/gsl_ntuple.h>
    #include <gsl/gsl_histogram.h>

    struct data
    {
      double x;
      double y;
      double z;
    };

    int sel_func (void *ntuple_data, void *params);
    double val_func (void *ntuple_data, void *params);

    int
    main (void)
    {
      struct data ntuple_row;

      gsl_ntuple *ntuple
        = gsl_ntuple_open ("test.dat", &ntuple_row,
                           sizeof (ntuple_row));
      double lower = 1.5;

      gsl_ntuple_select_fn S;
      gsl_ntuple_value_fn V;

      gsl_histogram *h = gsl_histogram_alloc (100);
      gsl_histogram_set_ranges_uniform(h, 0.0, 10.0);

      S.function = &sel_func;
      S.params = &lower;

      V.function = &val_func;
      V.params = 0;
```

```
    gsl_ntuple_project (h, ntuple, &V, &S);
    gsl_histogram_fprintf (stdout, h, "%f", "%f");
    gsl_histogram_free (h);
    gsl_ntuple_close (ntuple);

    return 0;
}

int
sel_func (void *ntuple_data, void *params)
{
  struct data * data = (struct data *) ntuple_data;
  double x, y, z, E2, scale;
  scale = *(double *) params;

  x = data->x;
  y = data->y;
  z = data->z;

  E2 = x * x + y * y + z * z;

  return E2 > scale;
}

double
val_func (void *ntuple_data, void *params)
{
  struct data * data = (struct data *) ntuple_data;
  double x, y, z;

  x = data->x;
  y = data->y;
  z = data->z;

  return x * x + y * y + z * z;
}
```

The following plot shows the distribution of the selected events. Note the cut-off at the lower bound.

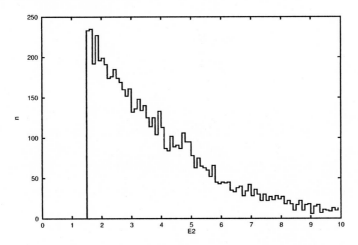

22.9 References and Further Reading

Further information on the use of ntuples can be found in the documentation for the CERN packages PAW and HBOOK (available online).

23 Monte Carlo Integration

This chapter describes routines for multidimensional Monte Carlo integration. These include the traditional Monte Carlo method and adaptive algorithms such as VEGAS and MISER which use importance sampling and stratified sampling techniques. Each algorithm computes an estimate of a multidimensional definite integral of the form,

$$ I = \int_{x_l}^{x_u} dx \int_{y_l}^{y_u} dy \, ... f(x, y, ...) $$

over a hypercubic region $((x_l, x_u), (y_l, y_u), ...)$ using a fixed number of function calls. The routines also provide a statistical estimate of the error on the result. This error estimate should be taken as a guide rather than as a strict error bound—random sampling of the region may not uncover all the important features of the function, resulting in an underestimate of the error.

The functions are defined in separate header files for each routine, gsl_monte_plain.h, 'gsl_monte_miser.h' and 'gsl_monte_vegas.h'.

23.1 Interface

All of the Monte Carlo integration routines use the same general form of interface. There is an allocator to allocate memory for control variables and workspace, a routine to initialize those control variables, the integrator itself, and a function to free the space when done.

Each integration function requires a random number generator to be supplied, and returns an estimate of the integral and its standard deviation. The accuracy of the result is determined by the number of function calls specified by the user. If a known level of accuracy is required this can be achieved by calling the integrator several times and averaging the individual results until the desired accuracy is obtained.

Random sample points used within the Monte Carlo routines are always chosen strictly within the integration region, so that endpoint singularities are automatically avoided.

The function to be integrated has its own datatype, defined in the header file 'gsl_monte.h'.

gsl_monte_function   Data Type

This data type defines a general function with parameters for Monte Carlo integration.

double (* f) (double * x, size_t *dim*, void * *params*)
> this function should return the value $f(x, params)$ for the argument x and parameters *params*, where x is an array of size *dim* giving the coordinates of the point where the function is to be evaluated.

size_t dim the number of dimensions for x.

void * params
> a pointer to the parameters of the function.

Here is an example for a quadratic function in two dimensions,

$$f(x,y) = ax^2 + bxy + cy^2$$

with $a = 3$, $b = 2$, $c = 1$. The following code defines a gsl_monte_function F which you could pass to an integrator:

```
struct my_f_params { double a; double b; double c; };

double
my_f (double x[], size_t dim, void * p) {
   struct my_f_params * fp = (struct my_f_params *)p;

   if (dim != 2)
      {
         fprintf (stderr, "error: dim != 2");
         abort ();
      }

   return  fp->a * x[0] * x[0]
             + fp->b * x[0] * x[1]
                + fp->c * x[1] * x[1];
}

gsl_monte_function F;
struct my_f_params params = { 3.0, 2.0, 1.0 };

F.f = &my_f;
F.dim = 2;
F.params = &params;
```

The function $f(x)$ can be evaluated using the following macro,

```
#define GSL_MONTE_FN_EVAL(F,x)
   (*((F)->f))(x,(F)->dim,(F)->params)
```

23.2 PLAIN Monte Carlo

The plain Monte Carlo algorithm samples points randomly from the integration region to estimate the integral and its error. Using this algorithm the estimate of the integral $E(f; N)$ for N randomly distributed points x_i is given by,

$$E(f; N) = V\langle f \rangle = \frac{V}{N} \sum_i^N f(x_i)$$

where V is the volume of the integration region. The error on this estimate $\sigma(E; N)$ is calculated from the estimated variance of the mean,

$$\sigma^2(E; N) = \frac{V}{N} \sum_i^N (f(x_i) - \langle f \rangle)^2.$$

For large N this variance decreases asymptotically as $\mathrm{Var}(f)/N$, where $\mathrm{Var}(f)$ is the true variance of the function over the integration region. The error estimate itself should decrease as $\sigma(f)/\sqrt{N}$. The familiar law of errors decreasing as $1/\sqrt{N}$ applies—to reduce the error by a factor of 10 requires a 100-fold increase in the number of sample points.

The functions described in this section are declared in the header file 'gsl_monte_plain.h'.

gsl_monte_plain_state * gsl_monte_plain_alloc (size_t   Function
    dim)
This function allocates and initializes a workspace for Monte Carlo integration in *dim* dimensions.

int gsl_monte_plain_init (gsl_monte_plain_state* s)   Function
This function initializes a previously allocated integration state. This allows an existing workspace to be reused for different integrations.

int gsl_monte_plain_integrate (gsl_monte_function * f,   Function
    double * *xl*, double * *xu*, size_t *dim*, size_t *calls*,
    gsl_rng * r, gsl_monte_plain_state * s, double *
    result, double * *abserr*)
This routines uses the plain Monte Carlo algorithm to integrate the function f over the *dim*-dimensional hypercubic region defined by the lower and upper limits in the arrays *xl* and *xu*, each of size *dim*. The integration uses a fixed number of function calls *calls*, and obtains random sampling points using the random number generator r. A previously allocated workspace s must be supplied. The result of the integration is returned in *result*, with an estimated absolute error *abserr*.

void gsl_monte_plain_free (gsl_monte_plain_state * s)   Function
This function frees the memory associated with the integrator state s.

23.3 MISER

The MISER algorithm of Press and Farrar is based on recursive stratified sampling. This technique aims to reduce the overall integration error
by concentrating integration points in the regions of highest variance.

The idea of stratified sampling begins with the observation that for
two disjoint regions a and b with Monte Carlo estimates of the integral
$E_a(f)$ and $E_b(f)$ and variances $\sigma_a^2(f)$ and $\sigma_b^2(f)$, the variance $\mathrm{Var}(f)$ of
the combined estimate $E(f) = \frac{1}{2}(E_a(f) + E_b(f))$ is given by,

$$\mathrm{Var}(f) = \frac{\sigma_a^2(f)}{4N_a} + \frac{\sigma_b^2(f)}{4N_b}.$$

It can be shown that this variance is minimized by distributing the points
such that,

$$\frac{N_a}{N_a + N_b} = \frac{\sigma_a}{\sigma_a + \sigma_b}.$$

Hence the smallest error estimate is obtained by allocating sample points
in proportion to the standard deviation of the function in each sub-region.

The MISER algorithm proceeds by bisecting the integration region
along one coordinate axis to give two sub-regions at each step. The direction is chosen by examining all d possible bisections and selecting the one
which will minimize the combined variance of the two sub-regions. The
variance in the sub-regions is estimated by sampling with a fraction of the
total number of points available to the current step. The same procedure
is then repeated recursively for each of the two half-spaces from the best
bisection. The remaining sample points are allocated to the sub-regions
using the formula for N_a and N_b. This recursive allocation of integration
points continues down to a user-specified depth where each sub-region is
integrated using a plain Monte Carlo estimate. These individual values
and their error estimates are then combined upwards to give an overall
result and an estimate of its error.

The functions described in this section are declared in the header file
'gsl_monte_miser.h'.

gsl_monte_miser_state * gsl_monte_miser_alloc (size_t   Function
          dim)
This function allocates and initializes a workspace for Monte Carlo
integration in dim dimensions. The workspace is used to maintain the
state of the integration.

int **gsl_monte_miser_init** (gsl_monte_miser_state* s)   Function
This function initializes a previously allocated integration state. This allows an existing workspace to be reused for different integrations.

int **gsl_monte_miser_integrate** (gsl_monte_function * f,   Function
double * xl, double * xu, size_t dim, size_t calls,
gsl_rng * r, gsl_monte_miser_state * s, double *
result, double * abserr)
This routines uses the MISER Monte Carlo algorithm to integrate the function f over the dim-dimensional hypercubic region defined by the lower and upper limits in the arrays xl and xu, each of size dim. The integration uses a fixed number of function calls calls, and obtains random sampling points using the random number generator r. A previously allocated workspace s must be supplied. The result of the integration is returned in result, with an estimated absolute error abserr.

void **gsl_monte_miser_free** (gsl_monte_miser_state * s)   Function
This function frees the memory associated with the integrator state s.

The MISER algorithm has several configurable parameters. The following variables can be accessed through the gsl_monte_miser_state struct,

double **estimate_frac**   Variable
This parameter specifies the fraction of the currently available number of function calls which are allocated to estimating the variance at each recursive step. The default value is 0.1.

size_t **min_calls**   Variable
This parameter specifies the minimum number of function calls required for each estimate of the variance. If the number of function calls allocated to the estimate using estimate_frac falls below min_calls then min_calls are used instead. This ensures that each estimate maintains a reasonable level of accuracy. The default value of min_calls is 16 * dim.

size_t **min_calls_per_bisection**   Variable
This parameter specifies the minimum number of function calls required to proceed with a bisection step. When a recursive step has fewer calls available than min_calls_per_bisection it performs a plain Monte Carlo estimate of the current sub-region and terminates its branch of the recursion. The default value of this parameter is 32 * min_calls.

double alpha   Variable
This parameter controls how the estimated variances for the two sub-regions of a bisection are combined when allocating points. With recursive sampling the overall variance should scale better than $1/N$, since the values from the sub-regions will be obtained using a procedure which explicitly minimizes their variance. To accommodate this behavior the MISER algorithm allows the total variance to depend on a scaling parameter α,

$$\text{Var}(f) = \frac{\sigma_a}{N_a^\alpha} + \frac{\sigma_b}{N_b^\alpha}.$$

The authors of the original paper describing MISER recommend the value $\alpha = 2$ as a good choice, obtained from numerical experiments, and this is used as the default value in this implementation.

double dither   Variable
This parameter introduces a random fractional variation of size *dither* into each bisection, which can be used to break the symmetry of integrands which are concentrated near the exact center of the hypercubic integration region. The default value of dither is zero, so no variation is introduced. If needed, a typical value of *dither* is 0.1.

23.4 VEGAS

The VEGAS algorithm of Lepage is based on importance sampling. It samples points from the probability distribution described by the function $|f|$, so that the points are concentrated in the regions that make the largest contribution to the integral.

In general, if the Monte Carlo integral of f is sampled with points distributed according to a probability distribution described by the function g, we obtain an estimate $E_g(f; N)$,

$$E_g(f; N) = E(f/g; N)$$

with a corresponding variance,

$$\text{Var}_g(f; N) = \text{Var}(f/g; N).$$

If the probability distribution is chosen as $g = |f|/I(|f|)$ then it can be shown that the variance $V_g(f; N)$ vanishes, and the error in the estimate will be zero. In practice it is not possible to sample from the exact distribution g for an arbitrary function, so importance sampling algorithms aim to produce efficient approximations to the desired distribution.

The VEGAS algorithm approximates the exact distribution by making a number of passes over the integration region while histogramming the function f. Each histogram is used to define a sampling distribution for the next pass. Asymptotically this procedure converges to the desired distribution. In order to avoid the number of histogram bins growing like K^d the probability distribution is approximated by a separable function: $g(x_1, x_2, \ldots) = g_1(x_1)g_2(x_2)\ldots$ so that the number of bins required is only Kd. This is equivalent to locating the peaks of the function from the projections of the integrand onto the coordinate axes. The efficiency of VEGAS depends on the validity of this assumption. It is most efficient when the peaks of the integrand are well-localized. If an integrand can be rewritten in a form which is approximately separable this will increase the efficiency of integration with VEGAS.

VEGAS incorporates a number of additional features, and combines both stratified sampling and importance sampling. The integration region is divided into a number of "boxes", with each box getting a fixed number of points (the goal is 2). Each box can then have a fractional number of bins, but if the ratio of bins-per-box is less than two, Vegas switches to a kind variance reduction (rather than importance sampling).

gsl_monte_vegas_state * gsl_monte_vegas_alloc (size_t *dim***)**   Function

This function allocates and initializes a workspace for Monte Carlo integration in *dim* dimensions. The workspace is used to maintain the state of the integration.

int gsl_monte_vegas_init (gsl_monte_vegas_state* *s*)**   Function

This function initializes a previously allocated integration state. This allows an existing workspace to be reused for different integrations.

int gsl_monte_vegas_integrate (gsl_monte_function * *f*,** double * *xl***, double * *xu***, size_t** *dim***, size_t** *calls***, gsl_rng * *r***, gsl_monte_vegas_state * *s***, double *** *result***, double * *abserr***)**   Function

This routines uses the VEGAS Monte Carlo algorithm to integrate the function *f* over the *dim*-dimensional hypercubic region defined by the lower and upper limits in the arrays *xl* and *xu*, each of size *dim*. The integration uses a fixed number of function calls *calls*, and obtains random sampling points using the random number generator *r*. A previously allocated workspace *s* must be supplied. The result of the integration is returned in *result*, with an estimated absolute error *abserr*. The result and its error estimate are based on a weighted average of independent samples. The chi-squared per degree of freedom for the weighted average is returned via the state struct component, *s->chisq*, and must be consistent with 1 for the weighted average to be reliable.

void gsl_monte_vegas_free (gsl_monte_vegas_state * *s*)**   Function

This function frees the memory associated with the integrator state *s*.

The VEGAS algorithm computes a number of independent estimates of the integral internally, according to the iterations parameter described below, and returns their weighted average. Random sampling of the integrand can occasionally produce an estimate where the error is zero, particularly if the function is constant in some regions. An estimate with zero error causes the weighted average to break down and must be handled separately. In the original Fortran implementations of VEGAS the error estimate is made non-zero by substituting a small value (typically 1e-30). The implementation in GSL differs from this and avoids the use of an arbitrary constant—it either assigns the value a weight which is the average weight of the preceding estimates or discards it according to the following procedure,

current estimate has zero error, weighted average has finite error
> The current estimate is assigned a weight which is the average weight of the preceding estimates.

current estimate has finite error, previous estimates had zero error
> The previous estimates are discarded and the weighted averaging procedure begins with the current estimate.

current estimate has zero error, previous estimates had zero error
> The estimates are averaged using the arithmetic mean, but no error is computed.

The VEGAS algorithm is highly configurable. The following variables can be accessed through the gsl_monte_vegas_state struct,

double result   Variable
double sigma   Variable
These parameters contain the raw value of the integral *result* and its error *sigma* from the last iteration of the algorithm.

double chisq   Variable
This parameter gives the chi-squared per degree of freedom for the weighted estimate of the integral. The value of *chisq* should be close to 1. A value of *chisq* which differs significantly from 1 indicates that the values from different iterations are inconsistent. In this case the weighted error will be under-estimated, and further iterations of the algorithm are needed to obtain reliable results.

double alpha   Variable
The parameter alpha controls the stiffness of the rebinning algorithm. It is typically set between one and two. A value of zero prevents rebinning of the grid. The default value is 1.5.

`size_t iterations`   Variable

The number of iterations to perform for each call to the routine. The default value is 5 iterations.

`int stage`   Variable

Setting this determines the *stage* of the calculation. Normally, `stage` = 0 which begins with a new uniform grid and empty weighted average. Calling vegas with `stage` = 1 retains the grid from the previous run but discards the weighted average, so that one can "tune" the grid using a relatively small number of points and then do a large run with `stage` = 1 on the optimized grid. Setting `stage` = 2 keeps the grid and the weighted average from the previous run, but may increase (or decrease) the number of histogram bins in the grid depending on the number of calls available. Choosing `stage` = 3 enters at the main loop, so that nothing is changed, and is equivalent to performing additional iterations in a previous call.

`int mode`   Variable

The possible choices are GSL_VEGAS_MODE_IMPORTANCE, GSL_VEGAS_ MODE_STRATIFIED, GSL_VEGAS_MODE_IMPORTANCE_ONLY. This determines whether VEGAS will use importance sampling or stratified sampling, or whether it can pick on its own. In low dimensions VEGAS uses strict stratified sampling (more precisely, stratified sampling is chosen if there are fewer than 2 bins per box).

`int verbose`   Variable
`FILE * ostream`   Variable

These parameters set the level of information printed by VEGAS. All information is written to the stream *ostream*. The default setting of *verbose* is -1, which turns off all output. A *verbose* value of 0 prints summary information about the weighted average and final result, while a value of 1 also displays the grid coordinates. A value of 2 prints information from the rebinning procedure for each iteration.

23.5 Examples

The example program below uses the Monte Carlo routines to estimate
the value of the following 3-dimensional integral from the theory of random
walks,

$$I = \int_{-\pi}^{+\pi} \frac{dk_x}{2\pi} \int_{-\pi}^{+\pi} \frac{dk_y}{2\pi} \int_{-\pi}^{+\pi} \frac{dk_z}{2\pi} \frac{1}{(1 - \cos(k_x)\cos(k_y)\cos(k_z))}.$$

The analytic value of this integral can be shown to be $I = \Gamma(1/4)^4/(4\pi^3) =$
1.393203929685676859.... The integral gives the mean time spent at the
origin by a random walk on a body-centered cubic lattice in three dimensions.

For simplicity we will compute the integral over the region $(0,0,0)$ to
(π,π,π) and multiply by 8 to obtain the full result. The integral is slowly
varying in the middle of the region but has integrable singularities at the
corners $(0,0,0)$, $(0,\pi,\pi)$, $(\pi,0,\pi)$ and $(\pi,\pi,0)$. The Monte Carlo routines
only select points which are strictly within the integration region and so
no special measures are needed to avoid these singularities.

```
#include <stdlib.h>
#include <gsl/gsl_math.h>
#include <gsl/gsl_monte.h>
#include <gsl/gsl_monte_plain.h>
#include <gsl/gsl_monte_miser.h>
#include <gsl/gsl_monte_vegas.h>

/* Computation of the integral,

      I = int (dx dy dz)/(2pi)^3  1/(1-cos(x)cos(y)cos(z))

   over (-pi,-pi,-pi) to (+pi, +pi, +pi).  The exact answer
   is Gamma(1/4)^4/(4 pi^3).  This example is taken from
   C.Itzykson, J.M.Drouffe, "Statistical Field Theory -
   Volume 1", Section 1.1, p21, which cites the original
   paper M.L.Glasser, I.J.Zucker, Proc.Natl.Acad.Sci.USA 74
   1800 (1977) */

/* For simplicity we compute the integral over the region
   (0,0,0) -> (pi,pi,pi) and multiply by 8 */

double exact = 1.3932039296856768591842462603255;

double
g (double *k, size_t dim, void *params)
{
  double A = 1.0 / (M_PI * M_PI * M_PI);
  return A / (1.0 - cos (k[0]) * cos (k[1]) * cos (k[2]));
}
```

```
void
display_results (char *title, double result, double error)
{
  printf ("%s ==================\n", title);
  printf ("result = % .6f\n", result);
  printf ("sigma  = % .6f\n", error);
  printf ("exact  = % .6f\n", exact);
  printf ("error  = % .6f = %.1g sigma\n", result - exact,
          fabs (result - exact) / error);
}

int
main (void)
{
  double res, err;

  double xl[3] = { 0, 0, 0 };
  double xu[3] = { M_PI, M_PI, M_PI };

  const gsl_rng_type *T;
  gsl_rng *r;

  gsl_monte_function G = { &g, 3, 0 };

  size_t calls = 500000;

  gsl_rng_env_setup ();

  T = gsl_rng_default;
  r = gsl_rng_alloc (T);

  {
    gsl_monte_plain_state *s = gsl_monte_plain_alloc (3);
    gsl_monte_plain_integrate (&G, xl, xu, 3, calls, r, s,
                               &res, &err);
    gsl_monte_plain_free (s);

    display_results ("plain", res, err);
  }

  {
    gsl_monte_miser_state *s = gsl_monte_miser_alloc (3);
    gsl_monte_miser_integrate (&G, xl, xu, 3, calls, r, s,
                               &res, &err);
    gsl_monte_miser_free (s);

    display_results ("miser", res, err);
  }
```

```
{
  gsl_monte_vegas_state *s = gsl_monte_vegas_alloc (3);

  gsl_monte_vegas_integrate (&G, xl, xu, 3, 10000, r, s,
                             &res, &err);
  display_results ("vegas warm-up", res, err);

  printf ("converging...\n");

  do
    {
      gsl_monte_vegas_integrate (&G, xl, xu, 3, calls/5, r, s,
                                 &res, &err);
      printf ("result = % .6f sigma = % .6f "
              "chisq/dof = %.1f\n", res, err, s->chisq);
    }
  while (fabs (s->chisq - 1.0) > 0.5);

  display_results ("vegas final", res, err);

  gsl_monte_vegas_free (s);
}
  return 0;
}
```

With 500,000 function calls the plain Monte Carlo algorithm achieves a
fractional error of 0.6%. The estimated error sigma is consistent with the
actual error, and the computed result differs from the true result by about
one standard deviation,

```
plain ==================
result =   1.385867
sigma  =   0.007938
exact  =   1.393204
error  = -0.007337 = 0.9 sigma
```

The MISER algorithm reduces the error by a factor of two, and also correctly estimates the error,

```
miser ==================
result =   1.390656
sigma  =   0.003743
exact  =   1.393204
error  = -0.002548 = 0.7 sigma
```

In the case of the VEGAS algorithm the program uses an initial warm-up
run of 10,000 function calls to prepare, or "warm up", the grid. This
is followed by a main run with five iterations of 100,000 function calls.
The chi-squared per degree of freedom for the five iterations are checked

for consistency with 1, and the run is repeated if the results have not converged. In this case the estimates are consistent on the first pass.

```
vegas warm-up ==================
result =  1.386925
sigma  =  0.002651
exact  =  1.393204
error  = -0.006278 = 2 sigma
converging...
result =  1.392957 sigma =  0.000452 chisq/dof = 1.1
vegas final ==================
result =  1.392957
sigma  =  0.000452
exact  =  1.393204
error  = -0.000247 = 0.5 sigma
```

If the value of chisq had differed significantly from 1 it would indicate inconsistent results, with a correspondingly underestimated error. The final estimate from VEGAS (using a similar number of function calls) is significantly more accurate than the other two algorithms.

23.6 References and Further Reading

The MISER algorithm is described in the following article by Press and Farrar,

W.H. Press, G.R. Farrar, *Recursive Stratified Sampling for Multidimensional Monte Carlo Integration*, Computers in Physics, v4 (1990), pp190–195.

The VEGAS algorithm is described in the following papers,

G.P. Lepage, *A New Algorithm for Adaptive Multidimensional Integration*, Journal of Computational Physics 27, 192–203, (1978)

G.P. Lepage, *VEGAS: An Adaptive Multi-dimensional Integration Program*, Cornell preprint CLNS 80-447, March 1980

24 Simulated Annealing

Stochastic search techniques are used when the structure of a space is not well understood or is not smooth, so that techniques like Newton's method (which requires calculating Jacobian derivative matrices) cannot be used. In particular, these techniques are frequently used to solve combinatorial optimization problems, such as the traveling salesman problem.

The goal is to find a point in the space at which a real valued *energy function* (or *cost function*) is minimized. Simulated annealing is a minimization technique which has given good results in avoiding local minima; it is based on the idea of taking a random walk through the space at successively lower temperatures, where the probability of taking a step is given by a Boltzmann distribution.

The functions described in this chapter are declared in the header file 'gsl_siman.h'.

24.1 Simulated Annealing algorithm

The simulated annealing algorithm takes random walks through the problem space, looking for points with low energies; in these random walks, the probability of taking a step is determined by the Boltzmann distribution,

$$p = e^{-(E_{i+1} - E_i)/(kT)}$$

if $E_{i+1} > E_i$, and $p = 1$ when $E_{i+1} \leq E_i$.

In other words, a step will occur if the new energy is lower. If the new energy is higher, the transition can still occur, and its likelihood is proportional to the temperature T and inversely proportional to the energy difference $E_{i+1} - E_i$.

The temperature T is initially set to a high value, and a random walk is carried out at that temperature. Then the temperature is lowered very slightly according to a *cooling schedule*, for example: $T \to T/\mu_T$ where μ_T is slightly greater than 1.

The slight probability of taking a step that gives higher energy is what allows simulated annealing to frequently get out of local minima.

24.2 Simulated Annealing functions

void gsl_siman_solve (const gsl_rng * r, void * *x0_p*,   Function
        gsl_siman_Efunc_t *Ef*, gsl_siman_step_t *take_step*,
        gsl_siman_metric_t *distance*, gsl_siman_print_t
        print_position, gsl_siman_copy_t *copyfunc*,
        gsl_siman_copy_construct_t *copy_constructor*,
        gsl_siman_destroy_t *destructor*, size_t *element_size*,
        gsl_siman_params_t *params*)

This function performs a simulated annealing search through a given space. The space is specified by providing the functions *Ef* and *distance*. The simulated annealing steps are generated using the random number generator *r* and the function *take_step*.

The starting configuration of the system should be given by *x0_p*. The routine offers two modes for updating configurations, a fixed-size mode and a variable-size mode. In the fixed-size mode the configuration is stored as a single block of memory of size *element_size*. Copies of this configuration are created, copied and destroyed internally using the standard library functions malloc, memcpy and free. The function pointers *copyfunc*, *copy_constructor* and *destructor* should be null pointers in fixed-size mode. In the variable-size mode the functions *copyfunc*, *copy_constructor* and *destructor* are used to create, copy and destroy configurations internally. The variable *element_size* should be zero in the variable-size mode.

The *params* structure (described below) controls the run by providing the temperature schedule and other tunable parameters to the algorithm.

On exit the best result achieved during the search is placed in **x0_p*. If the annealing process has been successful this should be a good approximation to the optimal point in the space.

If the function pointer *print_position* is not null, a debugging log will be printed to stdout with the following columns:

        number_of_iterations temperature x x-(*x0_p) Ef(x)

and the output of the function *print_position* itself. If *print_position* is null then no information is printed.

The simulated annealing routines require several user-specified functions to define the configuration space and energy function. The prototypes for these functions are given below.

gsl_siman_Efunc_t   Data Type
    This function type should return the energy of a configuration *xp*.

        double (*gsl_siman_Efunc_t) (void *xp)

`gsl_siman_step_t`   Data Type

This function type should modify the configuration *xp* using a random step taken from the generator *r*, up to a maximum distance of *step_size*.

```
void (*gsl_siman_step_t) (const gsl_rng *r, void *xp,
                          double step_size)
```

`gsl_siman_metric_t`   Data Type

This function type should return the distance between two configurations *xp* and *yp*.

```
double (*gsl_siman_metric_t) (void *xp, void *yp)
```

`gsl_siman_print_t`   Data Type

This function type should print the contents of the configuration *xp*.

```
void (*gsl_siman_print_t) (void *xp)
```

`gsl_siman_copy_t`   Data Type

This function type should copy the configuration *source* into *dest*.

```
void (*gsl_siman_copy_t) (void *source, void *dest)
```

`gsl_siman_copy_construct_t`   Data Type

This function type should create a new copy of the configuration *xp*.

```
void * (*gsl_siman_copy_construct_t) (void *xp)
```

`gsl_siman_destroy_t`   Data Type

This function type should destroy the configuration *xp*, freeing its memory.

```
void (*gsl_siman_destroy_t) (void *xp)
```

`gsl_siman_params_t`   Data Type

These are the parameters that control a run of `gsl_siman_solve`. This structure contains all the information needed to control the search, beyond the energy function, the step function and the initial guess.

`int n_tries`
> The number of points to try for each step.

`int iters_fixed_T`
> The number of iterations at each temperature.

`double step_size`
> The maximum step size in the random walk.

`double k, t_initial, mu_t, t_min`
> The parameters of the Boltzmann distribution and cooling schedule.

24.3 Examples

The simulated annealing package is clumsy, and it has to be because it is written in C, for C callers, and tries to be polymorphic at the same time. But here we provide some examples which can be pasted into your application with little change and should make things easier.

24.3.1 Trivial example

The first example, in one dimensional cartesian space, sets up an energy function which is a damped sine wave; this has many local minima, but only one global minimum, somewhere between 1.0 and 1.5. The initial guess given is 15.5, which is several local minima away from the global minimum.

```
#include <math.h>
#include <stdlib.h>
#include <gsl/gsl_siman.h>

/* set up parameters for this simulated annealing run */

/* how many points do we try before stepping */
#define N_TRIES 200

/* how many iterations for each T? */
#define ITERS_FIXED_T 10

/* max step size in random walk */
#define STEP_SIZE 10

/* Boltzmann constant */
#define K 1.0

/* initial temperature */
#define T_INITIAL 0.002

/* damping factor for temperature */
#define MU_T 1.005
#define T_MIN 2.0e-6

gsl_siman_params_t params
  = {N_TRIES, ITERS_FIXED_T, STEP_SIZE,
     K, T_INITIAL, MU_T, T_MIN};

/* now some functions to test in one dimension */
double E1(void *xp)
{
  double x = * ((double *) xp);

  return exp(-pow((x-1.0),2.0))*sin(8*x);
```

```
}

double M1(void *xp, void *yp)
{
  double x = *((double *) xp);
  double y = *((double *) yp);

  return fabs(x - y);
}

void S1(const gsl_rng * r, void *xp, double step_size)
{
  double old_x = *((double *) xp);
  double new_x;

  double u = gsl_rng_uniform(r);
  new_x = u * 2 * step_size - step_size + old_x;

  memcpy(xp, &new_x, sizeof(new_x));
}

void P1(void *xp)
{
  printf ("%12g", *((double *) xp));
}

int
main(int argc, char *argv[])
{
  const gsl_rng_type * T;
  gsl_rng * r;

  double x_initial = 15.5;

  gsl_rng_env_setup();

  T = gsl_rng_default;
  r = gsl_rng_alloc(T);

  gsl_siman_solve(r, &x_initial, E1, S1, M1, P1,
                  NULL, NULL, NULL,
                  sizeof(double), params);
  return 0;
}
```

Here are a couple of plots that are generated by running `siman_test` in the following way:

```
$ ./siman_test | grep -v "^#"
  | xyplot -xyil -y -0.88 -0.83 -d "x...y"
  | xyps -d > siman-test.eps
$ ./siman_test | grep -v "^#"
  | xyplot -xyil -xl "generation" -yl "energy" -d "x..y"
  | xyps -d > siman-energy.eps
```

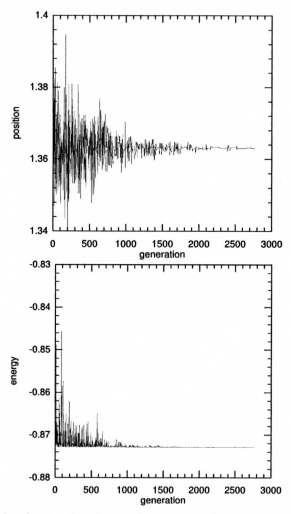

Example of a simulated annealing run: at higher temperatures (early in the plot) you see that the solution can fluctuate, but at lower temperatures it converges.

24.3.2 Traveling Salesman Problem

The TSP (*Traveling Salesman Problem*) is the classic combinatorial optimization problem. I have provided a very simple version of it, based on the coordinates of twelve cities in the southwestern United States. This should maybe be called the *Flying Salesman Problem*, since I am using the great-circle distance between cities, rather than the driving distance. Also: I assume the earth is a sphere, so I don't use geoid distances.

The `gsl_siman_solve` routine finds a route which is 3490.62 Kilometers long; this is confirmed by an exhaustive search of all possible routes with the same initial city.

The full code can be found in 'siman/siman_tsp.c', but I include here some plots generated in the following way:

```
$ ./siman_tsp > tsp.output
$ grep -v "^#" tsp.output
 | xyplot -xyil -d "x...............y"
    -lx "generation" -ly "distance"
    -lt "TSP -- 12 southwest cities"
 | xyps -d > 12-cities.eps
$ grep initial_city_coord tsp.output
 | awk '{print $2, $3, $4, $5}'
 | xyplot -xyil -lb0 -cs 0.8
    -lx "longitude (- means west)" -ly "latitude"
    -lt "TSP -- initial-order"
 | xyps -d > initial-route.eps
$ grep final_city_coord tsp.output
 | awk '{print $2, $3, $4, $5}'
 | xyplot -xyil -lb0 -cs 0.8
    -lx "longitude (- means west)" -ly "latitude"
    -lt "TSP -- final-order"
 | xyps -d > final-route.eps
```

This is the output showing the initial order of the cities; longitude is negative, since it is west and I want the plot to look like a map.

```
# initial coordinates of cities (longitude and latitude)
###initial_city_coord: -105.95 35.68 Santa Fe
###initial_city_coord: -112.07 33.54 Phoenix
###initial_city_coord: -106.62 35.12 Albuquerque
###initial_city_coord: -103.2 34.41 Clovis
###initial_city_coord: -107.87 37.29 Durango
###initial_city_coord: -96.77 32.79 Dallas
###initial_city_coord: -105.92 35.77 Tesuque
###initial_city_coord: -107.84 35.15 Grants
###initial_city_coord: -106.28 35.89 Los Alamos
###initial_city_coord: -106.76 32.34 Las Cruces
###initial_city_coord: -108.58 37.35 Cortez
###initial_city_coord: -108.74 35.52 Gallup
###initial_city_coord: -105.95 35.68 Santa Fe
```

The optimal route turns out to be:

```
# final coordinates of cities (longitude and latitude)
###final_city_coord: -105.95 35.68 Santa Fe
###final_city_coord: -106.28 35.89 Los Alamos
###final_city_coord: -106.62 35.12 Albuquerque
###final_city_coord: -107.84 35.15 Grants
###final_city_coord: -107.87 37.29 Durango
###final_city_coord: -108.58 37.35 Cortez
###final_city_coord: -108.74 35.52 Gallup
###final_city_coord: -112.07 33.54 Phoenix
###final_city_coord: -106.76 32.34 Las Cruces
###final_city_coord: -96.77 32.79 Dallas
###final_city_coord: -103.2 34.41 Clovis
###final_city_coord: -105.92 35.77 Tesuque
###final_city_coord: -105.95 35.68 Santa Fe
```

Initial and final (optimal) route for the 12 southwestern cities
Flying Salesman Problem.

Here's a plot of the cost function (energy) versus generation (point in the calculation at which a new temperature is set) for this problem:

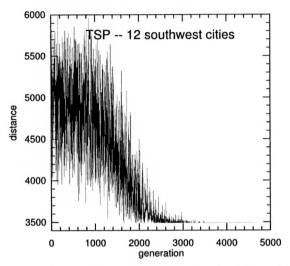

Example of a simulated annealing run for the 12 southwestern cities Flying Salesman Problem.

24.4 References and Further Reading

Further information is available in the following book,

Modern Heuristic Techniques for Combinatorial Problems, Colin R. Reeves (ed.), McGraw-Hill, 1995 (ISBN 0-07-709239-2).

25   Ordinary Differential Equations

This chapter describes functions for solving ordinary differential equation (ODE) initial value problems. The library provides a variety of low-level methods, such as Runge-Kutta and Bulirsch-Stoer routines, and higher-level components for adaptive step-size control. The components can be combined by the user to achieve the desired solution, with full access to any intermediate steps.

These functions are declared in the header file 'gsl_odeiv.h'.

25.1   Defining the ODE System

The routines solve the general n-dimensional first-order system,

$$\frac{dy_i(t)}{dt} = f_i(t, y_1(t), \ldots y_n(t))$$

for $i = 1, \ldots, n$. The stepping functions rely on the vector of derivatives f_i and the Jacobian matrix, $J_{ij} = \partial f_i(t, y(t))/\partial y_j$. A system of equations is defined using the gsl_odeiv_system datatype.

gsl_odeiv_system   Data Type

This data type defines a general ODE system with arbitrary parameters.

int (* function) (double t, const double y[], double dydt[], void * params)

> This function should store the vector elements of the derivatives $f_i(t, y, params)$ in the array *dydt*, for arguments (t, y) and parameters *params*. The function should return GSL_SUCCESS if the calculation was completed successfully. Any other return value indicates an error.

int (* jacobian) (double t, const double y[], double * dfdy, double dfdt[], void * params);

> This function should store the vector of derivative elements $\partial f_i(t, y, params)/\partial t$ in the array *dfdt* and the Jacobian matrix J_{ij} in the array *dfdy*, regarded as a row-ordered matrix J(i,j) = dfdy[i * dimension + j] where dimension is the dimension of the system. The function should return GSL_SUCCESS if the calculation was completed successfully. Any other return value indicates an error.

Some of the simpler solver algorithms do not make use of the Jacobian matrix, so it is not always strictly necessary to provide it (the `jacobian` element of the struct can be replaced by a null pointer for those algorithms). However, it is useful to provide the Jacobian to allow the solver algorithms to be interchanged—the best algorithms make use of the Jacobian.

`size_t dimension;`
This is the dimension of the system of equations.

`void * params`
This is a pointer to the arbitrary parameters of the system.

25.2 Stepping Functions

The lowest level components are the *stepping functions* which advance a solution from time t to $t + h$ for a fixed step-size h and estimate the resulting local error.

`gsl_odeiv_step * gsl_odeiv_step_alloc (const`   Function
     `gsl_odeiv_step_type * T, size_t dim)`
This function returns a pointer to a newly allocated instance of a stepping function of type T for a system of *dim* dimensions.

`int gsl_odeiv_step_reset (gsl_odeiv_step * s)`   Function
This function resets the stepping function *s*. It should be used whenever the next use of *s* will not be a continuation of a previous step.

`void gsl_odeiv_step_free (gsl_odeiv_step * s)`   Function
This function frees all the memory associated with the stepping function *s*.

`const char * gsl_odeiv_step_name (const gsl_odeiv_step` Function
     `* s)`
This function returns a pointer to the name of the stepping function. For example,

```
printf ("step method is '%s'\n",
        gsl_odeiv_step_name (s));
```
would print something like step method is 'rk4'.

`unsigned int gsl_odeiv_step_order (const`   Function
     `gsl_odeiv_step * s)`
This function returns the order of the stepping function on the previous step. This order can vary if the stepping function itself is adaptive.

int gsl_odeiv_step_apply (gsl_odeiv_step * s, double t,   Function
      double h, double y[], double yerr[], const double
      dydt_in[], double dydt_out[], const gsl_odeiv_system *
      dydt)

This function applies the stepping function s to the system of equations defined by dydt, using the step size h to advance the system from time t and state y to time t+h. The new state of the system is stored in y on output, with an estimate of the absolute error in each component stored in yerr. If the argument dydt_in is not null it should point an array containing the derivatives for the system at time t on input. This is optional as the derivatives will be computed internally if they are not provided, but allows the reuse of existing derivative information. On output the new derivatives of the system at time t+h will be stored in dydt_out if it is not null. Note that h can be positive or negative.

If the user-supplied functions defined in the system dydt return a status other than GSL_SUCCESS the step will be aborted. In this case, the elements of y will be restored to their pre-step values and the error code from the user-supplied function will be returned. To distinguish between error codes from the user-supplied functions and those from gsl_odeiv_step_apply itself, any user-defined return values should be distinct from the standard GSL error codes (see Section 3.2 [Error Codes], page 18).

The following algorithms are available,

gsl_odeiv_step_rk2   Step Type
      Embedded Runge-Kutta (2, 3) method.

gsl_odeiv_step_rk4   Step Type
      4th order (classical) Runge-Kutta.

gsl_odeiv_step_rkf45   Step Type
      Embedded Runge-Kutta-Fehlberg (4, 5) method. This method is a good general-purpose integrator.

gsl_odeiv_step_rkck   Step Type
      Embedded Runge-Kutta Cash-Karp (4, 5) method.

gsl_odeiv_step_rk8pd   Step Type
      Embedded Runge-Kutta Prince-Dormand (8,9) method.

gsl_odeiv_step_rk2imp   Step Type
      Implicit 2nd order Runge-Kutta at Gaussian points.

gsl_odeiv_step_rk4imp   Step Type
      Implicit 4th order Runge-Kutta at Gaussian points.

`gsl_odeiv_step_bsimp`   Step Type
    Implicit Bulirsch-Stoer method of Bader and Deuflhard. This algo-
    rithm requires the Jacobian.

`gsl_odeiv_step_gear1`   Step Type
    $M = 1$ implicit Gear method.

`gsl_odeiv_step_gear2`   Step Type
    $M = 2$ implicit Gear method.

25.3 Adaptive Step-size Control

The control function examines the proposed change to the solution
produced by a stepping function and attempts to determine the optimal
step-size for a user-specified level of error.

`gsl_odeiv_control * gsl_odeiv_control_standard_new`   Function
        (double *eps_abs*, double *eps_rel*, double *a_y*, double
        a_dydt)
    The standard control object is a four parameter heuristic based on
    absolute and relative errors *eps_abs* and *eps_rel*, and scaling factors *a_y*
    and *a_dydt* for the system state $y(t)$ and derivatives $y'(t)$ respectively.
    The step-size adjustment procedure for this method begins by com-
    puting the desired error level D_i for each component,

$$D_i = \epsilon_{abs} + \epsilon_{rel} * (a_y|y_i| + a_{dydt}|hy_i'|)$$

    and comparing it with the observed error $E_i = |yerr_i|$. If the observed
    error E exceeds the desired error level D by more than 10% for any
    component then the method reduces the step-size by an appropriate
    factor,

$$h_{new} = h_{old} * S * (E/D)^{-1/q}$$

    where q is the consistency order of the method (e.g. $q = 4$ for 4(5)
    embedded RK), and S is a safety factor of 0.9. The ratio E/D is taken
    to be the maximum of the ratios E_i/D_i.
    If the observed error E is less than 50% of the desired error level D for
    the maximum ratio E_i/D_i then the algorithm takes the opportunity to
    increase the step-size to bring the error in line with the desired level,

$$h_{new} = h_{old} * S * (E/D)^{-1/(q+1)}$$

    This encompasses all the standard error scaling methods. To avoid
    uncontrolled changes in the stepsize, the overall scaling factor is limited
    to the range 1/5 to 5.

gsl_odeiv_control * gsl_odeiv_control_y_new (double   Function
        eps_abs, double eps_rel)
This function creates a new control object which will keep the local
error on each step within an absolute error of eps_abs and relative
error of eps_rel with respect to the solution $y_i(t)$. This is equivalent
to the standard control object with a_y=1 and a_dydt=0.

gsl_odeiv_control * gsl_odeiv_control_yp_new (double   Function
        eps_abs, double eps_rel)
This function creates a new control object which will keep the local
error on each step within an absolute error of eps_abs and relative error
of eps_rel with respect to the derivatives of the solution $y_i'(t)$. This is
equivalent to the standard control object with a_y=0 and a_dydt=1.

gsl_odeiv_control * gsl_odeiv_control_scaled_new   Function
        (double eps_abs, double eps_rel, double a_y, double
        a_dydt, const double scale_abs[], size_t dim)
This function creates a new control object which uses the same algorithm as gsl_odeiv_control_standard_new but with an absolute
error which is scaled for each component by the array scale_abs. The
formula for D_i for this control object is,

$$D_i = \epsilon_{abs}s_i + \epsilon_{rel} * (a_y|y_i| + a_{dydt}|hy_i'|)$$

where s_i is the i-th component of the array scale_abs. The same error
control heuristic is used by the Matlab ODE suite.

gsl_odeiv_control * gsl_odeiv_control_alloc (const   Function
        gsl_odeiv_control_type * T)
This function returns a pointer to a newly allocated instance of a
control function of type T. This function is only needed for defining
new types of control functions. For most purposes the standard control
functions described above should be sufficient.

int gsl_odeiv_control_init (gsl_odeiv_control * c,   Function
        double eps_abs, double eps_rel, double a_y, double
        a_dydt)
This function initializes the control function c with the parameters
eps_abs (absolute error), eps_rel (relative error), a_y (scaling factor
for y) and a_dydt (scaling factor for derivatives).

void gsl_odeiv_control_free (gsl_odeiv_control * c)   Function
This function frees all the memory associated with the control function
c.

int gsl_odeiv_control_hadjust (gsl_odeiv_control * c,   Function
        gsl_odeiv_step * s, const double y[], const double
        yerr[], const double dydt[], double * h)

This function adjusts the step-size h using the control function c, and
the current values of y, yerr and dydt. The stepping function step
is also needed to determine the order of the method. If the error
in the y-values yerr is found to be too large then the step-size h is
reduced and the function returns GSL_ODEIV_HADJ_DEC. If the error is
sufficiently small then h may be increased and GSL_ODEIV_HADJ_INC is
returned. The function returns GSL_ODEIV_HADJ_NIL if the step-size is
unchanged. The goal of the function is to estimate the largest step-size
which satisfies the user-specified accuracy requirements for the current
point.

const char * gsl_odeiv_control_name (const   Function
        gsl_odeiv_control * c)

This function returns a pointer to the name of the control function.
For example,

        printf ("control method is '%s'\n",
                gsl_odeiv_control_name (c));

would print something like control method is 'standard'

25.4 Evolution

The highest level of the system is the evolution function which combines the results of a stepping function and control function to reliably
advance the solution forward over an interval (t_0, t_1). If the control function signals that the step-size should be decreased the evolution function
backs out of the current step and tries the proposed smaller step-size.
This process is continued until an acceptable step-size is found.

gsl_odeiv_evolve * gsl_odeiv_evolve_alloc (size_t dim)   Function

This function returns a pointer to a newly allocated instance of an
evolution function for a system of dim dimensions.

int gsl_odeiv_evolve_apply (gsl_odeiv_evolve * e,   Function
        gsl_odeiv_control * con, gsl_odeiv_step * step, const
        gsl_odeiv_system * dydt, double * t, double t1, double
        * h, double y[])

This function advances the system (e, dydt) from time t and position y
using the stepping function step. The new time and position are stored
in t and y on output. The initial step-size is taken as h, but this will be
modified using the control function c to achieve the appropriate error
bound if necessary. The routine may make several calls to step in order

to determine the optimum step-size. An estimate of the local error for the step can be obtained from the components of the array *e->yerr[]*. If the step-size has been changed the value of *h* will be modified on output. The maximum time *t1* is guaranteed not to be exceeded by the time-step. On the final time-step the value of *t* will be set to *t1* exactly. Note that systems with negative step-size *h* and *t1* < *t* are also supported.

If the user-supplied functions defined in the system *dydt* return a status other than GSL_SUCCESS the step will be aborted. In this case, *t* and *y* will be restored to their pre-step values and the error code from the user-supplied function will be returned. To distinguish between error codes from the user-supplied functions and those from gsl_odeiv_evolve_apply itself, any user-defined return values should be distinct from the standard GSL error codes.

int gsl_odeiv_evolve_reset (gsl_odeiv_evolve * e)   Function
This function resets the evolution function *e*. It should be used whenever the next use of *e* will not be a continuation of a previous step.

void gsl_odeiv_evolve_free (gsl_odeiv_evolve * e)   Function
This function frees all the memory associated with the evolution function *e*.

25.5 Examples

The following program solves the second-order nonlinear Van der Pol oscillator equation,

$$x''(t) + \mu x'(t)(x(t)^2 - 1) + x(t) = 0$$

This can be converted into a first order system suitable for use with the routines described in this chapter by introducing a separate variable for the velocity, $y = x'(t)$,

$$x' = y$$
$$y' = -x + \mu y(1 - x^2)$$

The program begins by defining functions for these derivatives and their Jacobian,

```
#include <stdio.h>
#include <gsl/gsl_errno.h>
#include <gsl/gsl_matrix.h>
#include <gsl/gsl_odeiv.h>

int
```

```
func (double t, const double y[], double f[],
     void *params)
{
  double mu = *(double *)params;
  f[0] = y[1];
  f[1] = -y[0] - mu*y[1]*(y[0]*y[0] - 1);
  return GSL_SUCCESS;
}

int
jac (double t, const double y[], double *dfdy,
     double dfdt[], void *params)
{
  double mu = *(double *)params;
  gsl_matrix_view dfdy_mat
    = gsl_matrix_view_array (dfdy, 2, 2);
  gsl_matrix * m = &dfdy_mat.matrix;
  gsl_matrix_set (m, 0, 0, 0.0);
  gsl_matrix_set (m, 0, 1, 1.0);
  gsl_matrix_set (m, 1, 0, -2.0*mu*y[0]*y[1] - 1.0);
  gsl_matrix_set (m, 1, 1, -mu*(y[0]*y[0] - 1.0));
  dfdt[0] = 0.0;
  dfdt[1] = 0.0;
  return GSL_SUCCESS;
}

int
main (void)
{
  const gsl_odeiv_step_type * T
    = gsl_odeiv_step_rk8pd;

  gsl_odeiv_step * s
    = gsl_odeiv_step_alloc (T, 2);
  gsl_odeiv_control * c
    = gsl_odeiv_control_y_new (1e-6, 0.0);
  gsl_odeiv_evolve * e
    = gsl_odeiv_evolve_alloc (2);

  double mu = 10;
  gsl_odeiv_system sys = {func, jac, 2, &mu};

  double t = 0.0, t1 = 100.0;
```

```
double h = 1e-6;
double y[2] = { 1.0, 0.0 };

while (t < t1)
  {
    int status = gsl_odeiv_evolve_apply (e, c, s,
                                          &sys,
                                          &t, t1,
                                          &h, y);

    if (status != GSL_SUCCESS)
        break;

    printf ("%.5e %.5e %.5e\n", t, y[0], y[1]);
  }

gsl_odeiv_evolve_free (e);
gsl_odeiv_control_free (c);
gsl_odeiv_step_free (s);
return 0;
}
```

For functions with multiple parameters, the appropriate information can be passed in through the *params* argument using a pointer to a struct.

The main loop of the program evolves the solution from $(y, y') = (1, 0)$ at $t = 0$ to $t = 100$. The step-size h is automatically adjusted by the controller to maintain an absolute accuracy of 10^{-6} in the function values y.

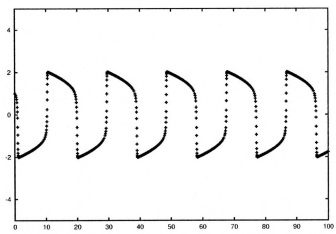

Numerical solution of the Van der Pol oscillator equation

using Prince-Dormand 8th order Runge-Kutta.

To obtain the values at regular intervals, rather than the variable spacings chosen by the control function, the main loop can be modified to advance the solution from one point to the next. For example, the following main loop prints the solution at the fixed points $t = 0, 1, 2, \ldots, 100$,

```
for (i = 1; i <= 100; i++)
  {
    double ti = i * t1 / 100.0;

    while (t < ti)
      {
        gsl_odeiv_evolve_apply (e, c, s,
                                &sys,
                                &t, ti, &h,
                                y);
      }

    printf ("%.5e %.5e %.5e\n", t, y[0], y[1]);
  }
```

It is also possible to work with a non-adaptive integrator, using only the stepping function itself. The following program uses the rk4 fourth-order Runge-Kutta stepping function with a fixed stepsize of 0.01,

```
int
main (void)
{
  const gsl_odeiv_step_type * T
    = gsl_odeiv_step_rk4;

  gsl_odeiv_step * s
    = gsl_odeiv_step_alloc (T, 2);

  double mu = 10;
  gsl_odeiv_system sys = {func, jac, 2, &mu};

  double t = 0.0, t1 = 100.0;
  double h = 1e-2;
  double y[2] = { 1.0, 0.0 }, y_err[2];
  double dydt_in[2], dydt_out[2];

  /* initialise dydt_in from system parameters */
  GSL_ODEIV_FN_EVAL(&sys, t, y, dydt_in);

  while (t < t1)
```

```
    {
        int status = gsl_odeiv_step_apply (s, t, h,
                                           y, y_err,
                                           dydt_in,
                                           dydt_out,
                                           &sys);

        if (status != GSL_SUCCESS)
            break;

        dydt_in[0] = dydt_out[0];
        dydt_in[1] = dydt_out[1];

        t += h;

        printf ("%.5e %.5e %.5e\n", t, y[0], y[1]);
    }

    gsl_odeiv_step_free (s);
    return 0;
}
```

The derivatives must be initialized for the starting point $t = 0$ before the
first step is taken. Subsequent steps use the output derivatives *dydt_out*
as inputs to the next step by copying their values into *dydt_in*.

25.6 References and Further Reading

Many of the basic Runge-Kutta formulas can be found in the Handbook of Mathematical Functions,

> Abramowitz & Stegun (eds.), *Handbook of Mathematical Functions*,
> Section 25.5.

The implicit Bulirsch-Stoer algorithm bsimp is described in the following
paper,

> G. Bader and P. Deuflhard, "A Semi-Implicit Mid-Point Rule for
> Stiff Systems of Ordinary Differential Equations.", Numer. Math.
> 41, 373–398, 1983.

26 Interpolation

This chapter describes functions for performing interpolation. The library provides a variety of interpolation methods, including Cubic splines and Akima splines. The interpolation types are interchangeable, allowing different methods to be used without recompiling. Interpolations can be defined for both normal and periodic boundary conditions. Additional functions are available for computing derivatives and integrals of interpolating functions.

The functions described in this section are declared in the header files 'gsl_interp.h' and 'gsl_spline.h'.

26.1 Introduction

Given a set of data points $(x_1, y_1) \ldots (x_n, y_n)$ the routines described in this section compute a continuous interpolating function $y(x)$ such that $y(x_i) = y_i$. The interpolation is piecewise smooth, and its behavior at the end-points is determined by the type of interpolation used. For periodic boundary conditions the first and last points data-points should satisfy $y_1 = y_n$.

26.2 Interpolation Functions

The interpolation function for a given dataset is stored in a gsl_interp object. These are created by the following functions.

gsl_interp * gsl_interp_alloc (const gsl_interp_type *   Function
         T, size_t size)
This function returns a pointer to a newly allocated interpolation object of type T for size data-points.

int gsl_interp_init (gsl_interp * interp, const double   Function
         xa[], const double ya[], size_t size)
This function initializes the interpolation object interp for the data (xa,ya) where xa and ya are arrays of size size. The interpolation object (gsl_interp) does not save the data arrays xa and ya and only stores the static state computed from the data. The xa data array is always assumed to be strictly ordered; the behavior for other arrangements is not defined.

void gsl_interp_free (gsl_interp * interp)   Function
This function frees the interpolation object interp.

26.3 Interpolation Types

The interpolation library provides five interpolation types:

`gsl_interp_linear`   *Interpolation Type*
    Linear interpolation. This interpolation method does not require any
    additional memory.

`gsl_interp_polynomial`   *Interpolation Type*
    Polynomial interpolation. This method should only be used for in-
    terpolating small numbers of points because polynomial interpolation
    introduces large oscillations, even for well-behaved datasets. The num-
    ber of terms in the interpolating polynomial is equal to the number of
    points.

`gsl_interp_cspline`   *Interpolation Type*
    Cubic spline with natural boundary conditions. The resulting curve
    is piecewise cubic on each interval, with matching first and second
    derivatives at the supplied data-points. The second derivative is chosen
    to be zero at the first point and last point.

`gsl_interp_cspline_periodic`   *Interpolation Type*
    Cubic spline with periodic boundary conditions. The resulting curve
    is piecewise cubic on each interval, with matching first and second
    derivatives at the supplied data-points. The derivatives at the first
    and last points are also matched. Note that the last point in the data
    must have the same y-value as the first point, otherwise the resulting
    periodic interpolation will have a discontinuity at the boundary.

`gsl_interp_akima`   *Interpolation Type*
    Non-rounded Akima spline with natural boundary conditions. This
    method uses the non-rounded corner algorithm of Wodicka.

`gsl_interp_akima_periodic`   *Interpolation Type*
    Non-rounded Akima spline with periodic boundary conditions. This
    method uses the non-rounded corner algorithm of Wodicka. Note that
    the last point in the data must have the same y-value as the first point,
    otherwise the resulting periodic interpolation will have a discontinuity
    at the boundary.

The following related functions are available:

`const char * gsl_interp_name (const gsl_interp * interp)`   *Function*
    This function returns the name of the interpolation type used by *interp*.
    For example,

```
printf ("interp uses '%s' interpolation.\n",
        gsl_interp_name (interp));
```

would print something like,

```
interp uses 'cspline' interpolation.
```

unsigned int gsl_interp_min_size (const gsl_interp *   Function
        interp)
This function returns the minimum number of points required by the
interpolation type of *interp*. For example, Akima spline interpolation
requires a minimum of 5 points.

26.4 Index Look-up and Acceleration

The state of searches can be stored in a gsl_interp_accel object,
which is a kind of iterator for interpolation lookups. It caches the previous
value of an index lookup. When the subsequent interpolation point falls
in the same interval its index value can be returned immediately.

size_t gsl_interp_bsearch (const double *x_array*[],   Function
        double *x*, size_t *index_lo*, size_t *index_hi*)
This function returns the index i of the array *x_array* such that x_
array[i] <= x < x_array[i+1]. The index is searched for in the range
[*index_lo*,*index_hi*].

gsl_interp_accel * gsl_interp_accel_alloc (void)   Function
This function returns a pointer to an accelerator object, which is a kind
of iterator for interpolation lookups. It tracks the state of lookups, thus
allowing for application of various acceleration strategies.

size_t gsl_interp_accel_find (gsl_interp_accel * a,   Function
        const double *x_array*[], size_t *size*, double *x*)
This function performs a lookup action on the data array *x_array* of
size *size*, using the given accelerator a. This is how lookups are performed during evaluation of an interpolation. The function returns an
index i such that x_array[i] <= x < x_array[i+1].

void gsl_interp_accel_free (gsl_interp_accel* *acc*)   Function
This function frees the accelerator object *acc*.

26.5 Evaluation of Interpolating Functions

double gsl_interp_eval (const gsl_interp * *interp*, const   Function
    double *xa*[], const double *ya*[], double *x*,
    gsl_interp_accel * *acc*)

int gsl_interp_eval_e (const gsl_interp * *interp*, const   Function
    double *xa*[], const double *ya*[], double *x*,
    gsl_interp_accel * *acc*, double * *y*)

These functions return the interpolated value of *y* for a given point *x*,
using the interpolation object *interp*, data arrays *xa* and *ya* and the
accelerator *acc*.

double gsl_interp_eval_deriv (const gsl_interp *   Function
    interp, const double *xa*[], const double *ya*[], double *x*,
    gsl_interp_accel * *acc*)

int gsl_interp_eval_deriv_e (const gsl_interp * *interp*,   Function
    const double *xa*[], const double *ya*[], double *x*,
    gsl_interp_accel * *acc*, double * *d*)

These functions return the derivative *d* of an interpolated function for
a given point *x*, using the interpolation object *interp*, data arrays *xa*
and *ya* and the accelerator *acc*.

double gsl_interp_eval_deriv2 (const gsl_interp *   Function
    interp, const double *xa*[], const double *ya*[], double *x*,
    gsl_interp_accel * *acc*)

int gsl_interp_eval_deriv2_e (const gsl_interp *   Function
    interp, const double *xa*[], const double *ya*[], double *x*,
    gsl_interp_accel * *acc*, double * *d2*)

These functions return the second derivative *d2* of an interpolated
function for a given point *x*, using the interpolation object *interp*,
data arrays *xa* and *ya* and the accelerator *acc*.

double gsl_interp_eval_integ (const gsl_interp *   Function
    interp, const double *xa*[], const double *ya*[], double *a*,
    double *b*, gsl_interp_accel * *acc*)

int gsl_interp_eval_integ_e (const gsl_interp * *interp*,   Function
    const double *xa*[], const double *ya*[], double *a*, double
    b, gsl_interp_accel * *acc*, double * *result*)

These functions return the numerical integral *result* of an interpolated
function over the range [*a*, *b*], using the interpolation object *interp*,
data arrays *xa* and *ya* and the accelerator *acc*.

26.6 Higher-level Interface

The functions described in the previous sections required the user to supply pointers to the x and y arrays on each call. The following functions are equivalent to the corresponding gsl_interp functions but maintain a copy of this data in the gsl_spline object. This removes the need to pass both xa and ya as arguments on each evaluation. These functions are defined in the header file 'gsl_spline.h'.

gsl_spline * gsl_spline_alloc (const gsl_interp_type * *T*, size_t *size*) — Function

int gsl_spline_init (gsl_spline * *spline*, const double xa[], const double ya[], size_t *size*) — Function

void gsl_spline_free (gsl_spline * *spline*) — Function

const char * gsl_spline_name (const gsl_spline * *spline*) — Function

unsigned int gsl_spline_min_size (const gsl_spline * *spline*) — Function

double gsl_spline_eval (const gsl_spline * *spline*, double x, gsl_interp_accel * *acc*) — Function

int gsl_spline_eval_e (const gsl_spline * *spline*, double x, gsl_interp_accel * *acc*, double * *y*) — Function

double gsl_spline_eval_deriv (const gsl_spline * *spline*, double x, gsl_interp_accel * *acc*) — Function

int gsl_spline_eval_deriv_e (const gsl_spline * *spline*, double x, gsl_interp_accel * *acc*, double * *d*) — Function

double gsl_spline_eval_deriv2 (const gsl_spline * *spline*, double x, gsl_interp_accel * *acc*) — Function

int gsl_spline_eval_deriv2_e (const gsl_spline * *spline*, double x, gsl_interp_accel * *acc*, double * *d2*) — Function

double gsl_spline_eval_integ (const gsl_spline * *spline*, double a, double b, gsl_interp_accel * *acc*) — Function

int gsl_spline_eval_integ_e (const gsl_spline * *spline*, double a, double b, gsl_interp_accel * *acc*, double * *result*) — Function

26.7 Examples

The following program demonstrates the use of the interpolation and spline functions. It computes a cubic spline interpolation of the 10-point dataset (x_i, y_i) where $x_i = i + \sin(i)/2$ and $y_i = i + \cos(i^2)$ for $i = 0 \ldots 9$.

```
#include <stdlib.h>
#include <stdio.h>
#include <math.h>
#include <gsl/gsl_errno.h>
#include <gsl/gsl_spline.h>

int
main (void)
{
  int i;
  double xi, yi, x[10], y[10];

  printf ("#m=0,S=2\n");

  for (i = 0; i < 10; i++)
    {
      x[i] = i + 0.5 * sin (i);
      y[i] = i + cos (i * i);
      printf ("%g %g\n", x[i], y[i]);
    }

  printf ("#m=1,S=0\n");

  {
    gsl_interp_accel *acc
      = gsl_interp_accel_alloc ();
    gsl_spline *spline
      = gsl_spline_alloc (gsl_interp_cspline, 10);

    gsl_spline_init (spline, x, y, 10);

    for (xi = x[0]; xi < x[9]; xi += 0.01)
      {
        yi = gsl_spline_eval (spline, xi, acc);
        printf ("%g %g\n", xi, yi);
      }
    gsl_spline_free (spline);
    gsl_interp_accel_free (acc);
  }
```

```
      return 0;
   }
```
The output is designed to be used with the GNU plotutils graph program,
```
   $ ./a.out > interp.dat
   $ graph -T ps < interp.dat > interp.ps
```

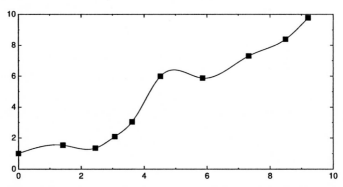

The result shows a smooth interpolation of the original points. The interpolation method can changed simply by varying the first argument of gsl_spline_alloc.

The next program demonstrates a periodic cubic spline with 4 data points. Note that the first and last points must be supplied with the same y-value for a periodic spline.

```
      #include <stdlib.h>
      #include <stdio.h>
      #include <math.h>
      #include <gsl/gsl_errno.h>
      #include <gsl/gsl_spline.h>

      int
      main (void)
      {
        int N = 4;

        /* Note: y[0] == y[N-1] for periodic data */

        double x[4] = {0.00, 0.10,  0.27,  0.30};
        double y[4] = {0.15, 0.70, -0.10,  0.15};

        gsl_interp_accel *acc = gsl_interp_accel_alloc ();
        const gsl_interp_type *t = gsl_interp_cspline_periodic;
        gsl_spline *spline = gsl_spline_alloc (t, N);
```

```
    int i; double xi, yi;

    printf ("#m=0,S=5\n");
    for (i = 0; i < N; i++)
      {
        printf ("%g %g\n", x[i], y[i]);
      }

    printf ("#m=1,S=0\n");
    gsl_spline_init (spline, x, y, N);

    for (i = 0; i <= 100; i++)
      {
        xi = (1 - i / 100.0) * x[0] + (i / 100.0) * x[N-1];
        yi = gsl_spline_eval (spline, xi, acc);
        printf ("%g %g\n", xi, yi);
      }

    gsl_spline_free (spline);
    gsl_interp_accel_free (acc);
    return 0;
  }
```

The output can be plotted with GNU graph.

```
$ ./a.out > interp.dat
$ graph -T ps < interp.dat > interp.ps
```

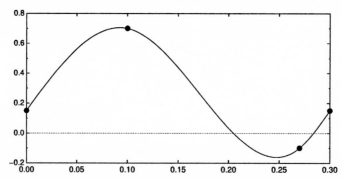

The result shows a periodic interpolation of the original points. The slope of the fitted curve is the same at the beginning and end of the data, and the second derivative is also.

26.8 References and Further Reading

Descriptions of the interpolation algorithms and further references can be found in the following books:

C.W. Ueberhuber, *Numerical Computation (Volume 1), Chapter 9 "Interpolation"*, Springer (1997), ISBN 3-540-62058-3.

D.M. Young, R.T. Gregory *A Survey of Numerical Mathematics (Volume 1), Chapter 6.8*, Dover (1988), ISBN 0-486-65691-8.

27 Numerical Differentiation

The routines described in this chapter compute numerical derivatives of user-defined functions by finite differencing. Starting from an initial user-supplied finite difference step-size, an adaptive algorithm is used to find the step-size which minimises the combined truncation and cancellation error, and to estimate the overall error in the derivative. These routines are declared in the header file 'gsl_deriv.h'.

To compute derivatives of a function defined by a discrete dataset, use the interpolation routines and their associated derivative functions as described in Section 26.5 [Evaluation of Interpolating Functions], page 386.

27.1 Functions

int gsl_deriv_central (const gsl_function * f, double   Function
        x, double h, double * result, double * abserr)

This function computes the numerical derivative of the function f at the point x using an adaptive central difference algorithm with a step-size of h. The derivative is returned in result and an estimate of its absolute error is returned in abserr.

The initial value of h is used to estimate an optimal step-size, based on the scaling of the truncation error and round-off error in the derivative calculation. The derivative is computed using a 5-point rule for equally spaced abscissae at $x - h$, $x - h/2$, x, $x + h/2$, $x + h$, with an error estimate taken from the difference between the 5-point rule and the corresponding 3-point rule $x - h$, x, $x + h$. Note that the value of the function at x does not contribute to the derivative calculation, so only 4-points are actually used.

int gsl_deriv_forward (const gsl_function * f, double   Function
        x, double h, double * result, double * abserr)

This function computes the numerical derivative of the function f at the point x using an adaptive forward difference algorithm with a step-size of h. The function is evaluated only at points greater than x, and never at x itself. The derivative is returned in result and an estimate of its absolute error is returned in abserr. This function should be used if $f(x)$ has a discontinuity at x, or is undefined for values less than x.

The initial value of h is used to estimate an optimal step-size, based on the scaling of the truncation error and round-off error in the derivative calculation. The derivative at x is computed using an "open" 4-point rule for equally spaced abscissae at $x + h/4$, $x + h/2$, $x + 3h/4$, $x + h$, with an error estimate taken from the difference between the 4-point rule and the corresponding 2-point rule $x + h/2$, $x + h$.

int gsl_deriv_backward (const gsl_function * f, double *Function* **x, double h, double * result, double * abserr)**
This function computes the numerical derivative of the function f at the point x using an adaptive backward difference algorithm with a step-size of h. The function is evaluated only at points less than x, and never at x itself. The derivative is returned in *result* and an estimate of its absolute error is returned in *abserr*. This function should be used if $f(x)$ has a discontinuity at x, or is undefined for values greater than x.

This function is equivalent to calling gsl_deriv_forward with a negative step-size.

27.2 Examples

The following code estimates the derivative of the function $f(x) = x^{3/2}$ at $x = 2$ and at $x = 0$. The function $f(x)$ is undefined for $x < 0$ so the derivative at $x = 0$ is computed using gsl_deriv_forward.

```
#include <stdio.h>
#include <gsl/gsl_math.h>
#include <gsl/gsl_deriv.h>

double f (double x, void * params)
{
  return pow (x, 1.5);
}

int
main (void)
{
  gsl_function F;
  double result, abserr;

  F.function = &f;
  F.params = 0;

  printf ("f(x) = x^(3/2)\n");

  gsl_deriv_central (&F, 2.0, 1e-8, &result, &abserr);
  printf ("x = 2.0\n");
  printf ("f'(x) = %.10f +/- %.10f\n", result, abserr);
  printf ("exact = %.10f\n\n", 1.5 * sqrt(2.0));
```

```
gsl_deriv_forward (&F, 0.0, 1e-8, &result, &abserr);
printf ("x = 0.0\n");
printf ("f'(x) = %.10f +/- %.10f\n", result, abserr);
printf ("exact = %.10f\n", 0.0);

return 0;
}
```

Here is the output of the program,

```
$ ./a.out
f(x) = x^(3/2)
x = 2.0
f'(x) = 2.1213203120 +/- 0.0000004064
exact = 2.1213203436

x = 0.0
f'(x) = 0.0000000160 +/- 0.0000000339
exact = 0.0000000000
```

27.3 References and Further Reading

The algorithms used by these functions are described in the following sources:

Abramowitz and Stegun, *Handbook of Mathematical Functions*, Section 25.3.4, and Table 25.5 (Coefficients for Differentiation).

S.D. Conte and Carl de Boor, *Elementary Numerical Analysis: An Algorithmic Approach*, McGraw-Hill, 1972.

28 Chebyshev Approximations

This chapter describes routines for computing Chebyshev approximations to univariate functions. A Chebyshev approximation is a truncation of the series $f(x) = \sum c_n T_n(x)$, where the Chebyshev polynomials
$T_n(x) = \cos(n \arccos x)$ provide an orthogonal basis of polynomials on the
interval $[-1, 1]$ with the weight function $1/\sqrt{1 - x^2}$. The first few Chebyshev polynomials are, $T_0(x) = 1$, $T_1(x) = x$, $T_2(x) = 2x^2 - 1$. For further
information see Abramowitz & Stegun, Chapter 22.

The functions described in this chapter are declared in the header file
'gsl_chebyshev.h'.

28.1 Definitions

A Chebyshev series is stored using the following structure,

```
typedef struct
{
    double * c;    /* coefficients  c[0] .. c[order] */
    int order;     /* order of expansion             */
    double a;      /* lower interval point           */
    double b;      /* upper interval point           */
    ...
} gsl_cheb_series
```

The approximation is made over the range $[a, b]$ using order+1 terms,
including the coefficient c[0]. The series is computed using the following
convention,

$$f(x) = \frac{c_0}{2} + \sum_{n=1} c_n T_n(x)$$

which is needed when accessing the coefficients directly.

28.2 Creation and Calculation of Chebyshev Series

gsl_cheb_series * gsl_cheb_alloc (const size_t n)   Function
    This function allocates space for a Chebyshev series of order n and
    returns a pointer to a new gsl_cheb_series struct.

void gsl_cheb_free (gsl_cheb_series * cs)   Function
    This function frees a previously allocated Chebyshev series cs.

int gsl_cheb_init (gsl_cheb_series * cs, const   Function
        gsl_function * f, const double a, const double b)
    This function computes the Chebyshev approximation cs for the func-
    tion f over the range (a, b) to the previously specified order. The com-
    putation of the Chebyshev approximation is an $O(n^2)$ process, and
    requires n function evaluations.

28.3 Chebyshev Series Evaluation

double gsl_cheb_eval (const gsl_cheb_series * cs,   Function
        double x)
    This function evaluates the Chebyshev series cs at a given point x.

int gsl_cheb_eval_err (const gsl_cheb_series * cs,   Function
        const double x, double * result, double * abserr)
    This function computes the Chebyshev series cs at a given point x,
    estimating both the series result and its absolute error abserr. The
    error estimate is made from the first neglected term in the series.

double gsl_cheb_eval_n (const gsl_cheb_series * cs,   Function
        size_t order, double x)
    This function evaluates the Chebyshev series cs at a given point n, to
    (at most) the given order order.

int gsl_cheb_eval_n_err (const gsl_cheb_series * cs,   Function
        const size_t order, const double x, double * result,
        double * abserr)
    This function evaluates a Chebyshev series cs at a given point x, es-
    timating both the series result and its absolute error abserr, to (at
    most) the given order order. The error estimate is made from the first
    neglected term in the series.

28.4 Derivatives and Integrals

The following functions allow a Chebyshev series to be differentiated or integrated, producing a new Chebyshev series. Note that the error estimate produced by evaluating the derivative series will be underestimated due to the contribution of higher order terms being neglected.

int gsl_cheb_calc_deriv (gsl_cheb_series * *deriv*, const   *Function*
       gsl_cheb_series * *cs*)

This function computes the derivative of the series *cs*, storing the derivative coefficients in the previously allocated *deriv*. The two series *cs* and *deriv* must have been allocated with the same order.

int gsl_cheb_calc_integ (gsl_cheb_series * *integ*, const   *Function*
       gsl_cheb_series * *cs*)

This function computes the integral of the series *cs*, storing the integral coefficients in the previously allocated *integ*. The two series *cs* and *integ* must have been allocated with the same order. The lower limit of the integration is taken to be the left hand end of the range a.

28.5 Examples

The following example program computes Chebyshev approximations to a step function. This is an extremely difficult approximation to make, due to the discontinuity, and was chosen as an example where approximation error is visible. For smooth functions the Chebyshev approximation converges extremely rapidly and errors would not be visible.

```
#include <stdio.h>
#include <gsl/gsl_math.h>
#include <gsl/gsl_chebyshev.h>

double
f (double x, void *p)
{
  if (x < 0.5)
    return 0.25;
  else
    return 0.75;
}

int
main (void)
{
  int i, n = 10000;
```

```
gsl_cheb_series *cs = gsl_cheb_alloc (40);

gsl_function F;

F.function = f;
F.params = 0;

gsl_cheb_init (cs, &F, 0.0, 1.0);

for (i = 0; i < n; i++)
  {
    double x = i / (double)n;
    double r10 = gsl_cheb_eval_n (cs, 10, x);
    double r40 = gsl_cheb_eval (cs, x);
    printf ("%g %g %g %g\n",
            x, GSL_FN_EVAL (&F, x), r10, r40);
  }

gsl_cheb_free (cs);

return 0;
}
```

The output from the program gives the original function, 10-th order approximation and 40-th order approximation, all sampled at intervals of 0.001 in x.

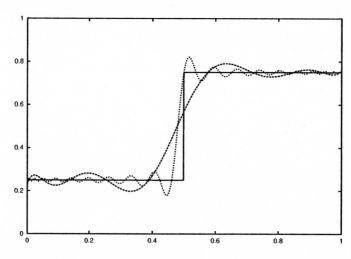

28.6 References and Further Reading

The following paper describes the use of Chebyshev series,

R. Broucke, "Ten Subroutines for the Manipulation of Chebyshev Series [C1] (Algorithm 446)". *Communications of the ACM* 16(4), 254–256 (1973)

29 Series Acceleration

The functions described in this chapter accelerate the convergence of a series using the Levin u-transform. This method takes a small number of terms from the start of a series and uses a systematic approximation to compute an extrapolated value and an estimate of its error. The u-transform works for both convergent and divergent series, including asymptotic series.

These functions are declared in the header file 'gsl_sum.h'.

29.1 Acceleration functions

The following functions compute the full Levin u-transform of a series with its error estimate. The error estimate is computed by propagating rounding errors from each term through to the final extrapolation.

These functions are intended for summing analytic series where each term is known to high accuracy, and the rounding errors are assumed to originate from finite precision. They are taken to be relative errors of order GSL_DBL_EPSILON for each term.

The calculation of the error in the extrapolated value is an $O(N^2)$ process, which is expensive in time and memory. A faster but less reliable method which estimates the error from the convergence of the extrapolated value is described in the next section. For the method described here a full table of intermediate values and derivatives through to $O(N)$ must be computed and stored, but this does give a reliable error estimate.

gsl_sum_levin_u_workspace * gsl_sum_levin_u_alloc   *Function*
        (size_t *n*)
This function allocates a workspace for a Levin u-transform of n terms. The size of the workspace is $O(2n^2 + 3n)$.

void gsl_sum_levin_u_free (gsl_sum_levin_u_workspace *   *Function*
        w)
This function frees the memory associated with the workspace *w*.

int gsl_sum_levin_u_accel (const double * *array*, size_t   *Function*
        array_size, gsl_sum_levin_u_workspace * *w*, double *
        sum_accel, double * *abserr*)
This function takes the terms of a series in *array* of size *array_size* and computes the extrapolated limit of the series using a Levin u-transform. Additional working space must be provided in *w*. The extrapolated sum is stored in *sum_accel*, with an estimate of the absolute error stored in *abserr*. The actual term-by-term sum is returned

in `w->sum_plain`. The algorithm calculates the truncation error (the difference between two successive extrapolations) and round-off error (propagated from the individual terms) to choose an optimal number of terms for the extrapolation.

29.2 Acceleration functions without error estimation

The functions described in this section compute the Levin u-transform of series and attempt to estimate the error from the "truncation error" in the extrapolation, the difference between the final two approximations. Using this method avoids the need to compute an intermediate table of derivatives because the error is estimated from the behavior of the extrapolated value itself. Consequently this algorithm is an $O(N)$ process and only requires $O(N)$ terms of storage. If the series converges sufficiently fast then this procedure can be acceptable. It is appropriate to use this method when there is a need to compute many extrapolations of series with similar convergence properties at high-speed. For example, when numerically integrating a function defined by a parameterized series where the parameter varies only slightly. A reliable error estimate should be computed first using the full algorithm described above in order to verify the consistency of the results.

`gsl_sum_levin_utrunc_workspace *`   *Function*
      `gsl_sum_levin_utrunc_alloc (size_t n)`
This function allocates a workspace for a Levin u-transform of n terms, without error estimation. The size of the workspace is $O(3n)$.

`void gsl_sum_levin_utrunc_free`   *Function*
      `(gsl_sum_levin_utrunc_workspace * w)`
This function frees the memory associated with the workspace w.

`int gsl_sum_levin_utrunc_accel (const double * array,`   *Function*
      `size_t array_size, gsl_sum_levin_utrunc_workspace * w,`
      `double * sum_accel, double * abserr_trunc)`
This function takes the terms of a series in *array* of size *array_size* and computes the extrapolated limit of the series using a Levin u-transform. Additional working space must be provided in *w*. The extrapolated sum is stored in *sum_accel*. The actual term-by-term sum is returned in `w->sum_plain`. The algorithm terminates when the difference between two successive extrapolations reaches a minimum or is sufficiently small. The difference between these two values is used as estimate of the error and is stored in *abserr_trunc*. To improve the reliability of the algorithm the extrapolated values are replaced by

moving averages when calculating the truncation error, smoothing out any fluctuations.

29.3 Examples

The following code calculates an estimate of $\zeta(2) = \pi^2/6$ using the series,

$$\zeta(2) = 1 + 1/2^2 + 1/3^2 + 1/4^2 + \ldots$$

After N terms the error in the sum is $O(1/N)$, making direct summation of the series converge slowly.

```c
#include <stdio.h>
#include <gsl/gsl_math.h>
#include <gsl/gsl_sum.h>

#define N 20

int
main (void)
{
  double t[N];
  double sum_accel, err;
  double sum = 0;
  int n;

  gsl_sum_levin_u_workspace * w
    = gsl_sum_levin_u_alloc (N);

  const double zeta_2 = M_PI * M_PI / 6.0;

  /* terms for zeta(2) = \sum_{n=1}^{\infty} 1/n^2 */

  for (n = 0; n < N; n++)
    {
      double np1 = n + 1.0;
      t[n] = 1.0 / (np1 * np1);
      sum += t[n];
    }

  gsl_sum_levin_u_accel (t, N, w, &sum_accel, &err);

  printf ("term-by-term sum = % .16f using %d terms\n",
          sum, N);
```

```
      printf ("term-by-term sum = % .16f using %d terms\n",
             w->sum_plain, w->terms_used);

      printf ("exact value      = % .16f\n", zeta_2);
      printf ("accelerated sum  = % .16f using %d terms\n",
             sum_accel, w->terms_used);

      printf ("estimated error  = % .16f\n", err);
      printf ("actual error     = % .16f\n",
             sum_accel - zeta_2);

      gsl_sum_levin_u_free (w);
      return 0;
    }
```

The output below shows that the Levin u-transform is able to obtain an estimate of the sum to 1 part in 10^{10} using the first eleven terms of the series. The error estimate returned by the function is also accurate, giving the correct number of significant digits.

```
$ ./a.out
term-by-term sum =  1.5961632439130233 using 20 terms
term-by-term sum =  1.5759958390005426 using 13 terms
exact value      =  1.6449340668482264
accelerated sum  =  1.6449340668166479 using 13 terms
estimated error  =  0.0000000000508580
actual error     = -0.0000000000315785
```

Note that a direct summation of this series would require 10^{10} terms to achieve the same precision as the accelerated sum does in 13 terms.

29.4 References and Further Reading

The algorithms used by these functions are described in the following papers,

T. Fessler, W.F. Ford, D.A. Smith, HURRY: An acceleration algorithm for scalar sequences and series *ACM Transactions on Mathematical Software*, 9(3):346–354, 1983. and Algorithm 602 9(3):355–357, 1983.

The theory of the u-transform was presented by Levin,

D. Levin, Development of Non-Linear Transformations for Improving Convergence of Sequences, *Intern. J. Computer Math.* B3:371–388, 1973.

A review paper on the Levin Transform is available online,

Herbert H. H. Homeier, Scalar Levin-Type Sequence Transformations, http://arxiv.org/abs/math/0005209.

30 Wavelet Transforms

This chapter describes functions for performing Discrete Wavelet Transforms (DWTs). The library includes wavelets for real data in both one and two dimensions. The wavelet functions are declared in the header files 'gsl_wavelet.h' and 'gsl_wavelet2d.h'.

30.1 Definitions

The continuous wavelet transform and its inverse are defined by the relations,

$$w(s, \tau) = \int_{-\infty}^{\infty} f(t) * \psi_{s,\tau}^*(t)dt$$

and,

$$f(t) = \int_{0}^{\infty} ds \int_{-\infty}^{\infty} w(s, \tau) * \psi_{s,\tau}(t)d\tau$$

where the basis functions $\psi_{s,\tau}$ are obtained by scaling and translation from a single function, referred to as the *mother wavelet*.

The discrete version of the wavelet transform acts on equally-spaced samples, with fixed scaling and translation steps (s, τ). The frequency and time axes are sampled *dyadically* on scales of 2^j through a level parameter j. The resulting family of functions $\{\psi_{j,n}\}$ constitutes an orthonormal basis for square-integrable signals.

The discrete wavelet transform is an $O(N)$ algorithm, and is also referred to as the *fast wavelet transform*.

30.2 Initialization

The gsl_wavelet structure contains the filter coefficients defining the wavelet and any associated offset parameters.

gsl_wavelet * gsl_wavelet_alloc (const   *Function*
      gsl_wavelet_type * T, size_t k)
This function allocates and initializes a wavelet object of type T. The parameter k selects the specific member of the wavelet family. A null pointer is returned if insufficient memory is available or if a unsupported member is selected.

The following wavelet types are implemented:

gsl_wavelet_daubechies   Wavelet
gsl_wavelet_daubechies_centered   Wavelet
  The is the Daubechies wavelet family of maximum phase with $k/2$
  vanishing moments. The implemented wavelets are $k = 4, 6, \ldots, 20$,
  with k even.

gsl_wavelet_haar   Wavelet
gsl_wavelet_haar_centered   Wavelet
  This is the Haar wavelet. The only valid choice of k for the Haar
  wavelet is $k = 2$.

gsl_wavelet_bspline   Wavelet
gsl_wavelet_bspline_centered   Wavelet
  This is the biorthogonal B-spline wavelet family of order (i, j). The
  implemented values of $k = 100 * i + j$ are 103, 105, 202, 204, 206, 208,
  301, 303, 305 307, 309.

The centered forms of the wavelets align the coefficients of the various
sub-bands on edges. Thus the resulting visualization of the coefficients of
the wavelet transform in the phase plane is easier to understand.

const char * gsl_wavelet_name (const gsl_wavelet * w)   Function
  This function returns a pointer to the name of the wavelet family for
  w.

void gsl_wavelet_free (gsl_wavelet * w)   Function
  This function frees the wavelet object w.

  The gsl_wavelet_workspace structure contains scratch space of the
same size as the input data and is used to hold intermediate results during
the transform.

gsl_wavelet_workspace * gsl_wavelet_workspace_alloc   Function
          (size_t n)
  This function allocates a workspace for the discrete wavelet transform.
  To perform a one-dimensional transform on n elements, a workspace
  of size n must be provided. For two-dimensional transforms of n-by-
  n matrices it is sufficient to allocate a workspace of size n, since the
  transform operates on individual rows and columns.

void gsl_wavelet_workspace_free   Function
          (gsl_wavelet_workspace * work)
  This function frees the allocated workspace work.

30.3 Transform Functions

This sections describes the actual functions performing the discrete wavelet transform. Note that the transforms use periodic boundary conditions. If the signal is not periodic in the sample length then spurious coefficients will appear at the beginning and end of each level of the transform.

30.3.1 Wavelet transforms in one dimension

int gsl_wavelet_transform (const gsl_wavelet * w,   *Function*
       double * *data*, size_t *stride*, size_t *n*,
       gsl_wavelet_direction *dir*, gsl_wavelet_workspace *
       work)

int gsl_wavelet_transform_forward (const gsl_wavelet *   *Function*
       w, double * *data*, size_t *stride*, size_t *n*,
       gsl_wavelet_workspace * *work*)

int gsl_wavelet_transform_inverse (const gsl_wavelet *   *Function*
       w, double * *data*, size_t *stride*, size_t *n*,
       gsl_wavelet_workspace * *work*)

These functions compute in-place forward and inverse discrete wavelet transforms of length n with stride *stride* on the array *data*. The length of the transform n is restricted to powers of two. For the transform version of the function the argument *dir* can be either gsl_wavelet_forward $(+1)$ or gsl_wavelet_backward (-1). A workspace *work* of length n must be provided.

For the forward transform, the elements of the original array are replaced by the discrete wavelet transform $f_i \rightarrow w_{j,k}$ in a packed triangular storage layout, where j is the index of the level $j = 0 \ldots J - 1$ and k is the index of the coefficient within each level, $k = 0 \ldots 2^j - 1$. The total number of levels is $J = \log_2(n)$. The output data has the following form,

$$(s_{-1,0}, d_{0,0}, d_{1,0}, d_{1,1}, d_{2,0}, \cdots, d_{j,k}, \cdots, d_{J-1,2^{J-1}-1})$$

where the first element is the smoothing coefficient $s_{-1,0}$, followed by the detail coefficients $d_{j,k}$ for each level j. The backward transform inverts these coefficients to obtain the original data.

These functions return a status of GSL_SUCCESS upon successful completion. GSL_EINVAL is returned if n is not an integer power of 2 or if insufficient workspace is provided.

30.3.2 Wavelet transforms in two dimension

The library provides functions to perform two-dimensional discrete wavelet transforms on square matrices. The matrix dimensions must be an integer power of two. There are two possible orderings of the rows and columns in the two-dimensional wavelet transform, referred to as the "standard" and "non-standard" forms.

The "standard" transform performs a complete discrete wavelet transform on the rows of the matrix, followed by a separate complete discrete wavelet transform on the columns of the resulting row-transformed matrix. This procedure uses the same ordering as a two-dimensional fourier transform.

The "non-standard" transform is performed in interleaved passes on the rows and columns of the matrix for each level of the transform. The first level of the transform is applied to the matrix rows, and then to the matrix columns. This procedure is then repeated across the rows and columns of the data for the subsequent levels of the transform, until the full discrete wavelet transform is complete. The non-standard form of the discrete wavelet transform is typically used in image analysis.

The functions described in this section are declared in the header file 'gsl_wavelet2d.h'.

int gsl_wavelet2d_transform (const gsl_wavelet * w,   Function
            double * data, size_t tda, size_t size1, size_t size2,
            gsl_wavelet_direction dir, gsl_wavelet_workspace *
            work)

int gsl_wavelet2d_transform_forward (const gsl_wavelet   Function
            * w, double * data, size_t tda, size_t size1, size_t
            size2, gsl_wavelet_workspace * work)

int gsl_wavelet2d_transform_inverse (const gsl_wavelet   Function
            * w, double * data, size_t tda, size_t size1, size_t
            size2, gsl_wavelet_workspace * work)

These functions compute two-dimensional in-place forward and inverse discrete wavelet transforms in standard and non-standard forms on the array data stored in row-major form with dimensions size1 and size2 and physical row length tda. The dimensions must be equal (square matrix) and are restricted to powers of two. For the transform version of the function the argument dir can be either gsl_wavelet_forward (+1) or gsl_wavelet_backward (−1). A workspace work of the appropriate size must be provided. On exit, the appropriate elements of the array data are replaced by their two-dimensional wavelet transform.

The functions return a status of GSL_SUCCESS upon successful completion. GSL_EINVAL is returned if size1 and size2 are not equal and integer powers of 2, or if insufficient workspace is provided.

int gsl_wavelet2d_transform_matrix (const gsl_wavelet   Function
     * w, gsl_matrix * m, gsl_wavelet_direction dir,
     gsl_wavelet_workspace * work)

int gsl_wavelet2d_transform_matrix_forward (const   Function
     gsl_wavelet * w, gsl_matrix * m,
     gsl_wavelet_workspace * work)

int gsl_wavelet2d_transform_matrix_inverse (const   Function
     gsl_wavelet * w, gsl_matrix * m,
     gsl_wavelet_workspace * work)

These functions compute the two-dimensional in-place wavelet transform on a matrix a.

int gsl_wavelet2d_nstransform (const gsl_wavelet * w,   Function
     double * data, size_t tda, size_t size1, size_t size2,
     gsl_wavelet_direction dir, gsl_wavelet_workspace *
     work)

int gsl_wavelet2d_nstransform_forward (const   Function
     gsl_wavelet * w, double * data, size_t tda, size_t
     size1, size_t size2, gsl_wavelet_workspace * work)

int gsl_wavelet2d_nstransform_inverse (const   Function
     gsl_wavelet * w, double * data, size_t tda, size_t
     size1, size_t size2, gsl_wavelet_workspace * work)

These functions compute the two-dimensional wavelet transform in non-standard form.

int gsl_wavelet2d_nstransform_matrix (const   Function
     gsl_wavelet * w, gsl_matrix * m,
     gsl_wavelet_direction dir, gsl_wavelet_workspace *
     work)

int gsl_wavelet2d_nstransform_matrix_forward (const   Function
     gsl_wavelet * w, gsl_matrix * m,
     gsl_wavelet_workspace * work)

int gsl_wavelet2d_nstransform_matrix_inverse (const   Function
     gsl_wavelet * w, gsl_matrix * m,
     gsl_wavelet_workspace * work)

These functions compute the non-standard form of the two-dimensional in-place wavelet transform on a matrix a.

30.4 Examples

The following program demonstrates the use of the one-dimensional wavelet transform functions. It computes an approximation to an input signal (of length 256) using the 20 largest components of the wavelet transform, while setting the others to zero.

```
#include <stdio.h>
#include <math.h>
#include <gsl/gsl_sort.h>
#include <gsl/gsl_wavelet.h>

int
main (int argc, char **argv)
{
  int i, n = 256, nc = 20;
  double *data = malloc (n * sizeof (double));
  double *abscoeff = malloc (n * sizeof (double));
  size_t *p = malloc (n * sizeof (size_t));

  FILE * f;
  gsl_wavelet *w;
  gsl_wavelet_workspace *work;

  w = gsl_wavelet_alloc (gsl_wavelet_daubechies, 4);
  work = gsl_wavelet_workspace_alloc (n);

  f = fopen (argv[1], "r");
  for (i = 0; i < n; i++)
    {
      fscanf (f, "%lg", &data[i]);
    }
  fclose (f);

  gsl_wavelet_transform_forward (w, data, 1, n, work);

  for (i = 0; i < n; i++)
    {
      abscoeff[i] = fabs (data[i]);
    }

  gsl_sort_index (p, abscoeff, 1, n);

  for (i = 0; (i + nc) < n; i++)
    data[p[i]] = 0;
```

```
        gsl_wavelet_transform_inverse (w, data, 1, n, work);

        for (i = 0; i < n; i++)
          {
            printf ("%g\n", data[i]);
          }
      }
```

The output can be used with the GNU plotutils graph program,

```
$ ./a.out ecg.dat > dwt.dat
$ graph -T ps -x 0 256 32 -h 0.3 -a dwt.dat > dwt.ps
```

The graphs below show an original and compressed version of a sample ECG recording from the MIT-BIH Arrhythmia Database, part of the PhysioNet archive of public-domain of medical datasets.

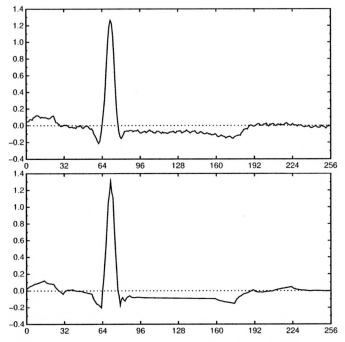

Original (upper) and wavelet-compressed (lower) ECG signals, using the 20 largest components of the Daubechies(4) discrete wavelet transform.

30.5 References and Further Reading

The mathematical background to wavelet transforms is covered in the original lectures by Daubechies,

> Ingrid Daubechies. Ten Lectures on Wavelets. *CBMS-NSF Regional Conference Series in Applied Mathematics* (1992), SIAM, ISBN 0898712742.

An easy to read introduction to the subject with an emphasis on the application of the wavelet transform in various branches of science is,

> Paul S. Addison. *The Illustrated Wavelet Transform Handbook*. Institute of Physics Publishing (2002), ISBN 0750306920.

For extensive coverage of signal analysis by wavelets, wavelet packets and local cosine bases see,

> S. G. Mallat. *A wavelet tour of signal processing* (Second edition). Academic Press (1999), ISBN 012466606X.

The concept of multiresolution analysis underlying the wavelet transform is described in,

> S. G. Mallat. Multiresolution Approximations and Wavelet Orthonormal Bases of $L^2(R)$. *Transactions of the American Mathematical Society*, 315(1), 1989, 69–87.

> S. G. Mallat. A Theory for Multiresolution Signal Decomposition— The Wavelet Representation. *IEEE Transactions on Pattern Analysis and Machine Intelligence*, 11, 1989, 674–693.

The coefficients for the individual wavelet families implemented by the library can be found in the following papers,

> I. Daubechies. Orthonormal Bases of Compactly Supported Wavelets. *Communications on Pure and Applied Mathematics*, 41 (1988) 909–996.

> A. Cohen, I. Daubechies, and J.-C. Feauveau. Biorthogonal Bases of Compactly Supported Wavelets. *Communications on Pure and Applied Mathematics*, 45 (1992) 485–560.

The PhysioNet archive of physiological datasets can be found online at http://www.physionet.org/ and is described in the following paper,

> Goldberger et al. PhysioBank, PhysioToolkit, and PhysioNet: Components of a New Research Resource for Complex Physiologic Signals. *Circulation* 101(23):e215-e220 2000.

31 Discrete Hankel Transforms

This chapter describes functions for performing Discrete Hankel Transforms (DHTs). The functions are declared in the header file 'gsl_dht.h'.

31.1 Definitions

The discrete Hankel transform acts on a vector of sampled data, where the samples are assumed to have been taken at points related to the zeroes of a Bessel function of fixed order; compare this to the case of the discrete Fourier transform, where samples are taken at points related to the zeroes of the sine or cosine function.

Specifically, let $f(t)$ be a function on the unit interval. Then the finite ν-Hankel transform of $f(t)$ is defined to be the set of numbers g_m given by,

$$g_m = \int_0^1 t\,dt\, J_\nu(j_{\nu,m}t) f(t),$$

so that,

$$f(t) = \sum_{m=1}^{\infty} \frac{2 J_\nu(j_{\nu,m}x)}{J_{\nu+1}(j_{\nu,m})^2} g_m.$$

Suppose that f is band-limited in the sense that $g_m = 0$ for $m > M$. Then we have the following fundamental sampling theorem.

$$g_m = \frac{2}{j_{\nu,M}^2} \sum_{k=1}^{M-1} f\left(\frac{j_{\nu,k}}{j_{\nu,M}}\right) \frac{J_\nu(j_{\nu,m}j_{\nu,k}/j_{\nu,M})}{J_{\nu+1}(j_{\nu,k})^2}.$$

It is this discrete expression which defines the discrete Hankel transform. The kernel in the summation above defines the matrix of the ν-Hankel transform of size $M - 1$. The coefficients of this matrix, being dependent on ν and M, must be precomputed and stored; the gsl_dht object encapsulates this data. The allocation function gsl_dht_alloc returns a gsl_dht object which must be properly initialized with gsl_dht_init before it can be used to perform transforms on data sample vectors, for fixed ν and M, using the gsl_dht_apply function. The implementation allows a scaling of the fundamental interval, for convenience, so that one can assume the function is defined on the interval $[0, X]$, rather than the unit interval.

Notice that by assumption $f(t)$ vanishes at the endpoints of the interval, consistent with the inversion formula and the sampling formula given above. Therefore, this transform corresponds to an orthogonal expansion in eigenfunctions of the Dirichlet problem for the Bessel differential equation.

31.2 Functions

`gsl_dht * gsl_dht_alloc (size_t size)`   Function
This function allocates a Discrete Hankel transform object of size *size*.

`int gsl_dht_init (gsl_dht * t, double nu, double xmax)`   Function
This function initializes the transform *t* for the given values of *nu* and *x*.

`gsl_dht * gsl_dht_new (size_t size, double nu, double`   Function
`        xmax)`
This function allocates a Discrete Hankel transform object of size *size* and initializes it for the given values of *nu* and *x*.

`void gsl_dht_free (gsl_dht * t)`   Function
This function frees the transform *t*.

`int gsl_dht_apply (const gsl_dht * t, double * f_in,`   Function
`        double * f_out)`
This function applies the transform *t* to the array *f_in* whose size is equal to the size of the transform. The result is stored in the array *f_out* which must be of the same length.

`double gsl_dht_x_sample (const gsl_dht * t, int n)`   Function
This function returns the value of the *n*-th sample point in the unit interval, $(j_{\nu,n+1}/j_{\nu,M})X$. These are the points where the function $f(t)$ is assumed to be sampled.

`double gsl_dht_k_sample (const gsl_dht * t, int n)`   Function
This function returns the value of the *n*-th sample point in "k-space", $j_{\nu,n+1}/X$.

31.3 References and Further Reading

The algorithms used by these functions are described in the following papers,

H. Fisk Johnson, Comp. Phys. Comm. 43, 181 (1987).

D. Lemoine, J. Chem. Phys. 101, 3936 (1994).

32 One dimensional Root-Finding

This chapter describes routines for finding roots of arbitrary one-dimensional functions. The library provides low level components for a variety of iterative solvers and convergence tests. These can be combined by the user to achieve the desired solution, with full access to the intermediate steps of the iteration. Each class of methods uses the same framework, so that you can switch between solvers at runtime without needing to recompile your program. Each instance of a solver keeps track of its own state, allowing the solvers to be used in multi-threaded programs.

The header file 'gsl_roots.h' contains prototypes for the root finding functions and related declarations.

32.1 Overview

One-dimensional root finding algorithms can be divided into two classes, *root bracketing* and *root polishing*. Algorithms which proceed by bracketing a root are guaranteed to converge. Bracketing algorithms begin with a bounded region known to contain a root. The size of this bounded region is reduced, iteratively, until it encloses the root to a desired tolerance. This provides a rigorous error estimate for the location of the root.

The technique of *root polishing* attempts to improve an initial guess to the root. These algorithms converge only if started "close enough" to a root, and sacrifice a rigorous error bound for speed. By approximating the behavior of a function in the vicinity of a root they attempt to find a higher order improvement of an initial guess. When the behavior of the function is compatible with the algorithm and a good initial guess is available a polishing algorithm can provide rapid convergence.

In GSL both types of algorithm are available in similar frameworks. The user provides a high-level driver for the algorithms, and the library provides the individual functions necessary for each of the steps. There are three main phases of the iteration. The steps are,

- initialize solver state, s, for algorithm T
- update s using the iteration T
- test s for convergence, and repeat iteration if necessary

The state for bracketing solvers is held in a `gsl_root_fsolver` struct. The updating procedure uses only function evaluations (not derivatives). The state for root polishing solvers is held in a `gsl_root_fdfsolver` struct. The updates require both the function and its derivative (hence the name `fdf`) to be supplied by the user.

32.2 Caveats

Note that root finding functions can only search for one root at a time. When there are several roots in the search area, the first root to be found will be returned; however it is difficult to predict which of the roots this will be. *In most cases, no error will be reported if you try to find a root in an area where there is more than one.*

Care must be taken when a function may have a multiple root (such as $f(x) = (x - x_0)^2$ or $f(x) = (x - x_0)^3$). It is not possible to use root-bracketing algorithms on even-multiplicity roots. For these algorithms the initial interval must contain a zero-crossing, where the function is negative at one end of the interval and positive at the other end. Roots with even-multiplicity do not cross zero, but only touch it instantaneously. Algorithms based on root bracketing will still work for odd-multiplicity roots (e.g. cubic, quintic, ...). Root polishing algorithms generally work with higher multiplicity roots, but at a reduced rate of convergence. In these cases the *Steffenson algorithm* can be used to accelerate the convergence of multiple roots.

While it is not absolutely required that f have a root within the search region, numerical root finding functions should not be used haphazardly to check for the *existence* of roots. There are better ways to do this. Because it is easy to create situations where numerical root finders can fail, it is a bad idea to throw a root finder at a function you do not know much about. In general it is best to examine the function visually by plotting before searching for a root.

32.3 Initializing the Solver

gsl_root_fsolver * gsl_root_fsolver_alloc (const   *Function*
      gsl_root_fsolver_type * T)

This function returns a pointer to a newly allocated instance of a solver of type T. For example, the following code creates an instance of a bisection solver,

```
const gsl_root_fsolver_type * T
  = gsl_root_fsolver_bisection;
gsl_root_fsolver * s
  = gsl_root_fsolver_alloc (T);
```

If there is insufficient memory to create the solver then the function returns a null pointer and the error handler is invoked with an error code of GSL_ENOMEM.

gsl_root_fdfsolver * gsl_root_fdfsolver_alloc (const   *Function*
        gsl_root_fdfsolver_type * *T*)

This function returns a pointer to a newly allocated instance of a derivative-based solver of type *T*. For example, the following code creates an instance of a Newton-Raphson solver,

```
const gsl_root_fdfsolver_type * T
  = gsl_root_fdfsolver_newton;
gsl_root_fdfsolver * s
  = gsl_root_fdfsolver_alloc (T);
```

If there is insufficient memory to create the solver then the function returns a null pointer and the error handler is invoked with an error code of GSL_ENOMEM.

int gsl_root_fsolver_set (gsl_root_fsolver * *s*,   *Function*
        gsl_function * *f*, double *x_lower*, double *x_upper*)

This function initializes, or reinitializes, an existing solver *s* to use the function *f* and the initial search interval [*x_lower*, *x_upper*].

int gsl_root_fdfsolver_set (gsl_root_fdfsolver * *s*,   *Function*
        gsl_function_fdf * *fdf*, double *root*)

This function initializes, or reinitializes, an existing solver *s* to use the function and derivative *fdf* and the initial guess *root*.

void gsl_root_fsolver_free (gsl_root_fsolver * *s*)   *Function*
void gsl_root_fdfsolver_free (gsl_root_fdfsolver * *s*)   *Function*

These functions free all the memory associated with the solver *s*.

const char * gsl_root_fsolver_name (const   *Function*
        gsl_root_fsolver * *s*)
const char * gsl_root_fdfsolver_name (const   *Function*
        gsl_root_fdfsolver * *s*)

These functions return a pointer to the name of the solver. For example,

```
printf ("s is a '%s' solver\n",
        gsl_root_fsolver_name (s));
```

would print something like s is a 'bisection' solver.

32.4 Providing the function to solve

You must provide a continuous function of one variable for the root finders to operate on, and, sometimes, its first derivative. In order to allow for general parameters the functions are defined by the following data types:

gsl_function   Data Type
    This data type defines a general function with parameters.

> double (* function) (double x, void * params)
> > this function should return the value $f(x, params)$ for argument x and parameters params

> void * params
> > a pointer to the parameters of the function

Here is an example for the general quadratic function,

$$f(x) = ax^2 + bx + c$$

with $a = 3$, $b = 2$, $c = 1$. The following code defines a gsl_function F which you could pass to a root finder:

```
struct my_f_params { double a; double b; double c; };

double
my_f (double x, void * p) {
   struct my_f_params * params
     = (struct my_f_params *)p;
   double a = (params->a);
   double b = (params->b);
   double c = (params->c);

   return  (a * x + b) * x + c;
}

gsl_function F;
struct my_f_params params = { 3.0, 2.0, 1.0 };

F.function = &my_f;
F.params = &params;
```

The function $f(x)$ can be evaluated using the following macro,

```
#define GSL_FN_EVAL(F,x)
     (*((F)->function))(x,(F)->params)
```

gsl_function_fdf   Data Type
This data type defines a general function with parameters and its first derivative.

double (* f) (double x, void * *params*)

> this function should return the value of $f(x, params)$ for argument x and parameters *params*

double (* df) (double x, void * *params*)

> this function should return the value of the derivative of f with respect to x, $f'(x, params)$, for argument x and parameters *params*

void (* fdf) (double x, void * *params*, double * f, double * df)

> this function should set the values of the function f to $f(x, params)$ and its derivative df to $f'(x, params)$ for argument x and parameters *params*. This function provides an optimization of the separate functions for $f(x)$ and $f'(x)$—it is always faster to compute the function and its derivative at the same time.

void * params

> a pointer to the parameters of the function

Here is an example where $f(x) = \exp(2x)$:

```
double
my_f (double x, void * params)
{
    return exp (2 * x);
}

double
my_df (double x, void * params)
{
    return 2 * exp (2 * x);
}

void
my_fdf (double x, void * params,
        double * f, double * df)
{
    double t = exp (2 * x);

    *f = t;
    *df = 2 * t;   /* uses existing value */
```

```
}
```

```
gsl_function_fdf FDF;
```

```
FDF.f = &my_f;
FDF.df = &my_df;
FDF.fdf = &my_fdf;
FDF.params = 0;
```

The function $f(x)$ can be evaluated using the following macro,

```
#define GSL_FN_FDF_EVAL_F(FDF,x)
        (*((FDF)->f))(x,(FDF)->params)
```

The derivative $f'(x)$ can be evaluated using the following macro,

```
#define GSL_FN_FDF_EVAL_DF(FDF,x)
        (*((FDF)->df))(x,(FDF)->params)
```

and both the function $y = f(x)$ and its derivative $dy = f'(x)$ can be evaluated at the same time using the following macro,

```
#define GSL_FN_FDF_EVAL_F_DF(FDF,x,y,dy)
        (*((FDF)->fdf))(x,(FDF)->params,(y),(dy))
```

The macro stores $f(x)$ in its y argument and $f'(x)$ in its dy argument—both of these should be pointers to double.

32.5 Search Bounds and Guesses

You provide either search bounds or an initial guess; this section explains how search bounds and guesses work and how function arguments control them.

A guess is simply an x value which is iterated until it is within the desired precision of a root. It takes the form of a double.

Search bounds are the endpoints of a interval which is iterated until the length of the interval is smaller than the requested precision. The interval is defined by two values, the lower limit and the upper limit. Whether the endpoints are intended to be included in the interval or not depends on the context in which the interval is used.

32.6 Iteration

The following functions drive the iteration of each algorithm. Each function performs one iteration to update the state of any solver of the corresponding type. The same functions work for all solvers so that different methods can be substituted at runtime without modifications to the code.

int gsl_root_fsolver_iterate (gsl_root_fsolver * s)   *Function*
int gsl_root_fdfsolver_iterate (gsl_root_fdfsolver *   *Function*
        s)

These functions perform a single iteration of the solver s. If the iteration encounters an unexpected problem then an error code will be returned,

GSL_EBADFUNC
            the iteration encountered a singular point where the function or its derivative evaluated to Inf or NaN.

GSL_EZERODIV
            the derivative of the function vanished at the iteration point, preventing the algorithm from continuing without a division by zero.

The solver maintains a current best estimate of the root at all times. The bracketing solvers also keep track of the current best interval bounding the root. This information can be accessed with the following auxiliary functions,

double gsl_root_fsolver_root (const gsl_root_fsolver *   *Function*
        s)
double gsl_root_fdfsolver_root (const   *Function*
        gsl_root_fdfsolver * s)

These functions return the current estimate of the root for the solver s.

double gsl_root_fsolver_x_lower (const   *Function*
        gsl_root_fsolver * s)
double gsl_root_fsolver_x_upper (const   *Function*
        gsl_root_fsolver * s)

These functions return the current bracketing interval for the solver s.

32.7 Search Stopping Parameters

A root finding procedure should stop when one of the following conditions is true:

- A root has been found to within the user-specified precision.
- A user-specified maximum number of iterations has been reached.
- An error has occurred.

The handling of these conditions is under user control. The functions below allow the user to test the precision of the current result in several standard ways.

int gsl_root_test_interval (double x_lower, double   Function
         x_upper, double epsabs, double epsrel)

This function tests for the convergence of the interval [x_lower, x_upper] with absolute error epsabs and relative error epsrel. The test returns GSL_SUCCESS if the following condition is achieved,

$$|a - b| < epsabs + epsrel \, \min(|a|, |b|)$$

when the interval $x = [a, b]$ does not include the origin. If the interval includes the origin then $\min(|a|, |b|)$ is replaced by zero (which is the minimum value of $|x|$ over the interval). This ensures that the relative error is accurately estimated for roots close to the origin.

This condition on the interval also implies that any estimate of the root r in the interval satisfies the same condition with respect to the true root r^*,

$$|r - r^*| < epsabs + epsrel \, r^*$$

assuming that the true root r^* is contained within the interval.

int gsl_root_test_delta (double x1, double x0, double   Function
         epsabs, double epsrel)

This function tests for the convergence of the sequence ..., x0, x1 with absolute error epsabs and relative error epsrel. The test returns GSL_SUCCESS if the following condition is achieved,

$$|x_1 - x_0| < epsabs + epsrel \, |x_1|$$

and returns GSL_CONTINUE otherwise.

int **gsl_root_test_residual** (double *f*, double *epsabs*)   Function
   This function tests the residual value *f* against the absolute error
   bound *epsabs*. The test returns GSL_SUCCESS if the following condition is achieved,

$$|f| < epsabs$$

and returns GSL_CONTINUE otherwise. This criterion is suitable for
situations where the precise location of the root, x, is unimportant
provided a value can be found where the residual, $|f(x)|$, is small
enough.

32.8 Root Bracketing Algorithms

   The root bracketing algorithms described in this section require an
initial interval which is guaranteed to contain a root—if a and b are the
endpoints of the interval then $f(a)$ must differ in sign from $f(b)$. This
ensures that the function crosses zero at least once in the interval. If a
valid initial interval is used then these algorithm cannot fail, provided the
function is well-behaved.

   Note that a bracketing algorithm cannot find roots of even degree,
since these do not cross the x-axis.

gsl_root_fsolver_bisection   Solver
   The *bisection algorithm* is the simplest method of bracketing the roots
   of a function. It is the slowest algorithm provided by the library, with
   linear convergence.

   On each iteration, the interval is bisected and the value of the function at the midpoint is calculated. The sign of this value is used to
   determine which half of the interval does not contain a root. That half
   is discarded to give a new, smaller interval containing the root. This
   procedure can be continued indefinitely until the interval is sufficiently
   small.

   At any time the current estimate of the root is taken as the midpoint
   of the interval.

gsl_root_fsolver_falsepos   Solver
   The *false position algorithm* is a method of finding roots based on
   linear interpolation. Its convergence is linear, but it is usually faster
   than bisection.

   On each iteration a line is drawn between the endpoints $(a, f(a))$ and
   $(b, f(b))$ and the point where this line crosses the x-axis taken as a
   "midpoint". The value of the function at this point is calculated and
   its sign is used to determine which side of the interval does not contain

a root. That side is discarded to give a new, smaller interval containing the root. This procedure can be continued indefinitely until the interval is sufficiently small.

The best estimate of the root is taken from the linear interpolation of the interval on the current iteration.

`gsl_root_fsolver_brent`   Solver

The *Brent-Dekker method* (referred to here as *Brent's method*) combines an interpolation strategy with the bisection algorithm. This produces a fast algorithm which is still robust.

On each iteration Brent's method approximates the function using an interpolating curve. On the first iteration this is a linear interpolation of the two endpoints. For subsequent iterations the algorithm uses an inverse quadratic fit to the last three points, for higher accuracy. The intercept of the interpolating curve with the x-axis is taken as a guess for the root. If it lies within the bounds of the current interval then the interpolating point is accepted, and used to generate a smaller interval. If the interpolating point is not accepted then the algorithm falls back to an ordinary bisection step.

The best estimate of the root is taken from the most recent interpolation or bisection.

32.9 Root Finding Algorithms using Derivatives

The root polishing algorithms described in this section require an initial guess for the location of the root. There is no absolute guarantee of convergence—the function must be suitable for this technique and the initial guess must be sufficiently close to the root for it to work. When these conditions are satisfied then convergence is quadratic.

These algorithms make use of both the function and its derivative.

`gsl_root_fdfsolver_newton`   Derivative Solver

Newton's Method is the standard root-polishing algorithm. The algorithm begins with an initial guess for the location of the root. On each iteration, a line tangent to the function f is drawn at that position. The point where this line crosses the x-axis becomes the new guess. The iteration is defined by the following sequence,

$$x_{i+1} = x_i - \frac{f(x_i)}{f'(x_i)}$$

Newton's method converges quadratically for single roots, and linearly for multiple roots.

`gsl_root_fdfsolver_secant`   Derivative Solver

The *secant method* is a simplified version of Newton's method which does not require the computation of the derivative on every step.

On its first iteration the algorithm begins with Newton's method, using the derivative to compute a first step,

$$x_1 = x_0 - \frac{f(x_0)}{f'(x_0)}$$

Subsequent iterations avoid the evaluation of the derivative by replacing it with a numerical estimate, the slope of the line through the previous two points,

$$x_{i+1} = x_i - \frac{f(x_i)}{f'_{est}} \text{ where } f'_{est} = \frac{f(x_i) - f(x_{i-1})}{x_i - x_{i-1}}$$

When the derivative does not change significantly in the vicinity of the root the secant method gives a useful saving. Asymptotically the secant method is faster than Newton's method whenever the cost of evaluating the derivative is more than 0.44 times the cost of evaluating the function itself. As with all methods of computing a numerical derivative the estimate can suffer from cancellation errors if the separation of the points becomes too small.

On single roots, the method has a convergence of order $(1 + \sqrt{5})/2$ (approximately 1.62). It converges linearly for multiple roots.

`gsl_root_fdfsolver_steffenson`   Derivative Solver

The *Steffenson Method* provides the fastest convergence of all the routines. It combines the basic Newton algorithm with an Aitken "delta-squared" acceleration. If the Newton iterates are x_i then the acceleration procedure generates a new sequence R_i,

$$R_i = x_i - \frac{(x_{i+1} - x_i)^2}{(x_{i+2} - 2x_{i+1} + x_i)}$$

which converges faster than the original sequence under reasonable conditions. The new sequence requires three terms before it can produce its first value so the method returns accelerated values on the second and subsequent iterations. On the first iteration it returns the ordinary Newton estimate. The Newton iterate is also returned if the denominator of the acceleration term ever becomes zero.

As with all acceleration procedures this method can become unstable if the function is not well-behaved.

32.10 Examples

For any root finding algorithm we need to prepare the function to be solved. For this example we will use the general quadratic equation described earlier. We first need a header file ('demo_fn.h') to define the function parameters,

```
struct quadratic_params
  {
    double a, b, c;
  };

double quadratic (double x, void *params);
double quadratic_deriv (double x, void *params);
void quadratic_fdf (double x, void *params,
                    double *y, double *dy);
```

We place the function definitions in a separate file ('demo_fn.c'),

```
double
quadratic (double x, void *params)
{
  struct quadratic_params *p
    = (struct quadratic_params *) params;

  double a = p->a;
  double b = p->b;
  double c = p->c;

  return (a * x + b) * x + c;
}

double
quadratic_deriv (double x, void *params)
{
  struct quadratic_params *p
    = (struct quadratic_params *) params;

  double a = p->a;
  double b = p->b;
  double c = p->c;

  return 2.0 * a * x + b;
}

void
```

```
quadratic_fdf (double x, void *params,
               double *y, double *dy)
{
  struct quadratic_params *p
    = (struct quadratic_params *) params;

  double a = p->a;
  double b = p->b;
  double c = p->c;

  *y = (a * x + b) * x + c;
  *dy = 2.0 * a * x + b;
}
```

The first program uses the function solver `gsl_root_fsolver_brent` for Brent's method and the general quadratic defined above to solve the following equation,

$$x^2 - 5 = 0$$

with solution $x = \sqrt{5} = 2.236068...$

```
#include <stdio.h>
#include <gsl/gsl_errno.h>
#include <gsl/gsl_math.h>
#include <gsl/gsl_roots.h>

#include "demo_fn.h"
#include "demo_fn.c"

int
main (void)
{
  int status;
  int iter = 0, max_iter = 100;
  const gsl_root_fsolver_type *T;
  gsl_root_fsolver *s;
  double r = 0, r_expected = sqrt (5.0);
  double x_lo = 0.0, x_hi = 5.0;
  gsl_function F;
  struct quadratic_params params = {1.0, 0.0, -5.0};

  F.function = &quadratic;
  F.params = &params;

  T = gsl_root_fsolver_brent;
```

```
s = gsl_root_fsolver_alloc (T);
gsl_root_fsolver_set (s, &F, x_lo, x_hi);

printf ("using %s method\n",
        gsl_root_fsolver_name (s));

printf ("%5s [%9s, %9s] %9s %10s %9s\n",
        "iter", "lower", "upper", "root",
        "err", "err(est)");

do
  {
     iter++;
     status = gsl_root_fsolver_iterate (s);
     r = gsl_root_fsolver_root (s);
     x_lo = gsl_root_fsolver_x_lower (s);
     x_hi = gsl_root_fsolver_x_upper (s);
     status = gsl_root_test_interval (x_lo, x_hi,
                                      0, 0.001);

     if (status == GSL_SUCCESS)
       printf ("Converged:\n");

     printf ("%5d [%.7f, %.7f] %.7f %+.7f %.7f\n",
             iter, x_lo, x_hi,
             r, r - r_expected,
             x_hi - x_lo);
  }
while (status == GSL_CONTINUE && iter < max_iter);
return status;
}
```

Here are the results of the iterations,

```
$ ./a.out
using brent method
 iter [    lower,     upper]       root        err  err(est)
    1 [1.0000000, 5.0000000] 1.0000000 -1.2360680 4.0000000
    2 [1.0000000, 3.0000000] 3.0000000 +0.7639320 2.0000000
    3 [2.0000000, 3.0000000] 2.0000000 -0.2360680 1.0000000
    4 [2.2000000, 3.0000000] 2.2000000 -0.0360680 0.8000000
    5 [2.2000000, 2.2366300] 2.2366300 +0.0005621 0.0366300
Converged:
    6 [2.2360634, 2.2366300] 2.2360634 -0.0000046 0.0005666
```

If the program is modified to use the bisection solver instead of Brent's method, by changing `gsl_root_fsolver_brent` to `gsl_root_fsolver_bisection` the slower convergence of the Bisection method can be observed,

```
$ ./a.out
using bisection method
iter [    lower,    upper]      root          err  err(est)
    1 [0.0000000, 2.5000000] 1.2500000 -0.9860680 2.5000000
    2 [1.2500000, 2.5000000] 1.8750000 -0.3610680 1.2500000
    3 [1.8750000, 2.5000000] 2.1875000 -0.0485680 0.6250000
    4 [2.1875000, 2.5000000] 2.3437500 +0.1076820 0.3125000
    5 [2.1875000, 2.3437500] 2.2656250 +0.0295570 0.1562500
    6 [2.1875000, 2.2656250] 2.2265625 -0.0095055 0.0781250
    7 [2.2265625, 2.2656250] 2.2460938 +0.0100258 0.0390625
    8 [2.2265625, 2.2460938] 2.2363281 +0.0002601 0.0195312
    9 [2.2265625, 2.2363281] 2.2314453 -0.0046227 0.0097656
   10 [2.2314453, 2.2363281] 2.2338867 -0.0021813 0.0048828
   11 [2.2338867, 2.2363281] 2.2351074 -0.0009606 0.0024414
Converged:
   12 [2.2351074, 2.2363281] 2.2357178 -0.0003502 0.0012207
```

The next program solves the same function using a derivative solver instead.

```c
#include <stdio.h>
#include <gsl/gsl_errno.h>
#include <gsl/gsl_math.h>
#include <gsl/gsl_roots.h>

#include "demo_fn.h"
#include "demo_fn.c"

int
main (void)
{
  int status;
  int iter = 0, max_iter = 100;
  const gsl_root_fdfsolver_type *T;
  gsl_root_fdfsolver *s;
  double x0, x = 5.0, r_expected = sqrt (5.0);
  gsl_function_fdf FDF;
  struct quadratic_params params = {1.0, 0.0, -5.0};

  FDF.f = &quadratic;
  FDF.df = &quadratic_deriv;
  FDF.fdf = &quadratic_fdf;
  FDF.params = &params;
```

```
T = gsl_root_fdfsolver_newton;
s = gsl_root_fdfsolver_alloc (T);
gsl_root_fdfsolver_set (s, &FDF, x);

printf ("using %s method\n",
        gsl_root_fdfsolver_name (s));

printf ("%-5s %10s %10s %10s\n",
        "iter", "root", "err", "err(est)");
do
  {
    iter++;
    status = gsl_root_fdfsolver_iterate (s);
    x0 = x;
    x = gsl_root_fdfsolver_root (s);
    status = gsl_root_test_delta (x, x0, 0, 1e-3);

    if (status == GSL_SUCCESS)
      printf ("Converged:\n");

    printf ("%5d %10.7f %+10.7f %10.7f\n",
            iter, x, x - r_expected, x - x0);
  }
while (status == GSL_CONTINUE && iter < max_iter);
return status;
}
```

Here are the results for Newton's method,

```
$ ./a.out
using newton method
iter        root         err    err(est)
   1   3.0000000  +0.7639320  -2.0000000
   2   2.3333333  +0.0972654  -0.6666667
   3   2.2380952  +0.0020273  -0.0952381
Converged:
   4   2.2360689  +0.0000009  -0.0020263
```

Note that the error can be estimated more accurately by taking the difference between the current iterate and next iterate rather than the previous iterate. The other derivative solvers can be investigated by changing gsl_root_fdfsolver_newton to gsl_root_fdfsolver_secant or gsl_root_fdfsolver_steffenson.

32.11 References and Further Reading

For information on the Brent-Dekker algorithm see the following two papers,

R. P. Brent, "An algorithm with guaranteed convergence for finding a zero of a function", *Computer Journal*, 14 (1971) 422–425

J. C. P. Bus and T. J. Dekker, "Two Efficient Algorithms with Guaranteed Convergence for Finding a Zero of a Function", *ACM Transactions of Mathematical Software*, Vol. 1 No. 4 (1975) 330–345

33 One dimensional Minimization

This chapter describes routines for finding minima of arbitrary one-dimensional functions. The library provides low level components for a variety of iterative minimizers and convergence tests. These can be combined by the user to achieve the desired solution, with full access to the intermediate steps of the algorithms. Each class of methods uses the same framework, so that you can switch between minimizers at runtime without needing to recompile your program. Each instance of a minimizer keeps track of its own state, allowing the minimizers to be used in multithreaded programs.

The header file 'gsl_min.h' contains prototypes for the minimization functions and related declarations. To use the minimization algorithms to find the maximum of a function simply invert its sign.

33.1 Overview

The minimization algorithms begin with a bounded region known to contain a minimum. The region is described by a lower bound a and an upper bound b, with an estimate of the location of the minimum x.

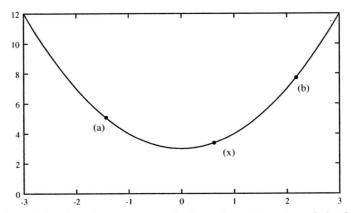

The value of the function at x must be less than the value of the function at the ends of the interval,

$$f(a) > f(x) < f(b)$$

This condition guarantees that a minimum is contained somewhere within the interval. On each iteration a new point x' is selected using one of the available algorithms. If the new point is a better estimate of the minimum, i.e. where $f(x') < f(x)$, then the current estimate of the minimum x is updated. The new point also allows the size of the bounded interval to be reduced, by choosing the most compact set of points which satisfies the constraint $f(a) > f(x) < f(b)$. The interval is reduced until it encloses the true minimum to a desired tolerance. This provides a best estimate of the location of the minimum and a rigorous error estimate.

Several bracketing algorithms are available within a single framework. The user provides a high-level driver for the algorithm, and the library provides the individual functions necessary for each of the steps. There are three main phases of the iteration. The steps are,

- initialize minimizer state, s, for algorithm T
- update s using the iteration T
- test s for convergence, and repeat iteration if necessary

The state for the minimizers is held in a `gsl_min_fminimizer` struct. The updating procedure uses only function evaluations (not derivatives).

33.2 Caveats

Note that minimization functions can only search for one minimum at a time. When there are several minima in the search area, the first minimum to be found will be returned; however it is difficult to predict which of the minima this will be. *In most cases, no error will be reported if you try to find a minimum in an area where there is more than one.*

With all minimization algorithms it can be difficult to determine the location of the minimum to full numerical precision. The behavior of the function in the region of the minimum x^* can be approximated by a Taylor expansion,

$$y = f(x^*) + \frac{1}{2}f''(x^*)(x - x^*)^2$$

and the second term of this expansion can be lost when added to the first term at finite precision. This magnifies the error in locating x^*, making it proportional to $\sqrt{\epsilon}$ (where ϵ is the relative accuracy of the floating point numbers). For functions with higher order minima, such as x^4, the magnification of the error is correspondingly worse. The best that can be achieved is to converge to the limit of numerical accuracy in the function values, rather than the location of the minimum itself.

33.3 Initializing the Minimizer

gsl_min_fminimizer * gsl_min_fminimizer_alloc (const   *Function*
      gsl_min_fminimizer_type * T)

This function returns a pointer to a newly allocated instance of a minimizer of type T. For example, the following code creates an instance of a golden section minimizer,

```
const gsl_min_fminimizer_type * T
  = gsl_min_fminimizer_goldensection;
gsl_min_fminimizer * s
  = gsl_min_fminimizer_alloc (T);
```

If there is insufficient memory to create the minimizer then the function returns a null pointer and the error handler is invoked with an error code of GSL_ENOMEM.

int gsl_min_fminimizer_set (gsl_min_fminimizer * s,   *Function*
      gsl_function * f, double x_minimum, double x_lower,
      double x_upper)

This function sets, or resets, an existing minimizer s to use the function f and the initial search interval [x_lower, x_upper], with a guess for the location of the minimum x_minimum.

If the interval given does not contain a minimum, then the function returns an error code of GSL_EINVAL.

int gsl_min_fminimizer_set_with_values   *Function*
      (gsl_min_fminimizer * s, gsl_function * f, double
      x_minimum, double f_minimum, double x_lower, double
      f_lower, double x_upper, double f_upper)

This function is equivalent to gsl_min_fminimizer_set but uses the values f_minimum, f_lower and f_upper instead of computing f(x_minimum), f(x_lower) and f(x_upper).

void gsl_min_fminimizer_free (gsl_min_fminimizer * s)   *Function*

This function frees all the memory associated with the minimizer s.

const char * gsl_min_fminimizer_name (const   *Function*
      gsl_min_fminimizer * s)

This function returns a pointer to the name of the minimizer. For example,

```
printf ("s is a '%s' minimizer\n",
        gsl_min_fminimizer_name (s));
```

would print something like s is a 'brent' minimizer.

33.4 Providing the function to minimize

You must provide a continuous function of one variable for the minimizers to operate on. In order to allow for general parameters the functions are defined by a `gsl_function` data type (see Section 32.4 [Providing the function to solve], page 422).

33.5 Iteration

The following functions drive the iteration of each algorithm. Each function performs one iteration to update the state of any minimizer of the corresponding type. The same functions work for all minimizers so that different methods can be substituted at runtime without modifications to the code.

`int gsl_min_fminimizer_iterate (gsl_min_fminimizer *`   *Function*
           `s)`

This function performs a single iteration of the minimizer *s*. If the iteration encounters an unexpected problem then an error code will be returned,

`GSL_EBADFUNC`

> the iteration encountered a singular point where the function evaluated to `Inf` or `NaN`.

`GSL_FAILURE`

> the algorithm could not improve the current best approximation or bounding interval.

The minimizer maintains a current best estimate of the position of the minimum at all times, and the current interval bounding the minimum. This information can be accessed with the following auxiliary functions,

`double gsl_min_fminimizer_x_minimum (const`   *Function*
           `gsl_min_fminimizer * s)`

This function returns the current estimate of the position of the minimum for the minimizer *s*.

`double gsl_min_fminimizer_x_upper (const`   *Function*
           `gsl_min_fminimizer * s)`
`double gsl_min_fminimizer_x_lower (const`   *Function*
           `gsl_min_fminimizer * s)`

These functions return the current upper and lower bound of the interval for the minimizer *s*.

```
double gsl_min_fminimizer_f_minimum (const          Function
        gsl_min_fminimizer * s)
double gsl_min_fminimizer_f_upper (const            Function
        gsl_min_fminimizer * s)
double gsl_min_fminimizer_f_lower (const            Function
        gsl_min_fminimizer * s)
```

These functions return the value of the function at the current estimate of the minimum and at the upper and lower bounds of the interval for the minimizer *s*.

33.6 Stopping Parameters

A minimization procedure should stop when one of the following conditions is true:

- A minimum has been found to within the user-specified precision.
- A user-specified maximum number of iterations has been reached.
- An error has occurred.

The handling of these conditions is under user control. The function below allows the user to test the precision of the current result.

```
int gsl_min_test_interval (double x_lower, double    Function
        x_upper, double epsabs, double epsrel)
```
This function tests for the convergence of the interval [x_lower, x_upper] with absolute error *epsabs* and relative error *epsrel*. The test returns GSL_SUCCESS if the following condition is achieved,

$$|a - b| < epsabs + epsrel \, \min(|a|, |b|)$$

when the interval $x = [a, b]$ does not include the origin. If the interval includes the origin then $\min(|a|, |b|)$ is replaced by zero (which is the minimum value of $|x|$ over the interval). This ensures that the relative error is accurately estimated for minima close to the origin.

This condition on the interval also implies that any estimate of the minimum x_m in the interval satisfies the same condition with respect to the true minimum x_m^*,

$$|x_m - x_m^*| < epsabs + epsrel \, x_m^*$$

assuming that the true minimum x_m^* is contained within the interval.

33.7 Minimization Algorithms

The minimization algorithms described in this section require an initial interval which is guaranteed to contain a minimum—if a and b are the endpoints of the interval and x is an estimate of the minimum then $f(a) > f(x) < f(b)$. This ensures that the function has at least one minimum somewhere in the interval. If a valid initial interval is used then these algorithms cannot fail, provided the function is well-behaved.

gsl_min_fminimizer_goldensection   Minimizer

The *golden section algorithm* is the simplest method of bracketing the minimum of a function. It is the slowest algorithm provided by the library, with linear convergence.

On each iteration, the algorithm first compares the subintervals from the endpoints to the current minimum. The larger subinterval is divided in a golden section (using the famous ratio $(3 - \sqrt{5})/2 = 0.3189660\ldots$) and the value of the function at this new point is calculated. The new value is used with the constraint $f(a') > f(x') < f(b')$ to a select new interval containing the minimum, by discarding the least useful point. This procedure can be continued indefinitely until the interval is sufficiently small. Choosing the golden section as the bisection ratio can be shown to provide the fastest convergence for this type of algorithm.

gsl_min_fminimizer_brent   Minimizer

The *Brent minimization algorithm* combines a parabolic interpolation with the golden section algorithm. This produces a fast algorithm which is still robust.

The outline of the algorithm can be summarized as follows: on each iteration Brent's method approximates the function using an interpolating parabola through three existing points. The minimum of the parabola is taken as a guess for the minimum. If it lies within the bounds of the current interval then the interpolating point is accepted, and used to generate a smaller interval. If the interpolating point is not accepted then the algorithm falls back to an ordinary golden section step. The full details of Brent's method include some additional checks to improve convergence.

33.8 Examples

The following program uses the Brent algorithm to find the minimum of the function $f(x) = \cos(x) + 1$, which occurs at $x = \pi$. The starting interval is $(0, 6)$, with an initial guess for the minimum of 2.

```
#include <stdio.h>
#include <gsl/gsl_errno.h>
#include <gsl/gsl_math.h>
#include <gsl/gsl_min.h>

double fn1 (double x, void * params)
{
  return cos(x) + 1.0;
}

int
main (void)
{
  int status;
  int iter = 0, max_iter = 100;
  const gsl_min_fminimizer_type *T;
  gsl_min_fminimizer *s;
  double m = 2.0, m_expected = M_PI;
  double a = 0.0, b = 6.0;
  gsl_function F;

  F.function = &fn1;
  F.params = 0;

  T = gsl_min_fminimizer_brent;
  s = gsl_min_fminimizer_alloc (T);
  gsl_min_fminimizer_set (s, &F, m, a, b);

  printf ("using %s method\n",
          gsl_min_fminimizer_name (s));

  printf ("%5s [%9s, %9s] %9s %10s %9s\n",
          "iter", "lower", "upper", "min",
          "err", "err(est)");

  printf ("%5d [%.7f, %.7f] %.7f %+.7f %.7f\n",
          iter, a, b,
          m, m - m_expected, b - a);
```

```
        do
          {
            iter++;
            status = gsl_min_fminimizer_iterate (s);

            m = gsl_min_fminimizer_x_minimum (s);
            a = gsl_min_fminimizer_x_lower (s);
            b = gsl_min_fminimizer_x_upper (s);

            status
              = gsl_min_test_interval (a, b, 0.001, 0.0);

            if (status == GSL_SUCCESS)
              printf ("Converged:\n");

            printf ("%5d [%.7f, %.7f] "
                    "%.7f %.7f %+.7f %.7f\n",
                    iter, a, b,
                    m, m_expected, m - m_expected, b - a);
          }
        while (status == GSL_CONTINUE && iter < max_iter);

        return status;
      }
```

Here are the results of the minimization procedure.

```
    $ ./a.out
         0 [0.0000000, 6.0000000] 2.0000000 -1.1415927 6.0000000
         1 [2.0000000, 6.0000000] 3.2758640 +0.1342713 4.0000000
         2 [2.0000000, 3.2831929] 3.2758640 +0.1342713 1.2831929
         3 [2.8689068, 3.2831929] 3.2758640 +0.1342713 0.4142862
         4 [2.8689068, 3.2831929] 3.2758640 +0.1342713 0.4142862
         5 [2.8689068, 3.2758640] 3.1460585 +0.0044658 0.4069572
         6 [3.1346075, 3.2758640] 3.1460585 +0.0044658 0.1412565
         7 [3.1346075, 3.1874620] 3.1460585 +0.0044658 0.0528545
         8 [3.1346075, 3.1460585] 3.1460585 +0.0044658 0.0114510
         9 [3.1346075, 3.1460585] 3.1424060 +0.0008133 0.0114510
        10 [3.1346075, 3.1424060] 3.1415885 -0.0000041 0.0077985
    Converged:
        11 [3.1415885, 3.1424060] 3.1415927 -0.0000000 0.0008175
```

33.9 References and Further Reading

Further information on Brent's algorithm is available in the following book,

Richard Brent, *Algorithms for minimization without derivatives*, Prentice-Hall (1973), republished by Dover in paperback (2002), ISBN 0-486-41998-3.

34 Multidimensional Root-Finding

This chapter describes functions for multidimensional root-finding (solving nonlinear systems with n equations in n unknowns). The library provides low level components for a variety of iterative solvers and convergence tests. These can be combined by the user to achieve the desired solution, with full access to the intermediate steps of the iteration. Each class of methods uses the same framework, so that you can switch between solvers at runtime without needing to recompile your program. Each instance of a solver keeps track of its own state, allowing the solvers to be used in multi-threaded programs. The solvers are based on the original Fortran library MINPACK.

The header file 'gsl_multiroots.h' contains prototypes for the multidimensional root finding functions and related declarations.

34.1 Overview

The problem of multidimensional root finding requires the simultaneous solution of n equations, f_i, in n variables, x_i,

$$f_i(x_1, \ldots, x_n) = 0 \qquad \text{for } i = 1 \ldots n.$$

In general there are no bracketing methods available for n dimensional systems, and no way of knowing whether any solutions exist. All algorithms proceed from an initial guess using a variant of the Newton iteration,

$$x \to x' = x - J^{-1} f(x)$$

where x, f are vector quantities and J is the Jacobian matrix $J_{ij} = \partial f_i / \partial x_j$. Additional strategies can be used to enlarge the region of convergence. These include requiring a decrease in the norm $|f|$ on each step proposed by Newton's method, or taking steepest-descent steps in the direction of the negative gradient of $|f|$.

Several root-finding algorithms are available within a single framework. The user provides a high-level driver for the algorithms, and the library provides the individual functions necessary for each of the steps. There are three main phases of the iteration. The steps are,

- initialize solver state, s, for algorithm T
- update s using the iteration T
- test s for convergence, and repeat iteration if necessary

The evaluation of the Jacobian matrix can be problematic, either because programming the derivatives is intractable or because computation of the n^2 terms of the matrix becomes too expensive. For these reasons the algorithms provided by the library are divided into two classes according to whether the derivatives are available or not.

The state for solvers with an analytic Jacobian matrix is held in a gsl_multiroot_fdfsolver struct. The updating procedure requires both the function and its derivatives to be supplied by the user.

The state for solvers which do not use an analytic Jacobian matrix is held in a gsl_multiroot_fsolver struct. The updating procedure uses only function evaluations (not derivatives). The algorithms estimate the matrix J or J^{-1} by approximate methods.

34.2 Initializing the Solver

The following functions initialize a multidimensional solver, either with or without derivatives. The solver itself depends only on the dimension of the problem and the algorithm, and can be reused for different problems.

gsl_multiroot_fsolver * gsl_multiroot_fsolver_alloc   Function
        (const gsl_multiroot_fsolver_type * T, size_t n)
This function returns a pointer to a newly allocated instance of a solver of type T for a system of n dimensions. For example, the following code creates an instance of a hybrid solver, to solve a 3-dimensional system of equations.

```
const gsl_multiroot_fsolver_type * T
  = gsl_multiroot_fsolver_hybrid;
gsl_multiroot_fsolver * s
  = gsl_multiroot_fsolver_alloc (T, 3);
```

If there is insufficient memory to create the solver then the function returns a null pointer and the error handler is invoked with an error code of GSL_ENOMEM.

gsl_multiroot_fdfsolver *   Function
        gsl_multiroot_fdfsolver_alloc (const
        gsl_multiroot_fdfsolver_type * T, size_t n)
This function returns a pointer to a newly allocated instance of a derivative solver of type T for a system of n dimensions. For example, the following code creates an instance of a Newton-Raphson solver, for a 2-dimensional system of equations.

```
const gsl_multiroot_fdfsolver_type * T
  = gsl_multiroot_fdfsolver_newton;
gsl_multiroot_fdfsolver * s =
    gsl_multiroot_fdfsolver_alloc (T, 2);
```

If there is insufficient memory to create the solver then the function
returns a null pointer and the error handler is invoked with an error
code of GSL_ENOMEM.

int gsl_multiroot_fsolver_set (gsl_multiroot_fsolver *   *Function*
      s, gsl_multiroot_function * *f*, gsl_vector * *x*)
This function sets, or resets, an existing solver *s* to use the function *f*
and the initial guess *x*.

int gsl_multiroot_fdfsolver_set   *Function*
      (gsl_multiroot_fdfsolver * *s*,
      gsl_multiroot_function_fdf * *fdf*, gsl_vector * *x*)
This function sets, or resets, an existing solver *s* to use the function
and derivative *fdf* and the initial guess *x*.

void gsl_multiroot_fsolver_free   *Function*
      (gsl_multiroot_fsolver * *s*)
void gsl_multiroot_fdfsolver_free   *Function*
      (gsl_multiroot_fdfsolver * *s*)
These functions free all the memory associated with the solver *s*.

const char * gsl_multiroot_fsolver_name (const   *Function*
      gsl_multiroot_fsolver * *s*)
const char * gsl_multiroot_fdfsolver_name (const   *Function*
      gsl_multiroot_fdfsolver * *s*)
These functions return a pointer to the name of the solver. For example,

```
printf ("s is a '%s' solver\n",
        gsl_multiroot_fdfsolver_name (s));
```

would print something like s is a 'newton' solver.

34.3 Providing the function to solve

You must provide n functions of n variables for the root finders to operate on. In order to allow for general parameters the functions are defined by the following data types:

gsl_multiroot_function   Data Type
    This data type defines a general system of functions with parameters.

>   int (* f) (const gsl_vector * x, void * params, gsl_vector * f)

>>   this function should store the vector result $f(x, params)$ in f for argument x and parameters params, returning an appropriate error code if the function cannot be computed.

>   size_t n   the dimension of the system, i.e. the number of components of the vectors x and f.

>   void * params
>>   a pointer to the parameters of the function.

Here is an example using Powell's test function,

$$f_1(x) = Ax_0x_1 - 1, \quad f_2(x) = \exp(-x_0) + \exp(-x_1) - (1 + 1/A)$$

with $A = 10^4$. The following code defines a gsl_multiroot_function system F which you could pass to a solver:

```
struct powell_params { double A; };

int
powell (gsl_vector * x, void * p, gsl_vector * f) {
   struct powell_params * params
     = *(struct powell_params *)p;
   const double A = (params->A);
   const double x0 = gsl_vector_get(x,0);
   const double x1 = gsl_vector_get(x,1);

   gsl_vector_set (f, 0, A * x0 * x1 - 1);
   gsl_vector_set (f, 1, (exp(-x0) + exp(-x1)
                          - (1.0 + 1.0/A)));
   return GSL_SUCCESS
}

gsl_multiroot_function F;
struct powell_params params = { 10000.0 };
```

```
F.f = &powell;
F.n = 2;
F.params = &params;
```

`gsl_multiroot_function_fdf`   Data Type

This data type defines a general system of functions with parameters and the corresponding Jacobian matrix of derivatives,

`int (* f) (const gsl_vector * x, void * params, gsl_vector * f)`

> this function should store the vector result $f(x, params)$ in f for argument x and parameters params, returning an appropriate error code if the function cannot be computed.

`int (* df) (const gsl_vector * x, void * params, gsl_matrix * J)`

> this function should store the n-by-n matrix result $J_{ij} = \partial f_i(x, params)/\partial x_j$ in J for argument x and parameters params, returning an appropriate error code if the function cannot be computed.

`int (* fdf) (const gsl_vector * x, void * params, gsl_vector * f, gsl_matrix * J)`

> This function should set the values of the f and J as above, for arguments x and parameters params. This function provides an optimization of the separate functions for $f(x)$ and $J(x)$—it is always faster to compute the function and its derivative at the same time.

`size_t n`   the dimension of the system, i.e. the number of components of the vectors x and f.

`void * params`

> a pointer to the parameters of the function.

The example of Powell's test function defined above can be extended to include analytic derivatives using the following code,

```
int
powell_df (gsl_vector * x, void * p, gsl_matrix * J)
{
   struct powell_params * params
     = *(struct powell_params *)p;
   const double A = (params->A);
   const double x0 = gsl_vector_get(x,0);
   const double x1 = gsl_vector_get(x,1);
   gsl_matrix_set (J, 0, 0, A * x1);
```

```
    gsl_matrix_set (J, 0, 1, A * x0);
    gsl_matrix_set (J, 1, 0, -exp(-x0));
    gsl_matrix_set (J, 1, 1, -exp(-x1));
    return GSL_SUCCESS
}

int
powell_fdf (gsl_vector * x, void * p,
            gsl_matrix * f, gsl_matrix * J) {
  struct powell_params * params
    = *(struct powell_params *)p;
  const double A = (params->A);
  const double x0 = gsl_vector_get(x,0);
  const double x1 = gsl_vector_get(x,1);

  const double u0 = exp(-x0);
  const double u1 = exp(-x1);

  gsl_vector_set (f, 0, A * x0 * x1 - 1);
  gsl_vector_set (f, 1, u0 + u1 - (1 + 1/A));

  gsl_matrix_set (J, 0, 0, A * x1);
  gsl_matrix_set (J, 0, 1, A * x0);
  gsl_matrix_set (J, 1, 0, -u0);
  gsl_matrix_set (J, 1, 1, -u1);
  return GSL_SUCCESS
}

gsl_multiroot_function_fdf FDF;

FDF.f = &powell_f;
FDF.df = &powell_df;
FDF.fdf = &powell_fdf;
FDF.n = 2;
FDF.params = 0;
```

Note that the function powell_fdf is able to reuse existing terms from the function when calculating the Jacobian, thus saving time.

34.4 Iteration

The following functions drive the iteration of each algorithm. Each function performs one iteration to update the state of any solver of the corresponding type. The same functions work for all solvers so that different methods can be substituted at runtime without modifications to the code.

int gsl_multiroot_fsolver_iterate   *Function*
    (gsl_multiroot_fsolver * s)
int gsl_multiroot_fdfsolver_iterate   *Function*
    (gsl_multiroot_fdfsolver * s)

These functions perform a single iteration of the solver s. If the iteration encounters an unexpected problem then an error code will be returned,

GSL_EBADFUNC

        the iteration encountered a singular point where the function or its derivative evaluated to Inf or NaN.

GSL_ENOPROG

        the iteration is not making any progress, preventing the algorithm from continuing.

The solver maintains a current best estimate of the root at all times. This information can be accessed with the following auxiliary functions,

gsl_vector * gsl_multiroot_fsolver_root (const   *Function*
    gsl_multiroot_fsolver * s)
gsl_vector * gsl_multiroot_fdfsolver_root (const   *Function*
    gsl_multiroot_fdfsolver * s)

These functions return the current estimate of the root for the solver s.

gsl_vector * gsl_multiroot_fsolver_f (const   *Function*
    gsl_multiroot_fsolver * s)
gsl_vector * gsl_multiroot_fdfsolver_f (const   *Function*
    gsl_multiroot_fdfsolver * s)

These functions return the function value $f(x)$ at the current estimate of the root for the solver s.

gsl_vector * gsl_multiroot_fsolver_dx (const   *Function*
    gsl_multiroot_fsolver * s)
gsl_vector * gsl_multiroot_fdfsolver_dx (const   *Function*
    gsl_multiroot_fdfsolver * s)

These functions return the last step dx taken by the solver s.

34.5 Search Stopping Parameters

A root finding procedure should stop when one of the following conditions is true:

- A multidimensional root has been found to within the user-specified precision.
- A user-specified maximum number of iterations has been reached.
- An error has occurred.

The handling of these conditions is under user control. The functions below allow the user to test the precision of the current result in several standard ways.

int gsl_multiroot_test_delta (const gsl_vector * *dx*,   Function
        const gsl_vector * *x*, double *epsabs*, double *epsrel*)

This function tests for the convergence of the sequence by comparing the last step *dx* with the absolute error *epsabs* and relative error *epsrel* to the current position *x*. The test returns GSL_SUCCESS if the following condition is achieved,

$$|dx_i| < epsabs + epsrel \, |x_i|$$

for each component of *x* and returns GSL_CONTINUE otherwise.

int gsl_multiroot_test_residual (const gsl_vector * *f*,   Function
        double *epsabs*)

This function tests the residual value *f* against the absolute error bound *epsabs*. The test returns GSL_SUCCESS if the following condition is achieved,

$$\sum_i |f_i| < epsabs$$

and returns GSL_CONTINUE otherwise. This criterion is suitable for situations where the precise location of the root, *x*, is unimportant provided a value can be found where the residual is small enough.

34.6 Algorithms using Derivatives

The root finding algorithms described in this section make use of both the function and its derivative. They require an initial guess for the location of the root, but there is no absolute guarantee of convergence—the function must be suitable for this technique and the initial guess must be sufficiently close to the root for it to work. When the conditions are satisfied then convergence is quadratic.

`gsl_multiroot_fdfsolver_hybridsj`   Derivative Solver

This is a modified version of Powell's Hybrid method as implemented in the HYBRJ algorithm in MINPACK. Minpack was written by Jorge J. Moré, Burton S. Garbow and Kenneth E. Hillstrom. The Hybrid algorithm retains the fast convergence of Newton's method but will also reduce the residual when Newton's method is unreliable.

The algorithm uses a generalized trust region to keep each step under control. In order to be accepted a proposed new position x' must satisfy the condition $|D(x' - x)| < \delta$, where D is a diagonal scaling matrix and δ is the size of the trust region. The components of D are computed internally, using the column norms of the Jacobian to estimate the sensitivity of the residual to each component of x. This improves the behavior of the algorithm for badly scaled functions.

On each iteration the algorithm first determines the standard Newton step by solving the system $J dx = -f$. If this step falls inside the trust region it is used as a trial step in the next stage. If not, the algorithm uses the linear combination of the Newton and gradient directions which is predicted to minimize the norm of the function while staying inside the trust region,

$$dx = -\alpha J^{-1} f(x) - \beta \nabla |f(x)|^2.$$

This combination of Newton and gradient directions is referred to as a *dogleg step*.

The proposed step is now tested by evaluating the function at the resulting point, x'. If the step reduces the norm of the function sufficiently then it is accepted and size of the trust region is increased. If the proposed step fails to improve the solution then the size of the trust region is decreased and another trial step is computed.

The speed of the algorithm is increased by computing the changes to the Jacobian approximately, using a rank-1 update. If two successive attempts fail to reduce the residual then the full Jacobian is recomputed. The algorithm also monitors the progress of the solution and returns an error if several steps fail to make any improvement,

GSL_ENOPROG
> the iteration is not making any progress, preventing the algorithm from continuing.

GSL_ENOPROGJ
> re-evaluations of the Jacobian indicate that the iteration is not making any progress, preventing the algorithm from continuing.

gsl_multiroot_fdfsolver_hybridj   Derivative Solver
This algorithm is an unscaled version of hybridsj. The steps are controlled by a spherical trust region $|x' - x| < \delta$, instead of a generalized region. This can be useful if the generalized region estimated by hybridsj is inappropriate.

gsl_multiroot_fdfsolver_newton   Derivative Solver
Newton's Method is the standard root-polishing algorithm. The algorithm begins with an initial guess for the location of the solution. On each iteration a linear approximation to the function F is used to estimate the step which will zero all the components of the residual. The iteration is defined by the following sequence,

$$x \to x' = x - J^{-1} f(x)$$

where the Jacobian matrix J is computed from the derivative functions provided by f. The step dx is obtained by solving the linear system,

$$J\, dx = -f(x)$$

using LU decomposition.

gsl_multiroot_fdfsolver_gnewton   Derivative Solver
This is a modified version of Newton's method which attempts to improve global convergence by requiring every step to reduce the Euclidean norm of the residual, $|f(x)|$. If the Newton step leads to an increase in the norm then a reduced step of relative size,

$$t = (\sqrt{1 + 6r} - 1)/(3r)$$

is proposed, with r being the ratio of norms $|f(x')|^2/|f(x)|^2$. This procedure is repeated until a suitable step size is found.

34.7 Algorithms without Derivatives

The algorithms described in this section do not require any derivative information to be supplied by the user. Any derivatives needed are approximated by finite differences. Note that if the finite-differencing step size chosen by these routines is inappropriate, an explicit user-supplied numerical derivative can always be used with the algorithms described in the previous section.

gsl_multiroot_fsolver_hybrids   Solver
This is a version of the Hybrid algorithm which replaces calls to the Jacobian function by its finite difference approximation. The finite difference approximation is computed using gsl_multiroots_fdjac with a relative step size of GSL_SQRT_DBL_EPSILON. Note that this step size will not be suitable for all problems.

gsl_multiroot_fsolver_hybrid   Solver
This is a finite difference version of the Hybrid algorithm without internal scaling.

gsl_multiroot_fsolver_dnewton   Solver
The *discrete Newton algorithm* is the simplest method of solving a multidimensional system. It uses the Newton iteration

$$x \to x - J^{-1}f(x)$$

where the Jacobian matrix J is approximated by taking finite differences of the function f. The approximation scheme used by this implementation is,

$$J_{ij} = (f_i(x + \delta_j) - f_i(x))/\delta_j$$

where δ_j is a step of size $\sqrt{\epsilon}|x_j|$ with ϵ being the machine precision ($\epsilon \approx 2.22 \times 10^{-16}$). The order of convergence of Newton's algorithm is quadratic, but the finite differences require n^2 function evaluations on each iteration. The algorithm may become unstable if the finite differences are not a good approximation to the true derivatives.

gsl_multiroot_fsolver_broyden   Solver
The *Broyden algorithm* is a version of the discrete Newton algorithm which attempts to avoids the expensive update of the Jacobian matrix on each iteration. The changes to the Jacobian are also approximated, using a rank-1 update,

$$J^{-1} \to J^{-1} - (J^{-1}df - dx)dx^T J^{-1}/dx^T J^{-1}df$$

where the vectors *dx* and *df* are the changes in *x* and *f*. On the first iteration the inverse Jacobian is estimated using finite differences, as in the discrete Newton algorithm.

This approximation gives a fast update but is unreliable if the changes are not small, and the estimate of the inverse Jacobian becomes worse as time passes. The algorithm has a tendency to become unstable unless it starts close to the root. The Jacobian is refreshed if this instability is detected (consult the source for details).

This algorithm is included only for demonstration purposes, and is not recommended for serious use.

34.8 Examples

The multidimensional solvers are used in a similar way to the one-dimensional root finding algorithms. This first example demonstrates the hybrids scaled-hybrid algorithm, which does not require derivatives. The program solves the Rosenbrock system of equations,

$$f_1(x, y) = a(1 - x), \quad f_2(x, y) = b(y - x^2)$$

with $a = 1, b = 10$. The solution of this system lies at $(x, y) = (1, 1)$ in a narrow valley.

The first stage of the program is to define the system of equations,

```
#include <stdlib.h>
#include <stdio.h>
#include <gsl/gsl_vector.h>
#include <gsl/gsl_multiroots.h>

struct rparams
  {
    double a;
    double b;
  };

int
rosenbrock_f (const gsl_vector * x, void *params,
              gsl_vector * f)
{
  double a = ((struct rparams *) params)->a;
  double b = ((struct rparams *) params)->b;

  const double x0 = gsl_vector_get (x, 0);
  const double x1 = gsl_vector_get (x, 1);
```

```
        const double y0 = a * (1 - x0);
        const double y1 = b * (x1 - x0 * x0);

        gsl_vector_set (f, 0, y0);
        gsl_vector_set (f, 1, y1);

        return GSL_SUCCESS;
    }
```

The main program begins by creating the function object f, with the arguments (x,y) and parameters (a,b). The solver s is initialized to use this function, with the hybrids method.

```
    int
    main (void)
    {
      const gsl_multiroot_fsolver_type *T;
      gsl_multiroot_fsolver *s;

      int status;
      size_t i, iter = 0;

      const size_t n = 2;
      struct rparams p = {1.0, 10.0};
      gsl_multiroot_function f = {&rosenbrock_f, n, &p};

      double x_init[2] = {-10.0, -5.0};
      gsl_vector *x = gsl_vector_alloc (n);

      gsl_vector_set (x, 0, x_init[0]);
      gsl_vector_set (x, 1, x_init[1]);

      T = gsl_multiroot_fsolver_hybrids;
      s = gsl_multiroot_fsolver_alloc (T, 2);
      gsl_multiroot_fsolver_set (s, &f, x);

      print_state (iter, s);

      do
        {
          iter++;
          status = gsl_multiroot_fsolver_iterate (s);

          print_state (iter, s);
```

```
            if (status)    /* check if solver is stuck */
              break;

            status =
              gsl_multiroot_test_residual (s->f, 1e-7);
          }
        while (status == GSL_CONTINUE && iter < 1000);

        printf ("status = %s\n", gsl_strerror (status));

        gsl_multiroot_fsolver_free (s);
        gsl_vector_free (x);
        return 0;
      }
```

Note that it is important to check the return status of each solver step, in case the algorithm becomes stuck. If an error condition is detected, indicating that the algorithm cannot proceed, then the error can be reported to the user, a new starting point chosen or a different algorithm used.

The intermediate state of the solution is displayed by the following function. The solver state contains the vector s->x which is the current position, and the vector s->f with corresponding function values.

```
      int
      print_state (size_t iter, gsl_multiroot_fsolver * s)
      {
        printf ("iter = %3u x = % .3f % .3f "
                "f(x) = % .3e % .3e\n",
                iter,
                gsl_vector_get (s->x, 0),
                gsl_vector_get (s->x, 1),
                gsl_vector_get (s->f, 0),
                gsl_vector_get (s->f, 1));
      }
```

Here are the results of running the program. The algorithm is started at $(-10, -5)$ far from the solution. Since the solution is hidden in a narrow valley the earliest steps follow the gradient of the function downhill, in an attempt to reduce the large value of the residual. Once the root has been approximately located, on iteration 8, the Newton behavior takes over and convergence is very rapid.

```
      iter =  0 x = -10.000   -5.000   f(x) = 1.100e+01  -1.050e+03
      iter =  1 x = -10.000   -5.000   f(x) = 1.100e+01  -1.050e+03
      iter =  2 x =  -3.976   24.827   f(x) = 4.976e+00   9.020e+01
      iter =  3 x =  -3.976   24.827   f(x) = 4.976e+00   9.020e+01
      iter =  4 x =  -3.976   24.827   f(x) = 4.976e+00   9.020e+01
```

```
iter =  5 x =  -1.274   -5.680   f(x) = 2.274e+00 -7.302e+01
iter =  6 x =  -1.274   -5.680   f(x) = 2.274e+00 -7.302e+01
iter =  7 x =   0.249    0.298   f(x) = 7.511e-01  2.359e+00
iter =  8 x =   0.249    0.298   f(x) = 7.511e-01  2.359e+00
iter =  9 x =   1.000    0.878   f(x) = 1.268e-10 -1.218e+00
iter = 10 x =   1.000    0.989   f(x) = 1.124e-11 -1.080e-01
iter = 11 x =   1.000    1.000   f(x) = 0.000e+00  0.000e+00
status = success
```

Note that the algorithm does not update the location on every iteration. Some iterations are used to adjust the trust-region parameter, after trying a step which was found to be divergent, or to recompute the Jacobian, when poor convergence behavior is detected.

The next example program adds derivative information, in order to accelerate the solution. There are two derivative functions rosenbrock_ df and rosenbrock_fdf. The latter computes both the function and its derivative simultaneously. This allows the optimization of any common terms. For simplicity we substitute calls to the separate f and df functions at this point in the code below.

```
int
rosenbrock_df (const gsl_vector * x, void *params,
               gsl_matrix * J)
{
   const double a = ((struct rparams *) params)->a;
   const double b = ((struct rparams *) params)->b;

   const double x0 = gsl_vector_get (x, 0);

   const double df00 = -a;
   const double df01 = 0;
   const double df10 = -2 * b  * x0;
   const double df11 = b;

   gsl_matrix_set (J, 0, 0, df00);
   gsl_matrix_set (J, 0, 1, df01);
   gsl_matrix_set (J, 1, 0, df10);
   gsl_matrix_set (J, 1, 1, df11);

   return GSL_SUCCESS;
}


int
rosenbrock_fdf (const gsl_vector * x, void *params,
                gsl_vector * f, gsl_matrix * J)
{
```

```
      rosenbrock_f (x, params, f);
      rosenbrock_df (x, params, J);

      return GSL_SUCCESS;
    }
```

The main program now makes calls to the corresponding fdfsolver versions of the functions,

```
    int
    main (void)
    {
      const gsl_multiroot_fdfsolver_type *T;
      gsl_multiroot_fdfsolver *s;

      int status;
      size_t i, iter = 0;

      const size_t n = 2;
      struct rparams p = {1.0, 10.0};
      gsl_multiroot_function_fdf f = {&rosenbrock_f,
                                      &rosenbrock_df,
                                      &rosenbrock_fdf,
                                      n, &p};

      double x_init[2] = {-10.0, -5.0};
      gsl_vector *x = gsl_vector_alloc (n);

      gsl_vector_set (x, 0, x_init[0]);
      gsl_vector_set (x, 1, x_init[1]);

      T = gsl_multiroot_fdfsolver_gnewton;
      s = gsl_multiroot_fdfsolver_alloc (T, n);
      gsl_multiroot_fdfsolver_set (s, &f, x);

      print_state (iter, s);

      do
        {
          iter++;

          status = gsl_multiroot_fdfsolver_iterate (s);

          print_state (iter, s);
```

```
              if (status)
                break;

              status = gsl_multiroot_test_residual (s->f, 1e-7);
            }
          while (status == GSL_CONTINUE && iter < 1000);

          printf ("status = %s\n", gsl_strerror (status));

          gsl_multiroot_fdfsolver_free (s);
          gsl_vector_free (x);
          return 0;
        }
```

The addition of derivative information to the hybrids solver does not
make any significant difference to its behavior, since it able to approximate the Jacobian numerically with sufficient accuracy. To illustrate the
behavior of a different derivative solver we switch to gnewton. This is a
traditional Newton solver with the constraint that it scales back its step
if the full step would lead "uphill". Here is the output for the gnewton
algorithm,

```
        iter = 0 x =  -10.000   -5.000 f(x) =   1.100e+01 -1.050e+03
        iter = 1 x =   -4.231  -65.317 f(x) =   5.231e+00 -8.321e+02
        iter = 2 x =    1.000  -26.358 f(x) =  -8.882e-16 -2.736e+02
        iter = 3 x =    1.000    1.000 f(x) =  -2.220e-16 -4.441e-15
        status = success
```

The convergence is much more rapid, but takes a wide excursion out to
the point $(-4.23, -65.3)$. This could cause the algorithm to go astray in
a realistic application. The hybrid algorithm follows the downhill path to
the solution more reliably.

34.9 References and Further Reading

The original version of the Hybrid method is described in the following
articles by Powell,

> M.J.D. Powell, "A Hybrid Method for Nonlinear Equations" (Chap 6,
> p 87–114) and "A Fortran Subroutine for Solving systems of Nonlin-
> ear Algebraic Equations" (Chap 7, p 115–161), in *Numerical Meth-
> ods for Nonlinear Algebraic Equations*, P. Rabinowitz, editor. Gor-
> don and Breach, 1970.

The following papers are also relevant to the algorithms described in this
section,

J.J. Moré, M.Y. Cosnard, "Numerical Solution of Nonlinear Equations", *ACM Transactions on Mathematical Software*, Vol 5, No 1, (1979), p 64–85

C.G. Broyden, "A Class of Methods for Solving Nonlinear Simultaneous Equations", *Mathematics of Computation*, Vol 19 (1965), p 577–593

J.J. Moré, B.S. Garbow, K.E. Hillstrom, "Testing Unconstrained Optimization Software", ACM Transactions on Mathematical Software, Vol 7, No 1 (1981), p 17–41

35 Multidimensional Minimization

This chapter describes routines for finding minima of arbitrary multidimensional functions. The library provides low level components for a variety of iterative minimizers and convergence tests. These can be combined by the user to achieve the desired solution, while providing full access to the intermediate steps of the algorithms. Each class of methods uses the same framework, so that you can switch between minimizers at runtime without needing to recompile your program. Each instance of a minimizer keeps track of its own state, allowing the minimizers to be used in multi-threaded programs. The minimization algorithms can be used to maximize a function by inverting its sign.

The header file 'gsl_multimin.h' contains prototypes for the minimization functions and related declarations.

35.1 Overview

The problem of multidimensional minimization requires finding a point x such that the scalar function,

$$f(x_1, \ldots, x_n)$$

takes a value which is lower than at any neighboring point. For smooth functions the gradient $g = \nabla f$ vanishes at the minimum. In general there are no bracketing methods available for the minimization of n-dimensional functions. The algorithms proceed from an initial guess using a search algorithm which attempts to move in a downhill direction.

Algorithms making use of the gradient of the function perform a one-dimensional line minimisation along this direction until the lowest point is found to a suitable tolerance. The search direction is then updated with local information from the function and its derivatives, and the whole process repeated until the true n-dimensional minimum is found.

The Nelder-Mead Simplex algorithm applies a different strategy. It maintains $n + 1$ trial parameter vectors as the vertices of a n-dimensional simplex. In each iteration step it tries to improve the worst vertex by a simple geometrical transformation until the size of the simplex falls below a given tolerance.

Both types of algorithms use a standard framework. The user provides a high-level driver for the algorithms, and the library provides the individual functions necessary for each of the steps. There are three main phases of the iteration. The steps are,

- initialize minimizer state, s, for algorithm T

- update s using the iteration T
- test s for convergence, and repeat iteration if necessary

Each iteration step consists either of an improvement to the line-minimisation in the current direction or an update to the search direction itself. The state for the minimizers with derivatives is held in a `gsl_multimin_fdfminimizer` struct, and the state for minimizers using function values only is held in a `gsl_multimin_fminimizer` struct.

35.2 Caveats

Note that the minimization algorithms can only search for one local minimum at a time. When there are several local minima in the search area, the first minimum to be found will be returned; however it is difficult to predict which of the minima this will be. In most cases, no error will be reported if you try to find a local minimum in an area where there is more than one.

It is also important to note that the minimization algorithms find local minima; there is no way to determine whether a minimum is a global minimum of the function in question.

35.3 Initializing the Multidimensional Minimizer

The following function initializes a multidimensional minimizer. The minimizer itself depends only on the dimension of the problem and the algorithm, and can be reused for different problems.

`gsl_multimin_fdfminimizer *`   Function
        `gsl_multimin_fdfminimizer_alloc (const`
        `gsl_multimin_fdfminimizer_type * T, size_t n)`
`gsl_multimin_fminimizer *`   Function
        `gsl_multimin_fminimizer_alloc (const`
        `gsl_multimin_fminimizer_type * T, size_t n)`
This function returns a pointer to a newly allocated instance of a minimizer of type T for an n-dimension function. If there is insufficient memory to create the minimizer then the function returns a null pointer and the error handler is invoked with an error code of `GSL_ENOMEM`.

int gsl_multimin_fdfminimizer_set   *Function*
        (gsl_multimin_fdfminimizer * s,
        gsl_multimin_function_fdf * fdf, const gsl_vector * x,
        double step_size, double tol)

This function initializes the minimizer s to minimize the function fdf starting from the initial point x. The size of the first trial step is given by step_size. The accuracy of the line minimization is specified by tol. The precise meaning of this parameter depends on the method used. Typically the line minimization is considered successful if the gradient of the function g is orthogonal to the current search direction p to a relative accuracy of tol, where $p \cdot g < tol|p||g|$.

int gsl_multimin_fminimizer_set   *Function*
        (gsl_multimin_fminimizer * s, gsl_multimin_function *
        f, const gsl_vector * x, const gsl_vector * step_size)

This function initializes the minimizer s to minimize the function f, starting from the initial point x. The size of the initial trial steps is given in vector step_size. The precise meaning of this parameter depends on the method used.

void gsl_multimin_fdfminimizer_free   *Function*
        (gsl_multimin_fdfminimizer * s)
void gsl_multimin_fminimizer_free   *Function*
        (gsl_multimin_fminimizer * s)

This function frees all the memory associated with the minimizer s.

const char * gsl_multimin_fdfminimizer_name (const   *Function*
        gsl_multimin_fdfminimizer * s)
const char * gsl_multimin_fminimizer_name (const   *Function*
        gsl_multimin_fminimizer * s)

This function returns a pointer to the name of the minimizer. For example,

        printf ("s is a '%s' minimizer\n",
                gsl_multimin_fdfminimizer_name (s));

would print something like s is a 'conjugate_pr' minimizer.

35.4 Providing a function to minimize

You must provide a parametric function of n variables for the minimizers to operate on. You may also need to provide a routine which calculates the gradient of the function and a third routine which calculates both the function value and the gradient together. In order to allow for general parameters the functions are defined by the following data types:

`gsl_multimin_function_fdf`   Data Type

This data type defines a general function of n variables with parameters and the corresponding gradient vector of derivatives,

`double (* f) (const gsl_vector * x, void * params)`

> this function should return the result $f(x, params)$ for argument x and parameters params.

`void (* df) (const gsl_vector * x, void * params, gsl_vector * g)`

> this function should store the n-dimensional gradient $g_i = \partial f(x, params)/\partial x_i$ in the vector g for argument x and parameters params, returning an appropriate error code if the function cannot be computed.

`void (* fdf) (const gsl_vector * x, void * params, double * f, gsl_vector * g)`

> This function should set the values of the f and g as above, for arguments x and parameters params. This function provides an optimization of the separate functions for $f(x)$ and $g(x)$—it is always faster to compute the function and its derivative at the same time.

`size_t n`   the dimension of the system, i.e. the number of components of the vectors x.

`void * params`

> a pointer to the parameters of the function.

`gsl_multimin_function`   Data Type

This data type defines a general function of n variables with parameters,

`double (* f) (const gsl_vector * x, void * params)`

> this function should return the result $f(x, params)$ for argument x and parameters params.

`size_t n`   the dimension of the system, i.e. the number of components of the vectors x.

`void * params`

> a pointer to the parameters of the function.

The following example function defines a simple paraboloid with two parameters,

```
/* Paraboloid centered on (dp[0],dp[1]) */

double
my_f (const gsl_vector *v, void *params)
{
  double x, y;
  double *dp = (double *)params;

  x = gsl_vector_get(v, 0);
  y = gsl_vector_get(v, 1);

  return 10.0 * (x - dp[0]) * (x - dp[0]) +
          20.0 * (y - dp[1]) * (y - dp[1]) + 30.0;
}

/* The gradient of f, df = (df/dx, df/dy). */
void
my_df (const gsl_vector *v, void *params,
        gsl_vector *df)
{
  double x, y;
  double *dp = (double *)params;

  x = gsl_vector_get(v, 0);
  y = gsl_vector_get(v, 1);

  gsl_vector_set(df, 0, 20.0 * (x - dp[0]));
  gsl_vector_set(df, 1, 40.0 * (y - dp[1]));
}

/* Compute both f and df together. */
void
my_fdf (const gsl_vector *x, void *params,
         double *f, gsl_vector *df)
{
  *f = my_f(x, params);
  my_df(x, params, df);
}
```

The function can be initialized using the following code,

```
gsl_multimin_function_fdf my_func;

double p[2] = { 1.0, 2.0 }; /* center at (1,2) */

my_func.f = &my_f;
my_func.df = &my_df;
my_func.fdf = &my_fdf;
my_func.n = 2;
my_func.params = (void *)p;
```

35.5 Iteration

The following functions drive the iterations of each algorithm. The functions perform one iteration to update the state of the minimizer. The same functions work for all minimizers of a given type, so that different methods can be substituted at runtime without modifications to the code.

int gsl_multimin_fdfminimizer_iterate   *Function*
      (gsl_multimin_fdfminimizer * s)
int gsl_multimin_fminimizer_iterate   *Function*
      (gsl_multimin_fminimizer * s)

These functions perform a single iteration of the minimizer s. If the iteration encounters an unexpected problem then an error code will be returned.

The minimizer maintains a current best estimate of the minimum at all times. This information can be accessed with the following auxiliary functions,

gsl_vector * gsl_multimin_fdfminimizer_x (const   *Function*
      gsl_multimin_fdfminimizer * s)
double gsl_multimin_fdfminimizer_minimum (const   *Function*
      gsl_multimin_fdfminimizer * s)
gsl_vector * gsl_multimin_fdfminimizer_gradient   *Function*
      (const gsl_multimin_fdfminimizer * s)

These functions return the current best estimates of the location of the minimum, the value of the function at that point and its gradient, for the minimizer s (with derivatives).

gsl_vector * gsl_multimin_fminimizer_x (const   Function
        gsl_multimin_fminimizer * s)
double gsl_multimin_fminimizer_minimum (const   Function
        gsl_multimin_fminimizer * s)
double gsl_multimin_fminimizer_size (const   Function
        gsl_multimin_fminimizer * s)

These functions return the current best estimate of the location of the minimum, the value of the function at that point, and the characteristic size of the minimizer s (without derivatives).

int gsl_multimin_fdfminimizer_restart   Function
        (gsl_multimin_fdfminimizer * s)

This function resets the minimizer s to use the current point as a new starting point.

35.6 Stopping Criteria

A minimization procedure should stop when one of the following conditions is true:

- A minimum has been found to within the user-specified precision.
- A user-specified maximum number of iterations has been reached.
- An error has occurred.

The handling of these conditions is under user control. The functions below allow the user to test the precision of the current result.

int gsl_multimin_test_gradient (const gsl_vector * g, Function
        double epsabs)

This function tests the norm of the gradient g against the absolute tolerance epsabs. The gradient of a multidimensional function goes to zero at a minimum. The test returns GSL_SUCCESS if the following condition is achieved,

$$|g| < epsabs$$

and returns GSL_CONTINUE otherwise. A suitable choice of epsabs can be made from the desired accuracy in the function for small variations in x. The relationship between these quantities is given by $\delta f = g\,\delta x$.

int gsl_multimin_test_size (const double size, double Function
        epsabs)

This function tests the minimizer specific characteristic size (if applicable to the used minimizer) against absolute tolerance epsabs. The test returns GSL_SUCCESS if the size is smaller than tolerance, otherwise GSL_CONTINUE is returned.

35.7 Algorithms with derivatives

There are several minimization methods available. The best choice of algorithm depends on the problem. All of the algorithms use the value of the function and its gradient at each evaluation point, except for the Simplex algorithm (described in the next section) which uses function values only.

`gsl_multimin_fdfminimizer_conjugate_fr`   Minimizer

This is the Fletcher-Reeves conjugate gradient algorithm. The conjugate gradient algorithm proceeds as a succession of line minimizations. The sequence of search directions is used to build up an approximation to the curvature of the function in the neighborhood of the minimum.

An initial search direction p is chosen using the gradient, and line minimization is carried out in that direction. The accuracy of the line minimization is specified by the parameter *tol*. The minimum along this line occurs when the function gradient g and the search direction p are orthogonal. The line minimization terminates when $p \cdot g < tol|p||g|$. The search direction is updated using the Fletcher-Reeves formula $p' = g' - \beta g$ where $\beta = -|g'|^2/|g|^2$, and the line minimization is then repeated for the new search direction.

`gsl_multimin_fdfminimizer_conjugate_pr`   Minimizer

This is the Polak-Ribiere conjugate gradient algorithm. It is similar to the Fletcher-Reeves method, differing only in the choice of the coefficient β. Both methods work well when the evaluation point is close enough to the minimum of the objective function that it is well approximated by a quadratic hypersurface.

`gsl_multimin_fdfminimizer_vector_bfgs`   Minimizer

This is the vector Broyden-Fletcher-Goldfarb-Shanno (BFGS) algorithm. It is a quasi-Newton method which builds up an approximation to the second derivatives of the function f using the difference between successive gradient vectors. By combining the first and second derivatives the algorithm is able to take Newton-type steps towards the function minimum, assuming quadratic behavior in that region.

`gsl_multimin_fdfminimizer_steepest_descent`   Minimizer

The steepest descent algorithm follows the downhill gradient of the function at each step. When a downhill step is successful the step-size is increased by a factor of two. If the downhill step leads to a higher function value then the algorithm backtracks and the step size is decreased using the parameter *tol*. A suitable value of *tol* for most applications is 0.1. The steepest descent method is inefficient and is included only for demonstration purposes.

35.8 Algorithms without derivatives

gsl_multimin_fminimizer_nmsimplex   Minimizer

This is the Simplex algorithm of Nelder and Mead. It constructs n vectors p_i from the starting vector x and the vector $step\_size$ as follows:

$$p_0 = (x_0, x_1, \cdots, x_n)$$
$$p_1 = (x_0 + step\_size_0, x_1, \cdots, x_n)$$
$$p_2 = (x_0, x_1 + step\_size_1, \cdots, x_n)$$
$$\cdots = \cdots$$
$$p_n = (x_0, x_1, \cdots, x_n + step\_size_n)$$

These vectors form the $n + 1$ vertices of a simplex in n dimensions. On each iteration the algorithm tries to improve the parameter vector p_i corresponding to the highest function value by simple geometrical transformations. These are reflection, reflection followed by expansion, contraction and multiple contraction. Using these transformations the simplex moves through the parameter space towards the minimum, where it contracts itself.

After each iteration, the best vertex is returned. Note, that due to the nature of the algorithm not every step improves the current best parameter vector. Usually several iterations are required.

The routine calculates the minimizer specific characteristic size as the average distance from the geometrical center of the simplex to all its vertices. This size can be used as a stopping criteria, as the simplex contracts itself near the minimum. The size is returned by the function gsl_multimin_fminimizer_size.

35.9 Examples

This example program finds the minimum of the paraboloid function defined earlier. The location of the minimum is offset from the origin in x and y, and the function value at the minimum is non-zero. The main program is given below, it requires the example function given earlier in this chapter.

```
int
main (void)
{
  size_t iter = 0;
  int status;

  const gsl_multimin_fdfminimizer_type *T;
  gsl_multimin_fdfminimizer *s;
```

```
/* Position of the minimum (1,2). */
double par[2] = { 1.0, 2.0 };

gsl_vector *x;
gsl_multimin_function_fdf my_func;

my_func.f = &my_f;
my_func.df = &my_df;
my_func.fdf = &my_fdf;
my_func.n = 2;
my_func.params = &par;

/* Starting point, x = (5,7) */
x = gsl_vector_alloc (2);
gsl_vector_set (x, 0, 5.0);
gsl_vector_set (x, 1, 7.0);

T = gsl_multimin_fdfminimizer_conjugate_fr;
s = gsl_multimin_fdfminimizer_alloc (T, 2);

gsl_multimin_fdfminimizer_set (s, &my_func, x, 0.01, 1e-4);

do
  {
    iter++;
    status = gsl_multimin_fdfminimizer_iterate (s);

    if (status)
      break;

    status = gsl_multimin_test_gradient (s->gradient, 1e-3);

    if (status == GSL_SUCCESS)
      printf ("Minimum found at:\n");

    printf ("%5d %.5f %.5f %10.5f\n", iter,
            gsl_vector_get (s->x, 0),
            gsl_vector_get (s->x, 1),
            s->f);

  }
while (status == GSL_CONTINUE && iter < 100);

gsl_multimin_fdfminimizer_free (s);
gsl_vector_free (x);

return 0;
}
```

The initial step-size is chosen as 0.01, a conservative estimate in this case, and the line minimization parameter is set at 0.0001. The program terminates when the norm of the gradient has been reduced below 0.001. The output of the program is shown below,

```
          x        y           f
   1  4.99629  6.99072   687.84780
   2  4.98886  6.97215   683.55456
   3  4.97400  6.93501   675.01278
   4  4.94429  6.86073   658.10798
   5  4.88487  6.71217   625.01340
   6  4.76602  6.41506   561.68440
   7  4.52833  5.82083   446.46694
   8  4.05295  4.63238   261.79422
   9  3.10219  2.25548    75.49762
  10  2.85185  1.62963    67.03704
  11  2.19088  1.76182    45.31640
  12  0.86892  2.02622    30.18555
Minimum found at:
  13  1.00000  2.00000    30.00000
```

Note that the algorithm gradually increases the step size as it successfully moves downhill, as can be seen by plotting the successive points.

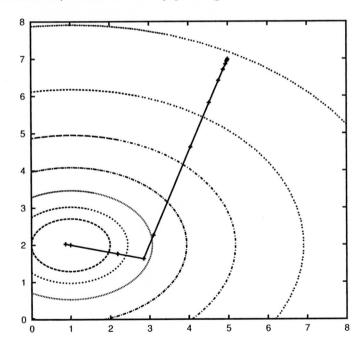

The conjugate gradient algorithm finds the minimum on its second direction because the function is purely quadratic. Additional iterations would be needed for a more complicated function.

Here is another example using the Nelder-Mead Simplex algorithm to minimize the same example object function, as above.

```
int
main(void)
{
    size_t np = 2;
    double par[2] = {1.0, 2.0};

    const gsl_multimin_fminimizer_type *T =
        gsl_multimin_fminimizer_nmsimplex;
    gsl_multimin_fminimizer *s = NULL;
    gsl_vector *ss, *x;
    gsl_multimin_function minex_func;

    size_t iter = 0, i;
    int status;
    double size;

    /* Initial vertex size vector */
    ss = gsl_vector_alloc (np);

    /* Set all step sizes to 1 */
    gsl_vector_set_all (ss, 1.0);

    /* Starting point */
    x = gsl_vector_alloc (np);

    gsl_vector_set (x, 0, 5.0);
    gsl_vector_set (x, 1, 7.0);

    /* Initialize method and iterate */
    minex_func.f = &my_f;
    minex_func.n = np;
    minex_func.params = (void *)&par;

    s = gsl_multimin_fminimizer_alloc (T, np);
    gsl_multimin_fminimizer_set (s, &minex_func, x, ss);

    do
      {
        iter++;
        status = gsl_multimin_fminimizer_iterate(s);

        if (status)
          break;
```

```
      size = gsl_multimin_fminimizer_size (s);
      status = gsl_multimin_test_size (size, 1e-2);

      if (status == GSL_SUCCESS)
        {
          printf ("converged to minimum at\n");
        }

      printf ("%5d ", iter);
      for (i = 0; i < np; i++)
        {
          printf ("%10.3e ", gsl_vector_get (s->x, i));
        }
      printf ("f = %7.3f size = %.3f\n", s->fval, size);
    }
  while (status == GSL_CONTINUE && iter < 100);

  gsl_vector_free(x);
  gsl_vector_free(ss);
  gsl_multimin_fminimizer_free (s);

  return status;
}
```

The minimum search stops when the Simplex size drops to 0.01. The output is shown below.

```
 1  6.500e+00 5.000e+00 f = 512.500 size = 1.082
 2  5.250e+00 4.000e+00 f = 290.625 size = 1.372
 3  5.250e+00 4.000e+00 f = 290.625 size = 1.372
 4  5.500e+00 1.000e+00 f = 252.500 size = 1.372
 5  2.625e+00 3.500e+00 f = 101.406 size = 1.823
 6  3.469e+00 1.375e+00 f = 98.760  size = 1.526
 7  1.820e+00 3.156e+00 f = 63.467  size = 1.105
 8  1.820e+00 3.156e+00 f = 63.467  size = 1.105
 9  1.016e+00 2.812e+00 f = 43.206  size = 1.105
10  2.041e+00 2.008e+00 f = 40.838  size = 0.645
11  1.236e+00 1.664e+00 f = 32.816  size = 0.645
12  1.236e+00 1.664e+00 f = 32.816  size = 0.447
13  5.225e-01 1.980e+00 f = 32.288  size = 0.447
14  1.103e+00 2.073e+00 f = 30.214  size = 0.345
15  1.103e+00 2.073e+00 f = 30.214  size = 0.264
16  1.103e+00 2.073e+00 f = 30.214  size = 0.160
17  9.864e-01 1.934e+00 f = 30.090  size = 0.132
18  9.190e-01 1.987e+00 f = 30.069  size = 0.092
19  1.028e+00 2.017e+00 f = 30.013  size = 0.056
20  1.028e+00 2.017e+00 f = 30.013  size = 0.046
21  1.028e+00 2.017e+00 f = 30.013  size = 0.033
```

```
22  9.874e-01 1.985e+00 f = 30.006  size = 0.028
23  9.846e-01 1.995e+00 f = 30.003  size = 0.023
24  1.007e+00 2.003e+00 f = 30.001  size = 0.012
converged to minimum at
25  1.007e+00 2.003e+00 f = 30.001  size = 0.010
```

The simplex size first increases, while the simplex moves towards the minimum. After a while the size begins to decrease as the simplex contracts around the minimum.

35.10 References and Further Reading

A brief description of multidimensional minimization algorithms and further references can be found in the following book,

> C.W. Ueberhuber, *Numerical Computation (Volume 2)*, Chapter 14, Section 4.4 "Minimization Methods", p. 325–335, Springer (1997), ISBN 3-540-62057-5.

The simplex algorithm is described in the following paper,

> J.A. Nelder and R. Mead, *A simplex method for function minimization*, Computer Journal vol. 7 (1965), 308–315.

36 Linear Least-Squares Fitting

This chapter describes routines for performing least squares fits to experimental data using linear combinations of functions. The data may be weighted or unweighted, i.e. with known or unknown errors. For weighted data the functions compute the best fit parameters and their associated covariance matrix. For unweighted data the covariance matrix is estimated from the scatter of the points, giving a variance-covariance matrix.

The functions are divided into separate versions for simple one- or two-parameter regression and multiple-parameter fits. The functions are declared in the header file 'gsl_fit.h'.

For non-linear fitting, see Chapter 37 [Nonlinear Least-Squares Fitting], page 491.

36.1 Overview

Least-squares fits are found by minimizing χ^2 (chi-squared), the weighted sum of squared residuals over n experimental datapoints (x_i, y_i) for the model $Y(c, x)$,

$$\chi^2 = \sum_i w_i (Y(c, x_i) - y_i)^2$$

The p parameters of the model are $c = \{c_0, c_1, \ldots\}$. The weight factors w_i are given by $w_i = 1/\sigma_i^2$, where σ_i is the experimental error on the data-point y_i. The errors are assumed to be gaussian and uncorrelated. For unweighted data the chi-squared sum is computed without any weight factors.

The fitting routines return the best-fit parameters c and their $p \times p$ covariance matrix. The covariance matrix measures the statistical errors on the best-fit parameters resulting from the errors on the data, σ_i, and is defined as $C_{ab} = \langle \delta c_a \delta c_b \rangle$ where $\langle\ \rangle$ denotes an average over the gaussian error distributions of the underlying datapoints.

The covariance matrix is calculated by error propagation from the data errors σ_i. The change in a fitted parameter δc_a caused by a small change in the data δy_i is given by

$$\delta c_a = \sum_i \frac{\partial c_a}{\partial y_i} \delta y_i$$

allowing the covariance matrix to be written in terms of the errors on the data,

$$C_{ab} = \sum_{i,j} \frac{\partial c_a}{\partial y_i} \frac{\partial c_b}{\partial y_j} \langle \delta y_i \delta y_j \rangle$$

For uncorrelated data the fluctuations of the underlying datapoints satisfy $\langle \delta y_i \delta y_j \rangle = \sigma_i^2 \delta_{ij}$, giving a corresponding parameter covariance matrix of

$$C_{ab} = \sum_{i} \frac{1}{w_i} \frac{\partial c_a}{\partial y_i} \frac{\partial c_b}{\partial y_i}$$

When computing the covariance matrix for unweighted data, i.e. data with unknown errors, the weight factors w_i in this sum are replaced by the single estimate $w = 1/\sigma^2$, where σ^2 is the computed variance of the residuals about the best-fit model, $\sigma^2 = \sum(Y(c, x_i) - y_i)^2/(n - p)$. This is referred to as the *variance-covariance matrix*.

The standard deviations of the best-fit parameters are given by the square root of the corresponding diagonal elements of the covariance matrix, $\sigma_{c_a} = \sqrt{C_{aa}}$.

36.2 Linear regression

The functions described in this section can be used to perform least-squares fits to a straight line model, $Y(c, x) = c_0 + c_1 x$.

int gsl_fit_linear (const double * x, const size_t   Function
         xstride, const double * y, const size_t *ystride*, size_t
         n, double * c0, double * c1, double * cov00, double *
         cov01, double * cov11, double * sumsq)
This function computes the best-fit linear regression coefficients $(c0,c1)$ of the model $Y = c_0 + c_1 X$ for the dataset (x, y), two vectors of length n with strides *xstride* and *ystride*. The errors on y are assumed unknown so the variance-covariance matrix for the parameters $(c0, c1)$ is estimated from the scatter of the points around the best-fit line and returned via the parameters $(cov00, cov01, cov11)$. The sum of squares of the residuals from the best-fit line is returned in *sumsq*.

int gsl_fit_wlinear (const double * x, const size_t   Function
         xstride, const double * w, const size_t *wstride*, const
         double * y, const size_t *ystride*, size_t n, double * c0,
         double * c1, double * cov00, double * cov01, double *
         cov11, double * chisq)
This function computes the best-fit linear regression coefficients $(c0,c1)$ of the model $Y = c_0 + c_1 X$ for the weighted dataset (x, y), two vectors

of length n with strides *xstride* and *ystride*. The vector w, of length n and stride *wstride*, specifies the weight of each datapoint. The weight is the reciprocal of the variance for each datapoint in y.

The covariance matrix for the parameters $(c0, c1)$ is computed using the weights and returned via the parameters $(cov00, cov01, cov11)$. The weighted sum of squares of the residuals from the best-fit line, χ^2, is returned in *chisq*.

int gsl_fit_linear_est (double x, double $c0$, double $c1$,   Function
        double $c00$, double $c01$, double $c11$, double $* y$, double
        $* y\_err$)

This function uses the best-fit linear regression coefficients $(c0, c1)$ and their covariance $(cov00, cov01, cov11)$ to compute the fitted function y and its standard deviation y_err for the model $Y = c_0 + c_1 X$ at the point x.

36.3 Linear fitting without a constant term

The functions described in this section can be used to perform least-squares fits to a straight line model without a constant term, $Y = c_1 X$.

int gsl_fit_mul (const double $* x$, const size_t *xstride*,   Function
        const double $* y$, const size_t *ystride*, size_t n,
        double $* c1$, double $* cov11$, double $* sumsq$)

This function computes the best-fit linear regression coefficient $c1$ of the model $Y = c_1 X$ for the datasets (x, y), two vectors of length n with strides *xstride* and *ystride*. The errors on y are assumed unknown so the variance of the parameter $c1$ is estimated from the scatter of the points around the best-fit line and returned via the parameter *cov11*. The sum of squares of the residuals from the best-fit line is returned in *sumsq*.

int gsl_fit_wmul (const double $* x$, const size_t *xstride*,   Function
        const double $* w$, const size_t *wstride*, const double $*$
        y, const size_t *ystride*, size_t n, double $* c1$, double $*$
        $cov11$, double $* sumsq$)

This function computes the best-fit linear regression coefficient $c1$ of the model $Y = c_1 X$ for the weighted datasets (x, y), two vectors of length n with strides *xstride* and *ystride*. The vector w, of length n and stride *wstride*, specifies the weight of each datapoint. The weight is the reciprocal of the variance for each datapoint in y.

The variance of the parameter $c1$ is computed using the weights and returned via the parameter *cov11*. The weighted sum of squares of the residuals from the best-fit line, χ^2, is returned in *chisq*.

int gsl_fit_mul_est (double x, double c1, double c11,   Function
        double * y, double * y_err)

This function uses the best-fit linear regression coefficient $c1$ and its covariance $cov11$ to compute the fitted function y and its standard deviation y_err for the model $Y = c_1 X$ at the point x.

36.4 Multi-parameter fitting

The functions described in this section perform least-squares fits to a general linear model, $y = Xc$ where y is a vector of n observations, X is an n by p matrix of predictor variables, and the elements of the vector c are the p unknown best-fit parameters which are to be estimated. The chi-squared value is given by $\chi^2 = \sum_i w_i (\sum_j X_{ij} c_j - y_i)^2$.

This formulation can be used for fits to any number of functions and/or variables by preparing the n-by-p matrix X appropriately. For example, to fit to a p-th order polynomial in x, use the following matrix,

$$X_{ij} = x_i^j$$

where the index i runs over the observations and the index j runs from 0 to $p - 1$.

To fit to a linear combination of p sinusoidal functions with fixed frequencies $\omega_1, \omega_2, \ldots, \omega_p$, use,

$$X_{ij} = \sin(\omega_j x_i)$$

To fit k sinusoidal functions with arbitrary phase, use both sines and cosines as columns of the matrix X,

$$X = \begin{pmatrix} \cos(\omega_1 x_1) & \sin(\omega_1 x_1) & \ldots & \cos(\omega_k x_1) & \sin(\omega_k x_1) \\ \cos(\omega_1 x_2) & \sin(\omega_1 x_2) & \ldots & \cos(\omega_k x_2) & \sin(\omega_k x_2) \\ \ldots & \ldots & \ldots & \ldots & \ldots \\ \cos(\omega_1 x_n) & \sin(\omega_1 x_n) & \ldots & \cos(\omega_k x_n) & \sin(\omega_k x_n) \end{pmatrix}$$

where the total number of parameters is $p = 2k$. Note that indices in this matrix follow the normal mathematical convention (starting from 1). When calling the GSL routines, all indices begin with zero.

To fit to a linear combination of p independent variables $x_1, x_2, \ldots, x_p$, use,

$$X_{ij} = x_j(i)$$

where $x_j(i)$ is the i-th value of the predictor variable x_j.

The functions described in this section are declared in the header file 'gsl_multifit.h'.

The solution of the general linear least-squares system requires an additional working space for intermediate results, such as the singular value decomposition of the matrix X.

gsl_multifit_linear_workspace *   Function
        gsl_multifit_linear_alloc (size_t n, size_t p)
This function allocates a workspace for fitting a model to n observations using p parameters.

void gsl_multifit_linear_free   Function
        (gsl_multifit_linear_workspace * $work$)
This function frees the memory associated with the workspace w.

int gsl_multifit_linear (const gsl_matrix * X, const   Function
        gsl_vector * y, gsl_vector * c, gsl_matrix * cov,
        double * $chisq$, gsl_multifit_linear_workspace * $work$)
int gsl_multifit_linear_svd (const gsl_matrix * X,   Function
        const gsl_vector * y, double tol, size_t * $rank$,
        gsl_vector * c, gsl_matrix * cov, double * $chisq$,
        gsl_multifit_linear_workspace * $work$)
These functions compute the best-fit parameters c of the model $y = Xc$ for the observations y and the matrix of predictor variables X. The variance-covariance matrix of the model parameters cov is estimated from the scatter of the observations about the best-fit. The sum of squares of the residuals from the best-fit, χ^2, is returned in $chisq$.

The best-fit is found by singular value decomposition of the matrix X using the preallocated workspace provided in $work$. The modified Golub-Reinsch SVD algorithm is used, with column scaling to improve the accuracy of the singular values. Any components which have zero singular value (to machine precision) are discarded from the fit. In the second form of the function the components are discarded if the ratio of singular values s_i/s_0 falls below the user-specified tolerance tol, and the effective rank is returned in $rank$.

int gsl_multifit_wlinear (const gsl_matrix * X, const   Function
        gsl_vector * w, const gsl_vector * y, gsl_vector * c,
        gsl_matrix * cov, double * $chisq$,
        gsl_multifit_linear_workspace * $work$)
int gsl_multifit_wlinear_svd (const gsl_matrix * X,   Function
        const gsl_vector * w, const gsl_vector * y, double
        tol, size_t * $rank$, gsl_vector * c, gsl_matrix * cov,
        double * $chisq$, gsl_multifit_linear_workspace * $work$)
This function computes the best-fit parameters c of the weighted model $y = Xc$ for the observations y with weights w and the matrix of predictor variables X. The covariance matrix of the model parameters

cov is computed with the given weights. The weighted sum of squares of the residuals from the best-fit, χ^2, is returned in *chisq*.

The best-fit is found by singular value decomposition of the matrix X using the preallocated workspace provided in *work*. Any components which have zero singular value (to machine precision) are discarded from the fit. In the second form of the function the components are discarded if the ratio of singular values s_i/s_0 falls below the user-specified tolerance *tol*, and the effective rank is returned in *rank*.

int gsl_multifit_linear_est (const gsl_vector * x,   Function
     const gsl_vector * c, const gsl_matrix * cov, double *
     y, double * y_err)

This function uses the best-fit multilinear regression coefficients c and their covariance matrix *cov* to compute the fitted function value y and its standard deviation y_err for the model $y = x.c$ at the point x.

36.5 Examples

The following program computes a least squares straight-line fit to a simple dataset, and outputs the best-fit line and its associated one standard-deviation error bars.

```
#include <stdio.h>
#include <gsl/gsl_fit.h>

int
main (void)
{
  int i, n = 4;
  double x[4] = { 1970, 1980, 1990, 2000 };
  double y[4] = {   12,   11,   14,   13 };
  double w[4] = {  0.1,  0.2,  0.3,  0.4 };

  double c0, c1, cov00, cov01, cov11, chisq;

  gsl_fit_wlinear (x, 1, w, 1, y, 1, n,
                   &c0, &c1, &cov00, &cov01, &cov11,
                   &chisq);

  printf ("# best fit: Y = %g + %g X\n", c0, c1);
  printf ("# covariance matrix:\n");
  printf ("# [ %g, %g\n#   %g, %g]\n",
          cov00, cov01, cov01, cov11);
  printf ("# chisq = %g\n", chisq);
```

```
for (i = 0; i < n; i++)
  printf ("data: %g %g %g\n",
                 x[i], y[i], 1/sqrt(w[i]));

printf ("\n");

for (i = -30; i < 130; i++)
  {
    double xf = x[0] + (i/100.0) * (x[n-1] - x[0]);
    double yf, yf_err;

    gsl_fit_linear_est (xf,
                        c0, c1,
                        cov00, cov01, cov11,
                        &yf, &yf_err);

    printf ("fit: %g %g\n", xf, yf);
    printf ("hi : %g %g\n", xf, yf + yf_err);
    printf ("lo : %g %g\n", xf, yf - yf_err);
  }
return 0;
}
```

The following commands extract the data from the output of the program and display it using the GNU plotutils graph utility,

```
$ ./demo > tmp
$ more tmp
# best fit: Y = -106.6 + 0.06 X
# covariance matrix:
# [ 39602, -19.9
#    -19.9, 0.01]
# chisq = 0.8

$ for n in data fit hi lo ;
  do
    grep "^$n" tmp | cut -d: -f2 > $n ;
  done
$ graph -T X -X x -Y y -y 0 20 -m 0 -S 2 -Ie data
      -S 0 -I a -m 1 fit -m 2 hi -m 2 lo
```

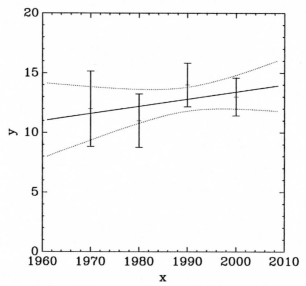

The next program performs a quadratic fit $y = c_0 + c_1 x + c_2 x^2$ to a weighted dataset using the generalised linear fitting function $\texttt{gsl\_multifit\_wlinear}$. The model matrix X for a quadratic fit is given by,

$$X = \begin{pmatrix} 1 & x_0 & x_0^2 \\ 1 & x_1 & x_1^2 \\ 1 & x_2 & x_2^2 \\ \ldots & \ldots & \ldots \end{pmatrix}$$

where the column of ones corresponds to the constant term c_0. The two remaining columns corresponds to the terms $c_1 x$ and $c_2 x^2$.

The program reads n lines of data in the format (x, y, err) where err is the error (standard deviation) in the value y.

```
#include <stdio.h>
#include <gsl/gsl_multifit.h>

int
main (int argc, char **argv)
{
  int i, n;
  double xi, yi, ei, chisq;
  gsl_matrix *X, *cov;
  gsl_vector *y, *w, *c;

  if (argc != 2)
    {
      fprintf (stderr,"usage: fit n < data\n");
```

```
        exit (-1);
    }

  n = atoi (argv[1]);

  X = gsl_matrix_alloc (n, 3);
  y = gsl_vector_alloc (n);
  w = gsl_vector_alloc (n);

  c = gsl_vector_alloc (3);
  cov = gsl_matrix_alloc (3, 3);

  for (i = 0; i < n; i++)
    {
      int count = fscanf (stdin, "%lg %lg %lg",
                              &xi, &yi, &ei);

      if (count != 3)
        {
          fprintf (stderr, "error reading file\n");
          exit (-1);
        }

      printf ("%g %g +/- %g\n", xi, yi, ei);

      gsl_matrix_set (X, i, 0, 1.0);
      gsl_matrix_set (X, i, 1, xi);
      gsl_matrix_set (X, i, 2, xi*xi);

      gsl_vector_set (y, i, yi);
      gsl_vector_set (w, i, 1.0/(ei*ei));
    }

  {
    gsl_multifit_linear_workspace * work
      = gsl_multifit_linear_alloc (n, 3);
    gsl_multifit_wlinear (X, w, y, c, cov,
                              &chisq, work);
    gsl_multifit_linear_free (work);
  }

#define C(i) (gsl_vector_get(c,(i)))
#define COV(i,j) (gsl_matrix_get(cov,(i),(j)))
```

```
          {
            printf ("# best fit: Y = %g + %g X + %g X^2\n",
                    C(0), C(1), C(2));

            printf ("# covariance matrix:\n");
            printf ("[ %+.5e, %+.5e, %+.5e  \n",
                       COV(0,0), COV(0,1), COV(0,2));
            printf ("  %+.5e, %+.5e, %+.5e  \n",
                       COV(1,0), COV(1,1), COV(1,2));
            printf ("  %+.5e, %+.5e, %+.5e ]\n",
                       COV(2,0), COV(2,1), COV(2,2));
            printf ("# chisq = %g\n", chisq);
          }
        return 0;
      }
```

A suitable set of data for fitting can be generated using the following
program. It outputs a set of points with gaussian errors from the curve
$y = e^x$ in the region $0 < x < 2$.

```
      #include <stdio.h>
      #include <math.h>
      #include <gsl/gsl_randist.h>

      int
      main (void)
      {
        double x;
        const gsl_rng_type * T;
        gsl_rng * r;

        gsl_rng_env_setup ();

        T = gsl_rng_default;
        r = gsl_rng_alloc (T);

        for (x = 0.1; x < 2; x+= 0.1)
          {
            double y0 = exp (x);
            double sigma = 0.1 * y0;
            double dy = gsl_ran_gaussian (r, sigma);

            printf ("%g %g %g\n", x, y0 + dy, sigma);
          }
```

```
    return 0;
 }
```

The data can be prepared by running the resulting executable program,

```
$ ./generate > exp.dat
$ more exp.dat
0.1 0.97935 0.110517
0.2 1.3359 0.12214
0.3 1.52573 0.134986
0.4 1.60318 0.149182
0.5 1.81731 0.164872
0.6 1.92475 0.182212
....
```

To fit the data use the previous program, with the number of data points given as the first argument. In this case there are 19 data points.

```
$ ./fit 19 < exp.dat
0.1 0.97935 +/- 0.110517
0.2 1.3359 +/- 0.12214
...
# best fit: Y = 1.02318 + 0.956201 X + 0.876796 X^2
# covariance matrix:
[ +1.25612e-02, -3.64387e-02, +1.94389e-02
  -3.64387e-02, +1.42339e-01, -8.48761e-02
  +1.94389e-02, -8.48761e-02, +5.60243e-02 ]
# chisq = 23.0987
```

The parameters of the quadratic fit match the coefficients of the expansion of e^x, taking into account the errors on the parameters and the $O(x^3)$ difference between the exponential and quadratic functions for the larger values of x. The errors on the parameters are given by the square-root of the corresponding diagonal elements of the covariance matrix. The chi-squared per degree of freedom is 1.4, indicating a reasonable fit to the data.

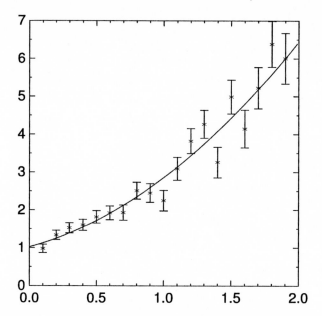

36.6 References and Further Reading

A summary of formulas and techniques for least squares fitting can be found in the "Statistics" chapter of the Annual Review of Particle Physics prepared by the Particle Data Group,

> *Review of Particle Properties*, R.M. Barnett et al., Physical Review D54, 1 (1996) http://pdg.lbl.gov/

The Review of Particle Physics is available online at the website given above.

The tests used to prepare these routines are based on the NIST Statistical Reference Datasets. The datasets and their documentation are available from NIST at the following website,

> http://www.nist.gov/itl/div898/strd/index.html.

37 Nonlinear Least-Squares Fitting

This chapter describes functions for multidimensional nonlinear least-squares fitting. The library provides low level components for a variety of iterative solvers and convergence tests. These can be combined by the user to achieve the desired solution, with full access to the intermediate steps of the iteration. Each class of methods uses the same framework, so that you can switch between solvers at runtime without needing to recompile your program. Each instance of a solver keeps track of its own state, allowing the solvers to be used in multi-threaded programs. The library reimplements the algorithms used in MINPACK, a non-linear minimization package written by Moré, Garbow and Hillstrom. Fortran code for MINPACK is available on Netlib.

The header file 'gsl_multifit_nlin.h' contains prototypes for the multidimensional nonlinear fitting functions and related declarations.

37.1 Overview

Nonlinear least-squares fitting is a minimization problem—the best fit to a dataset is found by choosing parameters which minimize the squared difference between the model and the data. This vector difference is referred to as the *residual*. The routines in this chapter minimize the norm of a general n-component vector, f_i, in p parameters, x_j,

$$\Phi(x) = \frac{1}{2}||F(x)||^2 = \frac{1}{2}\sum_{i=1}^{n} f_i(x_1, \dots, x_p)^2$$

The problem is formulated as a general minimization so the routines can be used to minimize the norm of any vector function, $||F(x)||$. Least-squares fitting of a model $Y(x)$ to data y minimizes the residual vector $F(x) = Y(x) - y$ with respect to the model parameters x. All algorithms proceed from an initial guess using the linearization,

$$\psi(p) = ||F(x+p)|| \approx ||F(x) + Jp||$$

where x is the initial point, p is the proposed step and J is the Jacobian matrix $J_{ij} = \partial f_i/\partial x_j$. Additional strategies are used to enlarge the region of convergence. These include requiring a decrease in the norm $||F||$ on each step or using a trust region to avoid steps which fall outside the linear regime.

To perform a weighted least-squares fit of a nonlinear model $Y(x, t)$ to data (t_i, y_i) with independent gaussian errors σ_i, use residual function components of the following form,

$$f_i = \frac{(Y_i(x, t_i) - y_i)}{\sigma_i}$$

With this definition the Jacobian is $J_{ij} = (1/\sigma_i)\partial Y_i/\partial x_j$, where $Y_i = Y_i(x, t_i)$.

Note that the model parameters are denoted by x in this chapter since the non-linear least-squares algorithms are described geometrically (i.e. finding the minimum of a surface). The independent variable of any data to be fitted is denoted by t. Unweighted fits can be computed using the appropriate definition of the residual function, f_i.

37.2 Initializing the Solver

gsl_multifit_fsolver * gsl_multifit_fsolver_alloc   Function
       (const gsl_multifit_fsolver_type * T, size_t n,
       size_t p)

This function returns a pointer to a newly allocated instance of a solver of type T for n observations and p parameters. The number of observations n must be greater than or equal to the number of parameters p.

If there is insufficient memory to create the solver then the function returns a null pointer and the error handler is invoked with an error code of GSL_ENOMEM.

gsl_multifit_fdfsolver * gsl_multifit_fdfsolver_alloc   Function
       (const gsl_multifit_fdfsolver_type * T, size_t n,
       size_t p)

This function returns a pointer to a newly allocated instance of a derivative solver of type T for n observations and p parameters. For example, the following code creates an instance of a Levenberg-Marquardt solver for 100 data points and 3 parameters,

```
const gsl_multifit_fdfsolver_type * T
    = gsl_multifit_fdfsolver_lmder;
gsl_multifit_fdfsolver * s
    = gsl_multifit_fdfsolver_alloc (T, 100, 3);
```

The number of observations n must be greater than or equal to parameters p.

If there is insufficient memory to create the solver then the function returns a null pointer and the error handler is invoked with an error code of GSL_ENOMEM.

int gsl_multifit_fsolver_set (gsl_multifit_fsolver *   Function
        s, gsl_multifit_function * *f*, gsl_vector * *x*)
This function initializes, or reinitializes, an existing solver *s* to use the
function *f* and the initial guess *x*.

int gsl_multifit_fdfsolver_set   Function
        (gsl_multifit_fdfsolver * *s*,
        gsl_multifit_function_fdf * *fdf*, gsl_vector * *x*)
This function initializes, or reinitializes, an existing solver *s* to use the
function and derivative *fdf* and the initial guess *x*.

void gsl_multifit_fsolver_free (gsl_multifit_fsolver *   Function
        s)
void gsl_multifit_fdfsolver_free   Function
        (gsl_multifit_fdfsolver * *s*)
These functions free all the memory associated with the solver *s*.

const char * gsl_multifit_fsolver_name (const   Function
        gsl_multifit_fsolver * *s*)
const char * gsl_multifit_fdfsolver_name (const   Function
        gsl_multifit_fdfsolver * *s*)
These functions return a pointer to the name of the solver. For example,

```
printf ("s is a '%s' solver\n",
        gsl_multifit_fdfsolver_name (s));
```

would print something like s is a 'lmder' solver.

37.3 Providing the Function to be Minimized

You must provide n functions of p variables for the minimization algorithms to operate on. In order to allow for arbitrary parameters the
functions are defined by the following data types:

gsl_multifit_function   Data Type
This data type defines a general system of functions with arbitrary
parameters.

    int (* f) (const gsl_vector * *x*, void * *params*, gsl_vector *
    f)
            this function should store the vector result $f(x, params)$
            in *f* for argument *x* and arbitrary parameters *params*,
            returning an appropriate error code if the function cannot
            be computed.

size_t n   the number of functions, i.e. the number of components of the vector f.

size_t p   the number of independent variables, i.e. the number of components of the vector x.

void * params
     a pointer to the arbitrary parameters of the function.

gsl_multifit_function_fdf   Data Type

This data type defines a general system of functions with arbitrary parameters and the corresponding Jacobian matrix of derivatives,

int (* f) (const gsl_vector * x, void * params, gsl_vector * f)
     this function should store the vector result $f(x, params)$ in f for argument x and arbitrary parameters params, returning an appropriate error code if the function cannot be computed.

int (* df) (const gsl_vector * x, void * params, gsl_matrix * J)
     this function should store the n-by-p matrix result $J_{ij} = \partial f_i(x, params)/\partial x_j$ in J for argument x and arbitrary parameters params, returning an appropriate error code if the function cannot be computed. Note that the Jacobian must match the supplied function f—if the sign differs, or the derivatives are incorrect, the algorithms will fail to converge.

int (* fdf) (const gsl_vector * x, void * params, gsl_vector * f, gsl_matrix * J)
     this function should set the values of the f and J as above, for arguments x and arbitrary parameters params. This function provides an optimization of the separate functions for $f(x)$ and $J(x)$—it is always faster to compute the function and its derivative at the same time.

size_t n   the number of functions, i.e. the number of components of the vector f.

size_t p   the number of independent variables, i.e. the number of components of the vector x.

void * params
     a pointer to the arbitrary parameters of the function.

Note that when fitting a non-linear model against experimental data, the data is passed to the functions above using the params argument and the trial best-fit parameters through the x argument.

37.4 Iteration

The following functions drive the iteration of each algorithm. Each function performs one iteration to update the state of any solver of the corresponding type. The same functions work for all solvers so that different methods can be substituted at runtime without modifications to the code.

int gsl_multifit_fsolver_iterate   *Function*
      (gsl_multifit_fsolver * *s*)
int gsl_multifit_fdfsolver_iterate   *Function*
      (gsl_multifit_fdfsolver * *s*)

These functions perform a single iteration of the solver *s*. If the iteration encounters an unexpected problem then an error code will be returned. The solver maintains a current estimate of the best-fit parameters at all times.

The solver struct *s* contains the following entries, which can be used to track the progress of the solution:

gsl_vector * x
> The current position.

gsl_vector * f
> The function value at the current position.

gsl_vector * dx
> The difference between the current position and the previous position, i.e. the last step, taken as a vector.

gsl_matrix * J
> The Jacobian matrix at the current position (for the gsl_multifit_fdfsolver struct only)

The best-fit information also can be accessed with the following auxiliary functions,

gsl_vector * gsl_multifit_fsolver_position (const   *Function*
      gsl_multifit_fsolver * *s*)
gsl_vector * gsl_multifit_fdfsolver_position (const   *Function*
      gsl_multifit_fdfsolver * *s*)

These functions return the current position (i.e. best-fit parameters) s->x of the solver *s*.

37.5 Search Stopping Parameters

A minimization procedure should stop when one of the following conditions is true:

- A minimum has been found to within the user-specified precision.
- A user-specified maximum number of iterations has been reached.
- An error has occurred.

The handling of these conditions is under user control. The functions below allow the user to test the current estimate of the best-fit parameters in several standard ways.

int gsl_multifit_test_delta (const gsl_vector * dx,   Function
        const gsl_vector * x, double epsabs, double epsrel)
This function tests for the convergence of the sequence by comparing the last step dx with the absolute error epsabs and relative error epsrel to the current position x. The test returns GSL_SUCCESS if the following condition is achieved,

$$|dx_i| < epsabs + epsrel\,|x_i|$$

for each component of x and returns GSL_CONTINUE otherwise.

int gsl_multifit_test_gradient (const gsl_vector * g,   Function
        double epsabs)
This function tests the residual gradient g against the absolute error bound epsabs. Mathematically, the gradient should be exactly zero at the minimum. The test returns GSL_SUCCESS if the following condition is achieved,

$$\sum_i |g_i| < epsabs$$

and returns GSL_CONTINUE otherwise. This criterion is suitable for situations where the precise location of the minimum, x, is unimportant provided a value can be found where the gradient is small enough.

int gsl_multifit_gradient (const gsl_matrix * J, const   Function
        gsl_vector * f, gsl_vector * g)
This function computes the gradient g of $\Phi(x) = (1/2)||F(x)||^2$ from the Jacobian matrix J and the function values f, using the formula $g = J^T f$.

37.6 Minimization Algorithms using Derivatives

The minimization algorithms described in this section make use of both the function and its derivative. They require an initial guess for the location of the minimum. There is no absolute guarantee of convergence—the function must be suitable for this technique and the initial guess must be sufficiently close to the minimum for it to work.

`gsl_multifit_fdfsolver_lmsder`   Derivative Solver

This is a robust and efficient version of the Levenberg-Marquardt algorithm as implemented in the scaled LMDER routine in MINPACK. Minpack was written by Jorge J. Moré, Burton S. Garbow and Kenneth E. Hillstrom.

The algorithm uses a generalized trust region to keep each step under control. In order to be accepted a proposed new position x' must satisfy the condition $|D(x' - x)| < \delta$, where D is a diagonal scaling matrix and δ is the size of the trust region. The components of D are computed internally, using the column norms of the Jacobian to estimate the sensitivity of the residual to each component of x. This improves the behavior of the algorithm for badly scaled functions.

On each iteration the algorithm attempts to minimize the linear system $|F + Jp|$ subject to the constraint $|Dp| < \Delta$. The solution to this constrained linear system is found using the Levenberg-Marquardt method.

The proposed step is now tested by evaluating the function at the resulting point, x'. If the step reduces the norm of the function sufficiently, and follows the predicted behavior of the function within the trust region, then it is accepted and the size of the trust region is increased. If the proposed step fails to improve the solution, or differs significantly from the expected behavior within the trust region, then the size of the trust region is decreased and another trial step is computed.

The algorithm also monitors the progress of the solution and returns an error if the changes in the solution are smaller than the machine precision. The possible error codes are,

GSL_ETOLF   the decrease in the function falls below machine precision

GSL_ETOLX   the change in the position vector falls below machine precision

GSL_ETOLG   the norm of the gradient, relative to the norm of the function, falls below machine precision

These error codes indicate that further iterations will be unlikely to change the solution from its current value. If the algorithm does not make any progress at all, check that the Jacobian is correct—in particular, that its sign corresponds correctly to derivative of the residual function.

gsl_multifit_fdfsolver_lmder   Derivative Solver
This is an unscaled version of the LMDER algorithm. The elements of the diagonal scaling matrix D are set to 1. This algorithm may be useful in circumstances where the scaled version of LMDER converges too slowly, or the function is already scaled appropriately.

37.7 Minimization Algorithms without Derivatives

There are no algorithms implemented in this section at the moment.

37.8 Computing the covariance matrix of best fit parameters

int gsl_multifit_covar (const gsl_matrix * J, double   Function
          epsrel, gsl_matrix * covar)
This function uses the Jacobian matrix J to compute the covariance matrix of the best-fit parameters. The covariance matrix is stored in covar on output. The parameter epsrel is used to remove linear-dependent columns when J is rank deficient.

The covariance matrix is given by,

$$C = (J^T J)^{-1}$$

and is computed by QR decomposition of J with column-pivoting. Any columns of R which satisfy

$$|R_{kk}| \leq epsrel|R_{11}|$$

are considered linearly-dependent and are excluded from the covariance matrix (the corresponding rows and columns of the covariance matrix are set to zero).

If the minimization uses the weighted least-squares function $f_i = (Y(x, t_i) - y_i)/\sigma_i$ then the covariance matrix above gives the statistical error on the best-fit parameters resulting from the gaussian errors σ_i on the underlying data y_i. This can be verified from the relation $\delta f = J\delta c$ and the fact that the fluctuations in f from the data y_i are normalized by σ_i and so satisfy $\langle \delta f \delta f^T \rangle = I$.

For an unweighted least-squares function, $f_i = (Y(x, t_i) - y_i)$, the covariance matrix above should be multiplied by the variance of the residuals about the best-fit $\sigma^2 = \sum (Y(x, t_i) - y_i)^2 / (n - p)$ to give the variance-covariance matrix $\sigma^2 C$. This estimates the statistical error on the best-fit parameters from the scatter of the underlying data.

For more information about covariance matrices see Section 36.1 [Fitting Overview], page 479.

37.9 Holding parameters constant

The MINPACK algorithms do not provide direct support for holding parameters constant (also known as *freezing* parameters). Models with different choices of parameters have to be supplied as separate implementations.

Alternatively, it is possible to create function and derivative routines where the parameter values are chosen dynamically, via a user-defined mapping of indices. In this case it is necessary to distinguish between the parameters of the model (both fixed and varying parameters) and the parameters of the minimization (the varying parameters). The minimization is carried out only for the reduced problem of the varying parameters, considered as a single vector x. This is mapped into the full model inside the user-supplied function and derivative calculations.

The index mapping can be passed to the functions f, df and fdf via the params argument, along with the data to be fitted, in a struct. The varying model parameters should then be updated from the algorithm-supplied trial vector x on each function or derivative call, the other parameters being left unchanged from their selected initial values. Note that the Jacobian matrix also has reduced dimensions so the derivatives must be computed with respect to the minimization parameters x rather than the full set of model parameters. The second example program in the following section demonstrates this technique.

37.10 Examples

The following example program fits a weighted exponential model with background $Y = A \exp(-\lambda t) + b$ to experimental data, (t_i, y_i, σ_i). The first part of the program sets up the functions expb_f and expb_df to compute the residual vector for the model and the corresponding Jacobian. The residual vector is given by,

$$f_i = ((A \exp(-\lambda t_i) + b) - y_i)/\sigma_i$$

where we have chosen uniform time steps $t_i = i$ in the program below. The Jacobian matrix J is the derivative of the residual functions with respect to the three parameters (A, λ, b). It is given by,

$$J_{ij} = \frac{\partial f_i}{\partial x_j}$$

where $x_0 = A$, $x_1 = \lambda$ and $x_2 = b$.

```
/* expfit.c -- compute residual for exponential
   +background model */

struct data {
  size_t n;
  double * y;
  double * sigma;
};

int
expb_f (const gsl_vector * x, void *data,
        gsl_vector * f)
{
  size_t n = ((struct data *)data)->n;
  double *y = ((struct data *)data)->y;
  double *sigma = ((struct data *) data)->sigma;

  double A = gsl_vector_get (x, 0);
  double lambda = gsl_vector_get (x, 1);
  double b = gsl_vector_get (x, 2);

  size_t i;

  for (i = 0; i < n; i++)
    {
      /* Model Yi = A * exp(-lambda * i) + b */
      double t = i;
      double Yi = A * exp (-lambda * t) + b;
      gsl_vector_set (f, i, (Yi - y[i])/sigma[i]);
    }

  return GSL_SUCCESS;
}

int
expb_df (const gsl_vector * x, void *data,
```

```
                gsl_matrix * J)
     {
       size_t n = ((struct data *)data)->n;
       double *sigma = ((struct data *) data)->sigma;

       double A = gsl_vector_get (x, 0);
       double lambda = gsl_vector_get (x, 1);

       size_t i;

       for (i = 0; i < n; i++)
         {
           /* Jacobian matrix J(i,j) = dfi / dxj, */
           /* where fi = (Yi - yi)/sigma[i],      */
           /*        Yi = A * exp(-lambda * i) + b  */
           /* and the xj are the parameters (A,lambda,b) */
           double t = i;
           double s = sigma[i];
           double e = exp(-lambda * t);
           gsl_matrix_set (J, i, 0, e/s);
           gsl_matrix_set (J, i, 1, -t * A * e/s);
           gsl_matrix_set (J, i, 2, 1/s);
         }
       return GSL_SUCCESS;
     }

     int
     expb_fdf (const gsl_vector * x, void *data,
               gsl_vector * f, gsl_matrix * J)
     {
       expb_f (x, data, f);
       expb_df (x, data, J);

       return GSL_SUCCESS;
     }
```

The main part of the program sets up a Levenberg-Marquardt solver and some simulated random data. The data uses the known parameters (1.0, 5.0, 0.1) combined with gaussian noise (standard deviation = 0.1) over a range of 40 timesteps. The initial guess for the parameters is chosen as (0.0, 1.0, 0.0).

```
#include <stdlib.h>
#include <stdio.h>
#include <gsl/gsl_rng.h>
#include <gsl/gsl_randist.h>
#include <gsl/gsl_vector.h>
#include <gsl/gsl_blas.h>
#include <gsl/gsl_multifit_nlin.h>

#include "expfit.c"

#define N 40

void print_state (size_t iter, gsl_multifit_fdfsolver * s);

int
main (void)
{
  const gsl_multifit_fdfsolver_type *T;
  gsl_multifit_fdfsolver *s;

  int status;
  size_t i, iter = 0;

  const size_t n = N;
  const size_t p = 3;

  gsl_matrix *covar = gsl_matrix_alloc (p, p);
  double y[N], sigma[N];
  struct data d = { n, y, sigma};
  gsl_multifit_function_fdf f;
  double x_init[3] = { 1.0, 0.0, 0.0 };
  gsl_vector_view x = gsl_vector_view_array (x_init, p);
  const gsl_rng_type * type;
  gsl_rng * r;

  gsl_rng_env_setup();

  type = gsl_rng_default;
  r = gsl_rng_alloc (type);

  f.f = &expb_f;
  f.df = &expb_df;
  f.fdf = &expb_fdf;
```

```
f.n = n;
f.p = p;
f.params = &d;

/* This is the data to be fitted */

for (i = 0; i < n; i++)
  {
    double t = i;
    y[i] = 1.0 + 5 * exp (-0.1 * t)
               + gsl_ran_gaussian (r, 0.1);
    sigma[i] = 0.1;
    printf ("data: %d %g %g\n", i, y[i], sigma[i]);
  };

T = gsl_multifit_fdfsolver_lmsder;
s = gsl_multifit_fdfsolver_alloc (T, n, p);
gsl_multifit_fdfsolver_set (s, &f, &x.vector);

print_state (iter, s);

do
  {
    iter++;
    status = gsl_multifit_fdfsolver_iterate (s);

    printf ("status = %s\n", gsl_strerror (status));

    print_state (iter, s);

    if (status)
      break;

    status = gsl_multifit_test_delta (s->dx, s->x,
                                      1e-4, 1e-4);
  }
while (status == GSL_CONTINUE && iter < 500);

gsl_multifit_covar (s->J, 0.0, covar);

#define FIT(i) gsl_vector_get(s->x, i)
#define ERR(i) sqrt(gsl_matrix_get(covar,i,i))
```

```
{
  double chi = gsl_blas_dnrm2(s->f);
  double dof = n - p;
  double c = GSL_MAX_DBL(1, chi / sqrt(dof));

  printf("chisq/dof = %g\n",  pow(chi, 2.0) / dof);

  printf ("A      = %.5f +/- %.5f\n", FIT(0), c*ERR(0));
  printf ("lambda = %.5f +/- %.5f\n", FIT(1), c*ERR(1));
  printf ("b      = %.5f +/- %.5f\n", FIT(2), c*ERR(2));
}

printf ("status = %s\n", gsl_strerror (status));

gsl_multifit_fdfsolver_free (s);
return 0;
}

void
print_state (size_t iter, gsl_multifit_fdfsolver * s)
{
  printf ("iter: %3u x = % 15.8f % 15.8f % 15.8f "
          "|f(x)| = %g\n",
          iter,
          gsl_vector_get (s->x, 0),
          gsl_vector_get (s->x, 1),
          gsl_vector_get (s->x, 2),
          gsl_blas_dnrm2 (s->f));
}
```

The iteration terminates when the change in x is smaller than 0.0001, as both an absolute and relative change. Here are the results of running the program:

```
iter: 0 x=1.00000000 0.00000000 0.00000000 |f(x)|=117.349
status=success
iter: 1 x=1.64659312 0.01814772 0.64659312 |f(x)|=76.4578
status=success
iter: 2 x=2.85876037 0.08092095 1.44796363 |f(x)|=37.6838
status=success
iter: 3 x=4.94899512 0.11942928 1.09457665 |f(x)|=9.58079
status=success
iter: 4 x=5.02175572 0.10287787 1.03388354 |f(x)|=5.63049
status=success
iter: 5 x=5.04520433 0.10405523 1.01941607 |f(x)|=5.44398
status=success
iter: 6 x=5.04535782 0.10404906 1.01924871 |f(x)|=5.44397
```

```
chisq/dof = 0.800996
A        = 5.04536 +/- 0.06028
lambda = 0.10405 +/- 0.00316
b        = 1.01925 +/- 0.03782
status = success
```

The approximate values of the parameters are found correctly, and the chi-squared value indicates a good fit (the chi-squared per degree of freedom is approximately 1). In this case the errors on the parameters can be estimated from the square roots of the diagonal elements of the covariance matrix.

If the chi-squared value shows a poor fit (i.e. $\chi^2/(n-p) \gg 1$) then the error estimates obtained from the covariance matrix will be too small. In the example program the error estimates are multiplied by $\sqrt{\chi^2/(n-p)}$ in this case, a common way of increasing the errors for a poor fit. Note that the use of an inappropriate model will cause even this scaled error to be underestimated if the assumption of gaussian errors breaks down.

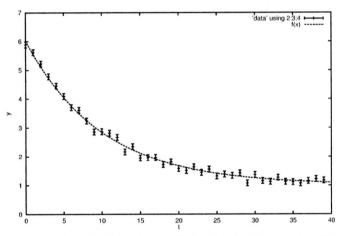

The next example shows how to hold model parameters constant, using an index mapping for the variables to be minimized over. We will fit the general rational approximation function,

$$Y(t) = \frac{t}{a_0 + a_1 t + a_2 t^2 + a_3 t^3 + a_4 t^4}$$

to $\tan(t)$ over twenty points in the range $[0, \pi/4]$, measuring the error by the unweighted sum of squared residuals $\chi^2 = \sum (Y(t_i) - y_i)^2$. Since $\tan(t)$ is an odd function we can choose to hold $a_1 = a_3 = 0$ so that $Y(-t) = -Y(t)$ and $a_0 = 1$ to fix the slope at the origin to the correct value, $Y'(t) = 1$. The parameters a_2 and a_4 will be the minimization parameters.

In the program below the integer array map selects the model parameters which are being minimized. The elements of this array are set as follows:

```
map[0] = 2;   /* x[0] corresponds to a_2 */
map[1] = 4;   /* x[1] corresponds to a_4 */
```

We perform the minimization in this reduced space with p=2. The array a[0..4] holds the full set of model parameters. The initial values of x[0] and x[1] are chosen as -0.1 and 0.0 respectively.

One feature of this program is that the function and derivative evaluations are performed in the single function rat_fdf. The individual routines for computing the function f and the Jacobian J make calls to rat_fdf with null pointer arguments for the quantities they do not require.

```
#include <stdlib.h>
#include <stdio.h>
#include <gsl/gsl_poly.h>
#include <gsl/gsl_vector.h>
#include <gsl/gsl_blas.h>
#include <gsl/gsl_multifit_nlin.h>

int rat_f (const gsl_vector * x, void *data, gsl_vector * f);
int rat_df (const gsl_vector * x, void *data, gsl_matrix * J);
int rat_fdf (const gsl_vector * x, void *data,
             gsl_vector * f, gsl_matrix * J);
void print_state (size_t iter, gsl_multifit_fdfsolver * s);

struct data
{
  size_t n, na;
  double *t, *y, *a;
  int *map;
};

int
rat_fdf (const gsl_vector * x, void *data, gsl_vector * f,
         gsl_matrix * J)
{
  struct data *p = (struct data *) data;
  size_t n = p->n;
  size_t i, j, k;

  /* Update full set of model parameters from x via map[] */

  for (j = 0; j < x->size; j++)
    {
      k = p->map[j];
      p->a[k] = gsl_vector_get (x, j);
```

```
          }

     for (i = 0; i < n; i++)
       {
         double ti = p->t[i], yi = p->y[i];
         double A = gsl_poly_eval (p->a, p->na, ti);
         double Yi = p->t[i] / A;

         /* Compute f_i = Yi-yi if required */

         if (f != NULL)
           {
             gsl_vector_set (f, i, Yi - yi);
           }

         /* Compute Jij = dY_i/dx_j if required */

         if (J != NULL)
           {
             for (j = 0; j < x->size; j++)
               {
                 k = p->map[j];
                 gsl_matrix_set (J, i, j, -Yi * pow (ti, k) / A);
               }
           }
       }

   return GSL_SUCCESS;
}

int
rat_f (const gsl_vector * x, void *data, gsl_vector * f)
{
  return rat_fdf (x, data, f, NULL);
}

int
rat_df (const gsl_vector * x, void *data, gsl_matrix * J)
{
  return rat_fdf (x, data, NULL, J);
}

int
main (void)
{
  const gsl_multifit_fdfsolver_type *T;
  gsl_multifit_fdfsolver *s;

  int status;
```

```
size_t i, iter = 0;
const size_t n = 20, na = 5;
double t[20], y[20], a[5];
const size_t p = 2;
int map[2];
double x_start[3];
gsl_multifit_function_fdf f;
struct data d;

d.n = n;
d.na = na;
d.t = t;
d.y = y;
d.a = a;
a[0] = 1.0; a[1] = 0; a[2] = 0; a[3] = 0; a[4] = 0;
d.map = map;
map[0] = 2; /* x[0] corresponds to a_2 */
map[1] = 4; /* x[1] corresponds to a_4 */

x_start[0] = -0.1;
x_start[1] = 0.0;

f.f = &rat_f;
f.df = &rat_df;
f.fdf = &rat_fdf;
f.n = n;
f.p = p;
f.params = &d;

/* Here is the data to be fitted: */

for (i = 0; i < n; i++)
  {
    t[i] = (0.25 * M_PI * i) / (n - 1.0);
    y[i] = tan (t[i]);
  };

T = gsl_multifit_fdfsolver_lmsder;
s = gsl_multifit_fdfsolver_alloc (T, n, p);

{
  gsl_vector_view x = gsl_vector_view_array (x_start, p);
  gsl_multifit_fdfsolver_set (s, &f, &x.vector);
}

print_state (iter, s);

do
  {
```

```
          iter++;
          status = gsl_multifit_fdfsolver_iterate (s);

          printf ("status = %s\n", gsl_strerror (status));
          print_state (iter, s);

          if (status)
            break;

          status = gsl_multifit_test_delta (s->dx, s->x,
                                            1e-4, 1e-4);
        }
      while (status == GSL_CONTINUE && iter < 500);

      printf ("status = %s\n", gsl_strerror (status));
      gsl_multifit_fdfsolver_free (s);

      return 0;
    }

    void
    print_state (size_t iter, gsl_multifit_fdfsolver * s)
    {
      printf ("iter: %u x= %+10.8f %+10.8f "
              "|f(x)|= %3.2e\n",
              iter,
              gsl_vector_get (s->x, 0),
              gsl_vector_get (s->x, 1), gsl_blas_dnrm2 (s->f));
    }
```

The output of running the program is shown below:

```
iter: 0 x= -0.10000000 +0.00000000 |f(x)|= 2.74e-01
status = success
iter: 1 x= -0.32450572 -0.11506345 |f(x)|= 5.37e-02
status = success
iter: 2 x= -0.33114513 -0.02980024 |f(x)|= 1.65e-03
status = success
iter: 3 x= -0.33286846 -0.02433166 |f(x)|= 4.25e-05
status = success
iter: 4 x= -0.33287116 -0.02432423 |f(x)|= 4.25e-05
status = success
```

The minimization converges on the solution $Y(t) = t/(1 - 0.33\,t^2 - 0.024\,t^4)$. This is in good agreement with the analytic Taylor series for $t/\tan(t)$,

$$t/\tan(t) = 1 - t^2/3 - t^4/45 - \ldots$$
$$= 1 - 0.33333\,t^2 - 0.022222\,t^4 + O(t^6)$$

37.11 References and Further Reading

The MINPACK algorithm is described in the following article,

J.J. Moré, *The Levenberg-Marquardt Algorithm: Implementation and Theory*, Lecture Notes in Mathematics, v630 (1978), ed G. Watson.

The following paper is also relevant to the algorithms described in this section,

J.J. Moré, B.S. Garbow, K.E. Hillstrom, "Testing Unconstrained Optimization Software", ACM Transactions on Mathematical Software, Vol 7, No 1 (1981), p 17–41.

38 Physical Constants

This chapter describes macros for the values of physical constants, such as the speed of light, c, and gravitational constant, G. The values are available in different unit systems, including the standard MKSA system (meters, kilograms, seconds, amperes) and the CGSM system (centimeters, grams, seconds, magnetic gauss), which is commonly used in Astronomy.

The definitions of constants in the MKSA system are available in the file 'gsl_const_mksa.h'. The constants in the CGSM system are defined in 'gsl_const_cgsm.h'. Dimensionless constants, such as the fine structure constant, which are pure numbers are defined in 'gsl_const_num.h'.

The full list of constants is described briefly below. Consult the header files themselves for the values of the constants used in the library.

38.1 Fundamental Constants

GSL_CONST_MKSA_SPEED_OF_LIGHT
> The speed of light in vacuum, c.

GSL_CONST_MKSA_VACUUM_PERMEABILITY
> The permeability of free space, μ_0. This constant is defined in the MKSA system only.

GSL_CONST_MKSA_VACUUM_PERMITTIVITY
> The permittivity of free space, ϵ_0. This constant is defined in the MKSA system only.

GSL_CONST_MKSA_PLANCKS_CONSTANT_H
> Planck's constant, h.

GSL_CONST_MKSA_PLANCKS_CONSTANT_HBAR
> Planck's constant divided by 2π, $\hbar$.

GSL_CONST_NUM_AVOGADRO
> Avogadro's number, N_a.

GSL_CONST_MKSA_FARADAY
> The molar charge of 1 Faraday.

GSL_CONST_MKSA_BOLTZMANN
> The Boltzmann constant, k.

GSL_CONST_MKSA_MOLAR_GAS
> The molar gas constant, R_0.

GSL_CONST_MKSA_STANDARD_GAS_VOLUME
> The standard gas volume, V_0.

GSL_CONST_MKSA_STEFAN_BOLTZMANN_CONSTANT
> The Stefan-Boltzmann radiation constant, σ.

GSL_CONST_MKSA_GAUSS
> The magnetic field of 1 Gauss.

38.2 Astronomy and Astrophysics

GSL_CONST_MKSA_ASTRONOMICAL_UNIT
> The length of 1 astronomical unit (mean earth-sun distance), au.

GSL_CONST_MKSA_GRAVITATIONAL_CONSTANT
> The gravitational constant, G.

GSL_CONST_MKSA_LIGHT_YEAR
> The distance of 1 light-year, ly.

GSL_CONST_MKSA_PARSEC
> The distance of 1 parsec, pc.

GSL_CONST_MKSA_GRAV_ACCEL
> The standard gravitational acceleration on Earth, g.

GSL_CONST_MKSA_SOLAR_MASS
> The mass of the Sun.

38.3 Atomic and Nuclear Physics

GSL_CONST_MKSA_ELECTRON_CHARGE
> The charge of the electron, e.

GSL_CONST_MKSA_ELECTRON_VOLT
> The energy of 1 electron volt, eV.

GSL_CONST_MKSA_UNIFIED_ATOMIC_MASS
> The unified atomic mass, amu.

GSL_CONST_MKSA_MASS_ELECTRON
> The mass of the electron, m_e.

GSL_CONST_MKSA_MASS_MUON
> The mass of the muon, m_μ.

GSL_CONST_MKSA_MASS_PROTON
> The mass of the proton, m_p.

GSL_CONST_MKSA_MASS_NEUTRON
>   The mass of the neutron, m_n.

GSL_CONST_NUM_FINE_STRUCTURE
>   The electromagnetic fine structure constant α.

GSL_CONST_MKSA_RYDBERG
>   The Rydberg constant, Ry, in units of energy. This is related
>   to the Rydberg inverse wavelength R by $Ry = hcR$.

GSL_CONST_MKSA_BOHR_RADIUS
>   The Bohr radius, a_0.

GSL_CONST_MKSA_ANGSTROM
>   The length of 1 angstrom.

GSL_CONST_MKSA_BARN
>   The area of 1 barn.

GSL_CONST_MKSA_BOHR_MAGNETON
>   The Bohr Magneton, μ_B.

GSL_CONST_MKSA_NUCLEAR_MAGNETON
>   The Nuclear Magneton, μ_N.

GSL_CONST_MKSA_ELECTRON_MAGNETIC_MOMENT
>   The absolute value of the magnetic moment of the electron,
> μ_e. The physical magnetic moment of the electron is nega-
>   tive.

GSL_CONST_MKSA_PROTON_MAGNETIC_MOMENT
>   The magnetic moment of the proton, μ_p.

GSL_CONST_MKSA_THOMSON_CROSS_SECTION
>   The Thomson cross section, σ_T.

GSL_CONST_MKSA_DEBYE
>   The electric dipole moment of 1 Debye, D.

38.4 Measurement of Time

GSL_CONST_MKSA_MINUTE
>   The number of seconds in 1 minute.

GSL_CONST_MKSA_HOUR
>   The number of seconds in 1 hour.

GSL_CONST_MKSA_DAY
>   The number of seconds in 1 day.

GSL_CONST_MKSA_WEEK
>   The number of seconds in 1 week.

38.5 Imperial Units

GSL_CONST_MKSA_INCH
> The length of 1 inch.

GSL_CONST_MKSA_FOOT
> The length of 1 foot.

GSL_CONST_MKSA_YARD
> The length of 1 yard.

GSL_CONST_MKSA_MILE
> The length of 1 mile.

GSL_CONST_MKSA_MIL
> The length of 1 mil (1/1000th of an inch).

38.6 Speed and Nautical Units

GSL_CONST_MKSA_KILOMETERS_PER_HOUR
> The speed of 1 kilometer per hour.

GSL_CONST_MKSA_MILES_PER_HOUR
> The speed of 1 mile per hour.

GSL_CONST_MKSA_NAUTICAL_MILE
> The length of 1 nautical mile.

GSL_CONST_MKSA_FATHOM
> The length of 1 fathom.

GSL_CONST_MKSA_KNOT
> The speed of 1 knot.

38.7 Printers Units

GSL_CONST_MKSA_POINT
> The length of 1 printer's point (1/72 inch).

GSL_CONST_MKSA_TEXPOINT
> The length of 1 TeX point (1/72.27 inch).

38.8 Volume, Area and Length

GSL_CONST_MKSA_MICRON
> The length of 1 micron.

GSL_CONST_MKSA_HECTARE
> The area of 1 hectare.

GSL_CONST_MKSA_ACRE
> The area of 1 acre.

GSL_CONST_MKSA_LITER
> The volume of 1 liter.

GSL_CONST_MKSA_US_GALLON
> The volume of 1 US gallon.

GSL_CONST_MKSA_CANADIAN_GALLON
> The volume of 1 Canadian gallon.

GSL_CONST_MKSA_UK_GALLON
> The volume of 1 UK gallon.

38.9 Mass and Weight

GSL_CONST_MKSA_POUND_MASS
> The mass of 1 pound.

GSL_CONST_MKSA_OUNCE_MASS
> The mass of 1 ounce.

GSL_CONST_MKSA_TON
> The mass of 1 ton.

GSL_CONST_MKSA_METRIC_TON
> The mass of 1 metric ton (1000 kg).

GSL_CONST_MKSA_UK_TON
> The mass of 1 UK ton.

GSL_CONST_MKSA_GRAM_FORCE
> The force of 1 gram weight.

GSL_CONST_MKSA_POUND_FORCE
> The force of 1 pound weight.

GSL_CONST_MKSA_KILOPOUND_FORCE
> The force of 1 kilopound weight.

GSL_CONST_MKSA_POUNDAL
> The force of 1 poundal.

38.10 Thermal Energy and Power

GSL_CONST_MKSA_CALORIE
>The energy of 1 calorie.

GSL_CONST_MKSA_BTU
>The energy of 1 British Thermal Unit, *btu*.

GSL_CONST_MKSA_THERM
>The energy of 1 Therm.

GSL_CONST_MKSA_HORSEPOWER
>The power of 1 horsepower.

38.11 Pressure

GSL_CONST_MKSA_BAR
>The pressure of 1 bar.

GSL_CONST_MKSA_STD_ATMOSPHERE
>The pressure of 1 standard atmosphere.

GSL_CONST_MKSA_TORR
>The pressure of 1 torr.

GSL_CONST_MKSA_METER_OF_MERCURY
>The pressure of 1 meter of mercury.

GSL_CONST_MKSA_INCH_OF_MERCURY
>The pressure of 1 inch of mercury.

GSL_CONST_MKSA_INCH_OF_WATER
>The pressure of 1 inch of water.

GSL_CONST_MKSA_PSI
>The pressure of 1 pound per square inch.

38.12 Viscosity

GSL_CONST_MKSA_POISE
>The dynamic viscosity of 1 poise.

GSL_CONST_MKSA_STOKES
>The kinematic viscosity of 1 stokes.

38.13 Light and Illumination

GSL_CONST_MKSA_STILB
>   The luminance of 1 stilb.

GSL_CONST_MKSA_LUMEN
>   The luminous flux of 1 lumen.

GSL_CONST_MKSA_LUX
>   The illuminance of 1 lux.

GSL_CONST_MKSA_PHOT
>   The illuminance of 1 phot.

GSL_CONST_MKSA_FOOTCANDLE
>   The illuminance of 1 footcandle.

GSL_CONST_MKSA_LAMBERT
>   The luminance of 1 lambert.

GSL_CONST_MKSA_FOOTLAMBERT
>   The luminance of 1 footlambert.

38.14 Radioactivity

GSL_CONST_MKSA_CURIE
>   The activity of 1 curie.

GSL_CONST_MKSA_ROENTGEN
>   The exposure of 1 roentgen.

GSL_CONST_MKSA_RAD
>   The absorbed dose of 1 rad.

38.15 Force and Energy

GSL_CONST_MKSA_NEWTON
>   The SI unit of force, 1 Newton.

GSL_CONST_MKSA_DYNE
>   The force of 1 Dyne = 10^{-5} Newton.

GSL_CONST_MKSA_JOULE
>   The SI unit of energy, 1 Joule.

GSL_CONST_MKSA_ERG
>   The energy 1 erg = 10^{-7} Joule.

38.16 Prefixes

These constants are dimensionless scaling factors.

GSL_CONST_NUM_YOTTA
10^{24}

GSL_CONST_NUM_ZETTA
10^{21}

GSL_CONST_NUM_EXA
10^{18}

GSL_CONST_NUM_PETA
10^{15}

GSL_CONST_NUM_TERA
10^{12}

GSL_CONST_NUM_GIGA
10^{9}

GSL_CONST_NUM_MEGA
10^{6}

GSL_CONST_NUM_KILO
10^{3}

GSL_CONST_NUM_MILLI
10^{-3}

GSL_CONST_NUM_MICRO
10^{-6}

GSL_CONST_NUM_NANO
10^{-9}

GSL_CONST_NUM_PICO
10^{-12}

GSL_CONST_NUM_FEMTO
10^{-15}

GSL_CONST_NUM_ATTO
10^{-18}

GSL_CONST_NUM_ZEPTO
10^{-21}

GSL_CONST_NUM_YOCTO
10^{-24}

38.17 Examples

The following program demonstrates the use of the physical constants in a calculation. In this case, the goal is to calculate the range of light-travel times from Earth to Mars.

The required data is the average distance of each planet from the Sun in astronomical units (the eccentricities and inclinations of the orbits will be neglected for the purposes of this calculation). The average radius of the orbit of Mars is 1.52 astronomical units, and for the orbit of Earth it is 1 astronomical unit (by definition). These values are combined with the MKSA values of the constants for the speed of light and the length of an astronomical unit to produce a result for the shortest and longest light-travel times in seconds. The figures are converted into minutes before being displayed.

```
#include <stdio.h>
#include <gsl/gsl_const_mksa.h>

int
main (void)
{
  double c  = GSL_CONST_MKSA_SPEED_OF_LIGHT;
  double au = GSL_CONST_MKSA_ASTRONOMICAL_UNIT;
  double minutes = GSL_CONST_MKSA_MINUTE;

  /* distance stored in meters */
  double r_earth = 1.00 * au;
  double r_mars  = 1.52 * au;

  double t_min, t_max;

  t_min = (r_mars - r_earth) / c;
  t_max = (r_mars + r_earth) / c;

  printf ("light travel time from Earth to Mars:\n");
  printf ("minimum = %.1f minutes\n", t_min / minutes);
  printf ("maximum = %.1f minutes\n", t_max / minutes);

  return 0;
}
```

Here is the output from the program,

```
light travel time from Earth to Mars:
minimum = 4.3 minutes
maximum = 21.0 minutes
```

38.18 References and Further Reading

The authoritative sources for physical constants are the 2002 CODATA recommended values, published in the articles below. Further information on the values of physical constants is also available from the cited articles and the NIST website.

Journal of Physical and Chemical Reference Data, 28(6), 1713-1852, 1999

Reviews of Modern Physics, 72(2), 351-495, 2000

http://www.physics.nist.gov/cuu/Constants/index.html

http://physics.nist.gov/Pubs/SP811/appenB9.html

39 IEEE floating-point arithmetic

This chapter describes functions for examining the representation of floating point numbers and controlling the floating point environment of your program. The functions described in this chapter are declared in the header file 'gsl_ieee_utils.h'.

39.1 Representation of floating point numbers

The IEEE Standard for Binary Floating-Point Arithmetic defines binary formats for single and double precision numbers. Each number is composed of three parts: a *sign bit* (s), an *exponent* (E) and a *fraction* (f). The numerical value of the combination (s, E, f) is given by the following formula,

$$(-1)^s(1 \cdot fffff\ldots)2^E$$

The sign bit is either zero or one. The exponent ranges from a minimum value E_{min} to a maximum value E_{max} depending on the precision. The exponent is converted to an unsigned number e, known as the *biased exponent*, for storage by adding a *bias* parameter, $e = E + bias$. The sequence $fffff\ldots$ represents the digits of the binary fraction f. The binary digits are stored in *normalized form*, by adjusting the exponent to give a leading digit of 1. Since the leading digit is always 1 for normalized numbers it is assumed implicitly and does not have to be stored. Numbers smaller than $2^{E_{min}}$ are be stored in *denormalized form* with a leading zero,

$$(-1)^s(0 \cdot fffff\ldots)2^{E_{min}}$$

This allows gradual underflow down to $2^{E_{min}-p}$ for p bits of precision. A zero is encoded with the special exponent of $2^{E_{min}-1}$ and infinities with the exponent of $2^{E_{max}+1}$.

The format for single precision numbers uses 32 bits divided in the following way,

```
seeeeeeeefffffffffffffffffffffff
```

```
s = sign bit, 1 bit
e = exponent, 8 bits   (E_min=-126, E_max=127, bias=127)
f = fraction, 23 bits
```

The format for double precision numbers uses 64 bits divided in the following way,

```
seeeeeeeeeeeeffffffffffffffffffffffffffffffffffffffffffffffffffffffff
```

```
s = sign bit, 1 bit
e = exponent, 11 bits   (E_min=-1022, E_max=1023, bias=1023)
f = fraction, 52 bits
```

It is often useful to be able to investigate the behavior of a calculation at the bit-level and the library provides functions for printing the IEEE representations in a human-readable form.

void gsl_ieee_fprintf_float (FILE * *stream*, const float   *Function*
        * *x*)

void gsl_ieee_fprintf_double (FILE * *stream*, const   *Function*
        double * *x*)

     These functions output a formatted version of the IEEE floating-point number pointed to by *x* to the stream *stream*. A pointer is used to pass the number indirectly, to avoid any undesired promotion from float to double. The output takes one of the following forms,

     NaN   the Not-a-Number symbol

     Inf, -Inf   positive or negative infinity

     1.fffff...*2^E, -1.fffff...*2^E
                a normalized floating point number

     0.fffff...*2^E, -0.fffff...*2^E
                a denormalized floating point number

     0, -0   positive or negative zero

     The output can be used directly in GNU Emacs Calc mode by preceding it with 2# to indicate binary. The GNU C Library also supports a similar printf %A specifier which displays IEEE floating-point numbers in hexadecimal format.

void gsl_ieee_printf_float (const float * *x*)   *Function*

void gsl_ieee_printf_double (const double * *x*)   *Function*

     These functions output a formatted version of the IEEE floating-point number pointed to by *x* to the stream stdout.

The following program demonstrates the use of the functions by printing the single and double precision representations of the fraction 1/3. For comparison the representation of the value promoted from single to double precision is also printed.

```
#include <stdio.h>
#include <gsl/gsl_ieee_utils.h>

int
main (void)
{
  float f = 1.0/3.0;
  double d = 1.0/3.0;

  double fd = f; /* promote from float to double */

  printf (" f="); gsl_ieee_printf_float(&f);
  printf ("\n");

  printf ("fd="); gsl_ieee_printf_double(&fd);
  printf ("\n");

  printf (" d="); gsl_ieee_printf_double(&d);
  printf ("\n");

  return 0;
}
```

The binary representation of $1/3$ is $0.01010101....$ The output below shows that the IEEE format normalizes this fraction to give a leading digit of 1,

```
f= 1.01010101010101010101011*2^-2
fd= 1.0101010101010101010101100000000000000000000000000000*2^-2
d= 1.0101010101010101010101010101010101010101010101010101*2^-2
```

The output also shows that a single-precision number is promoted to double-precision by adding zeros in the binary representation.

39.2 Setting up your IEEE environment

The IEEE standard defines several *modes* for controlling the behavior of floating point operations. These modes specify the important properties of computer arithmetic: the direction used for rounding (e.g. whether numbers should be rounded up, down or to the nearest number), the rounding precision and how the program should handle arithmetic exceptions, such as division by zero.

Many of these features can now be controlled via functions in the C standard library such as fpsetround, which should be used whenever they are available. Unfortunately in the past there has been no universal API for controlling their behavior—each system has had its own low-level way of accessing them. To help you write portable programs GSL allows you to specify modes in a platform-independent way using the environment variable GSL_IEEE_MODE. The library then takes care of all the necessary machine-specific initializations for you when you call the function gsl_ieee_env_setup.

void gsl_ieee_env_setup ()   Function
This function reads the environment variable GSL_IEEE_MODE and attempts to set up the corresponding specified IEEE modes. The environment variable should be a list of keywords, separated by commas, like this,

GSL_IEEE_MODE = "keyword,keyword,..."

where keyword is one of the following mode-names,

single-precision

double-precision

extended-precision

round-to-nearest

round-down

round-up

round-to-zero

mask-all

mask-invalid

mask-denormalized

mask-division-by-zero

mask-overflow

mask-underflow

trap-inexact

trap-common

If GSL_IEEE_MODE is empty or undefined then the function returns immediately and no attempt is made to change the system's IEEE mode. When the modes from GSL_IEEE_MODE are turned on the function prints a short message showing the new settings to remind you that the results of the program will be affected.

If the requested modes are not supported by the platform being used then the function calls the error handler and returns an error code of GSL_EUNSUP.

When options are specified using this method, the resulting mode is based on a default setting of the highest available precision (double precision or extended precision, depending on the platform) in round-to-nearest mode, with all exceptions enabled apart from the INEXACT exception. The INEXACT exception is generated whenever rounding occurs, so it must generally be disabled in scientific calculations. All other floating-point exceptions are enabled by default, including underflows and the use of denormalized numbers, for safety. They can be disabled with the individual mask- settings or together using mask-all.

The following adjusted combination of modes is convenient for many purposes,

```
GSL_IEEE_MODE="double-precision,"\
              "mask-underflow,"\
              "mask-denormalized"
```

This choice ignores any errors relating to small numbers (either denormalized, or underflowing to zero) but traps overflows, division by zero and invalid operations.

To clear and test exception flags in your own program, use the functions feclearexcept and fetestexcept declared in 'fenv.h' (part of the C99 standard).

To demonstrate the effects of different rounding modes consider the following program which computes e, the base of natural logarithms, by summing a rapidly-decreasing series,

$$e = 1 + \frac{1}{2!} + \frac{1}{3!} + \frac{1}{4!} + \ldots = 2.71828182846\ldots$$

```
#include <stdio.h>
#include <gsl/gsl_math.h>
#include <gsl/gsl_ieee_utils.h>

int
main (void)
{
  double x = 1, oldsum = 0, sum = 0;
  int i = 0;

  gsl_ieee_env_setup (); /* read GSL_IEEE_MODE */

  do
    {
      i++;

      oldsum = sum;
      sum += x;
      x = x / i;
```

```
printf ("i=%2d sum=%.18f error=%g\n",
        i, sum, sum - M_E);

    if (i > 30)
        break;
}
while (sum != oldsum);

    return 0;
}
```

Here are the results of running the program in round-to-nearest mode. This is the IEEE default so it isn't really necessary to specify it here,

```
$ GSL_IEEE_MODE="round-to-nearest" ./a.out
i= 1 sum=1.000000000000000000 error=-1.71828
i= 2 sum=2.000000000000000000 error=-0.718282
....
i=18 sum=2.718281828459045535 error=4.44089e-16
i=19 sum=2.718281828459045535 error=4.44089e-16
```

After nineteen terms the sum converges to within 4×10^{-16} of the correct value. If we now change the rounding mode to round-down the final result is less accurate,

```
$ GSL_IEEE_MODE="round-down" ./a.out
i= 1 sum=1.000000000000000000 error=-1.71828
....
i=19 sum=2.718281828459041094 error=-3.9968e-15
```

The result is about 4×10^{-15} below the correct value, an order of magnitude worse than the result obtained in the round-to-nearest mode.

If we change to rounding mode to round-up then the series no longer converges (the reason is that when we add each term to the sum the final result is always rounded up. This is guaranteed to increase the sum by at least one tick on each iteration). To avoid this problem we would need to use a safer convergence criterion, such as while (fabs(sum - oldsum) > epsilon), with a suitably chosen value of epsilon.

Finally we can see the effect of computing the sum using single-precision rounding, in the default round-to-nearest mode. In this case the program thinks it is still using double precision numbers but the CPU rounds the result of each floating point operation to single-precision accuracy. This simulates the effect of writing the program using single-precision float variables instead of double variables. The iteration stops after about half the number of iterations and the final result is much less accurate,

```
$ GSL_IEEE_MODE="single-precision" ./a.out
. . . .
i=12 sum=2.718281984329223633 error=1.5587e-07
```

with an error of $O(10^{-7})$, which corresponds to single precision accuracy (about 1 part in 10^7). Continuing the iterations further does not decrease the error because all the subsequent results are rounded to the same value.

39.3 References and Further Reading

The reference for the IEEE standard is,

ANSI/IEEE Std 754-1985, IEEE Standard for Binary Floating-Point Arithmetic.

A more pedagogical introduction to the standard can be found in the following paper,

David Goldberg: What Every Computer Scientist Should Know About Floating-Point Arithmetic. *ACM Computing Surveys*, Vol. 23, No. 1 (March 1991), pages 5–48.

Corrigendum: *ACM Computing Surveys*, Vol. 23, No. 3 (September 1991), page 413. and see also the sections by B. A. Wichmann and Charles B. Dunham in Surveyor's Forum: "What Every Computer Scientist Should Know About Floating-Point Arithmetic". *ACM Computing Surveys*, Vol. 24, No. 3 (September 1992), page 319.

A detailed textbook on IEEE arithmetic and its practical use is available from SIAM Press,

Michael L. Overton, *Numerical Computing with IEEE Floating Point Arithmetic*, SIAM Press, ISBN 0898715717.

Appendix A Debugging Numerical Programs

This chapter describes some tips and tricks for debugging numerical programs which use GSL.

A.1 Using gdb

Any errors reported by the library are passed to the function gsl_error. By running your programs under gdb and setting a breakpoint in this function you can automatically catch any library errors. You can add a breakpoint for every session by putting

```
break gsl_error
```

into your '.gdbinit' file in the directory where your program is started.

If the breakpoint catches an error then you can use a backtrace (bt) to see the call-tree, and the arguments which possibly caused the error. By moving up into the calling function you can investigate the values of variables at that point. Here is an example from the program fft/test_trap, which contains the following line,

```
status = gsl_fft_complex_wavetable_alloc (0, &complex_wavetable);
```

The function gsl_fft_complex_wavetable_alloc takes the length of an FFT as its first argument. When this line is executed an error will be generated because the length of an FFT is not allowed to be zero.

To debug this problem we start gdb, using the file '.gdbinit' to define a breakpoint in gsl_error,

```
$ gdb test_trap
```

```
GDB is free software and you are welcome to distribute copies
of it under certain conditions; type "show copying" to see
the conditions.  There is absolutely no warranty for GDB;
type "show warranty" for details.  GDB 4.16 (i586-debian-linux),
Copyright 1996 Free Software Foundation, Inc.
```

```
Breakpoint 1 at 0x8050b1e: file error.c, line 14.
```

When we run the program this breakpoint catches the error and shows the reason for it.

```
(gdb) run
Starting program: test_trap

Breakpoint 1, gsl_error (reason=0x8052b0d
    "length n must be positive integer",
    file=0x8052b04 "c_init.c", line=108, gsl_errno=1)
```

```
        at error.c:14
14              if (gsl_error_handler)
```

The first argument of `gsl_error` is always a string describing the error. Now we can look at the backtrace to see what caused the problem,

```
(gdb) bt
#0  gsl_error (reason=0x8052b0d
    "length n must be positive integer",
    file=0x8052b04 "c_init.c", line=108, gsl_errno=1)
    at error.c:14
#1  0x8049376 in gsl_fft_complex_wavetable_alloc (n=0,
    wavetable=0xbffff778) at c_init.c:108
#2  0x8048a00 in main (argc=1, argv=0xbffff9bc)
    at test_trap.c:94
#3  0x80488be in ___crt_dummy__ ()
```

We can see that the error was generated in the function `gsl_fft_complex_wavetable_alloc` when it was called with an argument of $n=0$. The original call came from line 94 in the file 'test_trap.c'.

By moving up to the level of the original call we can find the line that caused the error,

```
(gdb) up
#1  0x8049376 in gsl_fft_complex_wavetable_alloc (n=0,
    wavetable=0xbffff778) at c_init.c:108
108     GSL_ERROR ("length n must be positive integer", GSL_EDOM);
(gdb) up
#2  0x8048a00 in main (argc=1, argv=0xbffff9bc)
    at test_trap.c:94
94      status = gsl_fft_complex_wavetable_alloc (0,
            &complex_wavetable);
```

Thus we have found the line that caused the problem. From this point we could also print out the values of other variables such as `complex_wavetable`.

A.2 Examining floating point registers

The contents of floating point registers can be examined using the command `info float` (on supported platforms).

```
(gdb) info float
        st0: 0xc4018b895aa17a945000  Valid Normal -7.838871e+308
        st1: 0x3ff9ea3f50e4d7275000  Valid Normal 0.0285946
        st2: 0x3fe790c64ce27dad4800  Valid Normal 6.7415931e-08
        st3: 0x3ffaa3ef0df6607d7800  Spec  Normal 0.0400229
        st4: 0x3c028000000000000000  Valid Normal 4.4501477e-308
        st5: 0x3ffef5412c22219d9000  Zero  Normal 0.9580257
        st6: 0x3fff8000000000000000  Valid Normal 1
        st7: 0xc4028b65a1f6d243c800  Valid Normal -1.566206e+309
      fctrl: 0x0272 53 bit; NEAR; mask DENOR UNDER LOS;
```

```
fstat: 0xb9ba flags 0001; top 7; excep DENOR OVERF UNDER LOS
 ftag: 0x3fff
  fip: 0x08048b5c
  fcs: 0x051a0023
fopoff: 0x08086820
fopsel: 0x002b
```

Individual registers can be examined using the variables $reg, where reg
is the register name.

```
(gdb) p $st1
$1 = 0.0285946445426121210347719
```

A.3 Handling floating point exceptions

It is possible to stop the program whenever a SIGFPE floating point
exception occurs. This can be useful for finding the cause of an unexpected infinity or NaN. The current handler settings can be shown with
the command info signal SIGFPE.

```
(gdb) info signal SIGFPE
Signal  Stop  Print  Pass to program Description
SIGFPE  Yes   Yes    Yes             Arithmetic exception
```

Unless the program uses a signal handler the default setting should be
changed so that SIGFPE is not passed to the program, as this would cause
it to exit. The command handle SIGFPE stop nopass prevents this.

```
(gdb) handle SIGFPE stop nopass
Signal  Stop  Print  Pass to program Description
SIGFPE  Yes   Yes    No              Arithmetic exception
```

Depending on the platform it may be necessary to instruct the kernel to
generate signals for floating point exceptions. For programs using GSL
this can be achieved using the GSL_IEEE_MODE environment variable in
conjunction with the function gsl_ieee_env_setup as described in see
Chapter 39 [IEEE floating-point arithmetic], page 521.

```
(gdb) set env GSL_IEEE_MODE=double-precision
```

A.4 GCC warning options for numerical programs

Writing reliable numerical programs in C requires great care. The following GCC warning options are recommended when compiling numerical programs:

```
gcc -ansi -pedantic -Werror -Wall -W
    -Wmissing-prototypes -Wstrict-prototypes
    -Wtraditional -Wconversion -Wshadow
    -Wpointer-arith -Wcast-qual -Wcast-align
    -Wwrite-strings -Wnested-externs
    -fshort-enums -fno-common -Dinline= -g -O2
```

For details of each option consult the manual *Using and Porting GCC*. The following table gives a brief explanation of what types of errors these options catch.

-ansi -pedantic
: Use ANSI C, and reject any non-ANSI extensions. These flags help in writing portable programs that will compile on other systems.

-Werror
: Consider warnings to be errors, so that compilation stops. This prevents warnings from scrolling off the top of the screen and being lost. You won't be able to compile the program until it is completely warning-free.

-Wall
: This turns on a set of warnings for common programming problems. You need -Wall, but it is not enough on its own.

-O2
: Turn on optimization. The warnings for uninitialized variables in -Wall rely on the optimizer to analyze the code. If there is no optimization then these warnings aren't generated.

-W
: This turns on some extra warnings not included in -Wall, such as missing return values and comparisons between signed and unsigned integers.

-Wmissing-prototypes -Wstrict-prototypes
: Warn if there are any missing or inconsistent prototypes. Without prototypes it is harder to detect problems with incorrect arguments.

-Wtraditional
: This warns about certain constructs that behave differently in traditional and ANSI C. Whether the traditional or ANSI interpretation is used might be unpredictable on other compilers.

-Wconversion
>   The main use of this option is to warn about conversions
>   from signed to unsigned integers. For example, unsigned
>   int x = -1. If you need to perform such a conversion you
>   can use an explicit cast.

-Wshadow   This warns whenever a local variable shadows another local
>   variable. If two variables have the same name then it is a
>   potential source of confusion.

-Wpointer-arith -Wcast-qual -Wcast-align
>   These options warn if you try to do pointer arithmetic for
>   types which don't have a size, such as void, if you remove a
>   const cast from a pointer, or if you cast a pointer to a type
>   which has a different size, causing an invalid alignment.

-Wwrite-strings
>   This option gives string constants a const qualifier so that
>   it will be a compile-time error to attempt to overwrite them.

-fshort-enums
>   This option makes the type of enum as short as possible.
>   Normally this makes an enum different from an int. Conse-
>   quently any attempts to assign a pointer-to-int to a pointer-
>   to-enum will generate a cast-alignment warning.

-fno-common
>   This option prevents global variables being simultaneously
>   defined in different object files (you get an error at link time).
>   Such a variable should be defined in one file and referred to
>   in other files with an extern declaration.

-Wnested-externs
>   This warns if an extern declaration is encountered within a
>   function.

-Dinline=   The inline keyword is not part of ANSI C. Thus if you want
>   to use -ansi with a program which uses inline functions you
>   can use this preprocessor definition to remove the inline
>   keywords.

-g   It always makes sense to put debugging symbols in the exe-
>   cutable so that you can debug it using gdb. The only effect
>   of debugging symbols is to increase the size of the file, and
>   you can use the strip command to remove them later if
>   necessary.

A.5 References and Further Reading

The following books are essential reading for anyone writing and debugging numerical programs with GCC and GDB.

R.M. Stallman, *Using and Porting GNU CC*, Free Software Foundation, ISBN 1882114388

R.M. Stallman, R.H. Pesch, *Debugging with GDB: The GNU Source-Level Debugger*, Free Software Foundation, ISBN 1882114779

For a tutorial introduction to the GNU C Compiler and related programs, see

B.J. Gough, *An Introduction to GCC*, Network Theory Ltd, ISBN 0954161793

Appendix B Contributors to GSL

(See the AUTHORS file in the distribution for up-to-date information.)

Mark Galassi
> Conceived GSL (with James Theiler) and wrote the design document. Wrote the simulated annealing package and the relevant chapter in the manual.

James Theiler
> Conceived GSL (with Mark Galassi). Wrote the random number generators and the relevant chapter in this manual.

Jim Davies
> Wrote the statistical routines and the relevant chapter in this manual.

Brian Gough
> FFTs, numerical integration, random number generators and distributions, root finding, minimization and fitting, polynomial solvers, complex numbers, physical constants, permutations, vector and matrix functions, histograms, statistics, ieee-utils, revised CBLAS Level 2 & 3, matrix decompositions, eigensystems, cumulative distribution functions, testing, documentation and releases.

Reid Priedhorsky
> Wrote and documented the initial version of the root finding routines while at Los Alamos National Laboratory, Mathematical Modeling and Analysis Group.

Gerard Jungman
> Special Functions, Series acceleration, ODEs, BLAS, Linear Algebra, Eigensystems, Hankel Transforms.

Mike Booth
> Wrote the Monte Carlo library.

Jorma Olavi Tähtinen
> Wrote the initial complex arithmetic functions.

Thomas Walter
> Wrote the initial heapsort routines and cholesky decomposition.

Fabrice Rossi
> Multidimensional minimization.

Carlo Perassi
> Implementation of the random number generators in Knuth's *Seminumerical Algorithms*, 3rd Ed.

Szymon Jaroszewicz
> Wrote the routines for generating combinations.

Nicolas Darnis
> Wrote the initial routines for canonical permutations.

Jason H. Stover
> Wrote the major cumulative distribution functions.

Ivo Alxneit
> Wrote the routines for wavelet transforms.

Tuomo Keskitalo
> Improved the implementation of the ODE solvers.

Thanks to Nigel Lowry for help in proofreading the manual.

Appendix C Autoconf Macros

For applications using autoconf the standard macro AC_CHECK_LIB can be used to link with GSL automatically from a configure script. The library itself depends on the presence of a CBLAS and math library as well, so these must also be located before linking with the main libgsl file. The following commands should be placed in the 'configure.ac' file to perform these tests,

```
AC_CHECK_LIB(m,main)
AC_CHECK_LIB(gslcblas,main)
AC_CHECK_LIB(gsl,main)
```

It is important to check for libm and libgslcblas before libgsl, otherwise the tests will fail. Assuming the libraries are found the output during the configure stage looks like this,

```
checking for main in -lm... yes
checking for main in -lgslcblas... yes
checking for main in -lgsl... yes
```

If the library is found then the tests will define the macros HAVE_LIBGSL, HAVE_LIBGSLCBLAS, HAVE_LIBM and add the options -lgsl -lgslcblas -lm to the variable LIBS.

The tests above will find any version of the library. They are suitable for general use, where the versions of the functions are not important. An alternative macro is available in the file 'gsl.m4' to test for a specific version of the library. To use this macro simply add the following line to your 'configure.ac' file instead of the tests above:

```
AM_PATH_GSL(GSL_VERSION,
            [action-if-found],
            [action-if-not-found])
```

The argument GSL_VERSION should be the two or three digit MAJOR.MINOR or MAJOR.MINOR.MICRO version number of the release you require. A suitable choice for action-if-not-found is,

```
AC_MSG_ERROR(could not find required version of GSL)
```

Then you can add the variables GSL_LIBS and GSL_CFLAGS to your Makefile.am files to obtain the correct compiler flags. GSL_LIBS is equal to the output of the gsl-config --libs command and GSL_CFLAGS is equal to gsl-config --cflags command. For example,

```
libfoo_la_LDFLAGS = -lfoo $(GSL_LIBS) -lgslcblas
```
Note that the macro AM_PATH_GSL needs to use the C compiler so it should appear in the 'configure.ac' file before the macro AC_LANG_CPLUSPLUS for programs that use C++.

To test for inline the following test should be placed in your 'configure.ac' file,

```
AC_C_INLINE

if test "$ac_cv_c_inline" != no ; then
  AC_DEFINE(HAVE_INLINE,1)
  AC_SUBST(HAVE_INLINE)
fi
```
and the macro will then be defined in the compilation flags or by including the file 'config.h' before any library headers.

The following autoconf test will check for extern inline,

```
dnl Check for "extern inline", using a modified version
dnl of the test for AC_C_INLINE from acspecific.mt
dnl
AC_CACHE_CHECK([for extern inline], ac_cv_c_extern_inline,
[ac_cv_c_extern_inline=no
AC_TRY_COMPILE([extern $ac_cv_c_inline double foo(double x);
extern $ac_cv_c_inline double foo(double x) { return x+1.0; };
double foo (double x) { return x + 1.0; };],
[  foo(1.0)  ],
[ac_cv_c_extern_inline="yes"])
])

if test "$ac_cv_c_extern_inline" != no ; then
  AC_DEFINE(HAVE_INLINE,1)
  AC_SUBST(HAVE_INLINE)
fi
```
The substitution of portability functions can be made automatically if you use autoconf. For example, to test whether the BSD function hypot is available you can include the following line in the configure file 'configure.ac' for your application,

```
AC_CHECK_FUNCS(hypot)
```
and place the following macro definitions in the file 'config.h.in',

```
/* Substitute gsl_hypot for missing system hypot */

#ifndef HAVE_HYPOT
#define hypot gsl_hypot
#endif
```

The application source files can then use the include command #include <config.h> to substitute gsl_hypot for each occurrence of hypot when hypot is not available.

Appendix D GSL CBLAS Library

The prototypes for the low-level CBLAS functions are declared in the file gsl_cblas.h. For the definition of the functions consult the documentation available from Netlib (see Section 12.3 [BLAS References and Further Reading], page 164).

D.1 Level 1

float cblas_sdsdot (const int N, const float *alpha*,   Function
        const float * x, const int *incx*, const float * y, const
        int *incy*)

double cblas_dsdot (const int N, const float * x, const   Function
        int *incx*, const float * y, const int *incy*)

float cblas_sdot (const int N, const float * x, const   Function
        int *incx*, const float * y, const int *incy*)

double cblas_ddot (const int N, const double * x, const   Function
        int *incx*, const double * y, const int *incy*)

void cblas_cdotu_sub (const int N, const void * x,   Function
        const int *incx*, const void * y, const int *incy*, void *
        dotu)

void cblas_cdotc_sub (const int N, const void * x,   Function
        const int *incx*, const void * y, const int *incy*, void *
        dotc)

void cblas_zdotu_sub (const int N, const void * x,   Function
        const int *incx*, const void * y, const int *incy*, void *
        dotu)

void cblas_zdotc_sub (const int N, const void * x,   Function
        const int *incx*, const void * y, const int *incy*, void *
        dotc)

float cblas_snrm2 (const int N, const float * x, const   Function
        int *incx*)

float cblas_sasum (const int N, const float * x, const   Function
        int *incx*)

double cblas_dnrm2 (const int N, const double * x,   Function
        const int *incx*)

double cblas_dasum (const int *N*, const double * *x*,   Function
    const int *incx*)

float cblas_scnrm2 (const int *N*, const void * *x*, const   Function
    int *incx*)

float cblas_scasum (const int *N*, const void * *x*, const   Function
    int *incx*)

double cblas_dznrm2 (const int *N*, const void * *x*, const   Function
    int *incx*)

double cblas_dzasum (const int *N*, const void * *x*, const   Function
    int *incx*)

CBLAS_INDEX cblas_isamax (const int *N*, const float * *x*,   Function
    const int *incx*)

CBLAS_INDEX cblas_idamax (const int *N*, const double *   Function
    x, const int *incx*)

CBLAS_INDEX cblas_icamax (const int *N*, const void * *x*,   Function
    const int *incx*)

CBLAS_INDEX cblas_izamax (const int *N*, const void * *x*,   Function
    const int *incx*)

void cblas_sswap (const int *N*, float * *x*, const int   Function
    incx, float * *y*, const int *incy*)

void cblas_scopy (const int *N*, const float * *x*, const   Function
    int *incx*, float * *y*, const int *incy*)

void cblas_saxpy (const int *N*, const float *alpha*, const   Function
    float * *x*, const int *incx*, float * *y*, const int *incy*)

void cblas_dswap (const int *N*, double * *x*, const int   Function
    incx, double * *y*, const int *incy*)

void cblas_dcopy (const int *N*, const double * *x*, const   Function
    int *incx*, double * *y*, const int *incy*)

void cblas_daxpy (const int *N*, const double *alpha*,   Function
    const double * *x*, const int *incx*, double * *y*, const int
    incy)

void cblas_cswap (const int *N*, void * *x*, const int *incx*,   Function
    void * *y*, const int *incy*)

void cblas_ccopy (const int *N*, const void * *x*, const int   Function
    incx, void * *y*, const int *incy*)

void cblas_caxpy (const int N, const void * *alpha*, const void * x, const int *incx*, void * y, const int *incy*)   Function

void cblas_zswap (const int N, void * x, const int *incx*, void * y, const int *incy*)   Function

void cblas_zcopy (const int N, const void * x, const int *incx*, void * y, const int *incy*)   Function

void cblas_zaxpy (const int N, const void * *alpha*, const void * x, const int *incx*, void * y, const int *incy*)   Function

void cblas_srotg (float * a, float * b, float * c, float * s)   Function

void cblas_srotmg (float * $d1$, float * $d2$, float * $b1$, const float $b2$, float * P)   Function

void cblas_srot (const int N, float * x, const int *incx*, float * y, const int *incy*, const float c, const float s)   Function

void cblas_srotm (const int N, float * x, const int *incx*, float * y, const int *incy*, const float * P)   Function

void cblas_drotg (double * a, double * b, double * c, double * s)   Function

void cblas_drotmg (double * $d1$, double * $d2$, double * $b1$, const double $b2$, double * P)   Function

void cblas_drot (const int N, double * x, const int *incx*, double * y, const int *incy*, const double c, const double s)   Function

void cblas_drotm (const int N, double * x, const int *incx*, double * y, const int *incy*, const double * P)   Function

void cblas_sscal (const int N, const float *alpha*, float * x, const int *incx*)   Function

void cblas_dscal (const int N, const double *alpha*, double * x, const int *incx*)   Function

void cblas_cscal (const int N, const void * *alpha*, void * x, const int *incx*)   Function

void cblas_zscal (const int N, const void * *alpha*, void * x, const int *incx*)   Function

void cblas_csscal (const int N, const float *alpha*, void * x, const int *incx*)   Function

void cblas_zdscal (const int N, const double *alpha*, void * x, const int *incx*)   Function

D.2 Level 2

void cblas_sgemv (const enum CBLAS_ORDER *order*, const   Function
     enum CBLAS_TRANSPOSE *TransA*, const int *M*, const int
     N, const float *alpha*, const float * *A*, const int *lda*,
     const float * *x*, const int *incx*, const float *beta*,
     float * *y*, const int *incy*)

void cblas_sgbmv (const enum CBLAS_ORDER *order*, const   Function
     enum CBLAS_TRANSPOSE *TransA*, const int *M*, const int
     N, const int *KL*, const int *KU*, const float *alpha*,
     const float * *A*, const int *lda*, const float * *x*, const
     int *incx*, const float *beta*, float * *y*, const int *incy*)

void cblas_strmv (const enum CBLAS_ORDER *order*, const   Function
     enum CBLAS_UPLO *Uplo*, const enum CBLAS_TRANSPOSE
     TransA, const enum CBLAS_DIAG *Diag*, const int *N*,
     const float * *A*, const int *lda*, float * *x*, const int
     incx)

void cblas_stbmv (const enum CBLAS_ORDER *order*, const   Function
     enum CBLAS_UPLO *Uplo*, const enum CBLAS_TRANSPOSE
     TransA, const enum CBLAS_DIAG *Diag*, const int *N*,
     const int *K*, const float * *A*, const int *lda*, float * *x*,
     const int *incx*)

void cblas_stpmv (const enum CBLAS_ORDER *order*, const   Function
     enum CBLAS_UPLO *Uplo*, const enum CBLAS_TRANSPOSE
     TransA, const enum CBLAS_DIAG *Diag*, const int *N*,
     const float * *Ap*, float * *x*, const int *incx*)

void cblas_strsv (const enum CBLAS_ORDER *order*, const   Function
     enum CBLAS_UPLO *Uplo*, const enum CBLAS_TRANSPOSE
     TransA, const enum CBLAS_DIAG *Diag*, const int *N*,
     const float * *A*, const int *lda*, float * *x*, const int
     incx)

void cblas_stbsv (const enum CBLAS_ORDER *order*, const   Function
     enum CBLAS_UPLO *Uplo*, const enum CBLAS_TRANSPOSE
     TransA, const enum CBLAS_DIAG *Diag*, const int *N*,
     const int *K*, const float * *A*, const int *lda*, float * *x*,
     const int *incx*)

void cblas_stpsv (const enum CBLAS_ORDER *order*, const   Function
     enum CBLAS_UPLO *Uplo*, const enum CBLAS_TRANSPOSE
     TransA, const enum CBLAS_DIAG *Diag*, const int *N*,
     const float * *Ap*, float * *x*, const int *incx*)

void cblas_dgemv (const enum CBLAS_ORDER *order*, const   Function
    enum CBLAS_TRANSPOSE *TransA*, const int *M*, const int
    N, const double *alpha*, const double * *A*, const int
    lda, const double * *x*, const int *incx*, const double
    beta, double * *y*, const int *incy*)

void cblas_dgbmv (const enum CBLAS_ORDER *order*, const   Function
    enum CBLAS_TRANSPOSE *TransA*, const int *M*, const int
    N, const int *KL*, const int *KU*, const double *alpha*,
    const double * *A*, const int *lda*, const double * *x*,
    const int *incx*, const double *beta*, double * *y*, const
    int *incy*)

void cblas_dtrmv (const enum CBLAS_ORDER *order*, const   Function
    enum CBLAS_UPLO *Uplo*, const enum CBLAS_TRANSPOSE
    TransA, const enum CBLAS_DIAG *Diag*, const int *N*,
    const double * *A*, const int *lda*, double * *x*, const int
    incx)

void cblas_dtbmv (const enum CBLAS_ORDER *order*, const   Function
    enum CBLAS_UPLO *Uplo*, const enum CBLAS_TRANSPOSE
    TransA, const enum CBLAS_DIAG *Diag*, const int *N*,
    const int *K*, const double * *A*, const int *lda*, double *
    x, const int *incx*)

void cblas_dtpmv (const enum CBLAS_ORDER *order*, const   Function
    enum CBLAS_UPLO *Uplo*, const enum CBLAS_TRANSPOSE
    TransA, const enum CBLAS_DIAG *Diag*, const int *N*,
    const double * *Ap*, double * *x*, const int *incx*)

void cblas_dtrsv (const enum CBLAS_ORDER *order*, const   Function
    enum CBLAS_UPLO *Uplo*, const enum CBLAS_TRANSPOSE
    TransA, const enum CBLAS_DIAG *Diag*, const int *N*,
    const double * *A*, const int *lda*, double * *x*, const int
    incx)

void cblas_dtbsv (const enum CBLAS_ORDER *order*, const   Function
    enum CBLAS_UPLO *Uplo*, const enum CBLAS_TRANSPOSE
    TransA, const enum CBLAS_DIAG *Diag*, const int *N*,
    const int *K*, const double * *A*, const int *lda*, double *
    x, const int *incx*)

void cblas_dtpsv (const enum CBLAS_ORDER *order*, const   Function
    enum CBLAS_UPLO *Uplo*, const enum CBLAS_TRANSPOSE
    TransA, const enum CBLAS_DIAG *Diag*, const int *N*,
    const double * *Ap*, double * *x*, const int *incx*)

void cblas_cgemv (const enum CBLAS_ORDER *order*, const   Function
    enum CBLAS_TRANSPOSE *TransA*, const int *M*, const int
    N, const void * *alpha*, const void * *A*, const int *lda*,
    const void * *x*, const int *incx*, const void * *beta*, void
    * *y*, const int *incy*)

void cblas_cgbmv (const enum CBLAS_ORDER *order*, const   Function
    enum CBLAS_TRANSPOSE *TransA*, const int *M*, const int
    N, const int *KL*, const int *KU*, const void * *alpha*,
    const void * *A*, const int *lda*, const void * *x*, const
    int *incx*, const void * *beta*, void * *y*, const int *incy*)

void cblas_ctrmv (const enum CBLAS_ORDER *order*, const   Function
    enum CBLAS_UPLO *Uplo*, const enum CBLAS_TRANSPOSE
    TransA, const enum CBLAS_DIAG *Diag*, const int *N*,
    const void * *A*, const int *lda*, void * *x*, const int *incx*)

void cblas_ctbmv (const enum CBLAS_ORDER *order*, const   Function
    enum CBLAS_UPLO *Uplo*, const enum CBLAS_TRANSPOSE
    TransA, const enum CBLAS_DIAG *Diag*, const int *N*,
    const int *K*, const void * *A*, const int *lda*, void * *x*,
    const int *incx*)

void cblas_ctpmv (const enum CBLAS_ORDER *order*, const   Function
    enum CBLAS_UPLO *Uplo*, const enum CBLAS_TRANSPOSE
    TransA, const enum CBLAS_DIAG *Diag*, const int *N*,
    const void * *Ap*, void * *x*, const int *incx*)

void cblas_ctrsv (const enum CBLAS_ORDER *order*, const   Function
    enum CBLAS_UPLO *Uplo*, const enum CBLAS_TRANSPOSE
    TransA, const enum CBLAS_DIAG *Diag*, const int *N*,
    const void * *A*, const int *lda*, void * *x*, const int *incx*)

void cblas_ctbsv (const enum CBLAS_ORDER *order*, const   Function
    enum CBLAS_UPLO *Uplo*, const enum CBLAS_TRANSPOSE
    TransA, const enum CBLAS_DIAG *Diag*, const int *N*,
    const int *K*, const void * *A*, const int *lda*, void * *x*,
    const int *incx*)

void cblas_ctpsv (const enum CBLAS_ORDER *order*, const   Function
    enum CBLAS_UPLO *Uplo*, const enum CBLAS_TRANSPOSE
    TransA, const enum CBLAS_DIAG *Diag*, const int *N*,
    const void * *Ap*, void * *x*, const int *incx*)

void cblas_zgemv (const enum CBLAS_ORDER *order*, const   Function
   enum CBLAS_TRANSPOSE *TransA*, const int *M*, const int
   N, const void * *alpha*, const void * *A*, const int *lda*,
   const void * *x*, const int *incx*, const void * *beta*, void
   * *y*, const int *incy*)

void cblas_zgbmv (const enum CBLAS_ORDER *order*, const   Function
   enum CBLAS_TRANSPOSE *TransA*, const int *M*, const int
   N, const int *KL*, const int *KU*, const void * *alpha*,
   const void * *A*, const int *lda*, const void * *x*, const
   int *incx*, const void * *beta*, void * *y*, const int *incy*)

void cblas_ztrmv (const enum CBLAS_ORDER *order*, const   Function
   enum CBLAS_UPLO *Uplo*, const enum CBLAS_TRANSPOSE
   TransA, const enum CBLAS_DIAG *Diag*, const int *N*,
   const void * *A*, const int *lda*, void * *x*, const int *incx*)

void cblas_ztbmv (const enum CBLAS_ORDER *order*, const   Function
   enum CBLAS_UPLO *Uplo*, const enum CBLAS_TRANSPOSE
   TransA, const enum CBLAS_DIAG *Diag*, const int *N*,
   const int *K*, const void * *A*, const int *lda*, void * *x*,
   const int *incx*)

void cblas_ztpmv (const enum CBLAS_ORDER *order*, const   Function
   enum CBLAS_UPLO *Uplo*, const enum CBLAS_TRANSPOSE
   TransA, const enum CBLAS_DIAG *Diag*, const int *N*,
   const void * *Ap*, void * *x*, const int *incx*)

void cblas_ztrsv (const enum CBLAS_ORDER *order*, const   Function
   enum CBLAS_UPLO *Uplo*, const enum CBLAS_TRANSPOSE
   TransA, const enum CBLAS_DIAG *Diag*, const int *N*,
   const void * *A*, const int *lda*, void * *x*, const int *incx*)

void cblas_ztbsv (const enum CBLAS_ORDER *order*, const   Function
   enum CBLAS_UPLO *Uplo*, const enum CBLAS_TRANSPOSE
   TransA, const enum CBLAS_DIAG *Diag*, const int *N*,
   const int *K*, const void * *A*, const int *lda*, void * *x*,
   const int *incx*)

void cblas_ztpsv (const enum CBLAS_ORDER *order*, const   Function
   enum CBLAS_UPLO *Uplo*, const enum CBLAS_TRANSPOSE
   TransA, const enum CBLAS_DIAG *Diag*, const int *N*,
   const void * *Ap*, void * *x*, const int *incx*)

void cblas_ssymv (const enum CBLAS_ORDER *order*, const   Function
   enum CBLAS_UPLO *Uplo*, const int *N*, const float *alpha*,
   const float * *A*, const int *lda*, const float * *x*, const
   int *incx*, const float *beta*, float * *y*, const int *incy*)

void cblas_ssbmv (const enum CBLAS_ORDER *order*, const   Function
    enum CBLAS_UPLO *Uplo*, const int *N*, const int *K*, const
    float *alpha*, const float * *A*, const int *lda*, const
    float * *x*, const int *incx*, const float *beta*, float * *y*,
    const int *incy*)

void cblas_sspmv (const enum CBLAS_ORDER *order*, const   Function
    enum CBLAS_UPLO *Uplo*, const int *N*, const float *alpha*,
    const float * *Ap*, const float * *x*, const int *incx*,
    const float *beta*, float * *y*, const int *incy*)

void cblas_sger (const enum CBLAS_ORDER *order*, const int   Function
    M, const int *N*, const float *alpha*, const float * *x*,
    const int *incx*, const float * *y*, const int *incy*, float *
    A, const int *lda*)

void cblas_ssyr (const enum CBLAS_ORDER *order*, const   Function
    enum CBLAS_UPLO *Uplo*, const int *N*, const float *alpha*,
    const float * *x*, const int *incx*, float * *A*, const int
    lda)

void cblas_sspr (const enum CBLAS_ORDER *order*, const   Function
    enum CBLAS_UPLO *Uplo*, const int *N*, const float *alpha*,
    const float * *x*, const int *incx*, float * *Ap*)

void cblas_ssyr2 (const enum CBLAS_ORDER *order*, const   Function
    enum CBLAS_UPLO *Uplo*, const int *N*, const float *alpha*,
    const float * *x*, const int *incx*, const float * *y*, const
    int *incy*, float * *A*, const int *lda*)

void cblas_sspr2 (const enum CBLAS_ORDER *order*, const   Function
    enum CBLAS_UPLO *Uplo*, const int *N*, const float *alpha*,
    const float * *x*, const int *incx*, const float * *y*, const
    int *incy*, float * *A*)

void cblas_dsymv (const enum CBLAS_ORDER *order*, const   Function
    enum CBLAS_UPLO *Uplo*, const int *N*, const double *alpha*,
    const double * *A*, const int *lda*, const double * *x*,
    const int *incx*, const double *beta*, double * *y*, const
    int *incy*)

void cblas_dsbmv (const enum CBLAS_ORDER *order*, const   Function
    enum CBLAS_UPLO *Uplo*, const int *N*, const int *K*, const
    double *alpha*, const double * *A*, const int *lda*, const
    double * *x*, const int *incx*, const double *beta*, double *
    y, const int *incy*)

void cblas_dspmv (const enum CBLAS_ORDER *order*, const   Function
    enum CBLAS_UPLO *Uplo*, const int *N*, const double *alpha*,
    const double * *Ap*, const double * *x*, const int *incx*,
    const double *beta*, double * *y*, const int *incy*)

void cblas_dger (const enum CBLAS_ORDER *order*, const int   Function
    M, const int *N*, const double *alpha*, const double * *x*,
    const int *incx*, const double * *y*, const int *incy*,
    double * *A*, const int *lda*)

void cblas_dsyr (const enum CBLAS_ORDER *order*, const   Function
    enum CBLAS_UPLO *Uplo*, const int *N*, const double *alpha*,
    const double * *x*, const int *incx*, double * *A*, const int
    lda)

void cblas_dspr (const enum CBLAS_ORDER *order*, const   Function
    enum CBLAS_UPLO *Uplo*, const int *N*, const double *alpha*,
    const double * *x*, const int *incx*, double * *Ap*)

void cblas_dsyr2 (const enum CBLAS_ORDER *order*, const   Function
    enum CBLAS_UPLO *Uplo*, const int *N*, const double *alpha*,
    const double * *x*, const int *incx*, const double * *y*,
    const int *incy*, double * *A*, const int *lda*)

void cblas_dspr2 (const enum CBLAS_ORDER *order*, const   Function
    enum CBLAS_UPLO *Uplo*, const int *N*, const double *alpha*,
    const double * *x*, const int *incx*, const double * *y*,
    const int *incy*, double * *A*)

void cblas_chemv (const enum CBLAS_ORDER *order*, const   Function
    enum CBLAS_UPLO *Uplo*, const int *N*, const void * *alpha*,
    const void * *A*, const int *lda*, const void * *x*, const
    int *incx*, const void * *beta*, void * *y*, const int *incy*)

void cblas_chbmv (const enum CBLAS_ORDER *order*, const   Function
    enum CBLAS_UPLO *Uplo*, const int *N*, const int *K*, const
    void * *alpha*, const void * *A*, const int *lda*, const void
    * *x*, const int *incx*, const void * *beta*, void * *y*, const
    int *incy*)

void cblas_chpmv (const enum CBLAS_ORDER *order*, const   Function
    enum CBLAS_UPLO *Uplo*, const int *N*, const void * *alpha*,
    const void * *Ap*, const void * *x*, const int *incx*, const
    void * *beta*, void * *y*, const int *incy*)

void cblas_cgeru (const enum CBLAS_ORDER *order*, const   Function
    int *M*, const int *N*, const void * *alpha*, const void *
    x, const int *incx*, const void * *y*, const int *incy*, void
    * *A*, const int *lda*)

void cblas_cgerc (const enum CBLAS_ORDER *order*, const   Function
     int *M*, const int *N*, const void * *alpha*, const void *
     x, const int *incx*, const void * *y*, const int *incy*, void
     * *A*, const int *lda*)

void cblas_cher (const enum CBLAS_ORDER *order*, const   Function
     enum CBLAS_UPLO *Uplo*, const int *N*, const float *alpha*,
     const void * *x*, const int *incx*, void * *A*, const int *lda*)

void cblas_chpr (const enum CBLAS_ORDER *order*, const   Function
     enum CBLAS_UPLO *Uplo*, const int *N*, const float *alpha*,
     const void * *x*, const int *incx*, void * *A*)

void cblas_cher2 (const enum CBLAS_ORDER *order*, const   Function
     enum CBLAS_UPLO *Uplo*, const int *N*, const void * *alpha*,
     const void * *x*, const int *incx*, const void * *y*, const
     int *incy*, void * *A*, const int *lda*)

void cblas_chpr2 (const enum CBLAS_ORDER *order*, const   Function
     enum CBLAS_UPLO *Uplo*, const int *N*, const void * *alpha*,
     const void * *x*, const int *incx*, const void * *y*, const
     int *incy*, void * *Ap*)

void cblas_zhemv (const enum CBLAS_ORDER *order*, const   Function
     enum CBLAS_UPLO *Uplo*, const int *N*, const void * *alpha*,
     const void * *A*, const int *lda*, const void * *x*, const
     int *incx*, const void * *beta*, void * *y*, const int *incy*)

void cblas_zhbmv (const enum CBLAS_ORDER *order*, const   Function
     enum CBLAS_UPLO *Uplo*, const int *N*, const int *K*, const
     void * *alpha*, const void * *A*, const int *lda*, const void
     * *x*, const int *incx*, const void * *beta*, void * *y*, const
     int *incy*)

void cblas_zhpmv (const enum CBLAS_ORDER *order*, const   Function
     enum CBLAS_UPLO *Uplo*, const int *N*, const void * *alpha*,
     const void * *Ap*, const void * *x*, const int *incx*, const
     void * *beta*, void * *y*, const int *incy*)

void cblas_zgeru (const enum CBLAS_ORDER *order*, const   Function
     int *M*, const int *N*, const void * *alpha*, const void *
     x, const int *incx*, const void * *y*, const int *incy*, void
     * *A*, const int *lda*)

void cblas_zgerc (const enum CBLAS_ORDER *order*, const   Function
     int *M*, const int *N*, const void * *alpha*, const void *
     x, const int *incx*, const void * *y*, const int *incy*, void
     * *A*, const int *lda*)

void cblas_zher (const enum CBLAS_ORDER *order*, const   Function
       enum CBLAS_UPLO *Uplo*, const int N, const double *alpha*,
       const void * x, const int *incx*, void * A, const int *lda*)

void cblas_zhpr (const enum CBLAS_ORDER *order*, const   Function
       enum CBLAS_UPLO *Uplo*, const int N, const double *alpha*,
       const void * x, const int *incx*, void * A)

void cblas_zher2 (const enum CBLAS_ORDER *order*, const   Function
       enum CBLAS_UPLO *Uplo*, const int N, const void * *alpha*,
       const void * x, const int *incx*, const void * y, const
       int *incy*, void * A, const int *lda*)

void cblas_zhpr2 (const enum CBLAS_ORDER *order*, const   Function
       enum CBLAS_UPLO *Uplo*, const int N, const void * *alpha*,
       const void * x, const int *incx*, const void * y, const
       int *incy*, void * Ap)

D.3 Level 3

void cblas_sgemm (const enum CBLAS_ORDER *Order*, const   Function
       enum CBLAS_TRANSPOSE *TransA*, const enum
       CBLAS_TRANSPOSE *TransB*, const int M, const int N,
       const int K, const float *alpha*, const float * A, const
       int *lda*, const float * B, const int *ldb*, const float
       beta, float * C, const int *ldc*)

void cblas_ssymm (const enum CBLAS_ORDER *Order*, const   Function
       enum CBLAS_SIDE *Side*, const enum CBLAS_UPLO *Uplo*,
       const int M, const int N, const float *alpha*, const
       float * A, const int *lda*, const float * B, const int
       ldb, const float *beta*, float * C, const int *ldc*)

void cblas_ssyrk (const enum CBLAS_ORDER *Order*, const   Function
       enum CBLAS_UPLO *Uplo*, const enum CBLAS_TRANSPOSE
       Trans, const int N, const int K, const float *alpha*,
       const float * A, const int *lda*, const float *beta*, float
       * C, const int *ldc*)

void cblas_ssyr2k (const enum CBLAS_ORDER *Order*, const   Function
       enum CBLAS_UPLO *Uplo*, const enum CBLAS_TRANSPOSE
       Trans, const int N, const int K, const float *alpha*,
       const float * A, const int *lda*, const float * B, const
       int *ldb*, const float *beta*, float * C, const int *ldc*)

void cblas_strmm (const enum CBLAS_ORDER *Order*, const　　　Function
　　　enum CBLAS_SIDE *Side*, const enum CBLAS_UPLO *Uplo*,
　　　const enum CBLAS_TRANSPOSE *TransA*, const enum
　　　CBLAS_DIAG *Diag*, const int M, const int N, const
　　　float *alpha*, const float * A, const int *lda*, float * B,
　　　const int *ldb*)

void cblas_strsm (const enum CBLAS_ORDER *Order*, const　　　Function
　　　enum CBLAS_SIDE *Side*, const enum CBLAS_UPLO *Uplo*,
　　　const enum CBLAS_TRANSPOSE *TransA*, const enum
　　　CBLAS_DIAG *Diag*, const int M, const int N, const
　　　float *alpha*, const float * A, const int *lda*, float * B,
　　　const int *ldb*)

void cblas_dgemm (const enum CBLAS_ORDER *Order*, const　　　Function
　　　enum CBLAS_TRANSPOSE *TransA*, const enum
　　　CBLAS_TRANSPOSE *TransB*, const int M, const int N,
　　　const int K, const double *alpha*, const double * A,
　　　const int *lda*, const double * B, const int *ldb*, const
　　　double *beta*, double * C, const int *ldc*)

void cblas_dsymm (const enum CBLAS_ORDER *Order*, const　　　Function
　　　enum CBLAS_SIDE *Side*, const enum CBLAS_UPLO *Uplo*,
　　　const int M, const int N, const double *alpha*, const
　　　double * A, const int *lda*, const double * B, const int
　　　ldb, const double *beta*, double * C, const int *ldc*)

void cblas_dsyrk (const enum CBLAS_ORDER *Order*, const　　　Function
　　　enum CBLAS_UPLO *Uplo*, const enum CBLAS_TRANSPOSE
　　　Trans, const int N, const int K, const double *alpha*,
　　　const double * A, const int *lda*, const double *beta*,
　　　double * C, const int *ldc*)

void cblas_dsyr2k (const enum CBLAS_ORDER *Order*, const　　　Function
　　　enum CBLAS_UPLO *Uplo*, const enum CBLAS_TRANSPOSE
　　　Trans, const int N, const int K, const double *alpha*,
　　　const double * A, const int *lda*, const double * B,
　　　const int *ldb*, const double *beta*, double * C, const int
　　　ldc)

void cblas_dtrmm (const enum CBLAS_ORDER *Order*, const　　　Function
　　　enum CBLAS_SIDE *Side*, const enum CBLAS_UPLO *Uplo*,
　　　const enum CBLAS_TRANSPOSE *TransA*, const enum
　　　CBLAS_DIAG *Diag*, const int M, const int N, const
　　　double *alpha*, const double * A, const int *lda*, double *
　　　B, const int *ldb*)

void cblas_dtrsm (const enum CBLAS_ORDER *Order*, const   Function
        enum CBLAS_SIDE *Side*, const enum CBLAS_UPLO *Uplo*,
        const enum CBLAS_TRANSPOSE *TransA*, const enum
        CBLAS_DIAG *Diag*, const int *M*, const int *N*, const
        double *alpha*, const double * *A*, const int *lda*, double *
        B, const int *ldb*)

void cblas_cgemm (const enum CBLAS_ORDER *Order*, const   Function
        enum CBLAS_TRANSPOSE *TransA*, const enum
        CBLAS_TRANSPOSE *TransB*, const int *M*, const int *N*,
        const int *K*, const void * *alpha*, const void * *A*, const
        int *lda*, const void * *B*, const int *ldb*, const void *
        beta, void * *C*, const int *ldc*)

void cblas_csymm (const enum CBLAS_ORDER *Order*, const   Function
        enum CBLAS_SIDE *Side*, const enum CBLAS_UPLO *Uplo*,
        const int *M*, const int *N*, const void * *alpha*, const
        void * *A*, const int *lda*, const void * *B*, const int *ldb*,
        const void * *beta*, void * *C*, const int *ldc*)

void cblas_csyrk (const enum CBLAS_ORDER *Order*, const   Function
        enum CBLAS_UPLO *Uplo*, const enum CBLAS_TRANSPOSE
        Trans, const int *N*, const int *K*, const void * *alpha*,
        const void * *A*, const int *lda*, const void * *beta*, void
        * *C*, const int *ldc*)

void cblas_csyr2k (const enum CBLAS_ORDER *Order*, const   Function
        enum CBLAS_UPLO *Uplo*, const enum CBLAS_TRANSPOSE
        Trans, const int *N*, const int *K*, const void * *alpha*,
        const void * *A*, const int *lda*, const void * *B*, const
        int *ldb*, const void * *beta*, void * *C*, const int *ldc*)

void cblas_ctrmm (const enum CBLAS_ORDER *Order*, const   Function
        enum CBLAS_SIDE *Side*, const enum CBLAS_UPLO *Uplo*,
        const enum CBLAS_TRANSPOSE *TransA*, const enum
        CBLAS_DIAG *Diag*, const int *M*, const int *N*, const void
        * *alpha*, const void * *A*, const int *lda*, void * *B*, const
        int *ldb*)

void cblas_ctrsm (const enum CBLAS_ORDER *Order*, const   Function
        enum CBLAS_SIDE *Side*, const enum CBLAS_UPLO *Uplo*,
        const enum CBLAS_TRANSPOSE *TransA*, const enum
        CBLAS_DIAG *Diag*, const int *M*, const int *N*, const void
        * *alpha*, const void * *A*, const int *lda*, void * *B*, const
        int *ldb*)

void cblas_zgemm (const enum CBLAS_ORDER *Order*, const   Function
        enum CBLAS_TRANSPOSE *TransA*, const enum
        CBLAS_TRANSPOSE *TransB*, const int *M*, const int *N*,
        const int *K*, const void * *alpha*, const void * *A*, const
        int *lda*, const void * *B*, const int *ldb*, const void *
        beta, void * *C*, const int *ldc*)

void cblas_zsymm (const enum CBLAS_ORDER *Order*, const   Function
        enum CBLAS_SIDE *Side*, const enum CBLAS_UPLO *Uplo*,
        const int *M*, const int *N*, const void * *alpha*, const
        void * *A*, const int *lda*, const void * *B*, const int *ldb*,
        const void * *beta*, void * *C*, const int *ldc*)

void cblas_zsyrk (const enum CBLAS_ORDER *Order*, const   Function
        enum CBLAS_UPLO *Uplo*, const enum CBLAS_TRANSPOSE
        Trans, const int *N*, const int *K*, const void * *alpha*,
        const void * *A*, const int *lda*, const void * *beta*, void
        * *C*, const int *ldc*)

void cblas_zsyr2k (const enum CBLAS_ORDER *Order*, const   Function
        enum CBLAS_UPLO *Uplo*, const enum CBLAS_TRANSPOSE
        Trans, const int *N*, const int *K*, const void * *alpha*,
        const void * *A*, const int *lda*, const void * *B*, const
        int *ldb*, const void * *beta*, void * *C*, const int *ldc*)

void cblas_ztrmm (const enum CBLAS_ORDER *Order*, const   Function
        enum CBLAS_SIDE *Side*, const enum CBLAS_UPLO *Uplo*,
        const enum CBLAS_TRANSPOSE *TransA*, const enum
        CBLAS_DIAG *Diag*, const int *M*, const int *N*, const void
        * *alpha*, const void * *A*, const int *lda*, void * *B*, const
        int *ldb*)

void cblas_ztrsm (const enum CBLAS_ORDER *Order*, const   Function
        enum CBLAS_SIDE *Side*, const enum CBLAS_UPLO *Uplo*,
        const enum CBLAS_TRANSPOSE *TransA*, const enum
        CBLAS_DIAG *Diag*, const int *M*, const int *N*, const void
        * *alpha*, const void * *A*, const int *lda*, void * *B*, const
        int *ldb*)

void cblas_chemm (const enum CBLAS_ORDER *Order*, const   Function
        enum CBLAS_SIDE *Side*, const enum CBLAS_UPLO *Uplo*,
        const int *M*, const int *N*, const void * *alpha*, const
        void * *A*, const int *lda*, const void * *B*, const int *ldb*,
        const void * *beta*, void * *C*, const int *ldc*)

void cblas_cherk (const enum CBLAS_ORDER *Order*, const   Function
         enum CBLAS_UPLO *Uplo*, const enum CBLAS_TRANSPOSE
         Trans, const int *N*, const int *K*, const float *alpha*,
         const void * *A*, const int *lda*, const float *beta*, void *
         C, const int *ldc*)

void cblas_cher2k (const enum CBLAS_ORDER *Order*, const   Function
         enum CBLAS_UPLO *Uplo*, const enum CBLAS_TRANSPOSE
         Trans, const int *N*, const int *K*, const void * *alpha*,
         const void * *A*, const int *lda*, const void * *B*, const
         int *ldb*, const float *beta*, void * *C*, const int *ldc*)

void cblas_zhemm (const enum CBLAS_ORDER *Order*, const   Function
         enum CBLAS_SIDE *Side*, const enum CBLAS_UPLO *Uplo*,
         const int *M*, const int *N*, const void * *alpha*, const
         void * *A*, const int *lda*, const void * *B*, const int *ldb*,
         const void * *beta*, void * *C*, const int *ldc*)

void cblas_zherk (const enum CBLAS_ORDER *Order*, const   Function
         enum CBLAS_UPLO *Uplo*, const enum CBLAS_TRANSPOSE
         Trans, const int *N*, const int *K*, const double *alpha*,
         const void * *A*, const int *lda*, const double *beta*, void
         * *C*, const int *ldc*)

void cblas_zher2k (const enum CBLAS_ORDER *Order*, const   Function
         enum CBLAS_UPLO *Uplo*, const enum CBLAS_TRANSPOSE
         Trans, const int *N*, const int *K*, const void * *alpha*,
         const void * *A*, const int *lda*, const void * *B*, const
         int *ldb*, const double *beta*, void * *C*, const int *ldc*)

void cblas_xerbla (int *p*, const char * *rout*, const char *   Function
         form, ...)

D.4 Examples

The following program computes the product of two matrices using
the Level-3 BLAS function SGEMM,

$$\begin{pmatrix} 0.11 & 0.12 & 0.13 \\ 0.21 & 0.22 & 0.23 \end{pmatrix} \begin{pmatrix} 1011 & 1012 \\ 1021 & 1022 \\ 1031 & 1031 \end{pmatrix} = \begin{pmatrix} 367.76 & 368.12 \\ 674.06 & 674.72 \end{pmatrix}$$

The matrices are stored in row major order but could be stored in column
major order if the first argument of the call to cblas_sgemm was changed
to CblasColMajor.

```
#include <stdio.h>
#include <gsl/gsl_cblas.h>

int
main (void)
{
  int lda = 3;

  float A[] = { 0.11, 0.12, 0.13,
                0.21, 0.22, 0.23 };

  int ldb = 2;

  float B[] = { 1011, 1012,
                1021, 1022,
                1031, 1032 };

  int ldc = 2;

  float C[] = { 0.00, 0.00,
                0.00, 0.00 };

  /* Compute C = A B */

  cblas_sgemm (CblasRowMajor,
               CblasNoTrans, CblasNoTrans, 2, 2, 3,
               1.0, A, lda, B, ldb, 0.0, C, ldc);

  printf ("[ %g, %g\n", C[0], C[1]);
  printf ("  %g, %g ]\n", C[2], C[3]);

  return 0;
}
```

To compile the program use the following command line,

```
$ gcc -Wall demo.c -lgslcblas
```

There is no need to link with the main library -lgsl in this case as the CBLAS library is an independent unit. Here is the output from the program,

```
$ ./a.out
[ 367.76, 368.12
  674.06, 674.72 ]
```

Appendix E GPG verification

The official source-code releases of the GNU Scientific Library on ftp.gnu.org are digitally signed with gpg, the GNU Project's cryptography tool. You can verify the integrity of the GSL source code by checking its signature against the maintainer's key.

For the benefit of owners of this printed edition of the manual, the official fingerprint of the maintainer's key is reproduced here:

            D561 6F67 DF2F 5CCF 8A2B 6CA6 6E21 6FED 6406 9D5C

This fingerprint has been obtained directly from the GSL maintainer for inclusion in this printed manual. To check the GSL source code against the maintainer's key follow the procedure below, ensuring that exactly the same sequence of hexadecimal digits is shown as the fingerprint. In the event that the signing key changes, any new fingerprint will be printed in future editions of this manual.

Checking file signatures

To check a GSL release you will need the gpg and gpgv command-line tools installed, and the public key of the GSL maintainer, Brian Gough. This key is available from the Network Theory website—to download it use the GNU wget command like this,

    $ wget http://www.network-theory.co.uk/download/gpg.txt

The key will be stored in the file 'gpg.txt'. You will then need to check the fingerprint of the downloaded key against the one printed in this manual— the security of this procedure depends on this step. The command to display the fingerprint of the downloaded key is,

    $ gpg --with-fingerprint gpg.txt
    pub   1024D/64069D5C 2002-03-19 Brian Gough
                                        <bjg@network-theory.co.uk>
          Key fingerprint = ... hexadecimal digits ....
    sub   1024g/2E410647 2004-08-27

The hexadecimal digits of the key fingerprint in the output should match those printed in this manual. If there is any discrepancy, the downloaded key should not be used.[1]

---

[1] If the fingerprint does not match, please contact the publisher at info@network-theory.co.uk

Assuming the fingerprint is correct, import the key onto a keyring named 'gsl', ready for actual use:

```
$ gpg --no-default-keyring --keyring gsl --import gpg.txt
gpg: ~/.gnupg/gsl: keyring created
gpg: key 64069D5C: public key imported
gpg: Total number processed: 1
gpg:               imported: 1
```

You can now check the source code. You need both the tar file, e.g. 'gsl-1.8.tar.gz', and its signature file, e.g. 'gsl-1.8.tar.gz.sig'[2] from the 'gnu/gsl' directory on ftp.gnu.org.

The gpgv command is used to verify the file,

```
$ gpgv --keyring gsl gsl-1.8.tar.gz.sig
gpgv: Signature made Mon Apr 10 16:15:32 2006 BST
   using DSA key ID 64069D5C
gpgv: Good signature from "Brian Gough
   <bjg@network-theory.co.uk>"
```

If you see the message Good signature you can be confident that the file has not been tampered with (assuming the fingerprint displayed earlier matches the one printed in this manual).

---

[2] The file extension '.asc' is sometimes used instead, for signatures which are ascii-encoded.

Commercial support for GSL

Network Theory Ltd provides commercial support for the GNU Scientific Library. The company offers the following products and services:

- precompiled CDs for all platforms
- support by phone or email
- annual maintenance contracts

All software is backed by a 100% guarantee, with expert support from the developers of GSL. The money raised from the sales of CDs and maintenance contracts helps fund the development of the library.

For more information, visit the website www.network-theory.com or contact Dr. Brian Gough at

Address: Network Theory Limited
             15 Royal Park
             Bristol BS8 3AL
             United Kingdom

Telephone: +44 117 3179309 (or 0117 3179309 in the UK)

Fax: +44 117 9733323 (24 hour)

Email: sales@network-theory.com

Website: www.network-theory.com

GNU General Public License

Version 2, June 1991

Preamble

The licenses for most software are designed to take away your freedom to share and change it. By contrast, the GNU General Public License is intended to guarantee your freedom to share and change free software—to make sure the software is free for all its users. This General Public License applies to most of the Free Software Foundation's software and to any other program whose authors commit to using it. (Some other Free Software Foundation software is covered by the GNU Library General Public License instead.) You can apply it to your programs, too.

When we speak of free software, we are referring to freedom, not price. Our General Public Licenses are designed to make sure that you have the freedom to distribute copies of free software (and charge for this service if you wish), that you receive source code or can get it if you want it, that you can change the software or use pieces of it in new free programs; and that you know you can do these things.

To protect your rights, we need to make restrictions that forbid anyone to deny you these rights or to ask you to surrender the rights. These restrictions translate to certain responsibilities for you if you distribute copies of the software, or if you modify it.

For example, if you distribute copies of such a program, whether gratis or for a fee, you must give the recipients all the rights that you have. You must make sure that they, too, receive or can get the source code. And you must show them these terms so they know their rights.

We protect your rights with two steps: (1) copyright the software, and (2) offer you this license which gives you legal permission to copy, distribute and/or modify the software.

Also, for each author's protection and ours, we want to make certain that everyone understands that there is no warranty for this free software. If the software is modified by someone else and passed on, we want its recipients to know that what they have is not the original, so that any problems introduced by others will not reflect on the original authors' reputations.

Finally, any free program is threatened constantly by software patents. We wish to avoid the danger that redistributors of a free program will individually obtain patent licenses, in effect making the program proprietary. To prevent this, we have made it clear that any patent must be licensed for everyone's free use or not licensed at all.

The precise terms and conditions for copying, distribution and modification follow.

TERMS AND CONDITIONS FOR COPYING, DISTRIBUTION AND MODIFICATION

0. This License applies to any program or other work which contains a notice placed by the copyright holder saying it may be distributed under the terms of this General Public License. The "Program", below, refers to any such program or work, and a "work based on the Program" means either the Program or any derivative work under copyright law: that is to say, a work containing the Program or a portion of it, either verbatim or with modifications and/or translated into another language. (Hereinafter, translation is included without limitation in the term "modification".) Each licensee is addressed as "you".

    Activities other than copying, distribution and modification are not covered by this License; they are outside its scope. The act of running the Program is not restricted, and the output from the Program is covered only if its contents constitute a work based on the Program (independent of having been made by running the Program). Whether that is true depends on what the Program does.

1. You may copy and distribute verbatim copies of the Program's source code as you receive it, in any medium, provided that you conspicuously and appropriately publish on each copy an appropriate copyright notice and disclaimer of warranty; keep intact all the notices that refer to this License and to the absence of any warranty; and give any other recipients of the Program a copy of this License along with the Program.

    You may charge a fee for the physical act of transferring a copy, and you may at your option offer warranty protection in exchange for a fee.

2. You may modify your copy or copies of the Program or any portion of it, thus forming a work based on the Program, and copy and distribute such modifications or work under the terms of Section 1 above, provided that you also meet all of these conditions:

    a. You must cause the modified files to carry prominent notices stating that you changed the files and the date of any change.

    b. You must cause any work that you distribute or publish, that in whole or in part contains or is derived from the Program or any part thereof, to be licensed as a whole at no charge to all third parties under the terms of this License.

    c. If the modified program normally reads commands interactively when run, you must cause it, when started running for such interactive use in the most ordinary way, to print or display an announcement including an appropriate copyright notice and a notice that there is no warranty (or else, saying that you provide a warranty) and that users may redistribute the program under these conditions, and telling the user how to view a copy of this License. (Exception: if the Program itself is interactive but does not normally print such an announcement, your work based on the Program is not required to print an announcement.)

    These requirements apply to the modified work as a whole. If identifiable sections of that work are not derived from the Program, and can be reasonably considered independent and separate works in themselves, then this License, and its terms, do not apply to those sections when you distribute them as separate works. But when you distribute the same sections as part of a whole which is a work based on the Program, the distribution of the whole must be on the terms of this License, whose permissions for other licensees extend to the entire whole, and thus to each and every part regardless of who wrote it.

Thus, it is not the intent of this section to claim rights or contest your rights to work written entirely by you; rather, the intent is to exercise the right to control the distribution of derivative or collective works based on the Program.

In addition, mere aggregation of another work not based on the Program with the Program (or with a work based on the Program) on a volume of a storage or distribution medium does not bring the other work under the scope of this License.

3. You may copy and distribute the Program (or a work based on it, under Section 2) in object code or executable form under the terms of Sections 1 and 2 above provided that you also do one of the following:

    a. Accompany it with the complete corresponding machine-readable source code, which must be distributed under the terms of Sections 1 and 2 above on a medium customarily used for software interchange; or,

    b. Accompany it with a written offer, valid for at least three years, to give any third party, for a charge no more than your cost of physically performing source distribution, a complete machine-readable copy of the corresponding source code, to be distributed under the terms of Sections 1 and 2 above on a medium customarily used for software interchange; or,

    c. Accompany it with the information you received as to the offer to distribute corresponding source code. (This alternative is allowed only for noncommercial distribution and only if you received the program in object code or executable form with such an offer, in accord with Subsection b above.)

The source code for a work means the preferred form of the work for making modifications to it. For an executable work, complete source code means all the source code for all modules it contains, plus any associated interface definition files, plus the scripts used to control compilation and installation of the executable. However, as a special exception, the source code distributed need not include anything that is normally distributed (in either source or binary form) with the major components (compiler, kernel, and so on) of the operating system on which the executable runs, unless that component itself accompanies the executable.

If distribution of executable or object code is made by offering access to copy from a designated place, then offering equivalent access to copy the source code from the same place counts as distribution of the source code, even though third parties are not compelled to copy the source along with the object code.

4. You may not copy, modify, sublicense, or distribute the Program except as expressly provided under this License. Any attempt otherwise to copy, modify, sublicense or distribute the Program is void, and will automatically terminate your rights under this License. However, parties who have received copies, or rights, from you under this License will not have their licenses terminated so long as such parties remain in full compliance.

5. You are not required to accept this License, since you have not signed it. However, nothing else grants you permission to modify or distribute the Program or its derivative works. These actions are prohibited by law if you do not accept this License. Therefore, by modifying or distributing the Program (or any work based on the Program), you indicate your acceptance of this License to do so, and all its terms and conditions for copying, distributing or modifying the Program or works based on it.

6. Each time you redistribute the Program (or any work based on the Program), the recipient automatically receives a license from the original licensor to copy, distribute or modify the Program subject to these terms and conditions. You may not impose any further restrictions on the recipients' exercise of the rights granted herein. You are not responsible for enforcing compliance by third parties to this License.

7. If, as a consequence of a court judgment or allegation of patent infringement or for any other reason (not limited to patent issues), conditions are imposed on you (whether by court order, agreement or otherwise) that contradict the conditions of this License, they do not excuse you from the conditions of this License. If you cannot distribute so as to satisfy simultaneously your obligations under this License and any other pertinent obligations, then as a consequence you may not distribute the Program at all. For example, if a patent license would not permit royalty-free redistribution of the Program by all those who receive copies directly or indirectly through you, then the only way you could satisfy both it and this License would be to refrain entirely from distribution of the Program.

If any portion of this section is held invalid or unenforceable under any particular circumstance, the balance of the section is intended to apply and the section as a whole is intended to apply in other circumstances.

It is not the purpose of this section to induce you to infringe any patents or other property right claims or to contest validity of any such claims; this section has the sole purpose of protecting the integrity of the free software distribution system, which is implemented by public license practices. Many people have made generous contributions to the wide range of software distributed through that system in reliance on consistent application of that system; it is up to the author/donor to decide if he or she is willing to distribute software through any other system and a licensee cannot impose that choice.

This section is intended to make thoroughly clear what is believed to be a consequence of the rest of this License.

8. If the distribution and/or use of the Program is restricted in certain countries either by patents or by copyrighted interfaces, the original copyright holder who places the Program under this License may add an explicit geographical distribution limitation excluding those countries, so that distribution is permitted only in or among countries not thus excluded. In such case, this License incorporates the limitation as if written in the body of this License.

9. The Free Software Foundation may publish revised and/or new versions of the General Public License from time to time. Such new versions will be similar in spirit to the present version, but may differ in detail to address new problems or concerns.

Each version is given a distinguishing version number. If the Program specifies a version number of this License which applies to it and "any later version", you have the option of following the terms and conditions either of that version or of any later version published by the Free Software Foundation. If the Program does not specify a version number of this License, you may choose any version ever published by the Free Software Foundation.

10. If you wish to incorporate parts of the Program into other free programs whose distribution conditions are different, write to the author to ask for permission. For software which is copyrighted by the Free Software Foundation, write to the Free Software Foundation; we sometimes make exceptions for this. Our decision will be guided by the two goals of preserving the free status of all derivatives of our free software and of promoting the sharing and reuse of software generally.

NO WARRANTY

11. BECAUSE THE PROGRAM IS LICENSED FREE OF CHARGE, THERE IS NO WARRANTY FOR THE PROGRAM, TO THE EXTENT PERMITTED BY APPLICABLE LAW. EXCEPT WHEN OTHERWISE STATED IN WRITING THE COPYRIGHT HOLDERS AND/OR OTHER PARTIES PROVIDE THE PROGRAM "AS IS" WITHOUT WARRANTY OF ANY KIND, EITHER EXPRESSED OR IMPLIED, INCLUDING, BUT NOT LIMITED TO, THE IMPLIED WARRANTIES OF MERCHANTABILITY AND FITNESS FOR A PARTICULAR PURPOSE. THE ENTIRE RISK AS TO THE QUALITY AND PERFORMANCE OF THE PROGRAM IS WITH YOU. SHOULD THE PROGRAM PROVE DEFECTIVE, YOU ASSUME THE COST OF ALL NECESSARY SERVICING, REPAIR OR CORRECTION.

12. IN NO EVENT UNLESS REQUIRED BY APPLICABLE LAW OR AGREED TO IN WRITING WILL ANY COPYRIGHT HOLDER, OR ANY OTHER PARTY WHO MAY MODIFY AND/OR REDISTRIBUTE THE PROGRAM AS PERMITTED ABOVE, BE LIABLE TO YOU FOR DAMAGES, INCLUDING ANY GENERAL, SPECIAL, INCIDENTAL OR CONSEQUENTIAL DAMAGES ARISING OUT OF THE USE OR INABILITY TO USE THE PROGRAM (INCLUDING BUT NOT LIMITED TO LOSS OF DATA OR DATA BEING RENDERED INACCURATE OR LOSSES SUSTAINED BY YOU OR THIRD PARTIES OR A FAILURE OF THE PROGRAM TO OPERATE WITH ANY OTHER PROGRAMS), EVEN IF SUCH HOLDER OR OTHER PARTY HAS BEEN ADVISED OF THE POSSIBILITY OF SUCH DAMAGES.

END OF TERMS AND CONDITIONS

Appendix: How to Apply These Terms to Your New Programs

If you develop a new program, and you want it to be of the greatest possible use to the public, the best way to achieve this is to make it free software which everyone can redistribute and change under these terms.

To do so, attach the following notices to the program. It is safest to attach them to the start of each source file to most effectively convey the exclusion of warranty; and each file should have at least the "copyright" line and a pointer to where the full notice is found.

```
one line to give the program's name and a brief idea
of what it does.
Copyright (C) yyyy   name of author

This program is free software; you can redistribute it
and/or modify it under the terms of the GNU General Public
License as published by the Free Software Foundation; either
version 2 of the License, or (at your option) any later
version.

This program is distributed in the hope that it will be
useful, but WITHOUT ANY WARRANTY; without even the implied
warranty of MERCHANTABILITY or FITNESS FOR A PARTICULAR
PURPOSE.  See the GNU General Public License for more
details.

You should have received a copy of the GNU General Public
License along with this program; if not, write to the Free
Software Foundation, Inc., 59 Temple Place - Suite 330,
Boston, MA 02111-1307, USA.
```

Also add information on how to contact you by electronic and paper mail.

If the program is interactive, make it output a short notice like this when it starts in an interactive mode:

```
Gnomovision version 69, Copyright (C) 19yy name of author
Gnomovision comes with ABSOLUTELY NO WARRANTY; for details
type 'show w'.  This is free software, and you are welcome
to redistribute it under certain conditions; type 'show c'
for details.
```

The hypothetical commands 'show w' and 'show c' should show the appropriate parts of the General Public License. Of course, the commands you use may be called something other than 'show w' and 'show c'; they could even be mouse-clicks or menu items—whatever suits your program.

You should also get your employer (if you work as a programmer) or your school, if any, to sign a "copyright disclaimer" for the program, if necessary. Here is a sample; alter the names:

> Yoyodyne, Inc., hereby disclaims all copyright interest in the program 'Gnomovision' (which makes passes at compilers) written by James Hacker.
>
> *signature of Ty Coon*, 1 April 1989
> Ty Coon, President of Vice

This General Public License does not permit incorporating your program into proprietary programs. If your program is a subroutine library, you may consider it more useful to permit linking proprietary applications with the library. If this is what you want to do, use the GNU Library General Public License instead of this License.

GNU Free Documentation License

Version 1.2, November 2002

0. PREAMBLE

The purpose of this License is to make a manual, textbook, or other functional and useful document *free* in the sense of freedom: to assure everyone the effective freedom to copy and redistribute it, with or without modifying it, either commercially or noncommercially. Secondarily, this License preserves for the author and publisher a way to get credit for their work, while not being considered responsible for modifications made by others.

This License is a kind of "copyleft", which means that derivative works of the document must themselves be free in the same sense. It complements the GNU General Public License, which is a copyleft license designed for free software.

We have designed this License in order to use it for manuals for free software, because free software needs free documentation: a free program should come with manuals providing the same freedoms that the software does. But this License is not limited to software manuals; it can be used for any textual work, regardless of subject matter or whether it is published as a printed book. We recommend this License principally for works whose purpose is instruction or reference.

1. APPLICABILITY AND DEFINITIONS

This License applies to any manual or other work, in any medium, that contains a notice placed by the copyright holder saying it can be distributed under the terms of this License. Such a notice grants a world-wide, royalty-free license, unlimited in duration, to use that work under the conditions stated herein. The "Document", below, refers to any such manual or work. Any member of the public is a licensee, and is addressed as "you". You accept the license if you copy, modify or distribute the work in a way requiring permission under copyright law.

A "Modified Version" of the Document means any work containing the Document or a portion of it, either copied verbatim, or with modifications and/or translated into another language.

A "Secondary Section" is a named appendix or a front-matter section of the Document that deals exclusively with the relationship of the publishers or authors of the Document to the Document's overall subject (or to related matters) and contains nothing that could fall directly within that overall subject. (Thus, if the Document is in part a textbook of mathematics, a Secondary Section may not explain any mathematics.) The relationship could be a matter of historical connection with the subject or with related matters, or of legal, commercial, philosophical, ethical or political position regarding them.

The "Invariant Sections" are certain Secondary Sections whose titles are designated, as being those of Invariant Sections, in the notice that says that the Document is released under this License. If a section does not fit the above definition of Secondary then it is not allowed to be designated as Invariant. The Document may contain zero Invariant Sections. If the Document does not identify any Invariant Sections then there are none.

The "Cover Texts" are certain short passages of text that are listed, as Front-Cover Texts or Back-Cover Texts, in the notice that says that the Document is released under this License. A Front-Cover Text may be at most 5 words, and a Back-Cover Text may be at most 25 words.

A "Transparent" copy of the Document means a machine-readable copy, represented in a format whose specification is available to the general public, that is suitable for revising the document straightforwardly with generic text editors or (for images composed of pixels) generic paint programs or (for drawings) some widely available drawing editor, and that is suitable for input to text formatters or for automatic translation to a variety of formats suitable for input to text formatters. A copy made in an otherwise Transparent file format whose markup, or absence of markup, has been arranged to thwart or discourage subsequent modification by readers is not Transparent. An image format is not Transparent if used for any substantial amount of text. A copy that is not "Transparent" is called "Opaque".

Examples of suitable formats for Transparent copies include plain ASCII without markup, Texinfo input format, LaTeX input format, SGML or XML using a publicly available DTD, and standard-conforming simple HTML, PostScript or PDF designed for human modification. Examples of transparent image formats include PNG, XCF and JPG. Opaque formats include proprietary formats that can be read and edited only by proprietary word processors, SGML or XML for which the DTD and/or processing tools are not generally available, and the machine-generated HTML, PostScript or PDF produced by some word processors for output purposes only.

The "Title Page" means, for a printed book, the title page itself, plus such following pages as are needed to hold, legibly, the material this License requires to appear in the title page. For works in formats which do not have any title page as such, "Title Page" means the text near the most prominent appearance of the work's title, preceding the beginning of the body of the text.

A section "Entitled XYZ" means a named subunit of the Document whose title either is precisely XYZ or contains XYZ in parentheses following text that translates XYZ in another language. (Here XYZ stands for a specific section name mentioned below, such as "Acknowledgements", "Dedications", "Endorsements", or "History".) To "Preserve the Title" of such a section when you modify the Document means that it remains a section "Entitled XYZ" according to this definition.

The Document may include Warranty Disclaimers next to the notice which states that this License applies to the Document. These Warranty Disclaimers are considered to be included by reference in this License, but only as regards disclaiming warranties: any other implication that these Warranty Disclaimers may have is void and has no effect on the meaning of this License.

2. VERBATIM COPYING

You may copy and distribute the Document in any medium, either commercially or noncommercially, provided that this License, the copyright notices, and the license notice saying this License applies to the Document are reproduced in all copies, and that you add no other conditions whatsoever to those of this License. You may not use technical measures to obstruct or control the reading or further copying of the copies you make or distribute. However, you may accept compensation in exchange for copies. If you distribute a large enough number of copies you must also follow the conditions in section 3.

You may also lend copies, under the same conditions stated above, and you may publicly display copies.

3. COPYING IN QUANTITY

If you publish printed copies (or copies in media that commonly have printed covers) of the Document, numbering more than 100, and the Document's license notice requires Cover Texts, you must enclose the copies in covers that carry, clearly and legibly, all these Cover Texts: Front-Cover Texts on the front cover, and Back-Cover Texts on the back cover. Both covers must also clearly and legibly identify you as the publisher of these copies. The front cover must present the full title with all words of the title equally prominent and visible. You may add other material on the covers in addition. Copying with changes limited to the covers, as long as they preserve the title of the Document and satisfy these conditions, can be treated as verbatim copying in other respects.

If the required texts for either cover are too voluminous to fit legibly, you should put the first ones listed (as many as fit reasonably) on the actual cover, and continue the rest onto adjacent pages.

If you publish or distribute Opaque copies of the Document numbering more than 100, you must either include a machine-readable Transparent copy along with each Opaque copy, or state in or with each Opaque copy a computer-network location from which the general network-using public has access to download using public-standard network protocols a complete Transparent copy of the Document, free of added material. If you use the latter option, you must take reasonably prudent steps, when you begin distribution of Opaque copies in quantity, to ensure that this Transparent copy will remain thus accessible at the stated location until at least one year after the last time you distribute an Opaque copy (directly or through your agents or retailers) of that edition to the public.

It is requested, but not required, that you contact the authors of the Document well before redistributing any large number of copies, to give them a chance to provide you with an updated version of the Document.

4. MODIFICATIONS

You may copy and distribute a Modified Version of the Document under the conditions of sections 2 and 3 above, provided that you release the Modified Version under precisely this License, with the Modified Version filling the role of the Document, thus licensing distribution and modification of the Modified Version to whoever possesses a copy of it. In addition, you must do these things in the Modified Version:

A. Use in the Title Page (and on the covers, if any) a title distinct from that of the Document, and from those of previous versions (which should, if there were any, be listed in the History section of the Document). You may use the same title as a previous version if the original publisher of that version gives permission.

B. List on the Title Page, as authors, one or more persons or entities responsible for authorship of the modifications in the Modified Version, together with at least five of the principal authors of the Document (all of its principal authors, if it has fewer than five), unless they release you from this requirement.

C. State on the Title page the name of the publisher of the Modified Version, as the publisher.

D. Preserve all the copyright notices of the Document.

E. Add an appropriate copyright notice for your modifications adjacent to the other copyright notices.

F. Include, immediately after the copyright notices, a license notice giving the public permission to use the Modified Version under the terms of this License, in the form shown in the Addendum below.

G. Preserve in that license notice the full lists of Invariant Sections and required Cover Texts given in the Document's license notice.

H. Include an unaltered copy of this License.

I. Preserve the section Entitled "History", Preserve its Title, and add to it an item stating at least the title, year, new authors, and publisher of the Modified Version as given on the Title Page. If there is no section Entitled "History" in the Document, create one stating the title, year, authors, and publisher of the Document as given on its Title Page, then add an item describing the Modified Version as stated in the previous sentence.

J. Preserve the network location, if any, given in the Document for public access to a Transparent copy of the Document, and likewise the network locations given in the Document for previous versions it was based on. These may be placed in the "History" section. You may omit a network location for a work that was published at least four years before the Document itself, or if the original publisher of the version it refers to gives permission.

K. For any section Entitled "Acknowledgements" or "Dedications", Preserve the Title of the section, and preserve in the section all the substance and tone of each of the contributor acknowledgements and/or dedications given therein.

L. Preserve all the Invariant Sections of the Document, unaltered in their text and in their titles. Section numbers or the equivalent are not considered part of the section titles.

M. Delete any section Entitled "Endorsements". Such a section may not be included in the Modified Version.

N. Do not retitle any existing section to be Entitled "Endorsements" or to conflict in title with any Invariant Section.

O. Preserve any Warranty Disclaimers.

If the Modified Version includes new front-matter sections or appendices that qualify as Secondary Sections and contain no material copied from the Document, you may at your option designate some or all of these sections as invariant. To do this, add their titles to the list of Invariant Sections in the Modified Version's license notice. These titles must be distinct from any other section titles.

You may add a section Entitled "Endorsements", provided it contains nothing but endorsements of your Modified Version by various parties—for example, statements of peer review or that the text has been approved by an organization as the authoritative definition of a standard.

You may add a passage of up to five words as a Front-Cover Text, and a passage of up to 25 words as a Back-Cover Text, to the end of the list of Cover Texts in the Modified Version. Only one passage of Front-Cover Text and one of Back-Cover Text may be added by (or through arrangements made by) any one entity. If the Document already includes a cover text for the same cover, previously added by you or by arrangement made by the same entity you are acting on behalf of, you may not add another; but you may replace the old one, on explicit permission from the previous publisher that added the old one.

The author(s) and publisher(s) of the Document do not by this License give permission to use their names for publicity for or to assert or imply endorsement of any Modified Version.

5. COMBINING DOCUMENTS

You may combine the Document with other documents released under this License, under the terms defined in section 4 above for modified versions, provided that you include in the combination all of the Invariant Sections of all of the original documents, unmodified, and list them all as Invariant Sections of your combined work in its license notice, and that you preserve all their Warranty Disclaimers.

The combined work need only contain one copy of this License, and multiple identical Invariant Sections may be replaced with a single copy. If there are multiple Invariant Sections with the same name but different contents, make the title of each such section unique by adding at the end of it, in parentheses, the name of the original author or publisher of that section if known, or else a unique number. Make the same adjustment to the section titles in the list of Invariant Sections in the license notice of the combined work.

In the combination, you must combine any sections Entitled "History" in the various original documents, forming one section Entitled "History"; likewise combine any sections Entitled "Acknowledgements", and any sections Entitled "Dedications". You must delete all sections Entitled "Endorsements."

6. COLLECTIONS OF DOCUMENTS

You may make a collection consisting of the Document and other documents released under this License, and replace the individual copies of this License in the various documents with a single copy that is included in the collection, provided that you follow the rules of this License for verbatim copying of each of the documents in all other respects.

You may extract a single document from such a collection, and distribute it individually under this License, provided you insert a copy of this License into the extracted document, and follow this License in all other respects regarding verbatim copying of that document.

7. AGGREGATION WITH INDEPENDENT WORKS

A compilation of the Document or its derivatives with other separate and independent documents or works, in or on a volume of a storage or distribution medium, is called an "aggregate" if the copyright resulting from the compilation is not used to limit the legal rights of the compilation's users beyond what the individual works permit. When the Document is included in an aggregate, this License does not apply to the other works in the aggregate which are not themselves derivative works of the Document.

If the Cover Text requirement of section 3 is applicable to these copies of the Document, then if the Document is less than one half of the entire aggregate, the Document's Cover Texts may be placed on covers that bracket the Document within the aggregate, or the electronic equivalent of covers if the Document is in electronic form. Otherwise they must appear on printed covers that bracket the whole aggregate.

8. TRANSLATION

Translation is considered a kind of modification, so you may distribute translations of the Document under the terms of section 4. Replacing Invariant Sections with translations requires special permission from their copyright holders, but you may include translations of some or all Invariant Sections in addition to the original versions of these Invariant Sections. You may include a translation of this License, and all the license notices in the Document, and any Warranty Disclaimers, provided that you also include the original English version of this License and the original versions of those notices and disclaimers. In case of a disagreement between the translation and the original version of this License or a notice or disclaimer, the original version will prevail.

If a section in the Document is Entitled "Acknowledgements", "Dedications", or "History", the requirement (section 4) to Preserve its Title (section 1) will typically require changing the actual title.

9. TERMINATION

You may not copy, modify, sublicense, or distribute the Document except as expressly provided for under this License. Any other attempt to copy, modify, sublicense or distribute the Document is void, and will automatically terminate your rights under this License. However, parties who have received copies, or rights, from you under this License will not have their licenses terminated so long as such parties remain in full compliance.

10. FUTURE REVISIONS OF THIS LICENSE

The Free Software Foundation may publish new, revised versions of the GNU Free Documentation License from time to time. Such new versions will be similar in spirit to the present version, but may differ in detail to address new problems or concerns. See http://www.gnu.org/copyleft/.

Each version of the License is given a distinguishing version number. If the Document specifies that a particular numbered version of this License "or any later version" applies to it, you have the option of following the terms and conditions either of that specified version or of any later version that has been published (not as a draft) by the Free Software Foundation. If the Document does not specify a version number of this License, you may choose any version ever published (not as a draft) by the Free Software Foundation.

ADDENDUM: How to use this License for your documents

To use this License in a document you have written, include a copy of the License in the document and put the following copyright and license notices just after the title page:

> Copyright (C) *year your name.*
> Permission is granted to copy, distribute and/or modify this document under the terms of the GNU Free Documentation License, Version 1.2 or any later version published by the Free Software Foundation; with no Invariant Sections, no Front-Cover Texts, and no Back-Cover Texts. A copy of the license is included in the section entitled ''GNU Free Documentation License''.

If you have Invariant Sections, Front-Cover Texts and Back-Cover Texts, replace the "with...Texts." line with this:

> with the Invariant Sections being *list their titles,* with the Front-Cover Texts being *list,* and with the Back-Cover Texts being *list.*

If you have Invariant Sections without Cover Texts, or some other combination of the three, merge those two alternatives to suit the situation.

If your document contains nontrivial examples of program code, we recommend releasing these examples in parallel under your choice of free software license, such as the GNU General Public License, to permit their use in free software.

Free Software Needs Free Documentation

The following article was written by Richard Stallman, founder of the GNU Project.

The biggest deficiency in the free software community today is not in the software—it is the lack of good free documentation that we can include with the free software. Many of our most important programs do not come with free reference manuals and free introductory texts. Documentation is an essential part of any software package; when an important free software package does not come with a free manual and a free tutorial, that is a major gap. We have many such gaps today.

Consider Perl, for instance. The tutorial manuals that people normally use are non-free. How did this come about? Because the authors of those manuals published them with restrictive terms—no copying, no modification, source files not available—which exclude them from the free software world.

That wasn't the first time this sort of thing happened, and it was far from the last. Many times we have heard a GNU user eagerly describe a manual that he is writing, his intended contribution to the community, only to learn that he had ruined everything by signing a publication contract to make it non-free.

Free documentation, like free software, is a matter of freedom, not price. The problem with the non-free manual is not that publishers charge a price for printed copies—that in itself is fine. (The Free Software Foundation sells printed copies of manuals, too.) The problem is the restrictions on the use of the manual. Free manuals are available in source code form, and give you permission to copy and modify. Non-free manuals do not allow this.

The criteria of freedom for a free manual are roughly the same as for free software. Redistribution (including the normal kinds of commercial redistribution) must be permitted, so that the manual can accompany every copy of the program, both on-line and on paper.

Permission for modification of the technical content is crucial too. When people modify the software, adding or changing features, if they are conscientious they will change the manual too—so they can provide accurate and clear documentation for the modified program. A manual that leaves you no choice but to write a new manual to document a changed version of the program is not really available to our community.

Some kinds of limits on the way modification is handled are acceptable. For example, requirements to preserve the original author's copyright notice, the distribution terms, or the list of authors, are ok. It is also no problem to require modified versions to include notice that they were modified. Even entire sections that may not be deleted or changed are acceptable, as long as they deal with nontechnical topics (like this one). These kinds of restrictions are acceptable because they don't obstruct the community's normal use of the manual.

However, it must be possible to modify all the *technical* content of the manual, and then distribute the result in all the usual media, through all the usual channels. Otherwise, the restrictions obstruct the use of the manual, it is not free, and we need another manual to replace it.

Please spread the word about this issue. Our community continues to lose manuals to proprietary publishing. If we spread the word that free software needs free reference manuals and free tutorials, perhaps the next person who wants to contribute by writing documentation will realize, before it is too late, that only free manuals contribute to the free software community.

If you are writing documentation, please insist on publishing it under the GNU Free Documentation License or another free documentation license. Remember that this decision requires your approval—you don't have to let the publisher decide. Some commercial publishers will use a free license if you insist, but they will not propose the option; it is up to you to raise the issue and say firmly that this is what you want. If the publisher you are dealing with refuses, please try other publishers. If you're not sure whether a proposed license is free, write to licensing@gnu.org.

You can encourage commercial publishers to sell more free, copylefted manuals and tutorials by buying them, and particularly by buying copies from the publishers that paid for their writing or for major improvements. Meanwhile, try to avoid buying non-free documentation at all. Check the distribution terms of a manual before you buy it, and insist that whoever seeks your business must respect your freedom. Check the history of the book, and try reward the publishers that have paid or pay the authors to work on it.

The Free Software Foundation maintains a list of free documentation published by other publishers:

http://www.fsf.org/doc/other-free-books.html

Other books from the publisher

Network Theory publishes books about free software under free documentation licenses. Our current catalogue includes the following titles:

- **An Introduction to GCC** by Brian J. Gough, foreword by Richard M. Stallman. (ISBN 0-9541617-9-3) $19.95 (£12.95)

  This manual provides a tutorial introduction to the GNU C and C++ compilers, gcc and g++. Many books teach the C and C++ languages, but this book explains how to use the compiler itself. Based on years of observation of questions posted on mailing lists, it guides the reader straight to the important options of GCC.

  Concisely written, with numerous easy-to-follow "Hello World" examples, this book features a special foreword by Richard M. Stallman, principal developer of GCC and founder of the GNU Project.

- **GNU Octave Manual** by John W. Eaton (ISBN 0-9541617-2-6) $29.99 (£19.99)

  This manual is the definitive guide to GNU Octave, an interactive environment for numerical computation with matrices and vectors. For each copy sold $1 is donated to the GNU Octave Development Fund.

- **An Introduction to R** by W.N. Venables, D.M. Smith and the R Development Core Team (ISBN 0-9541617-4-2) $19.95 (£12.95)

  This tutorial manual provides a comprehensive introduction to GNU R, a free software package for statistical computing and graphics.

- **The R Reference Manual—Base Package (Volume 1)** by the R Development Core Team (ISBN 0-9546120-0-0) $69.95 (£39.95)

  This manual is the first volume of the complete reference manual for the base package of GNU R, a free software environment for statistical computing and graphics. The main commands of the base package of R are described in this volume, while the other functions (such as graphics) are described in volume two.

  For each set of manuals sold (volumes 1 & 2), $10 is donated to the R Foundation.

- **The R Reference Manual—Base Package (Volume 2)** by the R Development Core Team (ISBN 0-9546120-1-9) $69.95 (£39.95)

This manual is the second volume of the complete reference manual for the base package of GNU R. The commands for graphics, mathematics, distributions and random numbers, models, time-series and datasets are described in this volume.

- **Comparing and Merging Files with GNU diff and patch** by David MacKenzie, Paul Eggert, and Richard Stallman (ISBN 0-9541617-5-0) $19.95 (£12.95)

  This manual describes how to compare and merge files using GNU diff and patch. It includes an extensive tutorial that guides the reader through all the options of the diff and patch commands. Later chapters cover powerful time-saving techniques such as automatic merging of divergent branches of a source tree.

  This is a printed copy of the official GNU diffutils manual. It documents all the diffutils programs (diff, cmp, sdiff, diff3), plus GNU patch. For each copy of this manual sold, $1 is donated to the Free Software Foundation.

- **Version Management with CVS** by Per Cederqvist et al. (ISBN 0-9541617-1-8) $29.95 (£19.95)

  This manual describes how to use CVS, the concurrent versioning system—one of the most widely-used source-code management systems available today. The manual provides tutorial examples for new users of CVS, as well as the definitive reference documentation for every CVS command and configuration option.

- **GNU Bash Reference Manual** by Chet Ramey and Brian Fox (ISBN 0-9541617-7-7) $29.95 (£19.95)

  This manual is the definitive reference for GNU Bash, the standard GNU command-line interpreter. GNU Bash is a complete implementation of the POSIX.2 Bourne shell specification, with additional features from the C-shell and Korn shell. For each copy of this manual sold, $1 is donated to the Free Software Foundation.

- **An Introduction to Python** by Guido van Rossum and Fred L. Drake, Jr. (ISBN 0-9541617-6-9) $19.95 (£12.95)

  This tutorial provides an introduction to Python, an easy to learn object oriented programming language. For each copy of this manual sold, $1 is donated to the Python Software Foundation.

- **Python Language Reference Manual** by Guido van Rossum and Fred L. Drake, Jr. (ISBN 0-9541617-8-5) $19.95 (£12.95)

   This manual is the official reference for the Python language itself. It describes the syntax of Python and its built-in datatypes in depth, This manual is suitable for readers who need to be familiar with the details and rules of the Python language and its object system. For each copy of this manual sold, $1 is donated to the Python Software Foundation.

All titles are available for order from bookstores worldwide.

Sales of the manuals fund the development of more free software and documentation.

For details, visit the website http://www.network-theory.co.uk/

Function and Macro Index

G

Type and Variable Index

Concept Index

M

Printed in the United States
61099LVS00003B/6